POSTMODERNIST
FICTION

POSTMODERNIST FICTION

Brian McHale

London and New York

First published in 1987 by
Methuen, Inc.

Published in Great Britain by
Methuen & Co. Ltd

Reprinted 1989, 1991, 1993, 1994, 1996, 1999, 2001
by Routledge
11 New Fetter Lane
London EC4P 4EE
29 West 35th Street
New York, NY 10001

Routledge is an imprint of the
Taylor & Francis Group

© 1987 Brian McHale

Photoset by Rowland Phototypesetting Ltd
Bury St Edmunds, Suffolk
Transferred to Digital Printing 2003

Library of Congress Cataloguing in Publication Data

McHale, Brian.
  Postmodernist fiction.
  Bibliography: p.
  Includes index.
  1. Fiction—20th century—History and criticism.
2. Post modernism. I. Title.
PN3503.M24 1987 809.3'04 86-31140

Printed and bound by Antony Rowe Ltd, Eastbourne

British Library Cataloguing in Publication Data

McHale, Brian.
  Postmodernist fiction.
  1. Fiction—20th century—History and criticism.
  I. Title.
  809.3 PN3503

ISBN 0-415-04513-4

In memory of
Robert J. McHale 1927–85
Steve Sloan 1952–85
Arthur A. Cohen 1928–86

Contents

ACKNOWLEDGMENTS

The author and publishers would like to thank the following copyright holders for permission to reproduce the extracts of concrete prose which appear on pp. 185–8.

Christine Brooke-Rose and Hamish Hamilton, London, for the extract from *Thru* (London, Hamish Hamilton, 1975).

Ronald Sukenick for the extract from his book *Long Talking Bad Conditions Blues* (New York, Fiction Collective, 1979).

Raymond Federman for the extract from his book *Take It or Leave It* (New York, Fiction Collective, 1976).

Raymond Federman and The Ohio University Press, Athens, for the extract from *Double or Nothing* (Chicago, Swallow Press, 1971).

PREFACE

Hofstadter's Law: It always takes longer than you expect, even when you take into account Hofstadter's Law.

> (Douglas R. Hofstadter, *Gödel, Escher, Bach: An Eternal Golden Braid*, 1979)

A book which does not include its opposite, or "counter-book," is considered incomplete.

> (Jorge Luis Borges, "Tlön, Uqbar, Orbis Tertius," from "The Garden of Forking Paths," 1941)

This book falls under the category of descriptive poetics (librarians and compilers of bibliographies, please note). That is, it does not aspire to contribute to literary theory, although there is plenty of theory in it – too much for some people, no doubt, and not nearly enough for others. Nor does it aim to establish interpretations of particular texts, although it incorporates a good deal of mostly incidental interpretation. But what this book primarily aspires to do is to construct the repertory of motifs and devices, and the system of relations and differences, shared by a particular class of texts. I emphasize "construct": my position is (consistently, I hope) nominalist rather than realist, as I have tried to make clear in my first chapter.

The project started its life (in my mind, at least) as a fairly slim handbook, but became over the course of several years a very hefty manuscript. I am most grateful for the generous and insightful recommendations of Kit Hume and Linda Hutcheon who helped me find the substantially thinner book that was inside that fat book signaling wildly to be let out. Originally the book was to be called *Postmodernist Writing* instead of *Postmodernist Fiction*, and the difference between "writing" and "fiction" indicates something of what has been left out to produce the slimmer book in front of you. Aside from superfluous examples and other redundancies, I have removed all the material on postmodernist poetry and theater (a good deal of the former and not much of the latter), as well as a longish historical essay on the prehistory (or "archeology") of postmodernism. I don't think this has left any voids in the argument at hand, which is a tribute to my readers' canniness; but of course I have hopes that some, at least, of this "lost" material will eventually appear in print elsewhere.

This is essentially a one-idea book – an admission that probably ought to embarrass me more than it in fact does. That idea is simply stated: postmodernist fiction differs from modernist fiction just as a poetics dominated by ontological issues differs from one dominated by epistemological issues. All the rest is merely a matter of dotting i's and crossing t's. I have been surprised (and my editors at Methuen dismayed) to find how many i's there have been to dot and t's to cross.

This idea is sufficiently straightforward that it would be astonishing if no one else had ever considered it before; and of course quite a number of critics and theorists have anticipated some more or less large part of my argument. I have tried to give them the credit that is their due, especially in my first two chapters, but elsewhere as well. I want in particular to mention the avant-garde poet Dick Higgins, whose essays and manifestoes (in *A Dialectic of Centuries*, 1978, and *Horizons: The Poetics and Theory of the Intermedia*, 1984) I came across only after my own book was already substantially finished. Higgins's opposition between "cognitive" and "post-cognitive" art is not identical with my own between modernist epistemological poetics and post-modernist ontological poetics, but it's close enough for jazz.

It will also be clear that I owe a particular debt to David Lodge, whose typology of postmodernist strategies in *The Modes of Modern Writing* (1977) is a source of my own typology in Chapters 3 through 13. More than that: this book draws much of its energy from my desire to find a better motivation or ground for Lodge's typology than Lodge himself provided. I do not mean to say, hubristically, that I have somehow or other "gone beyond" Lodge, but only that *The Modes of Modern Writing* has fulfilled the true function of any scholarly book, that of stimulating further thought.

I have carried this book around with me in one form or another now for longer than I care to calculate, and have trotted parts of it out from time to time to test on various friends and colleagues. I would like to acknowledge my debt to some of the ones who have had the greatest influence on it: Chaya and Shmuel Amir, Mieke Bal, Hadar Ben-Aharon, Ziva Ben-Porat, John Cartmell, Theo D'haen, Moshe Gilad, Susanne Greenhalgh, Benjamin Hrushovski, Uri Margolin, Bob Parker, Yael Renan, Moshe Ron, David Shumway, Meir Sternberg, Randall Stevenson, and Ernst van Alphen. Nor may I neglect to thank my gracious and long-suffering editors at Methuen, Janice Price and Merrilyn Julian, or Terence Hawkes, who first brought this project to their attention, or, last but by no means least, Ruth Buncher, who typed the final, slimmed-down draft. All these people are free to claim or disavow responsibility to whatever degree they please, with my blessing.

Unfortunately, this freedom does not extend to Esther Gottlieb: this book is her responsibility, whether she wants it or not, and by now she has every reason *not* to want it. She may, if she prefers, share it with our daughters, Alma and Lily, who have literally grown up alongside this book – with everything that that entails in the way of sibling rivalry.

Finally, I owe a special debt of gratitude to the authors of the books I discuss, a few of whom I have met. Two of them, Raymond Federman and Ron Sukenick, I count as friends. The very least I could hope for this book is that it not hinder their work in any way. The *most* I could hope – well, I had better quote John Ashbery (from "Litany," 1979):

> It behooves
> Our critics to make the poets more aware of
> What they're doing, so that the poets in turn
> Can stand back from their work and be enchanted by it
> And in this way make room for the general public
> To crowd around and be enchanted by it too. . . .

That is the most I could hope for it.

BMcH
Tel Aviv, July 1985
Pittsburgh, May 1986

PART ONE: PRELIMINARIES

The Cognitive Questions (asked by most artists of the 20th century, Platonic or Aristotelian, till around 1958):

"How can I interpret this world of which I am a part? And what am I in it?"

The Postcognitive Questions (asked by most artists since then):

"Which world is this? What is to be done in it? Which of my selves is to do it?"

(Dick Higgins, *A Dialectic of Centuries*, 1978)

1: FROM MODERNIST TO POSTMODERNIST FICTION: CHANGE OF DOMINANT*

I don't think the ideas were "in the air" . . . rather, all of us found ourselves at the same stoplights in different cities at the same time. When the lights changed, we all crossed the streets.

> (Steve Katz, in LeClair and McCaffery [eds], *Anything Can Happen*, 1983)

"Postmodernist"? Nothing about this term is unproblematic, nothing about it is entirely satisfactory. It is not even clear who deserves the credit – or the blame – for coining it in the first place: Arnold Toynbee? Charles Olson? Randall Jarrell? There are plenty of candidates.[1] But whoever is responsible, he or she has a lot to answer for.

"Postmodernist"? Nobody *likes* the term. "Post," grouses Richard Kostelanetz,

> is a petty prefix, both today and historically, for major movements are defined in their own terms, rather than by their relation to something else. . . . No genuine avant-garde artist would want to be "post" anything.[2]

John Barth finds the term

> awkward and faintly epigonic, suggestive less of a vigorous or even interesting new direction in the old art of storytelling than of something anti-climactic, feebly following a very hard act to follow.[3]

And even more pungently, the term "postmodernist," for Charles Newman, "inevitably calls to mind a band of vainglorious contemporary artists follow-ing the circus elephants of Modernism with snow shovels."[4] Nobody likes the term, yet people continue to prefer it over the even less satisfactory

* A different version of this chapter has appeared under the title "Change of dominant from modernist to postmodernist writing," in Hans Bertens and Douwe Fokkema (eds), *Approaching Postmodernism* (Amsterdam and Philadelphia, John Benjamins, 1986). I am grateful to the editors and publisher for permission to reprint this material here.

alternatives that have occasionally been proposed (such as Federman's "Surfiction," or Klinkowitz's "Post-Contemporary fiction"). And it becomes more and more difficult to avoid using it.

"Postmodernist"? The term does not even make sense. For if "modern" means "pertaining to the present," then "post-modern" can only mean "pertaining to the future," and in that case what could postmodernist fiction be except fiction that has not yet been written? Either the term is a solecism, or this "post" does not mean what the dictionary tells us it ought to mean, but only functions as a kind of intensifier. "In a world which values progress," says John Gardner, "'post-modern' in fact means *New! Improved!*"[5]; and Christine Brooke-Rose says that "it merely means moderner modern (most-modernism?)."[6]

"Postmodernist"? Whatever we may think of the term, however much or little we may be satisfied with it, one thing is certain: the referent of "postmodernism," the *thing* to which the term claims to refer, *does not exist*. It does not exist, however, *not* in Frank Kermode's sense, when he argues that so-called postmodernism is only the persistence of modernism into a third and fourth generation, thus deserving to be called, at best, "neo-modernism."[7] Rather, postmodernism, the thing, does not exist precisely in the way that "the Renaissance" or "romanticism" do not exist. There is no postmodernism "out there" in the world any more than there ever was a Renaissance or a romanticism "out there." These are all literary–historical fictions, discursive artifacts constructed either by contemporary readers and writers or retrospectively by literary historians. And since they are discursive constructs rather than real-world objects, it is possible to construct them in a variety of ways, making it necessary for us to discriminate among, say, the various constructions of romanticism, as A. O. Lovejoy once did.[8] Similarly we can discriminate among constructions of postmodernism, none of them any less "true" or less fictional than the others, since *all* of them are finally fictions. Thus, there is John Barth's postmodernism, the literature of replenishment; Charles Newman's postmodernism, the literature of an inflationary economy; Jean-François Lyotard's postmodernism, a general condition of knowledge in the contemporary informational regime; Ihab Hassan's postmodernism, a stage on the road to the spiritual unification of humankind; and so on.[9] There is even Kermode's construction of postmodernism, which in effect constructs it right out of existence.

Just because there are many possible constructions of postmodernism, however, this does not mean that all constructs are equally interesting or valuable, or that we are unable to choose among them. Various criteria for preferring one construction of postmodernism over the others might be proposed – the criterion of self-consistency and internal coherence, for instance. Or the criterion of scope: postmodernism should not be defined so liberally that it covers *all* modes of contemporary writing, for then it would be of no use in drawing distinctions, but neither should it be defined too narrowly. (If there is no true postmodernist poet except Paul Celan, as someone once proposed to me, then why not simply talk about the poetics of Paul Celan and eliminate this distracting term "postmodernism" altogether?) Another criterion might be productiveness: a superior construction of postmodernism would be one that produces new insights, new or richer connections, coherence of a different degree or kind, ultimately *more discourse*, in the form of follow-up research, new interpretations, criticisms and refinements of the construct itself, counter-proposals, refutations, polemics. Above all, a superior construction of postmodernism would be one that satisfied the criterion of *interest*. If as literary historians we construct the objects of our description ("the Renaissance," "romanticism," "postmodernism") in the very act of describing them, we should strive at the very least to construct *interesting* objects. Naturally I believe that the fiction of postmodernism which I have constructed in this book is a superior construction. I have tried to make it internally consistent; I believe its scope is appropriate, neither indiscriminately broad nor unhelpfully narrow; and I hope it will prove to be both productive and interesting.

"Postmodernist"? Since we seem to be saddled with the term, whether we like it or not, and since postmodernism is a discursive construct anyway, why not see if we can make the term itself work for us, rather than against us, in constructing its referent? Ihab Hassan helps us move in this direction when he prints the term so as to emphasize its prefix and suffix:

POSTmodernISM[10]

This ISM (to begin at the end) does double duty. It announces that the referent here is not merely a chronological division but an organized system – a poetics, in fact – while at the same time properly identifying what exactly it is that postmodernism is *post*. Postmodernism is not post modern, whatever that might mean, but post modern*ism*; it does not come *after the present* (a solecism), but after the *modernist movement*. Thus the term "postmodernism," if we take it literally enough, *à la lettre*, signifies a poetics which is the successor of, or possibly a reaction against, the poetics of early twentieth-century modernism, and not some hypothetical writing of the future.[11]

As for the prefix POST, here I want to emphasize the element of logical and historical *consequence* rather than sheer temporal *posteriority*. Postmodernism follows *from* modernism, in some sense, more than it follows *after* modernism. If the statements from Richard Kostelanetz, John Barth, and Charles Newman are any indication, it is this POST that has most bothered people about the term "postmodernism." It need not have. After all, the presence of the prefix *post* in literary nomenclature – or of *pre*, for that matter – merely signals the inevitable *historicity* of all literary phenomena. Every literary–historical moment is *post* some other moment, just as it is *pre* some other moment, though of course we are not in the position to say exactly what it is *pre* – what it precedes and prepares the way for – except retrospectively, while we are always able to say, in principle, what it is *post* – what it is the posterity of. Postmodernism is the posterity of modernism – this is tautological, just as saying that pre-romanticism is the predecessor of romanticism would be tautological. But there is more than mere tautology to the relation between modernism and postmodernism if we can construct an argument about how the posterior phenomenon emerges from its predecessor – about, in other words, historical *consequentiality*.

To capture this consequentiality, the POST of POSTmodernISM – which is this book's primary objective – we need a tool for describing how one set of literary forms emerges from a historically prior set of forms. That tool can be found in the Russian formalist concept of the dominant, to which I now turn.

The dominant

Jurij Tynjanov probably deserves the credit for this concept, but it is best known to us through a lecture of Roman Jakobson's, dating from 1935. I quote from the 1971 English translation:

> The dominant may be defined as the focusing component of a work of art: it rules, determines, and transforms the remaining components. It is the dominant which guarantees the integrity of the structure . . . . a poetic work [is] a structured system, a regularly ordered hierarchical set of artistic devices. Poetic evolution is a shift in this hierarchy . . . The image of . . . literary history substantially changes; it becomes incomparably richer and at the same time more monolithic, more synthetic and ordered, than were the *membra disjecta* of previous literary scholarship.[12]

"Hierarchical"? "Monolithic"? To pre-empt the deconstruction that such deterministic and imperialistic language, with its overtones of power and coercion, seems to call for, let me try to salvage Jakobson's dominant for my own uses by deconstructing it a bit myself. Or rather, let me observe that Jakobson has in effect already deconstructed it somewhat *himself*.

Despite his claim about the monolithic character of a literary history organized in terms of a series of dominants, Jakobson's concept of the dominant is in fact plural. In this brief but typically multifaceted lecture, Jakobson applies his concept of the dominant not only to the structure of the individual literary text and the synchronic and diachronic organization of the literary system, but also to the analysis of the verse medium in general (where rhyme, meter, and intonation are dominant at different historical periods), of verbal art in general (where the aesthetic function is a transhistorical dominant), and of cultural history (painting is the dominant art-form of the Renaissance, music the dominant of the romantic period, and so on). Clearly, then, there are *many* dominants, and different dominants may be distinguished depending upon the level, scope, and focus of the analysis. Furthermore, one and the same text will, we can infer, yield different dominants depending upon what aspect of it we are analyzing: as an example of verse, it is dominated by one or other of the historical dominants of verse; as an example of verbal art, its aesthetic function is dominant; as a document of a particular moment in cultural history, it is dominated by its period's dominant; as a unique text-structure, it possesses its own unique dominant; and so on. In short, different dominants emerge depending upon which questions we ask of the text, and the position from which we interrogate it.

Having defused somewhat the overly deterministic implications of Jakobson's language, we can now see, I think, what kinds of advantages the concept of the dominant offers. Many of the most insightful and interesting treatments of postmodernist poetics have taken the form of more or less heterogeneous catalogues of features – the *membra disjecta* of literary scholarship, as Jakobson calls them. While such catalogues do often help us to begin ordering the protean variety of postmodernist phenomena, they also beg important questions, such as the question of why *these* particular features should cluster in *this* particular way – in other words, the question of what *system* might underlie the catalogue – and the question of how in the course of literary history one system has given way to another. These questions cannot be answered without the intervention of something like a concept of the dominant.

Catalogues of postmodernist features are typically organized in terms of oppositions with features of modernist poetics. Thus, for instance, David Lodge lists five strategies (contradiction, discontinuity, randomness, excess, short circuit) by which postmodernist writing seeks to avoid having to choose either of the poles of metaphoric (modernist) or metonymic (antimodernist) writing. Ihab Hassan gives us seven modernist rubrics (urbanism, technologism, dehumanization, primitivism, eroticism, antinomianism, experimentalism), indicating how postmodernist aesthetics modifies or extends each of them. Peter Wollen, writing of cinema, and without actually using either of the terms "modernist" and "postmodernist," proposes six oppositions (narrative transitivity vs. intransitivity, identification vs. foregrounding, single vs. multiple diegesis, closure vs. aperture, pleasure vs. unpleasure, fiction vs. reality) which capture the difference between Godard's counter-cinema (paradigmatically postmodernist, in my view) and the poetics of "classic" Hollywood movies. And Douwe Fokkema outlines a number of compositional and semantic conventions of the period code of postmodernism (such as inclusiveness, deliberate indiscriminateness, non-selection or quasi-nonselection, logical impossibility), contrasting these generally with the conventions of the modernist code.[13] In all these cases, the oppositions tend to be piecemeal and unintegrated; that is, we can see how a particular postmodernist feature stands in opposition to its modernist counterpart, but we cannot see how postmodernist poetics as a whole stands in opposition to modernist poetics as a whole, since neither of the opposed sets of features has been interrogated for its underlying systematicity. Nor can we see how the literary system has managed to travel from the state reflected in the catalogue of modernist features to the state reflected in the postmodernist catalogue: these are static oppositions, telling us little or nothing about the mechanisms of historical change.

Enter the dominant. With the help of this conceptual tool, we can both elicit the systems underlying these heterogeneous catalogues, and begin to account for historical change. For to describe change of dominant is in effect to describe the process of literary-historical change. Here is Jakobson again:

> In the evolution of poetic form it is not so much a question of the disappearance of certain elements and the emergence of others as it is the question of shifts in the mutual relationship among the diverse components of the system, in other words, a question of the shifting dominant. Within a given complex of poetic norms in general, or especially within the set of poetic norms valid for a given poetic genre, elements which were

originally secondary become essential and primary. On the other hand, the elements which were originally the dominant ones become subsidiary and optional.[14]

If we interrogate modernist and postmodernist texts with a view to eliciting the shifts in the hierarchy of devices – remembering, of course, that a different kind of inquiry would be likely to yield a different dominant – then what emerges as the dominant of modernist fiction? of postmodernist fiction?

Let us try out our tool on Douwe Fokkema's formulation of the period code of modernism, taking as our exemplary modernist text William Faulkner's *Absalom, Absalom!* (1936), a high-water mark of modernist poetics. According to Fokkema, the compositional and syntactical conventions of the modernist code include textual indefiniteness or incompleteness, epistemological doubt, metalingual skepticism, and respect for the idiosyncrasies of the reader. Its semantic aspects are organized around issues of epistemological doubt and metalingual self-reflection.[15] All of these conventions, with the possible exception of the convention of respecting the reader's idiosyncrasies (which seems to me a poor and debatable formulation), are reflected in *Absalom, Absalom!* The story of the rise and fall of the Sutpen dynasty comes down to Quentin Compson and his room-mate Shreve in a state of radical incompleteness and indefiniteness – "a few old mouth old mouth-to-mouth tales," as Quentin's father says, "letters without salutation or signature"[16] – its indefiniteness only heightened by the successive interpretations imposed upon it by biased or underinformed or otherwise unreliable informants (Mr Compson, Miss Rosa Coldfield, ultimately Thomas Sutpen himself). At the later stages in this chain of unreliable transmission, if not at its earlier stages, epistemological doubt and metalingual skepticism are insistently thematized. The rhetoric of Miss Rosa Coldfield, one of the few surviving parties to the events, may seem free from doubt (although for her, too, there are impenetrable mysteries), but that of Mr Compson is permeated by doubt and skeptical self-reflection:

> It's just incredible. It just does not explain. Or perhaps that's it: they don't explain and we are not supposed to know. . . . we see dimly people, the people in whose living blood and seed we ourselves lay dormant and waiting, in this shadowy attenuation of time possessing now heroic proportions, performing their acts of simple passion and simple violence, impervious to time and inexplicable – Yes, Judith, Bon, Henry, Sutpen: all of them. They are there, yet something is missing; they are like a chemical formula exhumed along with the letters from the forgotten chest, carefully, the paper old and faded and falling to pieces, the writing faded, almost indecipherable, yet meaningful, familiar in shape and sense, the name and presence of volatile and sentient forces; you bring them together in the proportions called for, but nothing happens; you re-read, tedious and intent, poring, making sure that you have forgotten nothing, made no miscalculation; you bring them together again and again nothing happens: just the words, the symbols, the shapes themselves, shadowy inscrutable and serene, against the turgid background of a horrible and bloody mischancing of human affairs.[17]

And if it is not perhaps very satisfactory to say that Faulkner's modernist text respects its reader's idiosyncrasies (whatever that might mean), we can certainly say that it deeply implicates its reader in its own preoccupations, "transferring" to him or her (almost in the psychoanalysts' sense) the same problems of reconstructing a coherent story from a radically indefinite and doubtful text that beset its own characters.[18] Mr Compson's account of reading and re-reading the doubtful texts of the Sutpen story is, in short, a *mise-en-abyme*, applying to the reader *of Absalom, Absalom!* as much as it does to the readers *in Absalom, Absalom!*[19]

So far so good: there is demonstrably a close fit between Fokkema's formulation of the modernist code and Faulkner's actual practice in *Absalom, Absalom!* But what is the dominant that "rules, determines, and transforms" the components of this text, guaranteeing the integrity of its structure? Or, to put it differently, what is the common denominator of the conventions which constitute Fokkema's modernist code? This seems self-evident, so much so that it is surprising that Fokkema has not identified it explicitly himself. Fokkema's modernist code is a follow-the-dots puzzle, with every dot in its place and properly numbered, and all that remains for us to do is draw the connecting line in order for the dominant to emerge.

I will formulate it as a general thesis about modernist fiction: the dominant of modernist fiction is *epistemological*. That is, modernist fiction deploys strategies which engage and foreground questions such as those mentioned by Dick Higgins in my epigraph: "How can I interpret this world of which I am a part? And what am I in it?"[20] Other typical modernist questions might be added: What is there to be known?; Who knows it?; How do they know it, and with what degree of certainty?; How is knowledge transmitted from one knower to another, and with what degree of reliability?; How does the object of knowledge change as it passes from knower to knower?; What are the limits of the knowable? And so on.

I think there can be no doubt that Faulkner's *Absalom, Absalom!*, for example, has been designed to raise just such epistemological questions. Its logic is that of a detective story, the epistemological genre *par excellence*. Faulkner's protagonists, like characters in many classic modernist texts – Henry James's and Joseph Conrad's, for instance – sift through the evidence of witnesses of different degrees of reliability in order to reconstruct and solve a "crime" – except that in Faulkner's case the quotation-marks can be dropped from around the word crime, for there really is a murder-mystery to be solved here. *Absalom* foregrounds such epistemological themes as the accessibility and circulation of knowledge, the different structuring imposed on the "same" knowledge by different minds, and the problem of "unknowability" or the limits of knowledge. And it foregrounds these themes through the use of characteristically modernist (epistemological) devices: the multiplication and juxtaposition of perspectives, the focalization of all the evidence through a single "center of consciousness" (the character Quentin), virtuoso variants on interior monologue (especially in the case of Miss Rosa), and so on. Finally, in a typically modernist move, *Absalom* transfers the epistemological difficulties of its characters to its readers; its strategies of "impeded form" (dislocated chronology, withheld or indirectly-presented information, difficult "mind-styles," and so on) *simulate* for the reader the very same problems of accessibility, reliability, and limitation of knowledge that plague Quentin and Shreve.

So Faulkner in *Absalom, Absalom!* practices a poetics of the epistemological dominant – modernist poetics, in other words. Except perhaps in one chapter, where modernist poetics threatens to break down, or more than threatens, actually *does* break down. In Ch. 8, Quentin and Shreve reach the limit of their knowledge of the Sutpen murder-mystery; nevertheless they go on, beyond reconstruction into pure speculation. The signs of the narrative act fall away, and with them all questions of authority and reliability. The text passes from mimesis of the various characters' narrations to unmediated diegesis, from characters "telling" to the author directly "showing" us what happened between Sutpen, Henry, and Bon. The murder-mystery is "solved," however, not through epistemological processes of weighing evidence and making deductions, but through the imaginative projection of what *could* – and, the text insists, *must* – have happened. *"Shall I project a world?"* is Oedipa Maas' anguished cry when faced by the absolute limits of her knowledge in Pynchon's *The Crying of Lot 49* (1966). Quentin and Shreve project a world, apparently unanxiously. Abandoning the intractable problems of attaining to reliable knowledge of *our* world, they improvise a *possible world*; they *fictionalize*.[21]

In short, Ch. 8 of *Absalom, Absalom!* dramatizes the shift of dominant from problems of *knowing* to problems of *modes of being* – from an epistemological dominant to an *ontological one*. At this point Faulkner's novel touches and perhaps crosses the boundary between modernist and postmodernist writing.

This brings me to a second general thesis, this time about postmodernist fiction: the dominant of postmodernist fiction is *ontological*. That is, postmodernist fiction deploys strategies which engage and foreground questions like the ones Dick Higgins calls "post-cognitive": "Which world is this? What is to be done in it? Which of my selves is to do it?"[22] Other typical postmodernist questions bear either on the ontology of the literary text itself or on the ontology of the world which it projects, for instance: What is a world?; What kinds of world are there, how are they constituted, and how do they differ?; What happens when different kinds of world are placed in confrontation, or when boundaries between worlds are violated?; What is the mode of existence of a text, and what is the mode of existence of the world (or worlds) it projects?; How is a projected world structured? And so on.

Equipped with this thesis about the ontological dominant of postmodernist fiction, we could now return to the various catalogues of features proposed by Lodge, Hassan, Wollen, and Fokkema, and if we did, we would find, I think, that most (if not quite all) of these features could easily be seen as strategies for foregrounding ontological issues. In other words, it is the ontological dominant which explains the selection and clustering of these particular features; the ontological dominant is the principle of systematicity underlying these otherwise heterogeneous catalogues.

Furthermore, once we have identified the respective dominants of the modernist and postmodernist systems, we are in a good position to begin describing the dynamics of the change by which one system emerges from and supplants the other. There is a kind of inner logic or inner dynamics – or so the case of *Absalom, Absalom!* strongly suggests – governing the change of dominant from modernist to postmodernist fiction. Intractable epistemological uncertainty becomes at a certain point ontological plurality or instability: push epistemological questions far enough and they "tip over" into ontological questions. By the same token, push ontological questions far enough and they tip over into epistemological questions – the sequence is not linear and unidirectional, but bidirectional and reversible.

A philosopher might object that we cannot raise epistemological questions without immediately raising ontological questions, and vice versa, and of course he or she would be right. But even to formulate such an objection, the philosopher would have to mention one of these sets of questions *before* the other set – inevitably, since discourse, even a philosopher's discourse, is linear and temporal, and one cannot say two things at the same time. Literary discourse, in effect, only specifies which set of questions ought to be asked *first* of a particular text, and delays the asking of the second set of questions, *slowing down* the process by which epistemological questions entail ontological questions and vice versa. This in a nutshell is the function of the dominant: it specifies the *order* in which different aspects are to be attended to, so that, although it would be perfectly possible to interrogate a postmodernist text about its epistemological implications, it is more *urgent* to interrogate it about its ontological implications. In postmodernist texts, in other words, epistemology is *backgrounded*, as the price for foregrounding ontology.[22]

Steve Katz said it better, and a good deal more pithily, in the remark I have cited as my epigraph. The logic of literary history brought writers in various cities – cities in Europe and Latin America as well as in North America – to a crosswalk; when the stoplights changed, they had one of two options, either to remain on this side and continue to practice a modernist poetics of the epistemological dominant (as many of them have done, of course), or to cross to a postmodernist poetics of the ontological dominant. The streets were different, but the *crossing* was the same.

Faulkner made that crossing in Ch. 8 of *Absalom, Absalom!* This is an isolated event in his *oeuvre*, however; he did not stay on the postmodernist side of the street, but quickly returned to the practice of modernism. So Faulkner is not very representative of the change that has occurred throughout western literature in the years since the Second World War. The change of dominant appears in its most dramatic form in writers who in the course of their careers travel the entire trajectory from modernist to postmodernist poetics, marking in successive novels different stages of the crossing. By way of substantiating my claims about the change of dominant, I have chosen to examine some of the more familiar contemporary writers of whom this is true: Samuel Beckett, Alain Robbe-Grillet, Carlos Fuentes, Vladimir Nabokov, Robert Coover, and Thomas Pynchon.

Beckett

Samuel Beckett makes the transition from modernist to postmodernist poetics in the course of his trilogy of novels of the early 1950s, *Molloy* (French, 1950; English, 1955), *Malone Dies* (French, 1951; English, 1956) and *The Unnamable* (French, 1952; English, 1959). *Molloy* juxtaposes two different, contrasting minds, Molloy's and Moran's, exposing them to (apparently) one and the same object-world, and thus allowing us to gauge their dissimilarity. This is a minimal structure of modernist perspectivism – its *locus classicus* is the "Nausicaa" chapter of Joyce's *Ulysses* (1922) – and Beckett has further reduced and stylized it, converting a minimal structure to a minimal*ist* one. But if Beckett in *Molloy* continues to practice a (stylized) modernist poetics, it is not a straightforward or unruffled modernism. There are difficulties with the structure of Beckett's world, incipient internal contradictions, threatened violations of the law of the excluded middle. In particular, it appears that Moran both is and is not identical with Molloy – a blurring of identities that tends to destabilize the projected world, and consequently to foreground its ontological structure. Here, we might say, modernist poetics begins to *hemorrhage*, to leak away – though not fatally, since it is still (barely) possible to recuperate these internal contradictions by invoking the model of the "unreliable narrator," thus stabilizing the projected world and reasserting the epistemological dominant of the text.

This hard-won stability is revoked in the opening pages of the trilogy's second volume, *Malone Dies*. Here Malone retroactively alters the ontological status of Molloy's and Moran's world by claiming to have been its author; with this gesture he places it between brackets or, better, *sous rature*, under erasure.[23] Malone's claim to authorship of *Molloy* has the effect of foregrounding the act of projecting a world, of fictionalizing, as indeed do all his other acts of world-projection throughout the text. Malone's stories of Macmann (or Saposcat – the name-change is in itself a sign of Malone's authorial freedom) constitute a second, embedded ontological level, a world subordinated to and ontologically "weaker" than the world Malone himself occupies. Of course, this embedded world is still recuperable in epistemological terms, as a reflection or extension of Malone's consciousness – until the end, that is. For at the end of the text the secondary world "takes over": we "descend" from Malone's world to the world of Macmann, but without ever reascending to Malone's world again, the text breaking off while we are still at the level of the secondary world. We are invited (by the novel's title, if nothing else) to construe this as a sign of the author's (Malone's) death *in medias res*, so to speak; nevertheless, an ambiguity lingers over this ending, leaving us to wonder which was the "more real," the world in which Malone lives and (presumably) dies, or the world which he has projected, and within which the text ends. In other words, there is here some *hesitation* between an epistemological dominant and an ontological dominant. *Both* epistemological *and* ontological questions seem to be raised by this text, but which focus of attention *dominates* depends upon how we look at the text. In this respect, *Malone Dies* recalls the figure/ground paradoxes of the *Gestalt* psychologists: looked at one way, the picture seems to represent (say) a goblet, looked at another way it represents two faces. Analogously, looked at one way, *Malone*

Dies seems to be focused on epistemological issues, while looked at another way it seems to be focused on ontological issues. I would like to reserve for texts of this type – hesitant texts, goblet/face texts – the label of "limit-modernist," on the model of Alan Wilde's "late modernism."[24]

The Unnamable duplicates the opening gambit of *Malone Dies*, with the unnamed and unnamable narrator claiming to have been the author of Malone's world, *and* of Molloy's, and indeed of all the worlds of Beckett's earlier fictions as well. Like Malone, the Unnamable projects worlds, but he displays greater freedom of ontological improvisation than Malone ever did, constructing, revising, deconstructing, abolishing, and reconstructing his characters (Basil/Mahood, Worm) and their worlds, apparently at will. And he goes even further, extending the recursive structure of worlds-within-worlds "upwards" as well as (like Malone) "downwards." That is, the Unnamable not only imagines characters, he also tries to imagine himself *as the character of someone else*. But who? First, he can only imagine an un-differentiated *they*, a chorus of voices constituting the discourse that he transmits to us, and that makes him exist for us; but then he speculates that surely *they*, in their turn, must be determined by some being ontologically superior even to them, whom he calls *the master*; but surely the master too, in his turn, must be determined by some still *more* superior being, some "everlasting third party."

In *The Unnamable* Beckett has, in effect, written a grotesque parody of St Anselm's so-called "ontological argument" for the existence of God. God is that than which no greater can be thought, said Anselm. Now if that than which no greater can be thought existed only in the mind, then a greater could still be thought after all, namely a being who existed in extramental reality. Therefore, so runs the syllogism, God must exist not only mentally but also in reality. The Unnamable parodies this astonishing feat of pulling-oneself-up-by-one's-own-ontological-boot-straps by showing that no matter how "high" his imaginings go, no matter how many recursive authors and authors-above-authors and authors-above-authors-above-authors he projects, he can never get outside of his own imaginings to the reality of his ultimate creator. There is an absolute ontological "ceiling" above the Unnamable's head which retreats as he approaches it. The ultimate creator, the God whom the Unnamable can never reach, is of course Samuel Beckett himself, and the retreating ceiling is the unbreachable barrier between the fictional world of the Unnamable and the real world which Samuel Beckett shares with us, his readers. In short, *The Unnamable* foregrounds the fundamental ontological discontinuity between the fictional and the real, and does so in such a way as to *model* the discontinuity between our own mode of being and that of whatever divinity we may wish there were.

Robbe-Grillet

Evidently the watershed between modernist and postmodernist poetics, which I have been describing, coincides rather closely with the one between the *nouveau* and the *nouveau nouveau roman*, a distinction regularly made in recent French criticism. Exactly how closely, I can demonstrate most conveniently from the case of Alain Robbe-Grillet, in some sense the exemplary *nouveau romancier*. His *La Jalousie* (1957), a "classic" *nouveau roman*, is also, like Beckett's *Molloy*, a stylized modernist novel, employing with extreme rigor the modernist conventions of limited point of view – except, of course, that the character through whom the world of the novel is focalized has been effaced, leaving a gap where a center of consciousness should be. This gap is readily filled, however: from the textual evidence, the reader reconstructs the missing figure of the jealous husband who obsessively spies on his wife and her presumed lover. "Completed" by the reader in this way, the novel becomes an example of a modernist epistemological *topos*, that of the *voyeur*, whose narrow aperture of physical sight – here, the *jalousie* of the title – serves as a kind of objective correlative for limited point of view itself. The *locus classicus* is perhaps the opening episode of Proust's *Sodome et Gomorrhe* (*Cities of the Plain*, 1921), where Marcel spies upon the homosexual courtship of Charlus and Jupien; but voyeurism in its epistemological function also recurs throughout Henry James, especially in *The Sacred Fount* (1901).

Thus, though at first sight strange and intractable, *La Jalousie* actually puts up little resistance to a recuperation in epistemological terms. Or at least not from this quarter; for it *does* put up some resistance from another quarter, namely in its use of structures *en abyme* (most notoriously, the Blacks' song). *Mise-en-abyme*, wherever it occurs, disturbs the orderly hierarchy of ontological levels (worlds within worlds), in effect *short-circuiting* the ontological structure, and thus foregrounding it. In other words, *mise-en-abyme* in *La Jalousie* constitutes, like the internal contradictions in *Molloy*, a hemorrhage of modernist poetics – but, again as in *Molloy*, not a fatal one.

Resistance to recuperation is stronger in Robbe-Grillet's next novel, *Dans le labyrinthe* (1959). This text is recuperable if we are willing to attribute the instability and inconsistency of its world to the consciousness of the dying soldier who is its protagonist. A number of critics have been willing to do so, most recently Christine Brooke-Rose (1981). But this is an "expensive" reading, in the sense that it requires us to smooth over a good many difficulties and to repress the text's own resistance to being read this way, especially the resistance that comes from what we might call its "Klein-bottle" structure. A Klein bottle is a three-dimensional figure whose inside surface is indistinguishable from its outside; similarly, inside and outside are indistinguishable in *Dans le labyrinthe*, its secondary or embedded representations (viz. the engraving of "The Defeat of Reichenfels") becoming the "outside world," its world in turn collapsing back into a secondary representation (a world within a world), which is thus *embedded in itself*. The ontological focus of this structure competes with the epistemological focus of the dying-soldier motif; but which dominates? I am suggesting, in other words, that *Dans le labyrinthe* is, like *Malone Dies*, a text of limit-modernism.

Klein-bottle paradoxes proliferate in *La Maison de rendez-vous* (1965), to the point where the projected world is completely destabilized. Here there is no identifiable center of consciousness through which we may attempt to recuperate the text's paradoxical changes of level and other inconsistencies. This is an exemplary *nouveau nouveau roman*, in short, demonstrating the "practice of writing"; or, I would prefer to say, an exemplary postmodernist text, governed by the ontological dominant and designed to dramatize ontological issues.

One good measure of the change of dominant in Robbe-Grillet's writing from *La Jalousie* through *La Maison de rendez-vous* is his treatment of *space*. *La Jalousie*, of course, is notorious for the obsessive precision with which it specifies the spatial disposition of objects in and around the African bungalow (e.g. the counting of the banana-trees). This precision obviously relates to the text's epistemological motifs: on the one hand, it serves to position the effaced center of consciousness; on the other, it enables us to infer aspects of the husband's psychological profile. In *Dans le labyrinthe*, our loss of bearings as readers is paralleled by the soldier's loss of bearings in a city which is apparently uniform and repetitive. Urban space here is modular or *serial* (in the sense of "serial music"), like the law courts in Kafka's *The Trial* or the infinitely-repeated hexagonal galleries of Borges's "The Library of Babel" (which may well have been Robbe-Grillet's models). Finally, space in the "Oriental port" (Hong Kong or Singapore or wherever it is supposed to be) of *La Maison de rendez-vous* is simply impossible, defying our attempts at orderly reconstruction. Here projected space has been overwhelmed by paradox; and this is true not only of the exterior spaces of the city, but also of the interior space of its buildings, for instance the tenement housing Edouard Manneret's flat, through which Kim the Eurasian girl traces an impossible, paradoxical itinerary.

Fuentes

The pattern I have been tracing can also be discerned in some of the writers of the so-called Latin-American "boom." My example is the career of the Mexican novelist Carlos Fuentes from *La muerte de Artemio Cruz* (1962) through *Terra nostra* (1975). *Artemio Cruz* and the novel which follows it, *Zona sagrada* (1967), represent variants of the modernist interior monologue novel, which focuses on the characteristic grid which each mind imposes on the outside world, or through which it assimilates the outside world. Each of these novels employs a different situational *topos* associated with the interior monologue convention, a different type of distortion of the mental grid. In the case of *Artemio Cruz*, this is the deathbed monologue *topos*, to which *Malone Dies*, incidentally, also belongs, and which may be traced back through Broch's *Death of Virgil* and Hemingway's "Snows of Kilimanjaro" ultimately to Tolstoy's "Ivan Ilych." The deathbed *topos* has been complicated or aggravated in *Artemio Cruz* by the presence of the modernist (and subsequently postmodernist) theme of the multiplicity of the self, dramatized here through the fragmentation of the monologue into three discontinuous monologues each using a different grammatical person. The model for this may well be Dos Passos's *U.S.A* trilogy (1930, 1932, 1936), where in several places the "same" experience is attributed both to a third-person fictional character and to an autobiographical persona who is sometimes a first-person subject, sometimes a second-person self-addressee.

The interior monologue of *Zona sagrada* belongs to the *topos* of the mad monologuist, the speaker who progressively becomes, or is progressively revealed to be, insane. This type of interior monologue situation dates at least from Edgar Allan Poe (e.g. "The Tell-tale Heart," "The Black Cat"), and enters mainstream modernist poetics especially through the neogothic mad monologuists of Faulkner (e.g. Darl Bundren in *As I Lay Dying*, Quentin Compson in *The Sound and the Fury*; but see also Septimus Warren Smith in Virginia Woolf's *Mrs Dalloway*). Fuentes' use of this *topos* here is complicated by the presence of the epistemological theme *par excellence*, the theme of illusion and reality: the monologuist's madness expresses itself through his obsession with his film-star mother and the disparity (or lack of it) between her "real" self and her public and cinematic "image."

Cambio de piel (*Change of Skin*, 1967) is Fuentes' limit-modernist text. In it he adapts the ontological structure of the fantastic, a genre which he had already exploited in a "straight" fantastic story, "Aura" (1962). The fantastic genre (in a broad sense, not in Todorov's narrower sense) involves a confrontation between two worlds whose basic physical norms are mutually incompatible. A miracle is "Another world's intrusion into this one," according to a character in Pynchon's *The Crying of Lot 49*, and it is precisely the miraculous in this sense of the term that constitutes the ontological structure of the fantastic genre. Miracles do happen in *Cambio de piel* – sympathetic magic, the resurrection of the dead – but Fuentes is careful to leave a loophole by framing the fantastic story within the discourse of a mad monologuist. On its closing pages we learn that the text has been produced by one Freddy Lambert, inmate of an insane asylum. As in the German expressionist film *The Cabinet of Dr Caligari*, which uses this same strategy (and to which *Cambio de piel* actually alludes), the fantastic is recuperated at the last possible moment and converted into a subjective delusion; the ontological structure of "another world's intrusion into this one" collapses into an epistemological structure, that of the uncanny (in Todorov's sense). We may well wonder, as in the case of Robbe-Grillet's *Dans le labyrinthe*, whether such a recuperation is not after all too "expensive," whether it does not foreclose a bit too abruptly on the fantastic elements and their ontological dominant.

Fuentes' adaptation and integration of peripheral or sub-literary ontological genres continues and reaches its peak in *Terra nostra*. This novel is, along with Pynchon's *Gravity's Rainbow* (1973), one of the paradigmatic texts of postmodernist writing, literally an anthology of postmodernist themes and devices. Here Fuentes again exploits the conventions of the fantastic, as well as those of science fiction and the historical novel. Science fiction, we might say, is to postmodernism what detective fiction was to modernism: it is the ontological genre *par excellence* (as the detective story is the epistemological genre *par excellence*), and so serves as a source of materials and models for postmodernist writers (including William Burroughs, Kurt Vonnegut, Italo Calvino, Pynchon, even Beckett and Nabokov). The pertinence of the historical novel to postmodernism, by contrast, is not so immediately obvious, and needs some explaining.

All historical novels, even the most traditional, typically involve some violation of ontological boundaries. For instance, they often claim "transworld identity"[25] between characters in their projected worlds and real-world historical figures, e.g. Napoleon or Richard Nixon. Traditional historical novels strive to suppress these violations, to hide the ontological "seams" between fictional projections and real-world facts. They do so by tactfully avoiding contradictions between their versions of historical figures and the familiar facts of these figures' careers, and by making the background norms governing their projected worlds conform to accepted real-world norms. *Terra nostra*, by contrast, foregrounds its ontological seams by systematically transgressing these rules of its genre. Here familiar facts are tactlessly contradicted – Columbus discovers America a full century too late, Philip II of Spain marries Elizabeth of England, and so on – and the projected world is governed by fantastic norms. Fuentes thus converts the historical novel into a medium for raising ontological issues, as do other postmodernist historical novelists, including Pynchon, Günter Grass, Robert Coover, Ishmael Reed, and Salman Rushdie.

One measure of the change of dominant in Fuentes' writing is the different treatments of the same motif in the modernist novel *Zona sagrada* and in *Terra nostra*. This is the motif of the "transhistorical party," where characters apparently from disparate historical eras are brought together at the same time and place. Obviously a carnivalesque motif, in Baxtin's sense, it is also related to the typical modernist motif of the party that assembles, or re-assembles, all the characters of the novel at a single locus – for instance, the Guermantes party in *Le Temps retrouvé* (*The Past Recaptured*, 1927), Clarissa's party in *Mrs Dalloway*, or even the fiesta at Pamplona in *The Sun Also Rises*. In Fuentes' *Zona sagrada*, the transhistorical party is epistemologically moti-vated, and implicated in the theme of illusion and reality: Guillermo, the narrator-protagonist, stumbles into such a party at his friend's Italian villa, only to find that things are not what they seem, and that the party is really only a movie set for one of his mother's films, the figures from different historical eras only actors in period costumes. In *Terra nostra*, however, the party is real, Paris having been transformed into an immense transhistorical carnival by the appearance in its streets of time-travelers from past historical periods. This transhistorical party, in short, has been modeled on a science-fiction *topos*, that of the "time war" (see e.g. Fritz Leiber's *The Big Time*, 1958, or Philip Jose Farmer's *To Your Scattered Bodies Go*, 1971). The motivation here is ontological, a confrontation between our world and a world whose norms permit time-travel.

Moreover, at the center of the transhistorical carnival of *Terra nostra* stands another ontological motif, involving a different type of "transworld identity" from the one that is characteristic of historical fiction. A number of characters gather to play poker, including Pierre Menard, Buendía, Oliveira, the cousins Sofía and Esteban, and Cuba Venegas. These characters have, of course, been "lifted" from texts by *other* South-American "Boom" novelists – from Borges' "Pierre Menard, Author of Don Quixote," García Márquez's *Cien años de soledad* (*One Hundred Years of Solitude*, 1967), Cortázar's *Rayuela* (*Hopscotch*, 1963/7), Carpentier's *El siglo de las luces*, and Cabrera Infante's *Tres tristes tigres*, respectively. Here, in other words, we have a case of intertextual boundary-violation, transworld identity between characters belonging to different fictional worlds. Disparate, incommensurable worlds literally rub shoulders around this poker-table, creating a dense ontological "knot," as though the entire intertextual space of Latin-American postmodernist writing had somehow been folded *into* the projected world of *Terra nostra*. What conceivable space could such a poker-table occupy? Only the sort of space where fragments of a number of possible orders have been gathered together – the space which Michel Foucault (1966) has called a *heterotopia*.

Nabokov

The crossover from modernist to postmodernist writing also occurs during the middle years of Vladimir Nabokov's American career, specifically in the sequence *Lolita* (1955), *Pale Fire* (1962), *Ada* (1969). Humbert Humbert of *Lolita* belongs, of course, to the tradition of radically unreliable modernist narrators, joining the distinguished line that includes Dowell of Ford Madox Ford's *The Good Soldier* and Jason Compson of *The Sound and the Fury*, and whose founder, so to speak, is Dostoyevski's Underground Man. In *Pale Fire*, this familiar convention of narratorial unreliability has been pushed to the limit. Here we can be sure that the narrator is radically unreliable, but without being able to determine (as we still can in the case of Humbert Humbert) *in what ways* he is unreliable, or *to what degree*. Excluding minor variants, no fewer than *four* distinct hypotheses may be entertained about *Pale Fire*:[26]

1   that Kinbote (or Botkin, or whatever his name is) is telling the truth and nothing but the truth: John Shade's poem "Pale Fire" really is an allusive and heavily camouflaged biography of Kinbote himself, who secretly is none other than Charles the Beloved, exiled King of Zembla;
2   that Kinbote really is the exiled King of Zembla, and the Zemblan part of his story is true, but that he is deluded in believing that Shade's poem in any way reflects the events of his own life;
3   that Kinbote is really a Russian *émigré* academic named Botkin, the whole of the King of Zembla's adventures, possibly the very Kingdom of Zembla itself, having been hallucinated by Botkin (on this hypothesis, needless to say, Shade's poem *certainly* has nothing to do with the Zemblan story);
4   that *everything* – Zembla and its king, John Shade and his poem – has been concocted by someone who is neither Shade nor Kinbote/Botkin. By whom, then? Well, by Vladimir Nabokov at one level, it goes without saying; but ought we perhaps to reconstruct some intermediary figure who stands between the biographical Nabokov and the substance of *Pale Fire*, or is there insufficient warrant for this?

Pale Fire, in other words, is a text of absolute epistemological uncertainty: we know that something is happening here but we don't know what it is, as Bob Dylan said of Mister Jones. Inevitably, epistemological doubt as total as this has ontological consequences as well; in particular, the Kingdom of Zembla flickers in and out of existence, depending upon which hypothesis we choose to entertain (it exists according to hypotheses 1 and 2, but not according to 3 and 4). Thus, we not only hesitate among hypotheses, but also between an epistemological and an ontological focus, making *Pale Fire* a text of limit-modernism, perhaps the paradigmatic limit-modernist novel.

Epistemological preoccupations continue to be visible in *Ada*: the modernist theme of memory, the device of joint narration by Van and Ada, comically dramatizing the disparity between two perspectives on the same objective "facts," and so on. Nevertheless, the dominant has unmistakably been shifted away from these preoccupations in this text, and it is above all the strange, familiar-yet-alien make-up of the projected world that engrosses our attention, memory and perspectivism having been firmly displaced to the background. The world of *Ada* can be seen as the convergence of two ontological structures, one based on a science-fiction *topos*, the other extrapolated from the conventions of the *roman-à-clef*. On the one hand, the Antiterra of *Ada*, with its displaced and superimposed spaces, its skew place-names, and its oddly juggled chronology, incorporates the parallel-world *topos* of such science-fiction novels as Philip K. Dick's *The Man in the High Castle* (1962): this is our world as it *might have been* if at certain branchings in history's garden of forking paths some path *other* than the one which produced our world had been chosen. Alternatively, Nabokov's Antiterra can be seen as a sort of ontological variant on the *roman-à-clef*, in which Nabokov's complicated multi-national and multi-lingual autobiography has been, in effect, encoded in the structure of the projected world. Thus, all three of Nabokov's "nations" – Russia, France, the United States – have been superimposed on a single geographical space, the "Estotiland" of *Ada*, while three peak periods in his life – the pre-revolutionary years of his childhood, the years of his young manhood in the 1920s, and the years of his greatest post-war success – have been telescoped into a single present. Either way we look at it, *Ada* represents a case of sheer ontological improvisation more radical than anything Quentin and Shreve attempt in *Absalom, Absalom!*

Coover

Robert Coover's career, too, corresponds to the by-now familiar pattern of change of dominant. His first novel, *The Origin of the Brunists* (1966), deploys the repertoire of modernist devices – multiple focalization and juxtaposed perspectives, interior monologue, and so on – in a perfectly orthodox, if perhaps somewhat mechanical, way. As in classic modernist texts, these devices function to express epistemological themes, here stated with particular explicitness. Coover's themes are essentially those of Berger's and Luckmann's *The Social Construction of Reality* – subtitled, it will be recalled, *A Treatise in the Sociology of Knowledge* – which appeared, interestingly, the same year as *Origin of the Brunists* (something in the air?). In effect, *Brunists* recounts the process of consolidation of what Berger and Luckmann would call a new "subuniverse of meaning" – i.e. a breakaway religious sect – from the solipsistic private world-views of an assortment of mystics, paranoiacs, and cranks. This process is evaluated from the normative viewpoint of the newspaperman Tiger Miller, a pluralist and relativist, but also a spokesman for "paramount reality," to use Berger's and Luckmann's term, the shared world of normal social interaction. "Not the void within and ahead," thinks Tiger on the novel's closing pages, "but the immediate living space between two"; not, in other words, the self-contained and totalizing "esoteric enclave" (Berger and Luckmann again) of the Brunist cult, but the paramount reality of our everyday life with others, here and now.

Just as Nabokov in *Pale Fire* pushes the unreliable narrator convention of *Lolita* to its limit, so Coover pushes the epistemological themes of *Origin of the Brunists* to their limit – and beyond – in his next novel, *The Universal Baseball Association Inc., J. Henry Waugh, Prop.* (1968). *Brunists* sticks to the central area of Berger's and Luckmann's epistemological problematics, namely the tension between paramount reality and subuniverses of meaning. *J. Henry Waugh* shifts to the fringes of that area, focusing on one of the strategies of temporary (or, in this case, permanent) *withdrawal* from paramount reality, a topic pursued by Stanley Cohen and Laurie Taylor, sociologists following very much in the footsteps of Berger and Luckmann, in their book *Escape Attempts: The Theory and Practice of Resistance to Everyday Life* (1976). Cohen and Taylor actually cite Coover's J. Henry Waugh as an example of permanent escape from paramount reality into what they call an "activity enclave," namely the table-top baseball game that Waugh designs and obsessively plays in private. Waugh is the novel's center of consciousness, and we witness from inside, so to speak, his progressively deeper absorption in the solipsistic world of the game, his increasing alienation from the everyday concerns of "real life." Thus, we are very near here to the mad monologuist *topos* exemplified by Guillermo of Fuentes' *Zona sagrada*. However, just at the point where Waugh's obsession escalates into outright madness, the text itself goes mad, or so it would appear: the signs of Waugh's framing consciousness fall away, Waugh himself disappears from the text, and the world-within-the-world of Waugh's baseball game acquires an independent reality, even a history, becoming in effect a free-standing world of its own. In this astonishing final chapter, *J. Henry Waugh* duplicates the breakthrough in Chapter 8 of Faulkner's *Absalom, Absalom!* or the closing pages of Beckett's *Malone Dies*. With this gesture of pure ontological improvisation, it crosses over from a modernist poetics of the epistemological dominant to a postmodernist poetics of the ontological dominant.

In subsequent writings, Coover has extended and consolidated his practice of postmodernist poetics. His collection *Pricksongs and Descants* (1969), for instance, amounts to a mini-anthology of ontological motifs and devices. Granted, several of the texts it contains were written before *J. Henry Waugh*; nevertheless, it seems significant that these texts were not actually gathered together into a book until *after* the breakthrough to postmodernism had been dramatized in *J. Henry Waugh*. *Pricksongs* includes a number of revisionist and parodic adaptations of fairy-tale and Bible-story ontologies ("The Door," "The Magic Poker," "The Gingerbread House," "The Brother," "J.'s Marriage"), a strategy used by other postmodernist writers as well, including Donald Barthelme (e.g. *Snow White*, 1967) and Angela Carter (e.g. *The Bloody Chamber*, 1979). It also contains several self-contradictory or self-canceling fictions ("The Magic Poker," "The Elevator," "Quenby and Ola, Swede and Carl," "The Babysitter"), worlds under erasure that realize the possibilities inherent in Beckett's trilogy or in Borges's "The Garden of Forking Paths," in the process laying bare the ontological structure of the fictional text. Coover's *The Public Burning* (1977) resembles Fuentes' *Terra nostra* in its (ab)use of the conventions of the historical novel for ontological purposes. Like Fuentes, Coover here systematically contradicts well-known historical facts (e.g. Vice-President Richard Nixon is made to attempt the seduction of Ethel Rosenberg on the eve of her execution), and grafts historical characters onto a fantastic world, a mismatching of norms dramatized by Richard Nixon's sodomization (!) by the mythological Uncle Sam. The climactic scene of the carnivalesque public execution in Times Square constitutes an onto-logical knot like the poker-game of *Terra nostra*, although on a larger scale. Here characters of different and incompatible ontological statuses – real-world historical figures, corporate trade-marks (e.g. Betty Crocker) and national symbols (e.g. Uncle Sam), purely fictional characters – have been gathered together in an impossible, heterotopian locus which is also, according to Coover, "the ritual center of the Western World."

Pynchon

Christine Brooke-Rose has described Thomas Pynchon's first novel *V.* (1963) as a parody of classic realist fiction, and not a very satisfactory parody at that, since the crucial distance between the parody and the model being parodied is not scrupulously enough maintained.[27] I disagree; by my reading, *V.* is not a parody but a stylization, and not of classic realism but of modernist fiction – like *Molloy*, *La Jalousie*, *Lolita*, and other texts of stylized modernism. The distinction between parody and stylization upon which Brooke-Rose draws comes from Baxtin. Parody, for Baxtin, reverses the evaluative "direction" or "orientation" of the parodied model, while stylization retains the original "orientation," taking care, however, to keep the original and its stylization distinct.[28] Now, while this is hardly the most lucid or unproblematic formula-tion one could hope for, it can be improved a good deal by introducing the concept of the dominant: in a stylization, the dominant of the original (the model being stylized) is preserved, while in parody it is not.

   V. preserves the epistemological dominant of modernism. Its frame, the story of Herbert Stencil's pursuit of the endlessly elusive Lady V., takes the form of an epistemological quest, a detective story like those of Conrad, James, or Faulkner, but blown up to gargantuan proportions. Within that frame Pynchon has embedded a series of stylized imitations of characteristic modernist strategies. In one chapter, for instance (Ch. 3), he defracts his espionage melodrama through the extremely limited perspectives of no fewer than seven supernumerary characters, climaxing with the limit-case of per-spectivism, the so-called "camera eye" (a favorite of typologists of point-of-view, but rare almost to the point of nonexistence in actual practice). The point is driven home even more forcibly when one realizes that Pynchon had originally narrated this same spy-thriller, then called "Under the Rose" (1961), from a unitary, omniscient point of view, only later recasting it, using this perversely overelaborate perspectivist technique, for inclusion in *V.* In another chapter (Ch. 9) we get a tale of imperialist savagery from the heart of African darkness, employing a Conradian unreliable narration at two removes; in yet another (Ch. 11), a Proustian first-person memoir displaying the vagaries and instability of seifhood, studded with self-conscious allusions to Eliot's high-modernist poetry. Finally, there is Herbert Stencil himself, the hero (or anti-hero) of the quest, who practices "forcible dislocation of personality" by referring to himself in the third person, as Henry Adams does in *Education* or Norman Mailer does in *Armies of the Night* (or, for that matter, as one of Pynchon's own characters does in his 1960 short story "Entropy"). Stencil as third-person center of consciousness is unmistakably a kind of personification or literalization of a typical modernist strategy of interior discourse – used extensively by James, Woolf, and Joyce, among others – namely *style indirect libre* or free indirect discourse.

Here, too, however, as in *Molloy* or *La Jalousie*, modernist poetics develops a hemorrhage, not yet fatal but dangerous. The fantastic alternative reality which Stencil constructs in the course of his quest – a reality incorporating the "lost world" of Vheissu, a clockwork woman fabricated from prosthetic devices, and other gothic or science-fiction improbabilities – is all kept safely within the frame of Stencil's unreliable information and ill-founded or outright fictional speculations. Until the end, that is, when we readers – but *not* Stencil himself – are confronted with apparently reliable, authoritative information tending to confirm the existence of this alternative reality. It is at this point, in the epilogue of *V.*, that Pynchon's text threatens to break through into a postmodernist version of the fantastic.

Threatens to, but does not quite do so. As Pynchon's second novel, *The Crying of Lot 49*, also does not, although it goes even further in that direction. *Lot 49* begins with "a sunrise over the library slope at Cornell University that nobody out on it had seen because the slope faces west"[29] – a variant on Bishop Berkeley's classic epistemological conundrum of the tree that falls in the forest with no one to hear it. It ends teetering on the brink of what one character would have called an "anarchist miracle": "another world's intrusion into this one," "a kiss of cosmic pool balls."[30] Teetering on the brink of a miracle, but not the miracle itself; for the novel backs off at the last possible moment from this intrusion of another world, leaving the problem of Berkeley's epistemological skepticism – the problem of solipsism – suspended, finally unresolved.

Pynchon names his heroine Oedipa, suggesting that this novel, too, belongs to the genre of detective story – which it does, in a sense. Oedipa, like the classic private-eye, needs to know; she must struggle to bridge the gap between appearances and reality; she must question the reliability of every piece of information, every source. Set in California, *Lot 49* adheres rather faithfully to the conventions of the LA private-eye sub-genre practiced by Erle Stanley Gardner – whose lawyer-detective Perry Mason Pynchon several times invokes – or, better, by Raymond Chandler and Ross Macdonald.[31] As in Chandler or Macdonald, nearly everyone Oedipa encounters proves to have been complicit in the original crime, the crime itself meanwhile changing its identity, becoming in the course of her investigations larger, more ramified, more sinister – a conspiracy. The "crime" itself, the object of

Oedipa's epistemological inquiry, appears at the outset as merely a number of odd loose ends in the estate of Pierce Inverarity, a millionaire realestate developer who had once been Oedipa's lover and who, for reasons of his own, has made her the executor of his will. These loose ends, followed up by Oedipa with exemplary private-eye's assidulity, each lead to the Tristero System, which may or may not be an underground postal network, and may or may not be stripping away from Oedipa, by means not stopping short of murder, everyone she has been relying upon for support, leaving her isolated with her disturbing knowledge.

May or may not be: therein lies the dilemma. Classically modernist in its form, *The Crying of Lot 49* represents the mediating consciousness of Oedipa, and through her the happenings in its fictional world. Except for a few discreet deviations toward narratorial omniscience in early chapters, the novel remains rigorously within this mode, using free indirect discourse to render Oedipa's thought-processes. So the reader has no opportunity to view events from outside Oedipa's consciousness, no way to check on her reliability as medium for this story; the reader is bounded by the limits of her mind. But just how limited *is* Oedipa's consciousness? How reliable a witness is she? There are disconcerting indications from the outset that Oedipa fears her own dangerous capacity for solipsism, her tendency to believe that the external world has been fabricated by her own mind. She identifies unhappily with a surrealist triptych by Remedios Varro depicting women embroidering a tapestry which is our world[32], and recognizes a fellow-sufferer in the theater director Ronald Driblette when he tells her:

> I'm the projector at the planetarium, all the closed little universe visible in the circle of that stage is coming out of my mouth, eyes, sometimes other orifices also. . . . If I were to dissolve in here . . . be washed down the drain into the Pacific, what you saw tonight would vanish too. You, that part of you so concerned, God knows how, with that little world, would also vanish.[33]

This provokes Oedipa to ask herself, *"Shall I project a world?"*[34] Is Oedipa projecting the Tristero? Is the postal conspiracy only a solipsistic delusion with no reality in the world outside her mind? Nothing that we know about either Oedipa or the Tristero rules out this possibility.

Oedipa herself clearly recognizes this possibility, and others that are equally unpalatable, if not more so. She tells herself:

> Either you have stumbled indeed . . . onto a network by which X number of Americans are truly communicating whilst reserving their lies, recitations of routine, arid betrayals of spiritual poverty, for the official government delivery system; maybe even onto a real alternative to the exitlessness, to the absence of surprise to life, that harrows the head of everybody American you know, and you too, sweetie. Or you are hallucinating it. Or a plot has been mounted against you, so expensive and elaborate . . . so labyrinthine that it must have meaning beyond just a practical joke. Or you are fantasying some such plot, in which case you are a nut, Oedipa, out of your skull.

> Those, now that she was looking at them, she saw to be the alternatives. Those symmetrical four. She didn't like any of them, but hoped she was mentally ill; that that's all it was.[35]

Now, three of Oedipa's "symmetrical four" alternatives embody aspects of the epistemological cul-de-sac into which she has backed herself. Possibly she is allowing herself to be deceived by the shiftiness of appearances, failing to penetrate the veil of hoax that Inverarity has presumably thrown over the truth. Or, possibly, Oedipa is hallucinating either this elaborate hoax or the Tristero conspiracy itself. Or, finally, the fourth alternative, Oedipa actually sees the truth plain: this other order of being, America's secret double, really exists.

Obviously, Oedipa's fourfold analysis of her dilemma could be simplified still further. On the one hand, there are the epistemological solutions: Oedipa is either deceived or self-deceived, the victim either of a hoax or of her own paranoia. On the other hand, there is the ontological solution, to which Bishop Berkeley also resorted: God exists, and guarantees the existence of the perceived world; or, in this case, the Tristero exists:

> Ones and zeroes. So did the couples arrange themselves. . . . Another mode of meaning behind the obvious, or none. Either Oedipa in the orbiting ecstasy of a true paranoia, or a real Tristero.[36]

The alternatives are not very different from those which present themselves to readers of Henry James's notorious novella *The Turn of the Screw* (1898). As in *The Crying of Lot 49*, the reader is forced to hesitate between an explanation in terms of epistemological categories – the governess's vision of events is distorted from within, she is hallucinating the apparitions – and one which posits an alternative ontology – there are other orders of being, the ghosts really exist, this is a case of "another world's intrusion into this one." Also as in *Lot 49*, there is finally no way to decide between the alternatives. The evidence is so finely balanced that one hesitates between the epistemological and the ontological lines of explanation, without finally resolving the hesitation; hence the "fantastic" effect. The difference between *The Turn of the Screw* and *Lot 49* – and it is a crucial difference – is, of course, that James's governess is herself unaware of the alternatives, believing in the "ghostly" explanation from the outset; the teetering between alternatives goes on "above her head," a problem for students of literature but not for her. Whereas Oedipa is only too aware of her alternatives. Once a student of literature herself, she understands the ambiguity of her situation as clearly as her readers do. In this respect, as in others, she is an exemplary late-modernist heroine.

Oedipa is left, at the end of *The Crying of Lot 49*, in an auction-room waiting for the buyer deputed by the Tristero to declare himself – or not, as the case may be. If he does, it will be a true epiphany, a descent of the Holy Spirit – proof that an alternative reality exists. But Oedipa does not break through the closed circle of her solipsism in the pages of this novel; nor does Pynchon break through here to a mode of fiction beyond modernism and its epistemological premises. The Tristero remains only a possibility. The breakthrough will not come until Pynchon's next novel, *Gravity's Rainbow*, where, no longer constrained by the limits of modernism, he will freely exploit the artistic possibilities of the plurality of worlds, the transgression of boundaries between worlds, the "kiss of cosmic pool balls." The dead-ending of episte-mology in solipsism can be transcended, but only by shifting from a mod-ernist poetics of epistemology to a postmodernist poetics of ontology, from Oedipa's anguished cry, "Shall I project a world?," to the unconstrained projection of worlds in the plural.

Contemporary fiction, says Annie Dillard in a memorable phrase, gives us a pretext for doing "unlicensed metaphysics in a teacup."[37] She then goes on in her own book, *Living by Fiction* (1982), to do what amounts to unlicensed epistemology – quite rightly, in my view, since many of the texts that interest her are late- or limit-modernist texts, not what I would call postmodernist. Still, I admire her phrase enough to want to expropriate it for my own purposes. Postmodernist fiction, as I have argued, and will try to substantiate further in what follows, gives us a pretext for doing unlicensed ontology in a teacup. Like Dillard, I want mostly to talk about the teacups themselves – postmodernist novels and stories. But before we can get to that there are still some preliminary matters to be cleared up – such as, "ontology" in what sense? and, how does one "do" ontology, anyway?

2: SOME ONTOLOGIES OF FICTION

They consider metaphysics a branch of fantastic literature.
>   (Jorge Luis Borges, "Tlön, Uqbar, Orbis Tertius," from *The Garden of Forking Paths*, 1941)

Postmodernism's ontological dominant is not the same as the ontology *of* postmodernism. We can see the difference if we consider for a moment how Alan Wilde uses "ontology" in his account of postmodernist irony. Of Donald Barthelme, one of his exemplary postmodernist ironists, Wilde writes:

> Like the pop artists, Barthelme puts aside the central modernist preoccupation with the epistemology, and it may well be the absence of questions about how we know that has operated most strongly to "defamiliarize" his (and their) work. Barthelme's concerns are, rather, ontological in their acceptance of a world that is, willy-nilly, a given of experience.[1]

Obviously, I endorse Wilde's point about postmodernism's bracketing of modernist epistemological questions and the defamiliarizing effect of this move. But we part company when he specifies Barthelme's ontological concerns as acceptance of the world, especially if he means this to be a characterization of postmodernist ontological concerns in general. For there are other possible forms that these concerns might take. Indeed, Wilde's is a minority voice; much more typically, critics have characterized postmodernism in terms of its ontological instability or indeterminacy, the *loss* of a world that could be accepted, "willy-nilly," as a given of experience.[2] If acceptance and assent such as Wilde finds in Barthelme is one possible ontological attitude within postmodernism, there is also, at the opposite pole, Pynchon's or, even more acute, Beckett's anguish in the face of a world that seems without ontological grounding (unless, of course, Wilde would exclude Pynchon or Beckett from consideration as postmodernists for this very reason.)

In any case, however we characterize the ontology of postmodernism, whether in terms of acceptance of the world or in terms of ontological indeterminacy, we are not characterizing postmodernist poetics as such but only that *part* of its poetics that we might call postmodernist *thematics*. Clearly, a wide range of ontological themes or attitudes is available to postmodernist writers, and it is important to specify which writers display which attitudes. But it is equally important to recognize that these attitudes, whatever they may be, come to our attention only through the foregrounding of ontological concerns which is common to all postmodernist writers, and that to accomplish this foregrounding all postmodernists draw on the same repertoire of strategies. A philosophical thematics, specifying the ontology *of* postmodernist texts, will only tell us that there *is* foregrounding; it will not tell us how this foregrounding has been accomplished, what strategies have been deployed.

For this we must turn from philosophical thematics to poetics proper, specifically to theories of *literary* ontology. If postmodernist poetics foregrounds ontological issues of text and world, it can only do so by exploiting general ontological characteristics shared by *all* literary texts and fictional worlds, and it is only against the background of general theories of literary ontology that specific postmodernist practices can be identified and understood. So before we can begin to describe the postmodernist repertoire of foregrounding strategies, we need to review some of the classic ontological themes in poetics, from the Renaissance through the German romantics to Roman Ingarden and contemporary "possible-worlds" theorists.

First, though, a working definition, drawn from this tradition of literary ontology: an ontology, writes Thomas Pavel, is "a theoretical description of a universe."[3] This definition should lay to rest the objections of those who find the coupling of "postmodernist" with "ontology" in itself oxymoronic and self-contradictory, on the grounds that postmodernist discourse is precisely the discourse that denies the possibility of ontological grounding. For the operative word in Pavel's definition, from my point of view, is the indefinite article: an ontology is a description of *a* universe, not of *the* universe; that is, it may describe *any* universe, potentially a *plurality* of universes. In other words, to "do" ontology in this perspective is not necessarily to seek some grounding for *our* universe; it might just as appropriately involve describing *other* universes, including "possible" or even "impossible" universes – not least of all the other universe, or heterocosm, of fiction.

Heterocosm

Among the oldest of the classic ontological themes in poetics is that of the *otherness* of the fictional world, its separation from the real world of experience. This was already a commonplace of Renaissance poetics when Sir Philip Sidney recapitulated it in his *Defense* or *Apologie*, published in 1595. The poet, Sidney writes,

> doth grow, in effect, into another nature, in making things either better than nature bringeth forth, or, quite anew, forms such as never were in

nature, as the heroes, demi-gods, cyclops, chimeras, furies, and such like; so as he goeth hand in hand with nature, not enclosed within the narrow warrant of her gifts, but freely ranging within the zodiac of his own wit.[4]

The poet figures here as a kind of demiurge, "another nature," and the world he creates appears as a Ptolemaic sphere, enclosed, however, not by the celestial zodiac but by the figurative zodiac of the poet's own "wit." Thus Sidney launches the theme of the fictional world as heterocosm, a universe apart, upon its modern career. This theme persists in the twentieth century under the rubric of "fictionality." "Over every poem which looks like a poem is a sign which reads: This road does not go through to action: fictitious."[5] The metaphor here is John Crowe Ransom's, but the ontological opposition it captures goes back to Sidney's *Defense* and beyond.

One important consequence of approaching the fictional world as heterocosm is the sharp ontological boundary that this approach draws around the fictional world at the expense of whatever internal ontological differences may appear *within* this world. Thomas Pavel makes this point explicitly. "Fictional constructions," he writes,

> once granted the willing suspension of disbelief, generally propose unitary models. The ontological cut in fiction cannot be seen except from outside.[6]

In effect, the only ontological difference that the heterocosm approach admits is the opposition between fictional and real. This does not mean, however, that *no* relationship exists between the fictional heterocosm and the real world. Quite the contrary: Sidney's theory of poetry (to the degree that the *Defense* constitutes *a* theory, and not a kind of anthology of theoretical commonplaces) is, after all, a *mimetic* theory, and far from contradicting one another the heterocosm theme and the mimetic theme are mutually dependent and mutually implicating. For the real world to be reflected in the mirror of literary mimesis, the imitation must be distinguishable from the imitated: the mirror of art must stand apart from and opposite to the nature to be mirrored. A mimetic relation is one of similarity, not *identity*, and similarity implies difference – the difference between the original object and its reflection, between the real world and the fictional heterocosm.

Unfortunately, imitation or mirroring is not the only possible relation between the fictional world and reality. The problem is not "forms such as never were in nature," which the theory of heterocosm handles quite easily. Rather, it is the appearance in fictional worlds of individuals who *have* existed in the real world: people such as Napoleon or Richard Nixon, places such as Paris or Dublin, ideas such as dialectical materialism or quantum mechanics. These are not *reflected* in fiction so much as *incorporated*; they constitute enclaves of ontological *difference* within the otherwise ontologically homogeneous fictional heterocosm.

To handle such phenomena, a modified heterocosm theory is required, one that admits of a certain kind of overlap or interpenetration between the heterocosm and the real. Thus, for example, according to Benjamin Hrushovski all literary texts involve a "double-decker" structure of reference.[7] Literary texts project at least one internal field of reference, a universe or semantic continuum (loosely, a "world") constructed *in* and *by* the text itself. In addition, they inevitably refer *outside* their internal field to an external field of reference: the objective world, the body of historical fact or scientific theory, an ideology or philosophy, other texts, and so on. The internal and external fields constitute two parallel planes but, says Hrushovski, their geometry is non-Euclidean, for the planes overlap at many points without merging into one; that is, many referents are *shared* by the two planes, thus possessing a "dual referential allegiance." There are other ways of handling such interpenetration of worlds, as we shall see a bit further on, but however it is handled it spoils the simple geometry of the mirror held up to nature.

"The old analogy between Author and God"

The heterocosm theme has a corollary which loomed even larger in Sidney's thinking, namely the theme of the poet's freedom and power, his demiurgic or quasi-divine function:

> Neither let it be deemed too saucy a comparison to balance the highest point of man's wit with the efficacy of nature; but rather give right honor to the heavenly Maker of that maker, who, having made man to his own likeness, set him beyond and over all the works of that second nature. Which in nothing he showeth so much as in poetry, when with the force of a divine breath he bringeth things forth far surpassing her doings. (Sidney, 8–9)

This is the other classic ontological theme of Sidney's *Defense*: "The old analogy between Author and God, novel and world," as John Barth puts it.[8] This theme, too, has persisted down to the twentieth century, though often in skeptical and self-deprecatory forms, not only in Barth but also, for example, in William Gass. "Authors are gods," Gass writes, "– a little tinny sometimes, but omnipotent no matter what, and plausible on top of that, if they can manage it."[9]

Why the irony here? Actually, from a twentieth-century point of view it makes better sense to turn the question around: why the absence of irony in Sidney? Somehow Sidney seems able to assert the freedom of the poet without that assertion tending to undermine the ontological stability of his fictional world. If his claims seem improbably unironic and anxiety-free to us, this is because between Sidney's time and our own the theme of author as god had been transformed and problematized – first by the practice of writers such as Cervantes, Sterne, and Diderot, then by the aesthetic theories of the German romantics, especially Friedrich Schlegel.[10]

Paradoxically, the romantic theory of poet as God could only develop after man's sense of his position in the universe had begun to erode. The closed, orderly world-view of Sidney and the Renaissance had had to give way to what might be called a Pascalian world-view, characterized by the perceived disparity between man's finite mind and the unfathomably vast, ungraspably complex universe. How is the mind to defend itself against such oppressive infinitude? By turning the tables on the universe, reducing it by a kind of conceptual jiu-jitsu to a finite plaything subject to the whims of infinite mind; in other words, through irony. And if the world of the work of art is analogous to the real world, then, to follow out the analogy, the artist must take an ironic stance in relation to the poetic heterocosm. No longer content with invisibly exercising his freedom to create worlds, the artist now makes his freedom visible by thrusting himself into the foreground of his work. He represents himself in the act of making his fictional world – or unmaking it, which is also his prerogative. There is a catch, of course: the artist represented in the act of creation or destruction is himself inevitably a fiction. The *real* artist always occupies an ontological level superior to that of his projected, fictional self, and therefore *doubly* superior to the fictional world: behind Jacques and the world he occupies stands "the author," and somewhere behind "the author" stands the real Diderot. There is a possibility here of infinite regress, puppet-master behind puppet-master *ad infinitum*. The romantic godlike poet is, to revert to theological discourse, both immanent and transcendent, both *inside* his heterocosm and *above* it, simultaneously present and absent.

But if the fictional world now acquires a visible maker, its own status must inevitably change, too: it has become less the mirror of nature, more an *artifact*, visibly a *made* thing. As a corollary, then, to the artist's paradoxical self-representation, the artwork itself comes to be presented *as* an artwork. The devices of art are laid bare, to use the Russian formalist term. The poetry of romantic irony is about poetry – about itself – as much as it is about a world: "poetry squared," in D. C. Muecke's phrase.

Ingarden

Although the German theorists of romantic irony introduced a certain onto-logical tension into the classical model of poetic heterocosm, they continued to focus on the external ontological relations of fiction, especially fiction's relation to its author. They added little, however, to our understanding of the *internal* ontological constitution and articulation of the fictional text and its world. The shift of attention to internal ontological structure does not come about until the twentieth century, in particular with the work of the Polish phenomenologist Roman Ingarden. Ingarden gives us, for the first time, a picture of fiction's intrinsic ontological complexity. The complexity of the literary artwork, he tells us, lies first of all in its being *heteronomous*, existing both autonomously, in its own right, and at the same time depending upon the constitutive acts of consciousness of a reader. Secondly, the literary artwork is not ontologically uniform or monolithic, but *polyphonic, stratified*. Each of its layers has a somewhat different ontological status, and functions somewhat differently in the ontological make-up of the whole. Ingarden distinguishes four such strata:

1   The stratum of word-sounds. Ingarden has in mind not the concrete phonic materials, which vary with each reader's "performance" of the text and thus do not belong to its ontological structure, but rather the *essential*

("phonemic," the linguists say) configurations. These make the differentiation of word-meanings possible, and thus form the "material base" for higher levels of the text. And the word-sounds are in their turn based on graphic signs, that is, the autonomously-subsisting physical book and its typography. The physical book, together with the persistence of intersubjective, communally-accepted word-meanings, jointly guarantee the continuing existence of the fictional text.

2   The stratum of meaning-units. The word-meanings of nouns, according to Ingarden, actualize parts of our concepts of objects; sentence-meanings project "states of affairs," which are progressively and retrospectively modified by the higher units of meaning into which sentence-meanings enter. None of this occurs, however, unless these meaning-units become the intentional objects of a reader's consciousness, in other words, not unless some reader "concretizes" them. Thus, by contrast with Sidney or the German romantic aestheticians, who had emphasized the "maker's" relation to his fiction, Ingarden's ontology of fiction depends on the interaction between the *reader* and the artwork.

Sentences in fiction undergo what Ingarden calls a "quasi" modification: that is, they function not as true assertions or judgments or questions, but as quasi-assertions, quasi-judgments, quasi-questions. "This road does not go through to action," as John Crowe Ransom says; except that, where Ransom would post this warning over the poetic text as a whole, Ingarden in effect posts it over *each and every sentence* of the text. The basic fiction/real cut does not merely bound the fiction, but passes *through* every one of its sentences. This is a view which Ingarden shares with, among others, I. A. Richards, Käte Hamburger, and John Searle. Whether one prefers the term "quasi-assertion," or "pseudostatement," or "fictional speech-act," the concept is about the same: sentences in literary texts are formally identical with real-world sentences but ontologically different, "weaker" in some sense.

3   The stratum of presented objects. This is where Ingarden makes his most original and valuable contribution, capturing our intuitions as readers that fictional texts do more than carry information in articulated chains of signifiers and signifieds – they also project objects and worlds. Purely intentional objects, Ingarden says, are projected by the word-meanings of nouns, or presented or implied by states of affairs at the sentence-level or higher. In the aggregate these presented objects constitute an "ontic sphere" of their own – a world. This world is partly indeterminate:

> It is always as if a beam of light were illuminating a part of a region, the remainder of which disappears in an indeterminate cloud but is still there in its indeterminacy.[11]

If the ontic sphere as a whole is "cloudy" in character, so too are the individual objects that make it up. Compared to real-world objects, presented objects are strange and paradoxical. Real-world objects have no indeterminate points, ontologically speaking (although there may, of course, be *epistemological* blindspots, points that we happen not to know about), while presented objects in fiction have ontological *gaps*, some of them permanent, some filled in by readers in the act of concretizing the text. Gilbert Sorrentino in *Mulligan*

Stew (1979) has laid bare this aspect of fiction's ontological structure by making two characters explore some of the "cloudy" regions of their own ontic sphere:

> It is a rather odd house, to say the least. There is the living room and the den, but we have not been able to find any other rooms. It *seems* as if there are other rooms, but when we approach them, they are – I don't quite know how to put this – they are simply *not there!* There is no kitchen, no porch, no bedrooms, no bath. At the side of the living room, a staircase leads "nowhere." Oh, I don't mean to say that it disappears into empty space, it simply leads to a kind of . . . haziness, in which one knows there is *supposed* to be a hallway and bedroom doors: but there is absolutely nothing.[12]

All houses in fiction are like this, partly specified, partly left vague. Normally neither the reader nor the character who shares the same world with such a house notices this vagueness; Sorrentino's characters, however, are aware of being *inside* a fiction, and so find this house anomalous, with its permanent gaps where a real-world house would be ontologically determinate.

Ambiguous sentences may project ambiguous objects, objects which are not temporarily but permanently and irresolvably ambiguous. This is not a matter, in other words, of *choosing* between alternative states of affairs, but rather of an ontological oscillation, a flickering effect, or, to use Ingarden's own metaphor, an effect of "iridescence" or "opalescence." And "opalescence" is not restricted to single objects; entire *worlds* may flicker:

> It may also happen that ambiguity is sustained in a number of sentences with a certain consistency; then this opalescence applies to entire spheres of objects, so that, in a manner of speaking, two different worlds are struggling for supremacy, with neither of them capable of attaining it.[13]

4   The stratum of schematized aspects. Not only are presented objects and worlds partly indeterminate and potentially ambiguous, they are also inevitably schematic, lacking the plenitude and density of real objects in the real world. Linguistic categories *abstract* properties from the flux of experience, and the world they project is not a completely filled-in picture but more like a connect-the-dots puzzle, a grid through whose interstices the concreteness of the real world inevitably escapes. Of course, we do not actually experience a real-world object in its "all-overness" either, but piecemeal, through only one sensory channel rather than all of them at once (for example, through sight but not through touch, taste, or smell), from one point of view at a time, and so on. The literary artwork cannot hope to project objects that have the plenitude of real objects, but it certainly *can* duplicate this piecemeal and aspectual nature of our experience of objects, for instance by choosing one sensory channel through which to present an object, or by restricting the point of view. The literary artwork also has resources peculiar to itself. It can, for example, cast an emotional "coloration" over presented objects through sound-values on the stratum of word-sounds, thus projecting these objects in a particular aspect. Such special resources compensate somewhat for the inevitable schematism of the presented world.

The stratum of presented objects, mediated through schematized aspects, manifests what Ingarden calls the work's "metaphysical qualities" – the tragic, the sublime, the grotesque, the holy, and so on. Metaphysical qualities do not, however, constitute a separate stratum, ontologically speaking, but are a function of the presented objects and world.

Possible worlds

"The essential trope of fiction," writes the postmodernist novelist Ron Sukenick, "is hypothesis, provisional supposition, a technique that requires suspension of belief as well as of disbelief."[14] This captures informally an intuition about the special logical status of the fictional text, its condition of being in-between, amphibious – neither true nor false, suspended between belief and disbelief.[15] It turns out to be a sound intuition, corroborated by the more formal reasoning found in theories of possible worlds. Thus, Thomas Pavel has argued that readers do not evaluate the logical possibility of the propositions they find in literary texts in the light of the actual world – as logicians would require them to do[16] – but rather abandon the actual world and adopt (temporarily) the *ontological perspective* of the literary work.[17]

Or, to put it somewhat differently, fictional narratives are subject to certain *global semantic constraints*: all the sentences of a text are governed by the same logical modality, something like its logical key signature.[18] Classical logic recognizes three such modalities: necessity, possibility, impossibility. Propositions about the real world fall under the modality of necessity. Propositions in fiction, by contrast, are governed by the modality of possibility; they require, in short, "suspension of belief as well as of disbelief."

And what about the third category, impossibility? Can we speak of *impossible* worlds? Umberto Eco thinks not. He excludes logical impossibility from the propositions that constitute worlds: every proposition must be *either* true *or* false of a possible world, it cannot be *both* true *and* false. This is to say that possible worlds, according to Eco, obey the law of the excluded middle. Worlds which violate the law of the excluded middle, about which, in other words, certain propositions are both true and false, Eco refuses to regard as full-fledged, self-sustaining worlds. Rather, these self-contradictory constructs are more like subversive critiques of worlds and world-building, anti-worlds rather than worlds proper:

> the proper effect of such narrative constructions (be they sci-fi novels or avant-garde texts in which the very notion of self-identity is challenged) is just that of producing a sense of logical uneasiness and of narrative discomfort. So they arouse a sense of suspicion in respect to our common beliefs and affect our disposition to trust the most credited laws of the world of our encyclopedia. They *undermine* the world of our encyclopedia rather than build up another self-sustaining world.[19]

Lubomír Doležel, however, is willing to entertain the idea of worlds that violate the law of the excluded middle, "semiotic worlds suspended between existence and nonexistence."[20] Perhaps this is only a difference in terminology, Eco withholding the label of "world" from these problematical "suspended" constructs, while Doležel is willing to apply it to them. In any case, there are many of them in postmodernist writing, for example, Muriel Spark's *The Hothouse by the East River* (1973), in which the characters are both dead and not dead, and their world both exists and does not exist. An "opalescent" world, Ingarden would have called this.

Possible worlds depend on somebody's propositional attitude: that is, in order for them to *be* possible, they must be believed in, imagined, wished for etc., by some human agent. We do this every day, when we speculate or plan or daydream – but also, of course, when we read or view or write fictions. Characters *inside* fictional worlds are also capable of sustaining propositional attitudes and projecting possible worlds. Eco calls these possible-worlds-within-possible-worlds *subworlds*; Pavel prefers the term *narrative domains*. It is the tension and disparity among various characters' subworlds, and between their subworlds and the fictional "real" world, that formed the basis of modernist and, before that, realist epistemological poetics. Pavel gives as an example the two parallel sets of worlds in *Don Quixote*, the "actual-in-the-novel world" in which one Alonso Quijana suffers certain delusions, and the worlds *of* Quixote's delusions.[21]

Pavel's concept of narrative domains is not quite identical with Eco's subworlds, however, for he has extended it interestingly to include not only epistemological domains such as Quixote's delusional worlds, but also *ontological* domains. A single work, in Pavel's view, may be apportioned among several different ontologies. He cites the example of the confrontation in such Renaissance plays as Marlowe's *Dr Faustus* and Kyd's *Spanish Tragedy* between a bi-planar, other-worldly ontology and a single-plane, this-worldly ontology. Such ontologically complex, multiple-world texts undertake the "exploration of certain ontological propositions."[22]

The possible-worlds approach not only complicates fiction's internal ontological structure, it also weakens its external boundary or frame. Classical mimetic theories, as we have seen, had a vested interest in maintaining this conceptual boundary, since without a sharp initial distinction between fiction and reality there could be no relation of similarity or mirroring between the two, no re-presentation of reality *in* fiction. Logicians and philosophers of language, such as Bertrand Russell, Saul Kripke, and John Searle, have tended to reinforce and even more sharply define that boundary, throwing a sort of logical and ontological *cordon sanitaire* around fiction.[23] But possible-worlds theorists in poetics have, by contrast, blurred fiction's external boundaries. By doing so, they make it possible for us to understand the passage or circulation that occurs across that boundary. Fiction's epidermis, it appears, is not an impermeable but a semipermeable membrane:

> Far from being well-defined and sealed off, fictional borders appear to be variously accessible, sometimes easy to trespass, obeying different sorts of constraints in different contexts.[24]

For one thing, as we have already seen, fictional possible worlds and the real world inevitably overlap to some extent – often to quite a large extent. This is so, as Eco reminds us, because no world can be described exhaustively; instead of trying futilely to describe a world "from scratch," it is much more feasible simply to "borrow" entities and properties from the ready-made world of reality. There is another, more technical sense in which worlds may be "variously accessible" to one another. Given the structure of one possible world, another is said to be accessible to it if by manipulating the first world's entities and their properties one can generate the structure of the second world. Now this is not a very intuitively evident or graspable concept. Eco suggests that one way of thinking about accessibility intuitively would be in terms of psychological *conceivability*: a second world is accessible if it can be conceived by inhabitants of the first world.[25] Borges' doubly fictional world of Tlön neatly exemplifies accessibility in this sense. Tlön is accessible to our world because the encyclopedists who invented it obviously generated their ideal world by manipulating structures of the real world, "projecting a world which would not be too incompatible with the real world."[26] But Tlön is also a *conceivable* world – self-evidently, since its fictive inventors the encyclopedists, and its real author Borges, as well as we the readers have all been able to conceive it.

This means, in effect, that the "same" entity can exist in more than one world, if there is accessibility among the worlds in question. But "same" in what sense? Eco addresses this question too, formulating criteria for what he calls "transworld identity." If an entity in one world differs from its "prototype" in another world only in accidental properties, not in essentials, and if there is a one-to-one correspondence between the prototype and its other-world variant, then the two entities can be considered identical even though they exist in distinct worlds.[27] This formulation captures our intuitions as readers that a historical personage is in some sense the "same" as his fictional representation in a historical novel, or that the author and his acquaintances are the "same" as their fictionalized replicas in an autobiographical novel or *roman-à-clef*. Note, however, that in such cases of transworld identity between real prototypes and their fictional replicas, the relation between the worlds is one of *asymmetrical* accessibility. The fictional world is accessible to our real world, but the real world is not accessible to the world of the fiction; in other words, we can conceive of the fictional characters and their world, but they cannot conceive of us and ours. Of course, Eco is well aware of the counter-examples to this generalization, works of romantic irony such as Luigi Pirandello's *Six Characters in Search of an Author* (1921), in which fictional characters are presented as being capable of conceiving of the real-world author who has refused to write their drama. But, argues Eco, this is not a valid counterexample but *trompe-l'œil*, for the author these characters seek is himself a fiction, belonging to their world, not ours.[28] Nevertheless, even if this apparent case of symmetrical accessibility between the real and fictional worlds is no more than *trompe-l'œil*, it does accomplish what romantic irony always aims to accomplish: it foregrounds ontological boundaries and ontological structure.

If entities can migrate across the semipermeable membrane that divides a fictional world from the real, they can also migrate between two different fictional worlds. Cordelia is still Cordelia, still in some sense the "same," whether she appears in Shakespeare's original *King Lear* or Nahum Tate's eighteenth-century revision, even though in the original she suffers a tragic destiny while in the revision she ends happily.[29] The transworld identity of Cordelia, it appears, has been preserved. It is not always so. If a prototype and its replica differ in essential properties, and not just the accidental ones, then, according to Eco, this may be a case of mere *homonymy* rather than transworld identity.[30] Such homonymy is frequent in literary parodies: Richardson's *Pamela* and Fielding's *Shamela* are (quasi-) homonymous, certainly not identical. But what about Pamela and Lady Booby of *Joseph Andrews* – is this also a case of mere homonymy, or have enough essential properties been preserved to warrant our considering the two characters identical? Comparable postmodernist examples abound. For instance, in *Mulligan Stew* Gilbert Sorrentino "borrows" the character Ned Beaumont from Dashiell Hammett's *The Thin Man*, and Anthony Lamont from Flann O'Brien's *At Swim-Two-Birds* (1939). Are these "borrowed" characters transworld-identical with their prototypes, or merely homonymous? I would venture to say that the case of Beaumont might involve transworld identity, but not Lamont, who has been parodically deformed in the course of his transmigration from one text to another. Eco's criteria of transworld identity become slippery and difficult to apply in postmodernist examples such as this one.

So entities can pass back and forth across the semipermeable membrane between two texts, as well as between the real world and the world of fiction. There is, finally, another dimension of transworld migration, and that is its historical dimension. Entities can change their ontological status in the course of history, in effect migrating from one ontological realm or level to another. For instance, real world entities and happenings can undergo "mythification," moving from the profane realm to the realm of the sacred. Or mythological entities can, with the erosion of the belief-system that sustains them, lose their status of *superior* reality, "realer" than the real world, and deteriorate to the status of "mere" fictions.[31] The evidence of such historical processes as mythification and fictionalization forces us to broaden our perspective. The external cut of the fictional heterocosm, it appears, is not determined only by fiction's relation to the real world and to other fictional texts, but also by its place among the whole range of other "unreal" and "quasi-real" ontologies in a given culture.

The social construction of (un)reality

"It is useful," writes Thomas Pavel, "to set up a complex ontology, involving different domains, populated by different kinds of beings."[32] Pavel calls this complex ontology the "ontological landscape" of a culture.[33] Ontological landscapes may be double, as in the many cultures that distinguish sacred and profane levels of reality. In such cultures, the two levels typically "fuse" at certain prescribed places and times – temples, festivals, and so on. In other cultures, the fusion of the levels may be more or less total, either strongly fused, as in the case of medieval Catholic culture, or weakly fused, as in late-nineteenth-century European Protestant culture. Or the ontological landscape may occupy only a single plane, for instance in the strictly this-worldly "literal" ontology of hard-core positivism. Finally, ontological landscapes may also be plural rather than double, organized into a central ontology and several peripheral ontologies, including "leisure" ontologies such as fiction. In periods of rapid ontological change, cultures may display symptoms of what Pavel calls ontological stress. "Passeism" is one such symptom, that is, "playful ontological regression"; Pavel's example is Haydn's oratorio *The Creation*, which pretended to revive a medieval onto- logical landscape of angelic orders and a geocentric cosmology. Another symptom of ontological stress is anarchism, the refusal either to accept or to reject any of a plurality of available ontological orders. This, I would main- tain, is precisely the postmodernist condition: an anarchic landscape of worlds in the plural.

Pavel's account of ontological landscapes, undertaken from a position informed by the ideas of modal logic, converges strikingly with certain analyses of the "social construction of reality" from a sociological perspective. The most familiar, and undoubtedly the most influential, of such approaches is that of Peter L. Berger and Thomas Luckmann.[34] Berger and Luckmann regard reality as a kind of collective fiction, constructed and sustained by the processes of socialization, institutionalization, and everyday social inter- action, especially through the medium of language. This approach to social reality as a fictional construct has precursors going back at least as far as Hans Vaihinger's philosophy of "as if" (1924). For Vaihinger, however, the fictions of science and society (such as the atomic theory, or Adam Smith's economic fiction that self-interest alone motivates human behavior) are transparent and temporary expedients, deliberately constructed to enable us to surmount particular conceptual difficulties, and discarded as soon as they have served their purpose. By contrast, Berger's and Luckmann's fictions are relatively permanent (although subject to historical change, of course) and opaque, that is, accepted as *the* reality, except under the probing of sociological reflection.

Socially-constructed reality is, like Pavel's ontological landscape, complex, a jigsaw puzzle of "subuniverses of meaning": the jostling world-views of different social classes, castes, religious sects, occupations, etc. These "sub- universes" are the equivalent in the outside world of the subworlds or domains that Eco and Pavel distinguish in the interior of the poetic hetero- cosm. The subuniverses are integrated within a more or less all-embracing "symbolic universe" whose unity is guaranteed by such high-powered conceptual machinery of "universe-maintenance" as mythology, theology, philosophy, and science. Well below the threshold of conceptualization, however, lies the shared social reality of everyday life. While this shared reality constitutes the common ground of interaction among the members of society, these same members also experience a multiplicity of private or peripheral realities: dreaming, play, fiction, and so on. But these other realities are felt to be marginal; it is the shared reality that is "paramount":

> Compared to the reality of everyday life, other realities appear as finite provinces of meaning, enclaves within the paramount reality marked by circumscribed meanings and modes of experience. The paramount reality envelops them on all sides, as it were, and consciousness always returns to the paramount reality as from an excursion.[35]

"As from an excursion": an intriguing metaphor, and one taken seriously by Stanley Cohen and Laurie Taylor, sociologists working very much in the vein of Berger and Luckmann.[36] Where Berger and Luckmann had focused on the construction of "paramount reality," Cohen and Taylor concentrate on the relations between this reality and the other "finite provinces" or "enclaves," the peripheral realities that Pavel calls "leisure ontologies." These "escapes" from the world of paramount reality range from mental strategies of ironic disengagement ("the mental management of routine") through hobbies, games, gambling, sex, holidays, mass-media entertainment, therapy, the use of alcohol and drugs ("free areas," "activity enclaves," "mindscaping"), to the extreme of radical escapes such as religious conversion, Utopian alternative societies, and, ultimately, schizophrenia. However, Cohen's and Taylor's most interesting discussions bear not on the radical alternative worlds at the extreme end of the scale, but rather on the frequency and density of "escape attempts" in normal, everyday life. A "hypothetical daily sequence" would, they suggest, have to involve a great deal of "shuffling" among worlds: the world of a celebrity's love-life, as reported by the morning newspaper; the world of daydream reminiscences, triggered by an old song heard on the car radio while driving to work; the game-world of a conversation about sports with colleagues over lunch; the projected "new landscape" of a conversation about holiday plans with one's spouse over dinner; the fictional "leisure ontology" of a James Bond adventure movie after dinner; and so on.

> All around us – on advertisement hoardings, bookshelves, record covers, television screens – these miniature escape fantasies present themselves. This, it seems, is how we are destined to live, as split personalities in which the private life is disturbed by the promise of escape routes to another reality.[37]

Contemporary writing, says Steve Katz, "has to echo in its form the shape of American experience, the discontinuous drama, all climax, all boring intermissions in the lobbies of theaters built on the flight decks of exploding 747s."[38] "To echo in its form": postmodernist fiction turns out to be mimetic after all, but this imitation of reality is accomplished not so much at the level of its content, which is often manifestly un- or anti-realistic, as at the level of form. "The shape of American experience, the discontinuous drama": what postmodernist fiction imitates, the object of its mimesis, is the pluralistic and anarchistic ontological landscape of advanced industrial cultures – and not only in the United States. "All boring intermissions": one of the features of this ontological landscape is its permeation by secondary realities, especially mass-media fictions, and one of the most typical experiences of members of this culture is that of the transition from one of these fictional worlds to the paramount reality of everyday life, or from paramount reality to fiction.[39] "The flight decks of exploding 747s": if our culture's ontological landscape is unprecedented in human history – at least in the *degree* of its pluralism – it also incorporates one feature common to all cultures, all ontological landscapes, namely the ultimate ontological boundary between life and death.[40] Yet even

here our culture is innovative, for it alone has had to make room in its
ontological landscape for mass technological death – "exploding 747s" –
even, ultimately, global nuclear death.

So postmodernist fiction *does* hold the mirror up to reality; but that reality,
now more than ever before, is plural.

And how does postmodernist fiction achieve this modeling of our pluralistic ontological landscape? Precisely by foregrounding the ontological
themes and differences, internal and external, described by ontologists of
fiction from Sidney through Schlegel to Ingarden, Hrushovski, and the
possible-world theorists. Ingarden believed that the ontological structures of
the text could not themselves be of any aesthetic value or interest, although
they could, of course, *sustain* components of indubitable interest and value.
The strata belonged permanently to the background of the artwork, never to
rise above the threshold of perceptibility:

> the skeleton of the layers and the structural order of sequence in a literary
> work of art are of neutral artistic value; they form the axiologically neutral
> foundation of the work of art in which the artistically valent elements . . . of
> the work are grounded.[41]

But Ingarden was wrong; it is precisely by foregrounding the skeleton of
layers – as well as the double-decker structure of reference described by
Hrushovski, the transworld identity described by Eco, and so on – that
postmodernist fiction achieves its aesthetic effects and sustains interest, in
the process modeling the complex ontological landscape of our experience.
Ingarden, in other words, simply failed to foresee postmodernism.

In what follows I have attempted to describe the repertoire of strategies
upon which postmodernist fiction draws in order to foreground the ontological structure of text and world (or worlds in the plural). As an organizing
scheme, I have adapted Hrushovski's three-dimensional model of semiotic
objects, altering that model in one important respect.[42] Hrushovski's three
dimensions are the reconstructed world ("Worlds"), the text continuum
("Words"), and the dimension of speakers, voices, and positions. I have had
to reconceive this third dimension of semiotic objects in a way more congenial
to the special postmodernist objects I am trying to describe. The dimension of
speakers, voices, and positions is especially foregrounded in modernist
poetics, but, while of course still present and functional in postmodernist
poetics, relatively backgrounded there.[43] In place of modernist forms
of perspectivism, postmodernist fiction substitutes a kind of ontological
perspectivism, the "iridescence" or "opalescence" of which Ingarden has
written. This "flickering" effect intervenes between the text-continuum (the
language and style of the text) and the reader's reconstruction of its world. I
have treated this ontological perspectivism as a separate dimension in effect
straddling the dimensions of text-continuum and reconstructed world, and
for want of a better term have labeled it the dimension of "construction" – a
term appropriately ambiguous between the *process* of construction and its
product, the thing constructed.

Finally, I have also considered how postmodernist fiction exploits to
its own ends the ontological "groundings" which, in Ingarden's view,

guarantee the autonomous existence of the literary work of art. The literary work, according to Ingarden, subsists autonomously (that is, apart from the reader's constitutive consciousness) thanks to three factors: the language, which exists intersubjectively in the minds of its speakers; the material book; and the biographical author who originally produced the work. Post-modernist strategies involving the first of these factors have been absorbed into Part 4, "Words"; the strategies by which postmodernist fiction fore-grounds and problematizes the other two are covered in Chapters 12 and 13, respectively.

PART TWO: WORLDS

I am conscious of the world as consisting of multiple realities. As I move from one reality to another, I experience the transition as a kind of shock.
> (Peter L. Berger and Thomas Luckmann, *The Social Construction of Reality*, 1966)

Worlds, infinite worlds.
> (Guy Davenport, "The Dawn in Erewhon", from *Tatlin!*, 1974)

3: IN THE ZONE

Separations are proceeding. Each alternative Zone speeds away from all the others, in fated acceleration, red-shifting, fleeing the Center. . . . The single roost lost. . . . Each bird has his branch now, and each one is the Zone.
(Thomas Pynchon, *Gravity's Rainbow*, 1973).

The Empire of the Great Khan, in Italo Calvino's *Invisible Cities* (1972), contains a number of continuous cities, shapeless, sprawling urban agglomerations lacking internal articulation or even clear external boundaries. There is Penthesilea, a city of continuous suburbs, without a definite center; Cecilia, a city which over the years has engulfed all the surrounding territory; and Trude, a city indistinguishable from any other, to the point of identity:

> The world is covered by a sole Trude which does not begin and does not end. Only the name of the airport changes.[1]

Contradictions arise: how can three cities, each said to have absorbed the entire space of the Empire, coexist? If Trude is coextensive with the whole world, what room does that leave for Penthesilea or Cecilia, or indeed any of the other cities of the Empire? Perhaps Penthesilea, Cecilia and Trude are only different names for one and the same continuous city; but if so, why are their descriptions so dissimilar? What paradoxical kind of space does this Empire occupy? What kind of world is this?

A problematical world, that much is certain. It has been designed, as Thomas Pavel has said of certain Renaissance texts, for the purpose of exploring ontological propositions. Some of Calvino's invisible cities place the world of the living in confrontation with the "other world" of the dead; others confront the sacred world with the profane; still others confront the real-world city with its representation or model or double. Not all of the cities explore ontological propositions, however; some raise classic epistemological issues – appearance vs reality, multiplicity of perspectives, the distortions of desire and memory, and so on. One might be tempted to think that the frametale of *Invisible Cities* focuses on this sort of epistemological problem rather than on an ontological one. Certainly, the framing narrative does foreground the question of reliability or unreliability in Marco Polo's account of the cities he claims to have visited. By my reading, however, this issue is subordinate to ontological issues in the text as a whole, above all the issue of what kind of space is capable of accommodating so many incommensurable and mutually exclusive worlds.

What kind of space? A *heterotopia*. The concept comes from Michel Foucault:

> There is a worse kind of disorder than that of the *incongruous*, the linking together of things that are inappropriate; I mean the disorder in which fragments of a large number of possible orders glitter separately in the dimension, without law or geometry, of the *heteroclite*; . . . in such a state, things are "laid," "placed," "arranged" in sites so very different from one another that it is impossible to find a place of residence for them, to define a *common locus* beneath them all. . . . Heterotopias are disturbing, probably because they secretly undermine language, because they make it impossible to name this *and* that, because they destroy "syntax" in advance, and not only the syntax with which we construct sentences but also that less apparent syntax which causes words and things (next to and also opposite to one another) to "hold together."[2]

The empire of Calvino's Great Khan is just such a heterotopia. Radically discontinuous and inconsistent, it juxtaposes worlds of incompatible structure. It violates the law of the excluded middle: logically, *either* Trude is everywhere *or* Cecilia is everywhere; in the Empire of *Invisible Cities*, both are everywhere, and so are Penthesilea and the other continuous cities as well. Umberto Eco might refuse to consider this a "world" at all, since it fails to observe the basic rules of world-building. In deference to this view, we might try avoiding the use of the term "world" in this connection, and instead follow the practice of a number of postmodernist writers who have found a different name for this sort of heterotopian space. They call it "the zone."

There is Julio Cortázar's zone, William Burroughs's, Alasdair Gray's. Behind them all lies Apollinaire's poem "Zone" (from *Alcools*, 1913), whose speaker, strolling through the immigrant and red-light districts of Paris, finds in them an objective correlative for modern Europe and his own marginal, heterogeneous, and outlaw experience. Clearly derived from Apollinaire's, Cortázar's zone (in *62: A Model Kit*, 1968) is a space of overlapping subjectivities, including shared fantasies and nightmares, which comes into being whenever his cast of bohemians and cosmopolitans convenes somewhere in "the DMZ [demilitarized zone] atmosphere of cafés." Burroughs's zone, or interzone, is a vast, ramshackle structure in which all the world's architectural styles are fused and all its races and cultures mingle, the apotheosis of the Third World shanty-town. Sometimes it is located in Latin America or North Africa, sometimes (as in *The Ticket That Exploded*, 1962) on another planet, sometimes (as in *Cities of the Red Night*, 1981) in a lost civilization of the distant past. By contrast, Alasdair Gray's zone (in *Lanark*, 1981), a space of paradox modeled on the Wonderland and Looking-glass worlds of the Alice books, has been displaced to the ambiguous no man's land *between* cities.

Finally, combining elements of all these postmodernist zones, there is Thomas Pynchon's zone. "In the Zone," the title of the third and longest section of his *Gravity's Rainbow* (1973), refers to occupied Germany in the anarchic weeks and months immediately following the collapse of the Third Reich. "It is a great frontierless streaming out here," says Pynchon's narrator about the zone:[3] former national boundaries have been obliterated, the armies of the victorious Allies are jockeying for position, entire displaced nations are on the move, spies, black-marketeers, and free-lance adventurers dodge back and forth across the ruined landscape. So far, Pynchon's zone would seem to be a realistic construct, closely corresponding to historical fact, and a far cry from the heterotopian empire of Calvino's Great Khan. But the collapse of regimes and national boundaries, it turns out, is only the outward and visible sign of the collapse of *ontological* boundaries. As the novel unfolds, our world and the "other world" mingle with increasing intimacy, hallucinations and fantasies become real, metaphors become literal, the fictional worlds of the mass media – the movies, comic-books – thrust themselves into the midst of historical reality. The zone, in short, becomes plural:

> Isn't this an "interface" here? a meeting surface for two worlds . . . sure, but *which two*?[4]

In fact, Pynchon's zone is paradigmatic for the heterotopian space of postmodernist writing, more so than Gray's or Burroughs's or even Calvino's. Here (to paraphrase Foucault) a large number of fragmentary possible worlds coexist in an impossible space which is associated with occupied Germany, but which in fact is located nowhere but in the written text itself.

How to build a zone

The space of a fictional world is a construct, just as the characters and objects that occupy it are, or the actions that unfold within it. Typically, in realist and modernist writing, this spatial construct is organized around a perceiving subject, either a character or the viewing position adopted by a disembodied narrator.[5] The heterotopian zone of postmodernist writing cannot be organized in this way, however. Space here is less constructed than *deconstructed* by the text, or rather constructed and deconstructed at the same time. Postmodernist fiction draws upon a number of strategies for constructing/deconstructing space, among them *juxtaposition, interpolation, superimposition*, and *misattribution*.

Spaces which real-world atlases or encyclopedias show as noncontiguous and unrelated, when juxtaposed in written texts constitute a zone. For instance, Guy Davenport, in "The Haile Selassie Funeral Train" (from *Da Vinci's Bicycle*, 1979), sends his fictional funeral train on an impossible itinerary. Setting out from Deauville in Normandy, it passes through Barcelona, along the Dalmatian coast of present-day Yugoslavia, to Genoa, Madrid, Odessa, Atlanta (in the State of Georgia, USA!), and back to Deauville again. The spaces it traverses, simply by the fact of having traversed them, and in that order, constitute a zone. Not coincidentally, among the train's incongruous collection of passengers is Guillaume Apollinaire, one of the first to have conceived of modern Europe as a heterotopian zone.

The strategy of interpolation involves introducing an alien space *within* a familiar space, or *between* two adjacent areas of space where no such "between" exists. This strategy has a long history prior to its adaptation to postmodernist uses. It underlies the "Ruritanian" *topos* of the imaginary country, a staple of swashbuckling adventure-stories in the tradition of Anthony Hope's *The Prisoner of Zenda* (1894) or, in a more sophisticated, modernist form, Joseph Conrad's *Nostromo* (1904). Uqbar, the invented Near Eastern country in Borges' story, "Tlön, Uqbar, Orbis Tertius" (1941), and the African kingdoms of Raymond Roussel's *Impressions d'Afrique (Impressions of Africa*, 1910), exemplify the postmodernist adaptation of this Ruritanian *topos*. Apparently located somewhere in Asia Minor, Uqbar's exact geographical position is indeterminable. There is a "fundamental vagueness" in the encyclopedists' description of its frontiers, which are all fixed with reference to geographical formations *within* the space of Uqbar itself. Although certain identifiable place-names appear in the same context with Uqbar – Khurasan, Armenia, Erzurum – it is not clear how the interpolated space relates to them. Like Borges' Uqbar, Roussel's kingdoms of Ponukele and Drelshkaf are mentioned in the same context with a few place-names that belong to the real world and can be found on a map: Marseilles, Tripoli, Porto Novo, Bougie. But the exact geographical disposition of these kingdoms with respect to known places is impossible to determine, and Roussel has the Emperor of Ponukele's cartographer exploit the indeterminacy of *real* African frontiers around the turn of the century by extending Emperor Talu's zone in every direction:

> On both sides of the vast watercourse [The Congo River], a huge red area represented the state belonging to the all-powerful Talu.
>
> As a form of flattery, the designer of the garment had indefinitely extended this impressive territory, which submitted to the rule of a single sceptre and whose boundaries were, in any case, largely undetermined; the brilliant carmine stretched to the southernmost point, where the words, "Cape of Good Hope," were set out in large black letters.[6]

The interpolation of a spurious space between known spaces serves here as the opening wedge for a total assimilation of the known to the spurious: Africa is engulfed by the zone.

A third strategy is superimposition. Here two familiar spaces are placed one on top of the other, as in a photographic double-exposure, creating through their tense and paradoxical coexistence a third space identifiable with neither of the original two – a zone. The great precursor is William Blake, who in his long poem *Jerusalem* (1804–20) superimposed the counties of the United Kingdom and the Twelve Tribes of Old Testament Israel to generate a visionary space. "And did those feet in ancient time / Walk upon England's mountains green?" – yes, they did, and at the same time no, they did not: no law of excluded middles in Blake. Guy Davenport's materials in "The Invention of Photography in Toledo" (from *Da Vinci's Bicycle*) are a good deal

humbler, but the result is comparable. Exploiting the homonymy between
Toledo, Spain, and Toledo, Ohio, Davenport has superimposed the two
cities, their topographies, histories, cultures:

> A small town safe in its whereabouts, Titus Livy said of Toledo. It sits on a
> promontory at a convergence of rivers.
>   Has not a silver cornet band strutted down its streets in shakos and
> scarlet sashes, playing with brio and a kind of melancholy elation *Santa
> Ana's Retreat from Buena Vista?* Swan Creek flows through its downtown
> into the blue Maumee, which flows into Lake Erie. It bore the name of Port
> Lawrence until Marcus Fulvius Nobilor erected the *fasces* and eagles of the
> SPQR in 193. Originally a port of Michigan until Andrew Jackson gave his
> nod to Ohio's claim, the fierce violet of its stormy skies inspired El Greco to
> paint his famous view of the city. It was in Toledo that the Visigoths joined
> the church and made Spain Catholic. And in 1897 Samuel L. (Golden Rule)
> Jones was elected mayor on the Independent ticket. Its incredible sunsets
> began to appear in late Roman eclogues.[7]

The effect is that of a disorienting double-vision: Toledo is both a former bone
of contention between Ohio and Michigan and (in the same sentence) the
subject of a famous painting by El Greco; it is both associated with the
Visigoths and Marcus Fulvius Nobilor, and with Andrew Jackson and
"Golden Rule" Jones; it is both sited on the banks of Swan Creek and on a
promontory at the convergence of two Spanish rivers.
   Similar effects are achieved by Julio Cortázar in his story "The Other
Heaven" (from *All Fires the Fire and Other Stories*, 1966), where Buenos Aires of
the 1940s is superimposed on Paris of the 1860s; and on a much larger scale in
Nabokov's *Ada* (1970). The alternate world, or Antiterra, of *Ada* has been
constructed by superimposing Russia on the space occupied in our world by
Canada and the United States, Britain on our France, Central Asia on
European Russia, and so on. All of these geographical double-exposures are
elaborately motivated: at the level of the fiction, by the science-fiction *topos* of
the parallel world; at the level of the author's biography (which in a Nabokov
text cannot be ruled out as an irrelevance), by the complex layering of cultures and homelands – Russia, England, France, the United States – that
constituted Nabokov's personal experience.
   A fourth strategy of zone-construction is misattribution. Traditional catalogues of places and their attributes, such as those of Walt Whitman, in effect
transcribe the unwritten encyclopedia of conventional wisdom and common
knowledge. Every association is "automatic" – or at any rate would have been
in the mid-nineteenth century:

> At home on Kanadian snow-shoes or up in the bush,
>   or with fishermen off Newfoundland,
> At home in the fleet of ice-boats, sailing with
>   the rest and tacking,
> At home on the hills of Vermont or in the woods
>   of Maine, or the Texan ranch.[8]

Common knowledge automatically associates Canada with snowshoes, Newfoundland with fishing, Vermont with hills (in this case the attribute is etymologically contained in the name), and so on. It would in a sense be *ungrammatical* in this context to associate Vermont with ranches, or Texas with fishing or the woods, even though, objectively, there are certainly fishermen and woods in the real-world Texas. Ensuring its own intelligibility by copying the encyclopedia, Whitman's catalogue at the same time reinforces or corroborates the encyclopedia, reassuring us that our associations are correct, that the image we have of North American places corresponds to what is really to be found there.

Postmodernist fictions, by contrast, often strive to displace and rupture these automatic associations, parodying the encyclopedia and substituting for "encyclopedic" knowledge their own *ad hoc*, arbitrary, unsanctioned associations. Examples of such unsanctioned, skewed attribution may be found in Donald Barthelme's story "Up, Aloft in the Air" (from *Come Back, Dr Caligari*, 1964), where the cities of Ohio have been assigned attributes which, if not quite impossible, are certainly unlikely, anti-verisimilar: Cleveland is associated with dancing, Akron with transistor radios and "ill-designed love triangles," Cincinnati with "polo, canned peaches, *liaisons dangereuses*," and so on.[9] This skewing of attributions is a matter of degree. Thus, Barthelme's Ohio is unlikely, but Kenneth Patchen's in *The Journal of Albion Moonlight* (1941) is a bizarre impossibility, an exotic land where as recently as 1924 cannibalism was practiced.[10] Falling in much the same category is Chad in Walter Abish's *Alphabetical Africa* (1974), a country to which Abish has managed to assign a beach, although the real-world Chad is landlocked; and Israel in Ronald Sukenick's *98.6* (1975), a tissue of deliberate misattributions:

> In Israel there are places where the jungle comes down to the sea and this is where I like to eat lunch. They have beach cabanas there you can have a long leisurely meal cooled by the breezes coming in from the Mediterranean as you watch the submarine excavation projects. Despite the jungle and the deserts inland Israel has perfect weather all year round it has to do with air currents generated over the Afar Triangle on the Red Sea. . . . Here in Israel we have no need of cars. . . . Automobiles have long been exiled from the cities and towns where transportation depends on various beasts of burden camels burros oxen. . . . We have an extensive monorail system and colorful barges make their way among the canals.[11]

In Israel, of course, there are *no* places where the jungle comes down to the sea, for there is no jungle, nor any monorails or barges or canals either; no more than there are roasting pits for the preparation of human flesh in Ohio, despite what Kenneth Patchen says.

In short, Sukenick's Israel, like Patchen's Ohio or Abish's Chad, has the same status as the Paraguay of Barthelme's story by that name (from *City Life*, 1970):

> This Paraguay is not the Paraguay that exists on our maps. It is not to be found on the continent, South America; it is not a political subdivision of that continent, with a population of 2,161,000 and a capital named Asunción.[12]

This Paraguay of Barthelme's is the *negation* of the Paraguay of the encyclo-pedia – in this case, of the actual encyclopedia, the place where facts of the kind Barthelme cites (only to negate them) are to be found. "This Paraguay," Barthelme continues, "exists elsewhere." Precisely; it exists in the zone.

Ohio, Oz, and other zones

The zone sometimes appears where we least expect it. In Ohio, for instance. In the literary imagination and the popular imagination alike, Ohio has long maintained, as they say, a low profile. Its "image" is one of colorlessness and poverty of associations. It is middle-American in every sense: middling in its landscapes and natural phenomena, culturally middling, sociologically mid-dling – not, one would think, likely raw material for ontological improvisa-tion. Yet, as we have seen, a number of postmodernist writers *have* chosen to improvise on the theme of Ohio: Patchen in *The Journal of Albion Moonlight*, Barthelme in "Up, Aloft in the Air," Davenport in "The Invention of Photog-raphy in Toledo." The zone of Ohio, it would appear, is a recurrent feature of postmodernist writing, a *topos* in both senses, geographical as well as rhetor-ical. But why Ohio in particular? And, more generally, why do a few favored geographical areas seem to recur as zones throughout postmodernist fiction?

The reasons are various. Behind each of the recurrent zones lies a different historical-cultural explanation for its place in the repertoire of postmodernist *topoi*. For example, in order to understand why Ohio, of all places, belongs to the postmodernist repertoire, we need to take into account the semiotics of American space in the nineteenth and twentieth centuries. For early nineteenth-century culture, and its imaginative writers in particular, America was organized into two adjacent worlds, the world of "civilization" and that of the "wilderness," separated by an ambiguous and liminal space, the "frontier" – a prototypical zone. This frontier zone fascinated American writers, not just those like Fenimore Cooper who located their narratives on the frontier itself, but also those who transposed the liminality and ambiguity of the frontier from geographical space into other spheres – Charles Brockden Brown, Nathaniel Hawthorne, Herman Melville, even Edgar Allan Poe. The characteristic form for all these writers was the romance, which the critic and literary historian Richard Chase has described as

> a kind of "border" fiction, whether the field of action is in the neutral territory between civilization and the wilderness, as in the adventure tales of Cooper and Simms, or whether, as in Hawthorne and later romancers, the field of action is conceived not so much as a place as a state of mind – the borderland of the human mind where the actual and the imaginary intermingle.[13]

The geographical frontier retreated westward ahead of advancing settlement throughout the nineteenth century. With the closing of the frontier, and the effective absorption of the wilderness space by civilization, American writers were forced to reconceptualize and imaginatively restructure their country. This process of reimagining American space has continued well into the twentieth century, for instance in texts like Hemingway's "Big Two-Hearted

River" (from *In Our Time*, 1925), Faulkner's "The Bear" (from *Go Down, Moses*, 1942), Norman Mailer's *Why Are We in Vietnam?* (1967), and Thomas McGuane's *Nobody's Angel* (1982). Such texts have sought to recover the frontier, sometimes nostalgically or elegiacally, sometimes in an ironic mode.

But there is another approach to the reconceptualization of American space, one undertaken earlier than these modernist examples, and on the margins of the literary system rather than at its center. Its *locus classicus* is L. Frank Baum's *The Wizard of Oz* (1900), a book intended for children. The Land of Oz, as everyone must surely know, is a fantastic self-contained world, encompassing several dissimilar realms. Baum locates it somehow *within* the state of Kansas – an impossibility, since its land-area must surely exceed that of Kansas. In effect, Oz is the frontier zone, but a *displaced* frontier; no longer marking the extreme western limit of civilization, the zone now stands at its very center, the geographical middle of the continental United States. Baum has reacted to the closing of the frontier, and everything it stands for in American ideology, by *reopening* the frontier in Middle America.[14] This strategy of reimagining America as an *interior* frontier clearly struck a responsive chord in the popular imagination; witness the extraordinary mythological status of the Hollywood movie version of *The Wizard of Oz*, which both exploited and helped consolidate the status of Baum's original.

All this helps explain, I think, the function of Ohio in postmodernist writing. It has gained a place in the postmodernist repertoire not by virtue of being Ohio as such, but by virtue of being typically middle-American – like Baum's Kansas, which is its functional equivalent. The American zone is the "Zone of the Interior."[15] Its strangeness and liminality are foregrounded by its being located not on the edges of the continent, but at its center. It is the historical descendant of the frontier zone, transposed to the flat, middling (in every sense) American heartland.

It is this version of American space, the Oz version, so to speak, rather than the elegiac lost-frontier version, that recurs throughout postmodernist writing about America, for instance in Michel Butor's *Mobile* (1962), Ronald Sukenick's *Out* (1973), Raymond Federman's *Take It or Leave It* (1976), and Angela Carter's quasi-science-fiction picaresque novel *The Passion of New Eve* (1977). Federman's American zone is, like the Manhattan of Spark's *Hothouse by the East River* (1973), a world under erasure. His narrative promises a classic transcontinental journey like those in, say, Kerouac's *On the Road* (1957); his hero's itinerary from East Coast to West is even plotted on a map; but none of the westward journey ever actually materializes. Preempted by an arbitrary and unforeseen turn of events, the promised journey slips from its ontological status of anticipated fact into the limbo of the merely hypothetical; it is canceled, erased out of existence. In Butor's *Mobile*, the American zone is shaped by *homonymy*; here geography is at the mercy of the play of the signifier. Butor's text leaps back and forth across the continent, radically disrupting geographic continuity, its displacements triggered by *identity of place-names*: we leap from Concord, California, to Concord, North Carolina, at the other extreme of the American continent, then to Concord, Georgia, then Concord, Florida, and so on. As in Davenport's "Invention of Photography in Toledo," similarity or identity at the level of the linguistic signifier has been allowed to derange and remodel geographical space. Butor also uses the irregular spacing of typography on the pages of his text to represent or simulate geographical space in an oblique and distorted way. Sukenick in *Out* similarly constructs an analogy between page-space and geographical space, but his analogy is more straightforwardly iconic, less oblique than Butor's. As Sukenick's protagonist moves westward across the American continent, the pages of the text become increasingly blank, until the moment of his embarkation upon the Pacific Ocean, when the text literally vanishes into the void of the empty page. Finally, Angela Carter has constructed what may be the paradigmatic representation of America as the zone. The hero/heroine of *The Passion of New Eve* travels from east to west across a future America devolved into warring city-states, each zone-city embodying a different "possible order." Approaching the end of this journey, Carter's protagonist reflects that since leaving New York she/he has

> lived in systems which operated within a self-perpetuating reality; a series of enormous solipsisms, a tribute to the existential freedom of the land of free enterprise.[16]

"A series of enormous solipsisms": it could be a characterization of Calvino's Empire of the Great Khan, or Pynchon's zone – or, indeed, of the Land of Oz itself, the "innocent" precursor of postmodernist heterotopian America.

Other recurrent postmodernist zones have different historical roots. Take, for example, the postmodernist use of Latin-American space. We have already seen examples from Barthelme ("Paraguay") and Cortázar ("The Other Heaven"), and this does not even begin to take into account the other major writers of the so-called "boom" in South American writing, including García Márquez, Fuentes, and Alejo Carpentier, among others. Clearly, Latin America constitutes another postmodernist *topos*, a favored zone. Just as clearly, however, the historical conditions of Latin-American postmodernism differ radically from those in North America. The frontier experience has not left nearly as deep a mark on the conceptualization of Latin-American space as it did in North America; nor has Latin America yet joined the ontological landscape of advanced industrial society (described in the preceding chapter) as fully as the United States has. We must look elsewhere for the formative conditions of the Latin-American zone.

These can be found, I think, in two mechanisms which converge upon the reinvention of Latin America as a heterotopia. The first mechanism involves the conceptualization of Latin America as *opposite* to the European world (including Anglo-America), Europe's other, its alien double. This dualism, Europe vs Latin America, runs right through Latin-American culture itself, of course; indeed, it even runs through the personal experience of many of the Latin-American "boom" writers, a number of whom – including Cortázar, García Márquez, Fuentes – are or have been expatriates from their native lands. The theme of dualism is explicit in Alejo Carpentier's *El recurso del metodo* (*Reasons of State*, 1974), in which a Latin-American dictator, connoisseur of European (especially Parisian) culture, shuttles back and forth between the two continents. Elsewhere, however, the Europe/Latin America dualism appears at a deeper level than that of theme. It constitutes the ontological structure of a text like Cortázar's "The Other Heaven," or, on a much larger scale, his novel *Rayuela* (*Hopscotch*, 1963/7), or Fuentes's *Terra nostra* (1975). The organization of both *Hopscotch* and *Terra nostra* is that of an immense triptych. In each, the first "panel" is devoted to Europe – "The Old World" in Fuentes, "The Other Side" in Cortázar – while the second turns to Latin America – "The New World," "This Side." This division of the fictional universe into two opposed worlds–literally different ontologies in Fuentes's case, only figuratively so in Cortázar's – is not, however, the end of the process, but only its first step. Once the unity of the fictional ontology has been split, further splittings-off follow; duality of the fictional world gives rise, by a kind of chain-reaction, to a *plurality* of worlds. Thus, the third "panel" in both *Hopscotch* and *Terra nostra* belongs to neither Europe nor Latin America, but breaks up into multiple worlds. In *Hopscotch*, this "pluralization" affects mainly narrative structure, which dissolves into a collection of heterogeneous "expendable chapters," including citations from other texts, metafictional reflections on the nature of the novel, and narrative episodes "lost" from the main story. In *Terra nostra*, however, this pluralization is genuinely ontological: a plurality of worlds.

The second mechanism, complementary to this one, hinges upon the conceptualization of Latin America not in terms of its *external* difference from Europe, but in terms of its own *internal* differences, its inherent multiplicity. Objectively, Latin America is a mosaic of dissimilar and, on the face of it, incompatible cultures, languages, world-views, landscapes, ecological zones. Its condition is, we might even say, *intrinsically* postmodernist. Even a "straight" realistic representation of the continent would have to take this multiplicity into account; and from such a representation to a postmodernist one is only a few short steps. These steps beyond realism are explicit in the narratives (and even, in one case, the title) of Alejo Carpentier's late-modernist novels *Los pasos perdidos* (*The Lost Steps*, 1953), and *El siglo de las luces* (*Explosion in a Cathedral*, 1962), which approach but stop just short of postmodernist poetics. The protagonist of *The Lost Steps* travels up-country along one of the great rivers of the South American continent, passing successively through locales so disparate that they seem to belong, like the "invisible cities" of the Great Khan's empire, to different worlds: the Lands of the Horse, the Lands of the Dog, the Capital of the Forms, the Great Plateaus, and so on. An explicit analogy is drawn with *The Odyssey*, the paradigmatic travel narrative involving visits to disparate realms. The Homeric analogy could have been applied even more appropriately to the voyages of *Explosion in a Cathedral*, in which the realms visited are actually island-worlds scattered throughout the Caribbean, like the Mediterranean island-worlds of *The Odyssey*. This multi-world Caribbean zone comes very close to constituting a heterotopia similar to those in postmodernist texts. Exactly how close, we can see from the episode in which privateers, driven off course by a storm, discover a miniature scale-model of the Caribbean, a gulf full of tiny islands:

> Full of islands, but with the incredible difference that these islands were very small, mere designs or ideas for islands, which had accumulated here just as models, sketches and empty casts accumulate in a sculptor's studio. Not one of these islands resembled its neighbour, nor were any two

constituted of the same material. . . . this Magic Gulf was like an earlier version of the Antilles, a blue-print which contained, in miniature, every-thing that could be seen on a larger scale in the Archipelago.[17]

This is still a *naturalized* heterotopia, "magic realism" with the emphasis on the realism; but the slightest shift of emphasis would yield a magic universe like that of *Terra nostra* or *One Hundred Years of Solitude* (1967).

Africa, too, recurs as a zone in postmodernist fiction; we have already seen such examples as Roussel's *Impressions d'Afrique* and Abish's *Alphabetical Africa*. Both adopt the strategy we observed in Butor's *Mobile*, that of subordi-nating the representation of geographical space to the free-play of the linguistic signifier. In the case of Roussel, free-play means generating elabo-rate, implausible pseudo-African scenes from a set of arbitrary plays on words, puns which do not even appear at the surface of the text, and whose role in its composition we would not suspect, had Roussel not explained the process elsewhere (in *Comment j'ai écrit certains de mes livres*, 1935). Abish's linguistic strategies are more transparent, though no less arbitrary than Roussel's. His Africa, as his book's title suggests, is alphabetized: the first chapter is composed exclusively of words beginning with the letter *a*, the second chapter of *a*-words supplemented by *b*-words, the third of *a, b,* and *c*-words, and so on, until by the twenty-sixth chapter the entire lexicon has become available; after that, the process is reversed, the vocabulary dwind-ling gradually down to *a*-words again. In short, an arbitrary distribution of vocabulary, corresponding, at the level of the fictional world, to a strange, piecemeal representation of Africa, full of anomalies such as the non-existent beaches of landlocked Chad.

The result, in the case of both Roussel and Abish, is a redrawing of the map – literally. We saw above how Roussel's cartographer redraws the map of sub-Saharan Africa, flattering Emperor Talu by absorbing most of it into his Empire. Abish's characters, too, make maps:

> Life in Tanzania is predicated on the colored maps of Africa that hang in the place, courtesy of *National Geographic*. On the maps Tanzania is colored a bright orange. Neighboring Malawi is light blue. The maps are the key to our future prosperity. The maps keep everyone employed, says the Queen. . . . Each day one hundred thousand Tanzanians carrying ladders, buckets of orange paint and brushes, are driven and also flown to different sections of the country. They paint everything in sight. . . . The Queen also proudly explains that Malawi has also decided to conform to international mapping standards, and since Tanzania had a technological headstart, she could export a light blue paint to Malawi.[18]

These maps, Roussel's as well as Abish's, are constructions *en abyme*; that is, they reflect on a miniature scale the structure of the texts in which they appear. In Tanzania, and somewhat less literalistically in Talu's Empire, real space does not determine the map but the other way around, the map determines the real space: if the map of Tanzania is colored bright orange, so must the *real* Tanzania be colored orange. In an exactly analogous way, the play of the signifier in these texts determines the shape of the fictional world, and not, as we would normally assume, the other way around.

Africa, in short, appears in these texts by Roussel and Abish as a free, undetermined space, a playground for ontological improvisation. Their maps strangely echo an earlier, more familiar map of the African continent: the one in Joseph Conrad's *Heart of Darkness* (1902). Conrad's narrator, Marlow, recalls how as a "little chap" he used to be fascinated by the unexplored "blank spaces" on maps, in particular the blank space in the interior of Africa. The map of Africa appears here as a screen upon which the young Marlow projects his fantasies of adventure and (no doubt) conquest, "a white patch for a boy to dream gloriously over." Like Roussel's cartographer and Abish's Queen of Tanzania, Marlow confuses the map with the space it represents: if the map is blank, the corresponding area of the real world, too, must be a kind of empty space, offering minimal resistance to the realization of adventurous fantasies. *Heart of Darkness*, of course, recounts the collapse of this dangerous illusion about the blank space of Africa, for, far from offering no resistance to fantasy, Africa is apt to absorb the unwary adventurer into its own nightmare. In other words, this map stands at the center of a typical modernist structure, that of illusion and disillusionment. Roussel and Abish in effect parody the illusion/disillusion structure of *Heart of Darkness*, substituting ontological improvisation where Conrad had an epistemological motif.

This is not by any means an "innocent" parody. Conrad's map, and its function in the young Marlow's imagination, in effect constitute a psychological alibi for imperialist expansion: it is the very blankness of the map, the inherent fascination of the unknown, that provokes the imperial response. The postmodernist parody only substitutes one kind of imperialism for another, an "imperialism of the imagination," so to speak, for an imperialism in fact. In a sense, it has been *too easy* to re-invent Africa, and some, at least, of the postmodernist writers have displayed a troubled awareness of this fact. Abish, for one, seems sensitive to the imperialist dimension of his *Alphabetical Africa*. He projects into its fictional world a surrogate author-figure who seems to reflect some of his own internal contradictions. On the one hand, this character asserts his freedom to improvise an Africa that answers to his own will and desires:

> I am inventing another country and another "now" for my book. It is largely an African country, dark, lush, hot, green and inhabited by a multitude of giant ants. . . . If I were to invent Africa all over again, I would not change a thing. I'd introduce a few broad tree-lined avenues, an outdoor cafe, a puppet theater and a realistic cannon pointing at the airport.[19]

On the other hand, he admits that Africa exceeds his imaginings:

> Basically Africa doesn't need any inventions, doesn't even need new interpretation. . . In general authors are provided a certain liberty. I'm no exception, as everyone happily gives me a certain freedom, and anticipates fabulous distortions. But Africa is not my invention by any means. I have not made any concessions, I have not invented anything I've seen or done.[20]

There is here at least an implicit critique of non-African writers' imaginative expropriation of African space. Angela Carter's critique is more explicit. In

The Infernal Desire Machines of Dr Hoffman (1972), she has constructed an Africa wholly derived from European fantasy. She populates its coast with cannibal tribesmen straight out of party jokes, comic-strips, and slapstick comedy; while in the interior she places centaurs, in effect suppressing indigenous mythology in favor of an imported European myth. This is imperialism of the imagination, and Carter knows it; indeed, her purpose is to foreground it and expose it for what it is. Thus, we learn from her Dr Hoffman that nothing in the European castaways' experience of this Africa was real: the "hitherto unimaginable flora," the "herds of biologically dubious fauna," the "hitherto unformulated territory," all of it was only the reification of the castaways' desires.[21] Dr Hoffman's analysis might be extended to the African zones of Roussel, Abish and others: their Africas, too, appear to be reifications of European desire. Is present-day Africa, then, still what it was for Conrad's Marlow at the turn of the century, a particularly inviting blank space on the map, fodder for westerners' dreams and wish-fulfillments?

Mimesis, clearly, is alive and well in postmodernist fiction. Postmodernist texts such as *Impressions d'Afrique* or *Alphabetical Africa* may not reflect objective African realities, but they do faithfully reflect our culture's ontological landscape, which allots a certain space to an unreal zone called "Africa." In a similar, and equally disturbing way postmodernist fiction also reflects the disruption of that landscape by twentieth-century war. War in our century has forced us to rethink the received categories of space, conceptual as well as geographical space; it has taught us to think in terms of the zone. The lexicon of war is one of the sources of the term "zone," and certainly the postmodernists have borrowed many of the characteristics of their zone from the zones of military discourse – the war zone, the occupied zone, the demilitarized zone.

The zone of Pynchon's *Gravity's Rainbow*, I have said, is the paradigm of the occupied zone in postmodernist writing. Earlier, John Hawkes in *The Cannibal* (1949) had created a comparable zone, but on a drastically reduced scale. Where Pynchon's zone spans Central Europe from the North Sea to the Polish frontier, Hawkes telescopes his into a single German town, which he calls Spitzen-on-the-Dien. Spitzen-on-the-Dien concentrates within its narrow confines all the derangements of the occupied zone at large. Its local history recapitulates the history of the Third Reich, sometimes obliquely and symbolically, for instance when during the closing days of the war the insane-asylum inmates stage a revolt. The same migrating nationalities that sweep across Pynchon's zone also appear in Hawkes's, but reduced to a representative handful of displaced persons at a dance in the town. Spitzen-on-the-Dien even has its own "other world": on the town's outskirts, ghosts of English soldiers haunt a ruined tank. Kenneth Patchen's strategy in constructing the zone of *The Journal of Albion Moonlight* is equally bold. Patchen, like Guy Davenport or Julio Cortázar, superimposes one space upon another. His zone is a double-exposure of war-torn Europe and the still neutral, peace-time America of 1939–40. The result is a composite vision of the American landscape transfigured by war in the same way that the European landscape is transformed in the texts of Hawkes and Pynchon.

Patchen thus introduces the war zone into the American heartland. His

America, like Pynchon's, is a "Zone of the Interior," but in a somewhat different sense from the one we find in Pynchon. Or is it so different? It took a certain prescience for Patchen to imagine, in 1940, Middle America transformed by a war in its midst; Pynchon, looking back on the 1940s from the vantage-point of the 1970s, needed no such prescience, for by now we are all aware of the ease with which total war can be delivered to our doorsteps, in Middle America or anywhere else. Since the days of Patchen's *Albion Moonlight*, the war zone has expanded to embrace the entire globe, thanks to nuclear weaponry and the science of ballistics, and it is Pynchon who, on the last page of *Gravity's Rainbow*, has given us the most memorable symbol of that all-embracing zone: the missile suspended a hair's-breadth above the movie-theater in which we readers sit.[22]

Intertextual zones

The disparate worlds that constitute the zone occupy different, incompatible spaces; as Foucault says, it is impossible to find any common locus beneath them all. Nevertheless, there is a sense in which the worlds of the zone *do*, in most cases, occupy the same *kind* of space. That is, they all belong to the projected space of the fictional universe, the space concretized by readers in the process of reading the text. In this sense, the zone is not heterotopian after all, but *homo*topian. One could, however, break up this homotopia by constructing a zone that embraced or straddled *different kinds* of space, one which annexed to the space of the fictional universe the spaces of other ontological strata.

But what other kinds of space could there be, apart from the space of the fictional universe? For one thing, there is the physical space of the material book, in particular the two-dimensional space of the *page*. It should be possible to integrate this physical space in the structure of the zone – and indeed, we have seen a number of cases where this has been done, including Michel Butor's *Mobile* and Ronald Sukenick's *Out*, which in effect annex the space of the page to the represented space of the American zone. This type of space, and its uses in postmodernist writing, will be discussed in Chapter 12, "Worlds on paper" (see pp. 179–96). There is also the conceptual space of language itself. When we conceive of linguistic signs as being composed of a signifier and a signified, we have in effect *spatialized* language, introducing an *internal* space within the sign. This space between the signifier and the signified may be wider or narrower; there may be slippages, displacements of one tier *vis-à-vis* the other. These gaps and slippages are what permit the free-play of the signifier; and texts such as Butor's *Mobile*, Roussel's *Impressions d'Afrique*, or Abish's *Alphabetical Africa* which, as we have seen, exploit the play of the signifier, in effect annex linguistic space to the projected space of their fictional universes. This type of space is discussed in Chapter 10, "Styled worlds" (see pp. 148–61).

Finally, there is a third type of space which may be annexed to the zone: intertextual space. It has become commonplace since Eliot's "Tradition and the individual talent," and even more so since the French structuralists' work on intertextuality, to picture literature as a field or, better, a network whose nodes are the actual texts of literature. By this account, an intertextual space is constituted whenever we recognize the relations among two or more texts, or between specific texts and larger categories such as genre, school, period. There are a number of ways of foregrounding this intertextual space and integrating it in the text's structure, but none is more effective than the device of "borrowing" a character from another text – "transworld identity," Umberto Eco has called this, the transmigration of characters from one fictional universe to another.

Now, our normal literary intuitions would seem to suggest that this device of borrowing characters is not really permissible. Lubomír Doležel captures this intuition when he speaks of the "compossibility" of characters.[23] Two fictional characters are compossible, that is, capable of coexisting and interacting, only if they belong to the same text; characters belonging to one text are normally not compossible with characters from another. Thus, Emma Bovary is compossible with Rodolphe Boulanger, but not with Ivan Karamazov. There would appear to be only one regular exception to this norm, and that is in the case of *retour de personnages*, when the identical characters recur in different texts by the same author; the paradigmatic examples are Balzac's *Comédie Humaine* and Faulkner's Yoknapatawpha novels. Here, however, transworld identity is the tail that wags the textual dog: it is precisely *because* characters persist from text to text that we are disposed to redefine a series of novels as a single continuous text, a kind of "super-text," thus preserving by a stratagem the rule of compossibility of characters. Furthermore, far from damaging the realistic illusion by calling our attention to intertextuality, the device of *retour de personnages* actually *buttresses* realism. Thus, Robert Alter describes *retour de personnages* in Balzac as:

> a strategy for sustaining the imperative claim to life of his fantasies by writing a huge ensemble of overlapping novels in which the figures and actions invented in one are reinforced, in a sense confirmed, by their reappearance in other books.[24]

How far can the device of *retour de personnages* be pushed before it begins to have the opposite effect, destabilizing rather than consolidating fictional ontology? Clearly there is a limit, and postmodernist fiction has explored and sometimes violated that limit. Robbe-Grillet is an example. In his novels from *La Maison de rendez-vous* (1965) through *Djinn* (1981), a number of characters – Johnson, Manneret, Dr Morgan, King Boris, Jean (or Djinn), Laura – recur in more than one text, some in as many as three. But is this true transworld identity, or only what Eco calls homonymy, identity of names without any carry-over of essential properties from text to text? It is difficult to say. Because of the extreme instability of Robbe-Grillet's fictional worlds, characters are not even self-consistent within the *same* text, so they can hardly be expected to be consistent from one text to another. If the *retour de personnages* consolidates these texts into a "super-text," the world of that "super-text" is no unitary whole, no Yoknapatawpha, but an uneasy juxtaposition of incommensurable worlds – a zone, in fact, but an *intertextual* zone. Robbe-Grillet, by abusing the motif of recurrent characters in this way, in effect *parodies* this device, substituting for the unitary worlds of *La Comédie Humaine* or Yoknapatawpha a heterotopian intertextual zone.

John Barth, too, carries the *retour de personnages* too far, but through *exaggeration* rather than, as in the case of Robbe-Grillet, indeterminacy. In *LETTERS* (1979) he has written the collective sequel to *all six* of his previous novels, from *The Floating Opera* (1956) through *Chimera* (1972), reviving from each of them its major characters and reintegrating them in a new fictional world. In some cases this is unproblematic, but in others the *retour de personnages* places severe ontological strain on the fictional world of *LETTERS*. This is particularly true of the character Jerome Bray, who claims to be descended from Harold Bray, Grand Tutor of the University in the parallel universe of *Giles Goat-Boy* (1966) – a world radically incompatible with the more or less realistic world of *LETTERS*. Furthermore, all of the "revived" characters are obsessed, in various ways, with what one of them calls the "recycling" of their lives; in short, they are *aware* of living through a sequel, and even if this awareness is too vague to destroy the realistic illusion, it is more than enough to foreground the intertextual dimension of this text for the reader.

The annexation of intertextual space can proceed along other lines as well. "Characters," asserts the narrator of Flann O'Brien's *At Swim-Two-Birds* (1939),

> should be interchangeable as between one book and another. The entire corpus of existing literature should be regarded as a limbo from which discerning authors could draw their characters as required, creating only when they failed to find a suitable existing puppet. The modern novel should be largely a work of reference.[25]

Borrowed characters abound in postmodernism. Thus, for example, Italo Calvino has expropriated Dumas' characters Dantès and the Abbé Faria in his rewriting of "The Count of Monte Cristo," (1967) while Alejo Carpentier in *El recurso del metodo* has peopled his fictional Paris with characters borrowed from Proust (including Morel, Brichot, the painter Elstir, the composer Vinteuil, and Madame Verdurin). García Márquez in *One Hundred Years of Solitude* mentions the room in Paris where Rocamadour will die one day – but Rocamadour dies not in the world of *One Hundred Years of Solitude*, but in the world of Cortázar's *Hopscotch*, from which García Márquez has borrowed him. And Gilbert Sorrentino, in *Imaginative Qualities of Actual Things* (1971), arbitrarily marries off one of his male characters to – Lolita!

> I have a mildly interesting idea . . . for those readers – and they are, I understand, legion – who insist on a character they can "get ahold of." Let's say that Bart's wife is Lolita. I mean, she is the exact Lolita that Nabokov stitched together. O.K. Now you've got Bart's wife – there she is, already made, grown up, yes, as she is at the end of the book, with Humbert dead.[26]

Is this *retour de personnage*? Transworld identity? In a sense, yes, of course, but parodied in such a way as to spectacularly violate, and thereby foreground, the ontological boundaries between fictional worlds. World-boundaries having been overrun in this way, the result is a kind of between-worlds space – a zone.

4: WORLDS IN COLLISION

I draw the line as a rule between one solar system and another.
(Christine Brooke-Rose, *Such*, 1966)

Science fiction, like postmodernist fiction, is governed by the ontological dominant. Indeed, it is perhaps *the* ontological genre *par excellence*. We can think of science fiction as postmodernism's noncanonized or "low art" double, its sister-genre in the same sense that the popular detective thriller is modernist fiction's sister-genre. Darko Suvin has defined the science-fiction genre as "literature of cognitive estrangement." By "estrangement" he means very nearly the Russian formalists' *ostranenie*, but a specifically ontological *ostranenie*, confronting the empirical givens of our world with something *not* given, something from outside or beyond it, "a strange newness, a *novum*."[1] By qualifying this estrangement as "cognitive," Suvin means to eliminate purely mythopoeic projections that have no standing in a world-view founded on logic, reason, positive science. Robert Scholes, Suvin's disciple in this, offers an elegant paraphrase:

> Fabulation . . . is fiction that offers us a world clearly and radically discontinuous from the one we know, yet returns to confront that known world in some cognitive way. . . . Speculative fabulation [ie. science fiction] . . . is defined by the presence of at least one clear *representational* discontinuity with life as we know it.[2]

Actually, this is more than paraphrase, for Scholes here neatly plugs up a hole in Suvin's definition. *Any* fiction of *any* genre involves at least one *novum* – a character who did not exist in the empirical world, an event that did not really occur – and very likely involves many more than one. What distinguishes science fiction is the occurrence of this *novum* not (or not only) at the level of story and actors but in the structure of the represented world itself – Scholes's "representational discontinuity," as opposed to what he calls "narrational discontinuity." Or, better: not the occurrence of a single *novum*, but the projection of a *network* of innovations, with their implications and consequences;

in other words, the projection of a world different from our own yet, as Suvin and Scholes both specify, in confrontation with our world. Science fiction, by staging "close encounters" between different worlds, placing them in confrontation, foregrounds their respective structures and the disparities between them. It thus obeys the same underlying principles of ontological poetics as postmodernist fiction.

It obeys the same underlying principles but, in the course of its independent historical development, has evolved *topoi* of its own for working out these principles in practice, conventions that are specific to the science-fiction genre. How is one to place worlds into confrontation? How are these "close encounters" to be managed? The answer takes a variety of historically-determined forms within science-fiction writing. In general, as Darko Suvin and, following him, Mark Rose have both observed, we can distinguish two complementary strategies: the first is to transport (through space, time, or "other dimensions") representatives of our world to a different world; the second, its inverse, involves (to use Pynchon's phrase) "another world's intrusion into this one."[3]

In the most typical (and stereotypical) science-fiction contexts, "worlds" should be understood literally as *planets*, and "confrontation between worlds" as interplanetary travel. "Another world's intrusion into this one," in the interplanetary context, takes the form of invasion from outer space – whether malign, as in H. G. Wells's classic *War of the Worlds* (1898), or benign, as in Arthur C. Clarke's *Childhood's End* (1953). The complementary *topos*, that of the earthling's visit to an alien planet, occurs in a number of variants: the simplest, travel to a single other world (e.g. Wells's *The First Men in the Moon*, 1901, or Ray Bradbury's *The Martian Chronicles*, 1950); or "planet-hopping" from world to world, as in pulp-magazine "space operas" or their cinematic equivalents, such as *Star Trek* and *Star Wars*; or travel across a planet on which disparate life-forms, races, civilizations are juxtaposed, a multi-world world (e.g. Edgar Rice Burroughs' Martian romances, or C. S. Lewis's *Out of the Silent Planet*, 1938). The "zero degree" of the interplanetary motif involves projecting a different planet without any provision for intrusion in either direction, by its inhabitants into our world or by earthlings into their world: worlds in collision without the collision. A classic example is Frank Herbert's *Dune* (1965), which constructs an integral, self-contained planetary world, nowhere explicitly related to our Earth. Here the confrontation between the projected world and our empirical world is implicit, experienced by no representative character but *reconstructed* by the reader.

Many space-travel narratives, although by no means all of them, are projected into the future, for the obvious reason that they depend upon technologies which have been extrapolated from those of the present day. In other words, displacement in *space* is intimately bound up with displacement in *time*. They are, in fact, functionally equivalent: spatially distant other worlds may be brought into confrontation with our world, but so may *temporally* distant worlds, and with identical results of "cognitive estrangement." Science-fiction future worlds tend to gravitate either toward the *Utopian* pole (as in Edward Bellamy's *Looking Backward*, 1888) or, more frequently, toward the *dystopian* pole (as in Wells's *When the Sleeper Wakes*,

1899, Aldous Huxley's *Brave New World*, 1932, or George Orwell's *1984*, 1949). The mode of displacement from present to future falls into one or another of several categories: that of "future history," which narrates more or less continuously the unfolding of "things to come" (e.g. Olaf Stapledon's *Last and First Men*, 1930, or Isaac Asimov's *Foundation* trilogy, 1951–3); or the "sleeper wakes" motif of Wells and Bellamy (and Woody Allen!), in which an inhabitant of our time hibernates through the intervening centuries and awakens in the world of the future; or the time-machine motif inaugurated by Wells's novel *The Time Machine* (1895), and apparently not exhausted yet. As in the case of the interplanetary *topos*, there is also a "zero degree" of temporal displacement in which a future world is projected but without any inhabitant of our time visiting it, the confrontation between worlds being left to the reader to reconstruct.

Once we have accepted the pseudo-scientific premise of travel outside the three familiar dimensions of space, through the "fourth dimension" of time, there is nothing to prevent us from going on to imagine travel to worlds in dimensions *beyond* the fourth. Here the ontological confrontation occurs between our world and some other world or worlds somehow adjacent or parallel to our own, accessible across some kind of boundary or barrier. Just as Wells' time-travel conceit seems to be inexhaustible, so his contemporary Edwin Abbott's conceit of interdimensional travel in *Flatland: A Romance of Many Dimensions* (1884) continues to be exploited in science-fiction writing. The most intriguing variant of the other-dimension *topos* is the parallel- or alternate-world story based on historical speculation, the "what-if" premise so beloved of amateur historians – and of Borges. "He believed," writes Borges of the imaginary author of the novel *The Garden of Forking Paths*,

> in an infinite series of times, in a dizzily growing, ever spreading network of diverging, converging and parallel times. This web of time – the strands of which approach one another, bifurcate, intersect or ignore each other through the centuries – embraces *every* possibility.[4]

In history's "garden of forking paths," one fork will inevitably be chosen in preference to all the other forks that *might* have been chosen instead. But what if things had gone differently, what if one of the other forks had been chosen? What kind of world would have resulted if, for instance, the Axis Powers instead of the Allies had won the Second World War? This speculation generates the world of Philip K. Dick's classic parallel-world story, *The Man in the High Castle* (1962). Inevitably, such a story invites the reader to compare the real state of affairs in our world with the hypothetical state of affairs projected for the parallel world; implicitly it places our world and the parallel world in confrontation. And sometimes even explicitly: in Dick's *Man in the High Castle*, a science-fiction writer in the parallel world publishes his *own* parallel-world story, based on the premise that the Axis had *lost* the Second World War. The parallel world *of* a parallel world is *our* world.

Finally, we must not forget the "lost world" *topos* of science-fiction writing. Important in earlier periods of the genre's development, this variant has all but ceased to be productive today, since it requires "blank spaces" like those on young Marlow's maps of Africa, onto which the writer may project "lost" fragments of the Earth's past, or parallel civilizations cut off from the mainstream of human history. Examples include H. Rider Haggard's *She* (1886–7), Arthur Conan Doyle's *The Lost World* (1912), Edgar Rice Burroughs' *The Land That Time Forgot* (1924), and variants in which the lost world is projected into the interior of the hollow Earth, such as Jules Verne's *Journey to the Center of the Earth* (1864) and Burroughs' romances of Pellucidar.

Parallel lines

Invasions from outer space, visits to other planets, Utopian or dystopian futures, time-travel, parallel or lost worlds – all of these science-fiction *topoi* serve the purposes of an ontological poetics, but one that has developed almost entirely independently of postmodernism's ontological poetics. Science fiction and postmodernist fiction, it would appear, have advanced along parallel literary–historical tracks. Occasionally these separate but parallel lines of development have produced motifs and *topoi* which are strikingly similar. One of these is the *topos* of the closed-system world in both science fiction and postmodernist fiction;[5] another is the *topos* of the death-world or "world to come."

Philip José Farmer, in his science-fiction tetralogy of "Riverworld" novels (*To Your Scattered Bodies Go*, 1971; *The Fabulous Riverboat*, 1971; *The Dark Design*, 1977; *The Magic Labyrinth*, 1980), has constructed a simple but flexible closed-system world in which to stage a cycle of adventure-stories. The entire human race, in Farmer's fiction, has been resurrected by technological means on a planet especially prepared to receive it: the Riverworld, self-contained, self-regulating, a river-valley some ten million miles long through which flows a mile-wide river whose source and mouth are the same north-polar sea. No space has been allotted for raising food to feed the thirty-six billion or so human beings who occupy the banks of this river, so Farmer must breach his system at one end and introduce a providential food-supply, meals generated apparently *ex nihilos* by energy-matter converters ranged along the riverbanks. There is death on the Riverworld – death by accident or violence – but only temporarily: those killed since the simultaneous, general resurrection undergo a "little resurrection," rematerializing elsewhere along the river's vast length. So this astonishing eco-system recycles *souls* as well as bodies. The entire elegant contraption, it turns out, has been designed and set in motion by superior beings called Ethicals. Having collected the souls of human beings throughout mankind's history, the Ethicals have now regenerated mankind and placed it on this new, closed-system world in order to give it a second chance to attain superior ethical development.

Farmer's closed-system world bears comparison with the world of Samuel Beckett's postmodernist text, *The Lost Ones* (*Le Depeupleur*, 1971; English trans., 1972). The exact ontological status of this world, as with all of Beckett's fictional worlds since at least *The Unnamable* (1952), is indeterminable. Perhaps it is a version of the afterlife, an updated *Purgatorio* or *Inferno*, as an isolated allusion to Dante might lead one to believe; or perhaps its closest analogue is, rather, the science-fiction *topos* of the multiple-generation voyage to the stars (as in Robert Heinlein's story "Universe," 1941, or J. G. Ballard's "Thirteen for Centaurus"). Vague though its status might be, the structure of this world is remorselessly clear, mathematically exact. Picture a cylinder fifty meters in diameter and sixteen high, inhabited by a "tribe" of some two hundred individuals – one body per square meter of floor-space. There is no egress from the cylinder: *huis clos*. The tribe's environment is subject to a "twofold vibration" of light and temperature, non-synchronous swings from dim yellow light to darkness and back again, and from extreme heat to extreme cold, with irregular momentary breakdowns of the rhythm. Several types of behavior are observable: some of the lost ones queue up to climb ladders, from which they may explore niches in the cylinder's wall; others circulate restlessly, searching the faces of their fellows; still others have lapsed into temporary or permanent stasis. Each type of activity is apparently governed by fixed rules, which the text specifies.

Obviously, at one level of description Beckett's cylinder-world differs in almost every particular from Farmer's Riverworld. Farmer's world is all hyperbole – a river ten million miles long, with thirty-six billion inhabitants, a tetralogy of some 600,000 words – while Beckett's is all minimalist understatement – fifty meters by sixteen, two hundred inhabitants, 8,000 words. Behind this huge difference in scale lies, however, the same cybernetic principle of the self-regulating closed system, the world as machine. Substantive differences only appear when we ask to what narrative *use* the closed-system world-structure is put in the two texts. In Beckett's case the answer is, to no use whatsoever. There is no foreground narrative action in *The Lost Ones*; the condition of the cylinder is merely described. The only change – and without change, of course, there is no possibility for narrative – is a change from bad to worse in the overall condition, an increase in the system's entropy. Farmer, by contrast, uses his Riverworld in a fairly conventional way, as the backdrop to a foreground romance narrative. To do so, he must disrupt the stability and integrity of his closed system, replacing infinite recyclings with linear action – a plot. Like the designers of classical closed-world tragedies, Farmer has recourse to a *deus ex machina*: a renegade Ethical who sabotages the project and instigates a quest to the river's headwaters by the most adventurous and enterprising of the Riverworlders. Farmer thus satisfies the science-fiction genre's ontological imperatives while at the same time performing the duty which is incumbent on all popular writers – and science fiction is, after all, a popular genre – namely, the duty to tell a "good story."

If the most important differences between Farmer's and Beckett's worlds can be attributed to the different criteria for popular fiction as opposed to "art" writing – Farmer must tell a story, while Beckett need not – their similarities cannot, conversely, be traced to shared conventions. The appearance of the same closed-system world-structure in the two texts must be explained in terms of a different history and logic of development in each case. The various elements of Farmer's Riverworld can be traced back to *topoi* already in circulation in science fiction for decades: the interplanetary *topos* of supervision by superior beings (e.g. Clarke's *Childhood's End* (1953) and *2001* (1968)); the *topos* of a war fought among time-travelers from different epochs (e.g. Fritz Leiber's *The Big Time*, 1958); the "Robinson Crusoe" *topos* of ingenious technological improvisation by castaways (e.g. Verne's *Mysterious Island*, 1874); above all, the precedent for constructing a planetary eco-system, exemplified by Frank Herbert's *Dune* (1965). There is no need to refer to such science-fiction *topoi* to explain the appearance of an analogous closed-system world in Beckett's writing, no reason even to suppose the least familiarity with science fiction on Beckett's part. All the elements of Beckett's cylinder-world are already present in his own writings, or those of his precursors or postmodernist contemporaries, without his having to go further afield to find them. The cylinder extends Beckett's earlier experimentation with "art in a closed field"[6] – as in the "calculus of possibilities" of Mr Knott's movements around his room, or the systematic circulation of Molloy's sucking-stones – and combines it with the tendency toward minimalism in Beckett's later short fiction, toward "Lessness" (the title of one of those fictions). In short, this world appears in Beckett's text for reasons intrinsic to postmodernist writing, and not traceable to the influence of science fiction, just as the analogous world appears in Farmer's text for reasons intrinsic to science fiction, and not traceable to the influence of postmodernism. This is a clear case of parallel development, not mutual influence.

Independent but parallel development also explains the similarities between Philip K. Dick's science-fiction novel *Ubik* (1969) and Muriel Spark's postmodernist text *The Hothouse by the East River* (1973), both of which construct equivocal afterlifes, variants on the "world" to come. Dick projects his characters into a bizarrely deteriorating world, one in which the material culture seems to suffer a temporal regression, degenerating from the high technology of 1992 to a quaint 1939, while the eleven protagonists themselves die off one by one in a highly gothic manner, aging and decaying before their companions' eyes like Rider Haggard's Ayesha or Wilde's Dorian Gray. This world, it turns out, has all along been a state of death, or half-death: the eleven, killed at the outset by a terrorist bomb, have been kept in a state of suspended animation, and the world they have experienced has only been a kind of shared dream or hallucination. Their spectacular deaths by instantaneous aging represent, in fact, a second and "true" death, as the suspended-animation system fails.

Similarly, Spark in *The Hothouse by the East River* constructs the familiar, comfortable world of a group of upper-middle-class New Yorkers which, like the world of *Ubik*, deteriorates before our eyes. Inconsistencies and improbabilities begin to creep in, inexplicable events occur. This, too, it turns out, has been a death-world, but one initially coinciding at every point with the real-world Manhattan. Spark's dead, victims of the 1944 V-2 blitz of London, act out a perfect simulacrum of the life they *would have lived* had they survived until the 1970s, even to the extent of raising the children they *would have* raised. This conditional existence starts breaking down from the moment when the dead begin to realize that they have been dead all along; Spark's world, like Dick's, erases itself.[7]

The parallelisms are striking, but again, as in the case of Farmer and Beckett, arise independently in the two genres. Dick plays variations on a set of familiar science-fiction *topoi*, such as suspended animation, and uses a number of devices drawn from the repertoire of popular fiction to organize his plot: the "ten little Indians" structure, the red herring that delays the solution of the mystery, the twist at the end, and so on. Spark's death-world, so similar to Dick's, nevertheless derives not from science-fiction conventions but from developments within postmodernist fiction itself. It derives, in particular, from the postmodernist preoccupation with death as the ultimate ontological boundary, which may be traced through the many postmodernist variants (revisionist, parodic) on the venerable *topos* of the "world to come," including Flann O'Brien's *The Third Policeman* (written, 1940; published, 1967), Pynchon's *Gravity's Rainbow* (1973), Stanley Elkin's *The Living End* (1979), Alasdair Gray's *Lanark* (1981), and so on. And where Dick draws freely on the formal repertoire of popular writing, Spark's principal device belongs to the repertoire of distinctively postmodernist strategies, namely the strategy of placing projected objects – in this case, an entire projected world – *sous rature*, under erasure (see pp. 99–111). Here again we have evidence that the two ontological sister-genres, science fiction and postmodernist fiction, have been pursuing analogous but independent courses of development.

The science-fictionalization of postmodernism

If science fiction and postmodernist fiction have tended on the whole to advance along parallel but independent tracks, there has also been a tendency for postmodernist writing to absorb motifs and *topoi* from science fiction writing, mining science fiction for its raw materials.[8] The postmodernists have not always been gracious in acknowledging their borrowings from their sister-genre, presumably because of the "low art" stigma that still attaches to science fiction. "*I am not* writing science fiction!" protests the "author" in Alasdair Gray's *Lanark*, and Raymond Federman seconds this on the opening page of his *The Twofold Vibration* (1982), in the process compiling a fairly thorough (if dismissive) catalogue of pertinent science-fiction motifs:

> Call it exploratory or better yet extemporaneous fiction, that's right . . . but no futuristic crap, I mean pseudoscientific bullshit, space warfare, fake theories of probabilities, unsolvable equations, strange creatures from other planets, ludicrous busybodies with pointed ears, wings instead of arms or wheels instead of legs, none of that, a way to look at the self, at humanity, from a potential point of view, premembering the future rather than remembering the past, but no gadgetry, no crass emotionless robots . . . no none of that infantilism, at least within reason, no invasions of earth by superbrains, spaceship battles in the galaxies, worlds that collide, nothing spuriously progressive or regressive in this story, nothing prophetic or moralistic either.[9]

They protest too much. In fact, both *Lanark* and *The Twofold Vibration* are transparently indebted to science fiction for some of their materials, and many of the motifs dismissed by Federman in fact form a part of his own repertoire, as well as that of other postmodernist writers.

Among postmodernism's borrowings from science fiction, strikingly few have come from the part of the repertoire that is most closely associated, at least in the popular mind, with the science-fiction genre, namely its interplanetary motifs. Only William Burroughs has made very much use of these motifs, but he exploits them so extensively and so centrally as almost to make up for the other postmodernists' neglect. Nearly every variant of the inter-planetary *topos* can be found somewhere in Burroughs' *oeuvre*: the invasion from outer space (e.g. in *Nova Express*, 1964, and *The Ticket That Exploded*, 1962), the earthling's visit to an alien planet (in *The Ticket That Exploded*), and so on. Burroughs unabashedly seizes on the lowest common denominator of science-fiction conventions; his invaders from outer space are pulp-style bug-eyed monsters – insect people, scorpion electricals, crab guards, tele-pathic fish-boys. Italo Calvino, too, improvises on various interplanetary themes in the science-fiction fables of his *Cosmicomics* (1965) and *t zero* (1967).

On the whole, however, postmodernist writing has preferred to adapt science fiction's motifs of temporal displacement rather than its spatial displacements, projecting worlds of the future rather than worlds in distant galaxies. Similarly, in constructing future worlds, postmodernist writing tends to focus on social and institutional innovations rather than on the strictly technological innovations which are stereotypically associated with science fiction: "no gadgetry," Federman declares. Nevertheless, there is a good deal of gadgetry in postmodernist worlds of the future. Burroughs, for instance, projects an elaborate repertoire of advances in the biological sci-ences, including cloning (*Naked Lunch*, 1959; *The Wild Boys*, 1971), synthetic human beings (*The Soft Machine*, 1961; revised, 1966), and, obsessively, virus plagues and biological warfare (*Exterminator!* 1973; *Cities of the Red Night*, 1981). Don DeLillo's gadgets in *Ratner's Star* (1976) tend to be sly parodies of current technology – for instance, his Sony 747 miniaturized jet airliner, large enough to contain a rock-garden – but he also projects a number of disturbing and currently unthinkable innovations in the theoretical sciences: zorgs and Nūtean surfaces in mathematics, sylphing compounds in chemistry, and, in physics, Moholean relativity, which implies the dissolution of the physical sciences as we presently understand them. Often the postmodernists seem content to borrow science fiction's most hackneyed "advanced technolo-gies," using them simply as backdrops and not taking them very seriously: an example would be Federman's spaceport and gigantic spaceship in *The Twofold Vibration*. The spectacular exception to this is Raymond Roussel, a postmodernist precursor whose impossibly ingenious contraptions, derived from those of Jules Verne, are the end-all and be-all of his enigmatic texts (*Impressions d'Afrique*, 1910; *Locus Solus*, 1914).

In general, however, postmodernist writers are more interested in the social and institutional consequences of technological innovation, the social arrangements these advances give rise to, rather than in the innovations themselves. Actually, this has been true of much of the science-fiction writing of recent decades as well, so that Federman is being somewhat unfair when he dismisses science fiction as mere "gadgetry" by contrast with his own "exploratory" or "extemporaneous" fiction. Federman himself, for instance, speculates on future sexual and marital arrangements (*The Twofold Vibration*), while Alasdair Gray projects the welfare state of the future (*Lanark*), and Burroughs the Biologic Courts that will be needed to adjudicate among competing life-forms in a crowded and jostling universe (*Nova Express*). Many postmodernist texts are preoccupied with the "cartelization" of the future, the growth of international conglomerates that threaten to displace national governments and engulf the entire world. Examples include Burroughs' Trak Sex and Dream Utilities (*The Soft Machine*), the Consortium Hondurium in DeLillo's *Ratner's Star*, and the group of conglomerates known collectively as "the creature" in Gray's *Lanark*.

Most postmodernist futures, in other words, are grim dystopias – as indeed most science-fiction worlds of the future have been in recent years. The motif of a world after the holocaust or some apocalyptic breakdown recurs. For instance, Angela Carter in *The Passion of New Eve* (1977) and Sam Shepard in his play *The Tooth of Crime* (1972) project similar visions of a future America that has disintegrated into an anarchic landscape of warring private armies and desert marauders. Carlos Fuentes in *Terra nostra* (1975) imagines a world that has broken down under the pressure of the population explosion, Burroughs in *The Wild Boys* one that has regressed in the aftermath of the exhaustion of earth's fossil-fuel reserves. In particular, the *topos* of nuclear holocaust and its aftermath recurs; examples include *Gravity's Rainbow*, Angela Carter's *Heroes and Villains* (1969), Russell Hoban's *Riddley Walker* (1980), Maggie Gee's *Dying, in other words* (1981), and, in a slightly displaced form, Christine Brooke-Rose's *Out* (1964). Unlikely though it may seem, positive, Utopian treatments of this postapocalyptic motif are also possible. For instance, Richard Brautigan in *In Watermelon Sugar* (1968) projects a pastoral idyll apparently set some time after the collapse of industrial civilization. Another of the rare Utopian future worlds occurs in Monique Wittig's *Les Guérillères* (1969).

Dystopias or Utopias, postmodernist worlds of the future typically employ the "zero degree" of temporal displacement, projecting a future time but without making any particular provision for bridging the temporal gap between present and future; that bridge is left for the reader to build. There are a few exceptions, however. For instance, the *topos* of "future history" occurs in *The Twofold Vibration*, where in the early chapters Federman rather breathlessly reviews twentieth-century history and "premembers" future developments as far as New Year's Eve, 1999. Temporal displacement through time-travel, like its spatial analogue, interplanetary flight, has been too closely identified with science fiction as such for postmodernist writers to be able to use it with much freedom. Only Burroughs, as might have been expected, makes much substantial use of it (in *The Soft Machine*, *The Wild Boys*, and especially *Cities of the Red Night*). Time-travel, for Burroughs, provides the fictional frame, the motivating alibi, for the slippages and segues between one identity and another, one memory and another, one culture and another, which are staples of his writing. Time-travel also figures in Fuentes' *Terra nostra*. Here a late-twentieth-century Parisian travels back in time to Spain's Siglo de Oro, while interlopers from past times invade and overwhelm Paris in the closing days of the twentieth century. This influx of time-travelers goes well beyond the simple confrontation of present and future, or past and present, of most time-travel stories, approaching the extreme conflation of all epochs in such science-fiction texts as Farmer's "Riverworld" tetralogy or Fritz Leiber's *The Big Time*.

What if the Russians, rather than the British, had settled most of North America? What if France had remained part of a British Continental Empire? What if electrical energy had been banned, even verbal allusions to it becoming taboo? Returning to history's forkings and choosing the alternative paths that events *could* have taken, Vladimir Nabokov in *Ada* generates a parallel world lying, presumably, in some "dimension" adjacent to our own. His world of Demonia or Antiterra is "a distortive glass of our distorted globe."[10] The degree and direction of its distortions can be gauged, for instance, from its teasingly askew place-names – the New World Express goes "via Mephisto, El Paso, Meksikansk and the Panama Chunnel" to Brazilia, the African Express leaves from London and reaches the Cape "through Nigero, Rodosia or Ethiopia"[11] – and its alternative literary history – Proust is the author of *Les Malheurs de Swann*, "The Waistline" is "a satire in free verse on Anglo-American feeding habits,"[12] and *Anna Karenina* begins, "All happy families are more or less dissimilar; all unhappy ones are more or less alike."[13] Like Dick in *The Man in the High Castle*, Nabokov lays bare the "alternateness" of his Antiterra by allowing its science-fiction writers and psychotics to envision a world parallel to their own – Terra, the what-if premise of a what-if premise, the parallel world of a parallel world. Other postmodernist parallel-worlds include the oddly skewed Miami of Harry Mathews' *The Sinking of the Odradek Stadium* (1971–2), and the world of John Barth's *Giles Goat-Boy* (1966), in which the history of western civilization (including its literary history) has been displaced into the microcosmic history of a university.

Increasingly rare in modern science fiction, the "lost world" *topos* figures hardly at all in postmodernist writing. Perhaps the only candidate is the disturbing lost civilization of Vheissu, visited in Thomas Pynchon's *V.* (1963) by the explorer Godolphin. But in fact the case of Vheissu demonstrates in what ways *V.* is not, after all, a postmodernist text. Every piece of evidence about Vheissu reaches us at a second or third remove, refracted through successive unreliable sources and mediators: the aged Godolphin's traveler's yarn is narrated to interested parties, overheard by eavesdroppers, transmitted by them to Stencil, who reconstructs the original narrative according to his standard operating procedure of "inference, poetic license, forcible dislocation of personality," and finally transmitted by him to still *other* listeners. Thus, the reality of this alleged "lost world" is diluted by a succession of mediating minds, and we are left not with an ontological projection but an epistemological puzzle: who knows about Vheissu? What does he know? How does he know it? In short, here Pynchon has superimposed epistemological structures upon science fiction's onto-logical motifs. *V.* is a late-modernist text, not "science-fictionalized" postmodernism.

The postmodernization of science fiction

There is, then, ample evidence of postmodernist writing's indebtedness to the science fiction genre. But the indebtedness also runs in the opposite direction. Just as postmodernism has borrowed ontological motifs from science fiction, so science fiction has in recent years begun to borrow from postmodernism. As a noncanonical, subliterary genre, science fiction has inevitably tended to lag behind canonized or mainstream literature in its adoption of new literary modes. Thus, the first flowering of popular science fiction in the United States during the 1930s coincided with the years of American modernism's most profound formal innovations in the hands of Faulkner, Dos Passos and others, yet the poetics of 1930s science fiction was *not* that of modernism, but the realist poetics that modernism strove to supersede.[14] Science fiction's breakthrough to modernist poetics did not occur until the 1960s, with the so-called "new wave" in American and British science-fiction writing. Dating from the "new wave," however, the pace of change in science fiction has accelerated, so that already by the late 1960s and early 1970s we can begin to discern, in the work of certain seminal figures, if not in the genre as a whole, an increased openness to developments in postmodernist writing – in other words, a tendency toward the "post-modernization" of science fiction.

One of the agents of this change has been the British science-fiction writer J. G. Ballard. Ballard had already made an important contribution to science fiction's first breakthrough, the "new wave" breakthrough into modernism, with his apocalyptic narratives of the 1960s, including the novella "The Voices of Time" (1960) and the trilogy of *The Drowned World* (1962), *The Drought* (1965), and *The Crystal World* (1966). The vehicle through which Ballard had introduced modernist poetics into science-fiction narratives was stylization – specifically, the self-conscious adaptation and exaggeration of elements of Joseph Conrad's modernist poetics, including his perspectivism, his melodramatic rhetoric and symbolist imagery, and even elements from his represented world. Of course this aspect of late-modernist stylization coexists in Ballard's novels with the ontological motifs characteristic of science fiction, in particular the familiar *topos* of apocalypse and post-apocalyptic survival. Nevertheless, in all of these narratives of the early- and mid-1960s Ballard holds his ontological improvisations firmly in check by means of a carefully-constructed epistemological frame. In all of them except the earliest ("The Voices of Time"), the perspective is scrupulously restricted to a single observer, whose consciousness is the only one to which we have access, with the result that we are encouraged to wonder how much of the implausible external landscape might actually be due to this observer's projections and distortions.

In his story-sequence *The Atrocity Exhibition* (1969) Ballard finally frees his ontological projections from their epistemological constraints, producing what is essentially a postmodernist text based on science-fiction *topoi*. Like all literary breakthroughs, this one has a prehistory, which is readily traceable in the works leading up to *The Atrocity Exhibition*. Already in the apocalypses of the early- and mid-1960s we can discern a pattern of repetition-with-variation embracing the entire series. In each, Earth is subjected to a global disaster, whether a plague of sleeping-sickness, rising sea-level, a manmade drought, or the bizarre crystalization of living matter. In each, a researcher, called Powers or Kerans or Ransom or Sanders (the last three near-anagrams), becomes obsessed with the strange new conditions of existence, and is drawn deeper and deeper into them, to his own annihilation. In each, the researcher forms a liaison with a mysterious woman, and suffers persecution at the hands of a demonic male figure, in some sense his double; and so on. Ballard even begins to repeat proper names from text to text: Mount Royal, the devastated English city of *The Drought*, reappears as Mount Royal, the African settlement of *The Crystal World*. All of this suggests, in a somewhat veiled way, the game-like permutation of a fixed repertoire of motifs – "art in a closed field" – which is precisely the organizing principle of *The Atrocity Exhibition*, except that here it is not veiled at all but, appropriately enough, exhibited. The protagonists of these stories are all obsessed with the problem of isolating a "modulus," a single abstract form which is repeated in a series of unrelated and apparently formless or irregular phenomena: photographs, erotic poses, urban landscapes. This theme of the "modulus" at the level of story-content in *The Atrocity Exhibition* exactly duplicates the formal organization of the stories, in which a fixed repertoire of modules, many of them repeated from the earlier apocalyptic novels, are differently recombined and manipulated from story to story. The modules include: a mentally unbalanced researcher whose name always begins with the letter T (Travis, Talbot, Traven, Tallis, Trabert etc.); a woman whom he "experimentally" murders (in several instances she bears the name of the mysterious female companion in *The Drought*, Catherine Austin or Austen); a demonic former student of his, whose name always begins with the letter K (Kline, Koester, Koster; cf. Kaldren in "The Voices of Time"); abandoned or ruined urban landscapes; recurrent objects or backgrounds, such as art and photography exhibitions, wrecked automobiles, helicopters, billboard advertisements, film showings, etc.; recurrent allusions to Dadaist or surrealist or neo-expressionist art (Ernst, Tanguy, Duchamp, De Chirico, Matta, Bacon); and so on.[15]

This transparently formalistic, game-like "art in a closed field" complicates science fiction's ontological confrontation between the present and a dystopian future world by superimposing on top of it, so to speak, a characteristically postmodernist ontological confrontation between the text as formal object and the world that it projects (see Chapter 10, "Styled worlds" pp. 148–61). Analogous strategies of serialism and transparently artificial formalism can be found, for instance, in Claude Simon's *Les Corps conducteurs* (*Conducting Bodies*, 1971) and *Triptych* (1973) or in Walter Abish's short fictions from *Minds Meet* (1975) and *In the Future Perfect* (1977). Behind both Simon and Abish stands the precursor-figure of Raymond Roussel, and it is surely no coincidence that Ballard has titled one chapter of a story from *The Atrocity Exhibition* "Impressions of Africa," and a chapter of another story "Locus Solus." These allusions complete the trajectory of Ballard's progress: from Conrad he has moved to Roussel, from late-modernist stylization to postmodernism.

Samuel Delany's progress, in his two 'big' science-fiction novels of the mid-1970s, *Triton* (1976) and *Dhalgren* (1974), bears comparison with Ballard's. Like Ballard in his apocalyptic novels of the mid-1960s, Delany in *Triton* couples science fiction with modernist poetics, exploiting science fiction's ontological motifs yet holding them in check by means of a modernist epistemological frame. Ontological motifs in *Triton* include the "war of the worlds" *topos* and the motif of visiting an alien planet – here elegantly inverted, since the alien planet, from the point of view of a citizen of Triton, is Earth. Delany's projected future world, although inevitably involving a good deal of gadgetry, focuses primarily on areas that most interest the post-modernists, namely social and institutional extrapolations: living arrangements, norms of sexual behavior, religious cults, even future art-forms and boardgames. Ontologically oriented though it may be in these regards, *Triton*, like Ballard's apocalyptic novels, is nevertheless mediated through a single consistent center-of-consciousness, one Bron Helstrom, whose self-deceptions, recognitions and mis-recognitions, limitations and unreliability as a perceiver inevitably become the focus of our attention. In effect, the presence of Bron's mind as a refracting medium "tames" ontological improvisation to a characteristically modernist epistemological structure.[16]

The same sort of "taming" of ontological license might have been expected from *Dhalgren*, Delany's other "big" 1970s novel. Here, as in *Triton*, the perspective is rigorously limited to the point of view of the protagonist, the nameless drifter who comes to be known as Kid. Kid, with his history of mental disorder and institutionalization, supplies a motivating framework that could enable us to explain – and explain away – the bizarre conditions under which the citizens of Bellona, the urban setting of *Dhalgren*, apparently live. These conditions include Bellona's inexplicable isolation from the rest of the country; its impossibly fluid and unstable topography, so that, for instance, an apartment located on one occasion only a few short blocks from the river, on another occasion is miles from it; the similar instability and variability with which time unfolds there; and its spectacularly implausible astronomical phenomena, including the apparition of two moons and a gigantic red sun hundreds of times larger than normal. Are all these implausibilities, and others like them, merely subjective delusions experienced by Kid alone? Kid himself, for one, assumes that the apparition of the giant red sun occurred in a dream, and attributes the disparities between his experiences and those of others to solipsism.

But Bellona really does exist under some special dispensation which affects all who remain there, not Kid alone. The astronomical miracles, for instance, are no solipsistic dreams but shared experiences, corroborated by witnesses other than Kid. And, the most persuasive evidence of all, there is at least one bizarrely implausible event which Kid himself fails to notice, but which the reader can reconstruct from the text. Members of a women's commune flee the city once and for all near the beginning of Kid's experiences in Bellona, and the *same* women flee again near the *end* of his experiences there. Blatantly self-contradictory, these events undermine the ontological stability of the represented world. Though he transmits these events to us, Kid misses the self-contradiction in them, which in a sense guarantees their objective, and not merely subjective, reality. Thus, we are compelled to abandon the epistemological explanation for the impossibilities of *Dhalgren*. Bellona is not a state of mind but a state of being; an ontological condition, not the symptoms of a psychological one.[17]

In *Breakfast of Champions* (1973), the imaginary science-fiction author Kilgore Trout meets *his* author, Kurt Vonnegut, Jr. Vonnegut, who had already used Trout in two previous novels (*God Bless You, Mr Rosewater*, 1965, and *Slaughterhouse-Five*, 1969), here sets his character free from the prison-house of fiction. (Actually, Vonnegut will subsequently renege on his manumission of Trout, at least to the extent of reviving his *name* as a pseudonym for another imaginary writer in *Jailbird*, 1979.) This encounter can serve as a parable for the argument I have been trying to make about the interaction between science fiction and postmodernist writing. Kilgore Trout is Vonnegut's self-caricature, Vonnegut imagining himself as the more or less "straight" science-fiction writer that he had started out to be in early novels like *Player Piano* (1952), *The Sirens of Titan* (1959), and *Cat's Cradle* (1963). The Kurt Vonnegut who projects himself into the world of his novel in order to interview – and liberate! – his own character is practicing romantic irony, and thereby aligning himself with the postmodernist revival of romantic irony. So Trout, archetypal science-fiction writer, alter ego of the "early" Vonnegut, meets the "later," postmodernist Vonnegut – what could be more symbolic? Particularly since the occurrence of such a meeting in itself exhibits the postmodernism of *Breakfast of Champions*. Spokesman of one of the genres of ontological poetics, Trout finds himself inside a text belonging to the other ontological genre – this is the relation of science fiction to postmodernist writing, in a nutshell.

5: A WORLD NEXT DOOR

listen: there's a hell
of a good universe next door; let's go
    (e. e. cummings, "pity this busy monster, manunkind," 1944)

"You know what a miracle is. . . . another world's intrusion into this one.
Most of the time we coexist peacefully, but when we do touch there's
cataclysm."
    (Thomas Pynchon, *The Crying of Lot 49*, 1966)

If you took a confrontation between worlds, such as you might find in a
science-fiction novel, and could somehow fold or compress it to fit into the
interior space of a normal-sized house, what would you have? Perhaps you
would have Julio Cortázar's "House Taken Over," from *End of the Game (Final
del juego*, 1956), in which supernatural beings occupy the rear of a normal
suburban house, forcing its middle-class, middle-aged inhabitants, a brother
and sister, to retreat to the front half and seal off the back half behind a stout
oak door: "another world's intrusion into this one." Or you might have
Carlos Fuentes's "Aura" (1962), in which a young historian takes up resi-
dence in a Mexico City apartment occupied by an aged woman and her
double, the "ghost" of her younger self: *this* world's intrusion into the *other*
world. Or you might have Cortázar's "Bestiary" (from *Bestiavio*, 1951), or its
slapstick version, "The Tiger Lodgers" (from *Cronopios y famas*, 1962), or
Richard Brautigan's "gothic western," *The Hawkline Monster* (1974), another
slapstick version, or Mikhail Bulgakov's *The Master and Margarita* (begun,
1928; completed, 1940) or Cortázar's *62: Modelo para armar* (*62: A Model-Kit*)
(1968), not a house but a *city* taken over; and so on. Whatever the example, the
ontological structure of the projected world is essentially the same in every
case: a *dual* ontology, on one side our world of the normal and everyday, on
the other side the next-door world of the paranormal or supernatural, and
running between them the contested boundary separating the two worlds –
Cortázar's stout oak door.

What you would have, in short, is a "Gothic enclosure," to use Rosemary

Jackson's term;[1] or, in other words, a haunted house. The implications should be clear: postmodernist fiction has close affinities with the genre of the fantastic, much as it has affinities with the science-fiction genre, and it draws upon the fantastic for motifs and *topoi* much as it draws upon science fiction. It is able to draw upon the fantastic in this way because the fantastic genre, like science fiction and like postmodernist fiction itself, is governed by the ontological dominant.

Hesitation

The fantastic: a genre of ontological poetics? This proposition requires some defending, for the consensus in contemporary poetics favors, on the contrary, an *epistemological* approach to fantastic writing.

The most influential version of this epistemological account is, of course, Tzvetan Todorov's.[2] The fantastic, for Todorov, is less a genre than a transient *state* of texts which actually belong to one of two adjacent genres: either the genre of the uncanny, in which apparently supernatural events are ultimately explained in terms of the laws of nature (for instance, as deceptions or hallucinations); or that of the marvelous, in which supernatural events are ultimately accepted as such – where, in other words, the supernatural becomes the norm. An example of a fantastic narrative that ultimately resolves itself into the uncanny would be Poe's "The Fall of the House of Usher"; one that resolves itself into the marvelous would be any of H. P. Lovecraft's horror stories. A text belongs to the fantastic proper only as long as it *hesitates* between natural and supernatural explanations, between the uncanny and the marvelous. Hesitation, or "epistemological uncertainty,"[3] is thus the underlying principle of the fantastic according to Todorov.

Few texts manage to maintain this delicate balance to the end. One that does is James's *Turn of the Screw* (1898); another, I would argue, is Pynchon's *Crying of Lot 49* (1966). But if this is so, then to push *past* this point of poised epistemological uncertainty – as Pynchon does in the transition from *Lot 49* to *Gravity's Rainbow* (1973), and as other postmodernist writers do at various stages in their own careers – means to *exit* the fantastic genre and enter the marvelous. Postmodernist ontological fiction should, it would appear, lie by definition *outside* the fantastic genre proper. How, then, do I justify my claim of affinity between postmodernist fiction and the fantastic genre?

Todorov himself would be the first to acknowledge that there is something anomalous about the behavior of the fantastic in the twentieth century, from his point of view. The paradigm case is Kafka's story "Metamorphosis" (1916), a text characterized throughout by a most unfantastic tone of banality, and one in which none of the characters actually experiences any epistemological hesitation between natural and supernatural explanations.[4] Stymied, Todorov is forced to conclude that Kafka's text heralds the disappearance of the fantastic in twentieth-century literature. This disappearance, he tells us, is a consequence of the disappearance of representation in contemporary writing, for the possibility of producing the fantastic effect is dependent upon the possibility of representing the real; without the latter, the former is out of the question. The fantastic "charge" has been absorbed into contemporary writing in general; all writing is "hesitant" now, although no writing can be hesitant in the fantastic mode any longer.[5]

But this is jumping to conclusions. For one thing, neither the absence of a hesitant character *within* the fictional world, nor the unfantastic banality of that world, need count against "Metamorphosis," for neither of these are *necessary* criteria of Todorov's fantastic, but merely optional ones.[6] Granted that somebody must experience epistemological hesitation, otherwise there is no fantastic effect at all in Todorov's sense, then why not say that, in the absence of a character to do the hesitating, the reader himself or herself does it? – which indeed seems to be the case in "Metamorphosis." As for the charge of banality – granted, the sort of fantastic narrative with which we are most familiar typically transpires in an atmosphere fraught with threat, terror, the unexpected; nevertheless, this is a historically contingent fact about the fantastic, and not a logical or structural necessity.

Finally, reports of the disappearance of representation in twentieth-century literature have been greatly exaggerated – as have reports of the disappearance of fantastic writing, for that matter. Much postmodernist fiction continues to cast a "shadow," to use Roland Barthes's expression: it continues to have "a *bit* of ideology, a *bit* of representation, a *bit* of subject."[7] Indeed, it is precisely by preserving a *bit* of representation that postmodernist fiction can mount its challenge *to* representation. Todorov has failed to see that in the context of postmodernism the fantastic has been co-opted as one of a number of strategies of an ontological poetics that pluralizes the "real" and thus problematizes representation. The postmodernist fantastic can be seen as a sort of jiu-jitsu that uses representation itself to overthrow representation.

So the anomalies lie not in "Metamorphosis" or postmodernist fantastic fiction, but in Todorov's theory and its ability to handle such texts. Todorov's epistemological approach simply does not get to the bottom of the fantastic. That "bottom," the deep structure of the fantastic, is, I would argue, ontological rather than epistemological. Rosemary Jackson, taking her cue from Baxtin, has described the fantastic as *dialogical*, an interrogation of the "real" and of monological forms of realistic representation.[8] The fantastic, in other words, involves a face-to-face confrontation between the possible (the "real") and the impossible, the normal and the paranormal. Another world penetrates or encroaches upon our world (as in "House Taken Over"), or some representative of our world penetrates an outpost of the other world, the world next door (as in "Aura"). Either way, this precipitates a confrontation between real-world norms (the laws of nature) and other-worldly, supernatural norms. Sometimes the confrontation is understated to the point of bland acquiescence, and the fantastic flattens out into that tone of unfantastic banality that Todorov found so problematic; at other times, as we shall see, it is strenuously agonistic.

The fantastic, by this analysis, can still be seen as a zone of hesitation, a frontier – not, however, a frontier between the uncanny and the marvelous, but between this world and the world next door.[9] Todorov is right, of course, that for a certain historical period, running roughly from the rise of the gothic novel in the eighteenth century to Kafka's "Metamorphosis," a structure of epistemological hesitation was superimposed upon the underlying dual ontological structure of the fantastic, naturalizing and "psychologizing" it. But in the years since "Metamorphosis," this epistemological structure has tended to evaporate, leaving behind it the ontological deep structure of the fantastic still intact. Hence the practice of an ontological poetics of the fantastic by postmodernist writers.

Banality

"Acceptance of a world that is, willy-nilly, a given of experience": this is the ontological attitude that Alan Wilde has attributed to Barthelme and other postmodernist artists, and while it is far from the only attitude discernible among the postmodernists, it is certainly a characteristic one. Todorov found it in "Metamorphosis," and it is shared by many postmodernist fantastic texts whose tone is unfantastically banal and whose characters, like Kafka's Gregor Samsa and his family, are impossibly blasé in the face of miraculous violations of natural law.

Thus, for example, in T. Coraghessan Boyle's story "Bloodfall" (from *Descent of Man and Other Stories*, 1980), blood begins inexplicably raining from the sky, yet the comfortable counterculture types who people this story seem unable to muster any reaction more vigorous than vague irritation. Similarly, in Cortázar's "Bestiary," the unpredictable presence of a tiger in the house is accepted by the family with casual matter-of-factness. Brautigan carries this matter-of-factness even further in *In Watermelon Sugar* (1968). What does a little boy talk about with tigers – *talking* tigers, that is – who have just finished killing his parents? His arithmetic homework, of course:

> "What do you want to know?" one of the tigers said.
> "What's nine times nine?"
> "Eighty-one," a tiger said.
> "What's eight times eight?"
> "Fifty-six," a tiger said.
> I asked them half a dozen other questions: six times six, seven times four etc. I was having a lot of trouble with arithmetic. Finally the tigers got bored with my questions and told me to go away.[10]

"Finally the tigers got bored": it is easy to see how they might, but a good deal less easy to see why postmodernist fantastic writers like Brautigan, Cortázar, Boyle, or Kafka before them, should want to flatten out a fantastic situation in this way.

"We shall never be sufficiently amazed about this lack of amazement," Camus said of Kafka,[11] and much the same could be said of "Bloodfall" or "Bestiary" or *In Watermelon Sugar*. For this is precisely the point: the characters' failure to be amazed by paranormal happenings serves to heighten *our* amazement. The rhetoric of contrastive banality, we might call this. Far from smothering or neutralizing the fantastic effect, as Todorov apparently believed it would, this "banalization" of the fantastic actually sharpens and intensifies the confrontation between the normal and paranormal. Normality in the hippie household of "Bloodfall" or on the country estate of "Bestiary" is *exaggeratedly* normal, normal to the point of boredom ("Finally the tigers got bored"); therefore any encroachment of the fantastic upon it will be felt as supremely disruptive, provoking the sharpest dialogue between normal and paranormal. This helps to explain the recurrence throughout the postmodernist fantastic of that hoary gothic locale, the haunted house: nothing is more domestic, more normal, than a middle-class house, so nothing is more disruptive than other-worldly agents penetrating and "taking over" a house.

The rhetoric of contrastive banality is carried to its logical extreme in the worlds of texts such as Salman Rushdie's *Midnight's Children* (1981) or Gabriel García Márquez's *One Hundred Years of Solitude* (1967). The India of *Midnight's Children* is a world thoroughly pervaded by miracles – so thoroughly, indeed, that the miraculous comes to appear routine. Similarly, in García Márquez's Macondo, supernatural beings and happenings, including ghosts and apparitions, supernatural plagues of insomnia or amnesia or dead birds, and so on, are all accepted quite matter-of-factly. But García Márquez goes a step further than Rushdie, for the Macondoans' reactions are not merely inappropriate or out of proportion to the strangeness of the events, they are actually *inverted*. On the one hand, the gypsies' flying carpet and Remedios the Beauty's ascension into heaven are regarded as normal everyday occurrences; on the other hand, the natural phenomenon of ice and the all-too-explicable massacre of demonstrators appear implausible, paranormal, too fantastic to be believed. Thus, in Macondo not only does the fantastic become banal but, by a kind of chiasmus, the banal also becomes fantastic. Nevertheless, the dialogue between the normal and the paranormal still continues in *One Hundred Years of Solitude*, although their relative positions have been reversed. *One Hundred Years* is still, in my sense, a fantastic text despite – or indeed because of – its banalization of the fantastic.

Resistance

Thus, even in those postmodernist fictions which seem to acquiesce in the fantastic, reducing it to banality, some *resistance* of normality against the paranormal continues to be felt – if not by any of the characters, then at least by the reader. As long as such resistance is present, the dialogue between the normal and the paranormal will continue – more than that, it will have been heightened, foregrounded, by the contrastive banality of the characters' bland non-reaction. This is one of the means postmodernist writing uses to emphasize the ontological confrontation inherent in the fantastic. The other means is more direct: it involves *dramatizing* the confrontation, turning the resistance of normality against the paranormal into an agonistic struggle.

As always, Borges is ready with a parable. The purely ideal world of Tlön, in his story "Tlön, Uqbar, Orbis Tertius," first manifests itself within our world through the appearance of other-worldly objects, piecemeal intrusions, but in the end it seems on the verge of supplanting our world entirely: "Contact with Tlön and the ways of Tlön have disintegrated this world."[12]

Borges' narrator, at the story's close, doubts whether our world has the will to resist usurpation by the ideal world.

The fantastic invasion proceeds on many fronts throughout postmodernist fiction. Italo Calvino's "invisible city" of Theodora, having laboriously eliminated all its natural vermin – serpents, flies, termites, rats, and so on – succumbs to an invasion of fantastic fauna from its library – sphinxes, griffons, chimeras, dragons, unicorns. In Cortázar's *62: Modelo para armar*, a visit by two characters from our world to the next-door parallel world called the City triggers a massive counterinvasion, as the real-world cities of Paris and Vienna are invaded and overwhelmed by the fantastic. And in Fuentes' *Terra nostra* (1975) three brothers, identical triplets, serve as the shock-troops of a fantastic invasion. Cast up on the shore of Philip II's sixteenth-century Spain, each is an emissary from some other world beyond or next door to this one: one brother has just returned from discovering a new world peopled by the divinities of Aztec mythology; the second is a character from gothic fiction, offspring of a royal father and a she-wolf; and the third is an intertextual character, none other than Don Juan Tenorio. These brothers carry their incommensurable realities into the midst of Philip's closed and unitary Spain, shattering it into multiple, jostling, juxtaposed worlds, and opening the floodgates to an influx of the supernatural. Philip's palace of El Escorial is overrun by the fantastic and transformed into a gothic haunted castle; indeed, Spain itself becomes a gothic enclosure, a country invaded and "taken over" by the paranormal.

How are the denizens of our world to resist this fantastic invasion? In Bulgakov's *The Master and Margarita*, when Satan invades Moscow under the cover of a touring magic-show, Moscow officialdom attempts to organize resistance by constructing plausible rationalizations, explanatory frameworks within which to "naturalize" the satanic miracles. The aim, in effect, is to convert the fantastic into what Todorov would call the uncanny. The *topos* of fantastic invasion and rationalistic resistance is most fully dramatized, however, in Angela Carter's *The Infernal Desire Machines of Dr Hoffman* (1972). Here Dr Hoffman wages a "guerilla war" against the everyday reality of the City by projecting into its midst disruptive unrealities, "concretised desires":

> Since mirrors offer alternatives, the mirrors had all turned into fissures or crannies in the hitherto hard-edge world of here and now and through these fissures came slithering sideways all manner of amorphous spooks. And these spooks were Dr. Hoffman's guerillas, his soldiers in disguise who, though absolutely unreal, nevertheless, were.[13]

Dr Hoffman's assaults on reality include transforming the entire audience at a performance of *The Magic Flute* into peacocks – his "first disruptive coup"[14] – and blowing up the cathedral, which disintegrates into fireworks and music (the *Symphonie Fantastique*, naturally). Resistance to Hoffman's invasive unreality is organized by the Minister of Determination, an uncompromising empiricist who stands, one might say, for militant normality:

> He believed the criterion of reality was that a thing was determinate and the identity of a thing lay only in the extent to which it resembled itself . . . . He

believed that the city – which he took as a microcosm of the universe – contained a finite set of objects and a finite set of their combinations and therefore a list could be made of all possible distinct forms which were logically viable. These could be counted, organized into a conceptual framework and so form a kind of check list for the verification of all phenomena, instantly available by means of an information retrieval system.[15]

In short, Carter elaborates the ontological confrontation between this world and the "world next door" into a literal agonistic struggle, analogous to the science-fiction *topos* of the "war of the worlds."

From "worlds" to worlds

Thus postmodernist fiction co-opts the fantastic genre in much the same way that it has co-opted science fiction, developing the fantastic genre's inherent potential for ontological dialogue into a vehicle for a postmodernist ontological poetics. But this is not the only route by which postmodernism arrives at its own form of the fantastic. It also reaches the fantastic by literalizing a characteristic modernist metaphor. This is the metaphorical use of "world" in the sense of way of life, life-experience, or *Weltanschauung* – a familiar metaphorical extension of the literal ontological sense of "world" to embrace an epistemological, psychological, or sociological meaning.[16]

Stages in the literalization of this modernist metaphor of "world" can be traced to the early writings of Julio Cortázar. The modernist metaphor can be found in Cortázar's novel *Rayuela* (*Hopscotch*, 1963), whose protagonist, Oliveira, is obsessed with the classic Berkeleyan (and late-modernist) epistemological problems of solipsism:

> The most absurd thing about these lives we pretend to lead are the false contacts in them. Isolated orbits, from time to time two hands will shake, a five-minute chat, a day at the races, a night at the opera, a wake where everybody feels a little more united (and it's true, but then it's all over just when it's time for linking up). And all the same one lives convinced his friends are there, that contact does exist, that agreements or disagreements are profound and lasting. How we all hate each other, without being aware that endearment is the current form of that hatred, and how the reason behind profound hatred is this excentration, the unbridgeable space between me and you, between this and that. All endearment is an ontological clawing.[17]

"Isolated orbits," "excentration": Cortázar's planetary imagery here develops in a particularly concrete way the metaphor of the "worlds" of individual experiences and outlooks. If Oliveira despairs at the falseness of most supposed contacts between life-worlds, *Hopscotch* shows us that true contact tends to be violent and disruptive. The novelist Morelli, moving in the solipsistic world of his fictions, is "touched" by the outside world when he is knocked down by a car; Oliveira, newly returned to Buenos Aires from Paris, impinges disruptively upon the calm and orderly shared world of Traveler and Talita. The erratic behavior provoked by Oliveira's intrusion reaches an absurd climax when Talita is made literally to walk the plank between the third-floor windows of facing flats to deliver a package of *yerba maté* to Oliveira. A consequence of trying to bridge the "unbridgeable gap between me and you," this episode also, of course, dramatizes the idea of "bridging the gap" between solipsistic life-worlds.

As we move from *Hopscotch* to Cortázar's early short stories we see how he goes about literalizing this metaphor of "worlds." In *Hopscotch*, Oliveira and his lover La Mega are fascinated by aquariums, and one readily sees why. Interposing a transparent but nevertheless impenetrable barrier between one order of being and another, aquariums serve as an analogy for the solipsistic isolation of one individual consciousness, one life-world, from another, even (or perhaps especially) in the case of lovers. Isabel, the adolescent heroine of "Bestiary," is similarly fascinated by the animal-life behind the glass wall of her ant-farm, in which she no doubt recognizes an analogy for her own alienation.[18] But the more important analogy is with the "haunted house" in which she is spending the summer: just as the world of the ants is separated by a barrier from Isabel's world, so the house is partitioned between normal areas and off-limit areas "taken over" by the marauding tiger. Here, in other words, the confrontation between worlds is no longer a psychological and epistemological metaphor, but a literal ontological structure, a fantastic double ontology. Finally, the narrator in the short story "Axolotl" (from Cortázar's *End of the Game*) also confronts an alien order of being – this time, that of the axolotl, a type of salamander – across the glass barrier of an aquarium tank. But here the ontological barrier ultimately fails to keep incommensurable orders of being separate: there is an exchange of identities, the narrator's consciousness becoming that of the axolotl – "what was his obsession is now an axolotl."[19] Simultaneously with the breakdown of this boundary between worlds, the supernatural intrudes into the world of this story, and the metaphor of "worlds" becomes fantastically literal. This moment when metaphorical "worlds" merge, the world of the story itself shifting simultaneously into the fantastic mode, recurs throughout Cortázar's early short fiction: for instance in "The Distances" (from *End of the Game*), when a middle-class Argentine girl and a Budapest beggarwoman meet on a bridge and supernaturally exchange identities; or in "The Island at Noon" (from *All Fires the Fire*, 1966), in which an airline steward, obsessed by a Greek island glimpsed from the plane window, ventures into the island-world, only to converge there with his own alter ego, with fatal results. In all these cases the collapse of world-boundaries is violent, disruptive, catastrophic, as it is in *Hopscotch* – except that here, unlike in *Hopscotch*, this violent dialogue of worlds is not a trope but literal, fantastic reality.

Displaced fantastic

Despite what Todorov says, then, the fantastic has *not* been wholly absorbed into contemporary writing in general; it is still recognizably present in its various postmodernist transformations. Nevertheless, Todorov does have a point: the fantastic no longer seems to be the exclusive property of texts which are identifiably fantastic in their ontological structure; a generalized fantastic effect or "charge" seems to be diffused throughout postmodernist writing, making its presence felt in displaced forms in texts that are not formally fantastic at all. For some notion of how this displacement and generalization of the fantastic comes about, we might consider two puzzling short texts: Maurice Blanchot's *L'Arrêt de mort* (1948), and William Gass's "Order of Insects" (from *In the Heart of the Heart of the Country*, 1968).

Of the two, *L'Arrêt de mort* is the only one that might properly be considered fantastic on structural grounds. It contains a number of apparently supernatural events – a woman briefly revives from the dead at the narrator's bidding, then later returns to take demonic possession of his lover – for which rational, nonsupernatural explanations are also available. It hesitates, in short, between the natural and the supernatural, or between (in Todorov's terms) the uncanny and the marvelous. "Order of Insects," by contrast, need not be read as fantastic at all. In it the narrator, a middle-class American housewife, finds herself succumbing, like Isabel in "Bestiary" or the narrator of "Axolotl," to an unwholesome fascination with an alien, inhuman order of being, the "world" (in the metaphorical sense) of the bugs that mysteriously turn up dead on her carpet in the morning. Nothing occurs that is supernatural or even very extraordinary, and the narrator's fixation on the "order of insects" can easily be explained away as the onset of a nervous breakdown.

And yet, and yet . . . The fantastic structure of *L'Arrêt de mort* is severely undermined by the vagueness and incoherence with which the narrator presents the situation and its possible explanations. By contrast with "classically" hesitant fantastic texts such as *The Turn of the Screw* or *The Crying of Lot 49*, neither of the explanatory frames, natural or supernatural, emerges here with any clarity. The narrator's language is maddeningly evasive, almost ungraspable, as he hints at dark secrets that he refuses to disclose (or does not himself know?). It looks as if hesitation has been transferred from ontological structure to *language* in this text. Conversely, the apparently nonfantastic "Order of Insects" retains some irreducible element of strangeness, some residue of the fantastic that cannot readily be explained away. Here, too, the locus of strangeness is the language – not excessively vague and elusive, as in the case of *L'Arrêt de mort*, but on the contrary excessively mannered and *writerly*. Where has such an apparently unexceptional woman acquired such an improbably heightened, self-conscious style?

Let us say, then, that the mysteries of these texts are mysteries of language, not of their fictional worlds. In that case, what would dispose the reader to continue to regard them as in some way related to the fantastic genre? For one thing, the presence in both texts of that most characteristic of fantastic *topoi*, the haunted house or "gothic enclosure" – oddly transformed, to be sure, but nonetheless unmistakable. Throughout *L'Arrêt de mort*, domestic interiors are constantly being penetrated by aliens – not supernatural beings, but other characters. Natural as this may appear on the surface, each of these intrusions (I count nine of them in the course of an eighty-page text) accompanies or provokes aggressive or guilty or otherwise bizarre behavior on the part of the characters involved. The intruder's reasons, when he or she has any, are invariably inadequate or absurd, and the one intruded upon behaves as inexplicably as the intruder. No reader, I think, could fail to recognize in these uncanny episodes variants on the venerable gothic motif of the "house taken over."

The house in "Order of Insects" is also haunted, also "taken over": in one sense, by the mysterious (although perfectly natural) bugs; in another sense, by the woman whose obsession with these bugs transforms her life and that of her family. But the nature of this "haunting" cannot be understood completely unless we take into account the context in which "Order of Insects" appears. Two stories which precede "Order of Insects" in the volume *In the Heart of the Heart of the Country* also involve intrusions upon domestic spaces. In "The Pedersen Kid," the narrator, a country boy, enters a neighbor's house, where a killer is thought to be holed up, and suddenly, inexplicably, acquires an elaborate, highly self-conscious verbal style. In "Mrs Mean," the narrator does not actually succeed in penetrating his neighbor's house, but merely imagines himself doing so, which, nevertheless, is enough to release in him a similar flood of extravagant language. Finally, in "Order of Insects," the woman and her family have just moved into a "new" house – until recently, that is, somebody else's house; accordingly, here the verbal extravagance and self-consciousness begins with the first sentence of the text. The pattern should be clear: in *In the Heart of the Heart of the Country*, the penetration of someone else's domestic space – a displaced version of the gothic motif of haunting – corresponds to the acquisition of an extravagant language.

This suggests that the haunted house of "Order of Insects," and the apartments of *L'Arrêt de mort* as well, may in fact be haunted houses of fiction or even haunted prison-houses of language. In short, it is tempting, and possible, to read both texts as *allegories of writing*. *L'Arrêt de mort* is full of uncanny writings – deathbed letters, wills, hands that can be read (by a palmist) – all of them related to death or the return and persistence of the dead; the last text in this uncanny series is *L'Arrêt de mort* itself. Blanchot thus invites us to read *L'Arrêt de mort* as an allegory of the relations between death and writing: on the one hand, writing as a form of repetition of life, hence of survival beyond death; on the other hand, writing as the sign or guarantee of the writer's death. In "Order of Insects," the dead bugs are identified from the outset as being somehow related to writing: they appear "like ink stains" on the carpet; the housewife collects them in typewriter-ribbon tins; their desiccated shells survive after the interior flesh has decayed, in the same way that the "empty" signs of writing survive their author's death. The "order of insects," then, might well be the order of writing.

So here, we have two haunted-house stories that turn out really to be allegories of writing. But what can this mean – "really" allegories? Allegorical reading is possible here, perhaps even tempting, but it is not in any sense *necessary*: the literal level of both these texts seems perfectly self-contained, quite able to do without an allegorical level. We may well wonder whether an allegorical reading here would not be an imposition of our own. In short, these texts *hesitate* between the literal and the allegorical – just as, from another perspective, they hesitate between the representation of a world and the anti-representational foregrounding of language *for its own sake*. These are ontological oppositions, ontological hesitations, although not the oppositions and hesitations associated with traditional fantastic writing. Hesitation has been displaced from the frontier between this world and the "world next door," to the confrontation between different ontological levels in the structure of texts. This explains the general diffusion of fantastic "charge" throughout postmodernist writing: a displaced effect of the fantastic persists wherever a dialogue springs up between different ontological realms or levels.

6: REAL, COMPARED TO WHAT?*

"The Oranging of America" . . . is fiction, and its content derives entirely from my imagination. Where I have used real names or what seem to be physical descriptions of real people, it is done purely in the interest of fiction. In any serious sense any similarities between these stories and the real lives of any person living or dead are unintended and coincidental.

(Max Apple, *The Oranging of America and Other Stories*, 1976)

Everyone is familiar with the form of disclaimer that typically appears on the copyright page of works of fiction: "All the characters in this book are fictitious, and any resemblance to actual persons, living or dead, is purely coincidental," or something to that effect. A statement loaded with mimetic preconceptions, it is an obvious target for postmodernist parody, so it comes as no surprise to find postmodernist writers prefacing their anti-mimetic works with mock-disclaimers.[1] Max Apple's disclaimer from *The Oranging of America* is not a parody, however, as should be clear from its strange wording. "In any serious sense any similarities . . . are unintended and coincidental" – this formulation seems to recall John Searle's definition of fiction as "non-serious" utterances. The motive for such wording is transparently *legal*: Apple is trying to avoid libel actions being brought against him, for the very good reason that in his stories certain characters bear the names and some of the attributes of living or recently-deceased real-world persons. In the title-story, "The Oranging of America," there is a character named Howard Johnson, founder of a chain of roadside restaurants and motels, and another named Robert Frost, a famous poet residing on a farm in New Hampshire. In "Inside Norman Mailer," there is a pugnacious novelist and journalist named Norman Mailer, as well as a number of other literary hangers-on with names like Robert Penn Warren, Wayne Booth, Theodore White, and Richard

---

* This title is an outright theft from the jazz pianist and bandleader Les McCann, whose funky anthem, "Compared to What," contains the refrain: "Tryin' to make it real compared to what." Unavoidably, my punctuation has disambiguated his wonderfully ambiguous line.

I owe a special debt to my student Moshe Gilad for the treatment of historical fiction in this chapter.

Poirier. "Understanding Alvarado" features a Cuban dictator named Fidel Castro, and "Patty-Cake, Patty-Cake . . . A Memoir" an unnamed Michigan congressman, subsequently President of the United States, whose career matches that of the real-world Gerald Ford. Whether or not these examples constitute "transworld identities," in Eco's formal sense, between the real-world figures and the fictional characters, Apple is certainly flirting with the possibility of transworld identity. Enough attributes have been transferred from the real-world persons to make a law-suit plausible; hence the need for an especially evasive disclaimer on the copyright page.

But why play with fire in this way? Obviously because the bandying-about of celebrities' names holds a certain appeal for readers; it has the scent of scandal about it. And what, exactly, is the source of the scandal? Ultimately, its source is *ontological*: boundaries between worlds have been violated. There is an ontological scandal when a real-world figure is inserted in a fictional situation, where he interacts with purely fictional characters, as in Apple's "Understanding Alvarado," in which Castro pitches in a fictional baseball game whose prize will be the retired Cuban star of American baseball, Achilles "Archie" Alvarado, a fictional character. There is also an ontological scandal when two real-world figures interact in a fictional context, for instance when Howard Johnson is introduced to Robert Frost in "The Oranging of America," or Norman Mailer boxes with the story's author, Max Apple, in "Inside Norman Mailer." In general, the presence in a fictional world of a character who is transworld-identical with a real-world figure sends shock-waves throughout that world's ontological structure.

Apple, hardly a writer in the forefront of postmodernist innovation, nevertheless exemplifies strategies found throughout postmodernist fiction. Everywhere we find real-world historical figures inserted in fictional contexts, with much the same disorienting effect as in Apple's texts. For these purposes, highly "charged" figures are often preferred, figures rich in associations for most readers, able to excite strong reactions, whether of attraction or repulsion: the Kennedy brothers, Richard Nixon, Chairman Mao, Lenin, Trotsky, Sigmund Freud, Idi Amin, Che Guevara, Sanjay Gandhi, Norman Mailer, Malcolm X, Rudolph Hess, and the Duke and Duchess of Windsor.[2] Other real-world figures who have been manipulated this way include political figures such as Abraham Lincoln, Warren G. Harding, Walter Rathenau, Walter Mellon, and Nelson Rockefeller; artists such as Paul Klee, Chagall, and Picasso; writers and thinkers such as Rossetti, Swinburne, Ruskin, Kafka, Max Brod, Wittgenstein, Shklovsky, Marcel Proust, Gertrude Stein, Joyce, Lawrence, Yeats, Pound, Milton, and Lord Byron; and media "stars" such as Mickey Rooney, Walt Disney, and the tennis star Ilie Nastase.[3] Not only does the presence of such figures violate the real-world/fictional-world boundary, but these texts often compound the ontological offense by staging wholly unhistorical confrontations between two or more real-world figures: between Kafka and Wittgenstein in Davenport's "Aeroplanes at Brescia" (from *Tatlin!*, 1974); between young Jack Kennedy and Malcolm X in *Gravity's Rainbow* (1973); between Richard Nixon and Ethel Rosenberg in *The Public Burning* (1977); between Kennedy and Mailer in Abish's "The Istanbul Papers" (from *Minds Meet*, 1975); between

John Milton and Thomas Urquhart (the translator of Rabelais) in Alasdair Gray's "Logopandocy" (from *Unlikely Stories, Mostly*, 1983); and, in Doctorow's *Ragtime* (1975), between various pairs of historical personages – Evelyn Nesbit and Emma Goldmann, Harry K. Thaw and Harry Houdini, Houdini and the Archduke Franz Ferdinand, and so on.

Is there anything distinctively postmodernist in these examples of trans-world identity between fictional characters and real-world figures? After all, the presence of such transworld-identical characters is typical of many realistic historical novels as well. And the presence of historical characters in historical novels is itself only a special case of the universal structure of literary reference whereby an internal (fictional) field of reference and an external (real-world) field overlap and interpenetrate.[4] In terms of this "double-decker" structure of reference, there is nothing exceptional about, say, Robert Frost meeting Howard Johnson in Apple's text, or Evelyn Nesbit meeting Emma Goldmann in Doctorow's. There is a certain *tension* between the internal and external fields in such cases, for we know (or think we know) that in the external field these meetings never occurred. But tension between the two fields is not distinctively postmodernist; it also characterizes, for example, Tolstoy's treatment of Napoleon in *War and Peace*.

Bear in mind, however, that the "double-decker" model of literary reference aims at universal applicability. Within this universal norm we find local period and generic norms which may be more constraining. In other words, not every external referent need necessarily be admissible to the plane of the internal field of reference in all cultures, at all periods, in all genres. Transworld identity is a game with variable rules. Apple's disclaimer implicitly acknowledges the existence of one set of such rules, encoded in contemporary libel laws. Libel laws, in fact, constitute a rare example of a fully codified literary convention!

Constrained realemes

In principle, we ought to be able to reconstruct the different repertoires of real-world objects, individuals, and properties which are admissible to different genres of texts at different historical periods. Such repertoires are not, of course, made up of real-world things-in-themselves, things in the raw so to speak, but things as signifieds in a system of signification. We could call these semioticized things "realemes," using a neologism coined by Itamar Even-Zohar.[5] From the entire range of realemes available to a given culture and language, a certain subrange may be selected for the realeme repertoire of one class of text, a different subrange for a different class of text, while other subranges may be judged inadmissible and excluded from the repertoires of one or both of these text-classes. Judgments of admissibility and inadmissibility are culture-bound, not universal; realemes which one culture permits in its texts, another culture may exclude from the same text-class. Even-Zohar cites the example of the realeme "children," which Dutch commercial texts admit while the "equivalent" French commercial texts (for example, on EEC cornflakes packages) exclude. And what is true for differences between cultures will also be true, *mutatis mutandis*, for differences between periods or genres.

If this is so, then how is the repertoire of historical realemes constituted for "traditional" or "classic" historical fiction (Walter Scott, Fenimore Cooper, Hugo, Balzac, Thackeray, Tolstoy)? What constraints govern the insertion of historical realemes in this genre and period? And how does postmodernist practice measure up against the "classic" tradition?

Three constraints on the insertion of realemes seem to be characteristic of "classic" historical fiction:

1 Historical realemes – persons, events, specific objects, and so on – can only be introduced on condition that the properties and actions attributed to them in the text do not actually contradict the "official" historical record. This, of course, is a question-begging formulation; it leaves open questions of *which* version of history is to be regarded as the "official" one, of how the average reader's knowledge relates to the "official" account, and so on. Slippery though they may be, we do operate with intuitions about what is accepted historical "fact" and how far any fictional version deviates from that "fact." Another way of formulating this constraint would be to say that freedom to improvise actions and properties of historical figures is limited to the "dark areas" of history, that is, to those aspects about which the "official" record has nothing to report. *Within* the "dark areas," the historical novelist is permitted a relatively free hand. For example, history does not record that Queen Caroline ever interviewed a Scottish girl named Jeanie Deans sometime in the year 1736, through the intercession of the Duke of Argyle – but neither does it positively *rule out* such an encounter, so this episode of Scott's *Heart of Midlothian* (1818) satisfies the "dark areas" constraint. The "dark areas" are normally the times and places where real-world and purely fictional characters interact in "classic" historical fiction. Hrushovski observes that temporal references in fiction are often left "floating": we are given the day of the week on which an event supposedly transpires, but not the exact date, or the decade and month but not the exact year, and so on. This, says Hrushovski, is a mark of fictionality; more specifically, it creates a convenient dark area and allows the novelist some freedom to improvise.

Note, however, that there are at least two different norms for what constitutes a "dark area," some writers at some periods adhering to one norm, others to the other. Some historical novels treat the interior life of historical figures as dark areas – logically enough, since the "official" historical record cannot report on what went on *inside* a historical figure without fictionalizing to some extent. According to this norm, the novelist is free to introspect his historical characters, even to invent interior monologues for them; the classic example, of course, is Tolstoy's Napoleon. But the Tolstoyan example is not the only norm in this matter. Other historical novels regard the inner world of historical figures as inaccessible – inadmissible realemes, in other words – and therefore present them externally only, reserving the presentation of inner life for their wholly fictional characters; this is the norm that Scott, for example, follows.

2 The constraint on contradictions of the "official" historical record extends beyond specific realemes (persons, events) to the entire *system* of

realemes that constitutes a historical culture. Just as historical figures may not behave in ways that contradict the "official" record, so the entire material culture and *Weltanschauung* of a period may not be at variance with what "official" history tells us about the period. In effect, this is a constraint on *anachronism*. Constraints on anachronism, of course, are difficult to enforce. An acceptable degree of faithfulness to the material culture of the past is not so difficult to maintain – even the least sophisticated forms of historical fiction normally manage that (which is why we call them "costume dramas"). But few historical novels succeed in projecting the intellectual culture or ideology of a past period – its ethos, thought-styles, attitudes and tastes, and so on – without anachronism. Scott's Middle Ages, for example, capture little of any medieval *Weltanschauung*, but are permeated with nineteenth-century romantic ideology.

3 Finally, the most diffuse yet at the same time most profound constraint of all: the logic and physics of the fictional world must be compatible with those of reality if historical realemes are to be transferred from one realm to the other; otherwise, the text will be at radical variance with the norms of "classic" historical fiction. In Thomas Pavel's words:

> in order to be manageable, secondary ontologies have to respect as much as possible the inner structure of the primary ontologies they use as their ontic foundation.[6]

Or, to put it differently, historical fictions must be *realistic* fictions; a fantastic historical fiction is an anomaly.

These constraints are observed not only by nineteenth-century "classic" historical novelists – Scott, Cooper, Tolstoy and so on – but also by modernists and, for the most part, by late-modernists working in the "historical" mode as well. Consider Dos Passos in the *U.S.A.* trilogy (1930, 1932, 1936). His use of historical figures such as Big Bill Haywood or Woodrow Wilson in the fictional (as opposed to non-fictional and biographical) sections of his text is strictly governed by the "dark areas" constraint; he avoids anachronism; and his fictional world obeys real-world physics and logic. The same is by and large true of such late-modernist historical fictions as Barth's *The Sot-Weed Factor* (1960; revised, 1967), Doctorow's *Ragtime*, and Thomas's *The White Hotel* (1981), although in these cases we do begin to observe some deterioration or slippage in the "classic" norms. Thus, for example, although the notorious lesbian liaison between Evelyn Nesbit and Emma Goldmann in *Ragtime* actually occurs in a historical "dark area," and thus satisfies the "classic" paradigm, other events in this text violate the "dark areas" constraint, notably the fictional Coalhouse Walker's occupation of the Morgan Library. Similarly, Barth in *The Sot-Weed Factor* carefully avoids anachronisms of material culture, but seems positively to flaunt anachronisms of *Weltanschauung*. His Henry Burlingame is equipped with a full complement of late-twentieth-century intellectual attitudes and opinions – in cosmology, anthropology, sexuality, and even literary criticism. Finally, Thomas in *The White Hotel* has constructed a world whose norms, he invites us to think, *may be* fantastic, including the possibility of prophecy and a vision of the "other world." And to compound the violation, he has deeply implicated the historical figure of Freud and the historical event of the Babi Yar massacre in the fantastic dimension of his novel.

Now we can return to our examples of transworld identity from postmodernist writing. Many of these, it turns out, do indeed adhere to the "classic" paradigm of constraints on the insertion of historical realemes. Fowles's Pre-Raphaelite Brothers, for instance, are handled strictly according to the rules of the historical novelist's game, as are most of the historical figures in Grass's *Flounder* (Frederick the Great, the Brothers Grimm, Rosa Luxemburg, and so on), and many of the ones in Guy Davenport's stories. The fictional encounter between Kafka and Wittgenstein in Davenport's "Aeroplanes at Brescia," for instance, remains safely within the "dark areas" of both figures' "official" biographies. The same cannot be said, however, for Abish's Proust (in "How the Comb Gives Fresh Meaning to the Hair," from *Minds Meet*) or Boyle's Idi Amin (in "Dada," from *Descent of Man*). It is simply a stark contradiction of the historical record to place Proust in Albuquerque, New Mexico, as Abish does, or Amin at a neo-Dadaist exhibition in New York, as Boyle does. On the other hand, Coover's use of Richard Nixon as center-of-consciousness in the odd-numbered chapters of *The Public Burning* does not in itself violate the "dark areas" norm – or rather, it violates this norm as understood by Scott, but not as understood by Tolstoy. In terms of the Tolstoyan model, Nixon's consciousness constitutes a historical "dark area," and Coover is free to insert material claiming to represent Nixon's interior monologue. However, Coover violates the norms of "classic" historical fiction elsewhere: when he has Nixon try to seduce Ethel Rosenberg at Sing-Sing Prison on the eve of her execution, in visible contradiction of the historical record; and even more spectacularly when he has him sodomized by Uncle Sam himself in the novel's Epilogue, thus merging (!) historical fiction and the fantastic. Other illicit mergings of history and the fantastic occur, for instance, in Elkin's *The Living End*, in which the historical Ilie Nastase is overheard by the dead but still conscious Ladlehaus from his grave beside the tennis court, or in Rushdie's *Midnight's Children*, where the historical Sanjay Gandhi replicates or clones himself many times over, his features appearing on every one of the Sanjay Youth volunteers (whose duties during the Emergency involved promoting sterilizations and vasectomies). And what becomes of historical figures when they are inserted in self-consciously anachronistic texts such as Ishmael Reed's *Mumbo Jumbo* (1973) and *Flight to Canada* (1977)? President Warren G. Harding seems to escape "contamination," but only because his presence in *Mumbo Jumbo* is so marginal. The same cannot be said of President Abraham Lincoln in *Flight to Canada*, however. Already badly compromised by various violations of the "dark areas" constraint, Lincoln's historicity collapses entirely when in his presence another character *picks up a telephone* to call General Robert E. Lee. Once this has occurred, we can no longer be surprised when Lincoln's assassination is *televised* (in a transparent allusion to the Kennedy assassination and its aftermath), for we are clearly outside the "classic" paradigm of the historical novel.

Apocryphal history

"A character cannot walk out of a fictional house and show up in a real cafe," writes Hrushovski. Of course not; but historical fiction often strives to give the illusion that the *opposite* can happen, that a historical figure can walk out of a real cafe and show up in a fictional house – or that, say, the historical Col John Graham of Claverhouse in Scott's *Old Mortality* (1817) can ride away from the historical skirmish at Drumclog and show up at the fictional Tillietudlem Tower. When such migrations occur, an ontological boundary between the real and the fictional – or, in Hrushovski's terms, between an external and an internal field of reference – has been transgressed. "Classic" historical fiction from Scott through Barth tries to make this transgression as discreet, as nearly unnoticeable as possible, camouflaging the seam between historical reality and fiction in ways described above: by introducing pure fiction only in the "dark areas" of the historical record; by avoiding anachronism; by matching the "inner structure" of its fictional worlds to that of the real world. Postmodernist fiction, by contrast, seeks to foreground this seam by making the transition from one realm to the other as jarring as possible. This it does by violating the constraints on "classic" historical fiction: by visibly contradicting the public record of "official" history; by flaunting anachronisms; and by integrating history and the fantastic. Apocryphal history, creative anachronism, historical fantasy – these are the typical strategies of the postmodernist revisionist historical novel. The postmodernist historical novel is revisionist in two senses. First, it revises the *content* of the historical record, reinterpreting the historical record, often demystifying or debunking the orthodox version of the past. Secondly, it revises, indeed transforms, the conventions and norms of historical fiction itself.

The two meanings of revisionism converge especially in the postmodernist strategy of apocryphal or alternative history. Apocryphal history contradicts the official version in one of two ways: either it *supplements* the historical record, claiming to restore what has been lost or suppressed; or it *displaces* official history altogether. In the first of these cases, apocryphal history operates in the "dark areas" of history, apparently in conformity to the norms of "classic" historical fiction but in fact *parodying* them. In the second case, apocryphal history spectacularly violates the "dark areas" constraint. In both cases, the effect is to juxtapose the officially-accepted version of what happened and the way things were, with another, often radically dissimilar version of the world. The tension between these two versions induces a form of ontological flicker between the two worlds: one moment, the official version seems to be eclipsed by the apocryphal version; the next moment, it is the apocryphal version that seems mirage-like, the official version appearing solid, irrefutable.

What is official history the history of? Of the winners, says Stanley Elkin; of the male sex, says Grass. So each attempts to redress the balance of the historical record of writing histories of the excluded, those relegated permanently to history's dark areas. Elkin in *George Mills* (1982) narrates episodes from the long history of a family of perpetual losers, the blue-collar Millses, who never cross the threshold into official history. If a Mills is involved in a great historical event – such as the First Crusade – it is as page to a noble youngest son who never gets nearer to the Holy Land than Poland; if a Mills encounters a historical figure, it is as unsuccessful candidate for the privilege of driving King George IV's carriage. Grass, in the same vein, writes the history of cooks, the women who fed and cared for history's "great men" and were left in historical anonymity for their pains. Clearly this form of apocryphal history responds to the same impulse to restore "lost" groups (the peasantry and working-class, women, minorities) to the historical record that animates historical research itself in our time.

A related form of apocryphal history might be called "secret history." "Someone once said that beneath or behind all political and cultural warfare lies a struggle between secret societies," writes Ishmael Reed in *Mumbo Jumbo*,[7] where he tries to convince us that beneath or behind all western history lies the struggle between the Atonist Order and the agents of the Osirian-Dionysian mysteries. The latest manifestation of this centuries-long struggle is the attempt by the white elite of the Wallflower Order to suppress jazz dancing in the 1920s. According to Reed, the Great Depression was a conspiracy to keep Americans from being able to afford radios, thus restricting their access to subversive Black music, while the Second World War was an "extravaganza" staged by the Wallflower Order. History as paranoiac conspiracy-theory – this is what Reed offers in *Mumbo Jumbo*, and it is a vision of history that he shares with many other postmodernist revisionist historical novelists, including Thomas Pynchon. In his late-modernist text *V.* (1963), Pynchon makes his characters suspect that the perpetual crises of the twentieth century might be the fruit of some vast conspiracy operating in the "dark areas" of history, while in *The Crying of Lot 49* (1966) he confronts Oedipa Maas with the possibility that America might be the battlefield for "a struggle between secret societies." But it is of course in *Gravity's Rainbow* that Pynchon practices to the fullest his paranoiac mode of secret history, uncovering layer upon layer of conspiracy behind the official historical facts of the Second World War. Is the war a plot by the great international corporations and cartels? by the technologies themselves, a struggle not so much between secret societies as between plastics, electronics, aircraft? by inscrutable forces from the "other world"? The facts, as reinterpreted by Pynchon, might sustain one or more of these theories, but no final conclusion is possible; we are left with a kind of free-floating paranoia.

Equally paranoiac, although not quite so cosmic in its implications, is the secret history constructed by John Barth in *LETTERS* (1979). Already in *The Sot-Weed Factor* he had given us a paradigmatic secret history, actually entitled *Secret Historie of the Voiage Up the Bay of Chesapeake*. This apocryphal narrative by the historical Capt. John Smith debunks the pious legend of Smith's rescue by Pocahontas, substituting bawdy for gallantry and opportunism for heroics. In its demystificatory impulse it is typical of much postmodernist revisionist historical fiction, although it lacks postmodernism's paranoiac vision. This lack is rectified in *LETTERS*, in which the Cook/Burlingame family, carried over from *The Sot-Weed Factor*, appear as hereditary conspirators either for or against the Government of the United States. Alternating in their allegiances from one generation to the next – or in some cases, from the first half of their careers to the second – the Cooks/Burlingames interfere in most of the major crises of nineteenth-century America: Pontiac's conspiracy in the French and Indian War, the treachery of Benedict Arnold in the Revolutionary War, Aaron Burr's plot and Tecumseh's Indian confederacy, the burning of Washington and the siege of Baltimore in the war of 1812, the supposed rescue of Napoleon from St Helena to New Jersey, and so on. "Action Historiography," one of the twentieth-century Cooks calls this.

The Cooks/Burlingames manage to keep their names out of the official historical record, appearing there, if at all, under the guise of various avatars or surrogates: Joseph Brant, Benedict Arnold, Major Andre, Aaron Burr. So, too, do Pynchon's conspirators (whether corporations, technologies, or angels and spirits) avoid the full light of history. But Reed's apocryphal history spills over from the "dark areas" of the historical record; his conspiracy "goes public," making an impact that *had* to have found its way into official history. It is one thing to claim that the Depression and World War II were manipulated behind the scenes by secret societies, and that these facts have been suppressed, but quite another thing to tell of the progress of an epidemic of irresistible jazz dancing, precipitating a national crisis in the early 1920s. If this crisis occurred, it should belong to our general historical knowledge; so Reed's history no longer supplements official history, filling in its blank spots, but actually *displaces* it. Comparable displacements of official history occur in *Flight to Canada*, Reed's revisionist history of the Civil War, and in *The Public Burning*, Robert Coover's alternative version of the Rosenberg execution. But the most grandiose postmodernist revision of official history is Carlos Fuentes's *Terra nostra* (1975). An alternative history of Spain and Spanish America, Fuentes's text has Felipe II of Spain marrying Elizabeth Tudor of England and bringing her to live with him at El Escorial, the New World being discovered a century later than in official history and its vast economic and political consequences unfolding in a drastically foreshortened span of time (days rather than decades), Cervantes being condemned to the galleys for heresy and writing Kafka's "Metamorphosis" centuries prematurely, and so on. Fuentes reflects on his own revisionist method through the episode of Valerio Camillo's Theater of Memory ("lifted" from Frances Yates' books on the art of memory). Camillo's theater projects images from memory, not memory of the past, however, but "the most absolute of memories: the memory of what could have been but was not."[8] In the theater of memory, Calpurnia dissuades Caesar from attending the Senate on the Ides of March, a baby girl is born in a stable in Palestine during the reign of Augustus, Socrates refuses the offer of suicide, Columbus travels eastward to the court of the Great Khan on camelback, and so on.[9] As for Spain, "there will never be in history, monsignore," says Camillo to his Spanish visitor, "nations more needful of a second opportunity to be what they were not than these that speak and that will speak your tongue."[10] The second opportunity is provided by Camillo's theater:

> History repeats itself only because we are unaware of the alternate possibility for each historic event: what that event could have been but was not. Knowing, we can insure that history does not repeat itself; that the alternate possibility is the one that occurs for the first time.[11]

And of course that "alternate possibility" is *Terra nostra* itself, Fuentes's apocryphal counterhistory of the Spanish.

Creative anachronism

Valerio Camillo's Theater of Memory, it gradually dawns on us, is a cinema – a glaring anachronism in Renaissance Venice. Thus, in addition to the ontological tension between the official and apocryphal versions of the world, there is here a tension between past and present, the material culture of the twentieth century having been superimposed on the sixteenth to produce an impossible hybrid. Anachronism in material culture is rare even among the postmodernists, however. Exceptions occur, as we have already seen, in Reed's *Flight to Canada*, where twentieth-century technology (telephone, television, automobile, aircraft) is superimposed on nineteenth-century history; and also in *Mumbo Jumbo*, where the secret Wallflower Order is already credited in the 1920s with possessing post-World War II technology, including television, synthetic materials ("polyurethane, Polystyrene, Lucite, Plexiglas, acrylate, Mylar, Teflon, phenolic, polycarbonate")[12] and the potential for space-flight. More typical is creative anachronism in world-view and ideology. "Classic" historical fiction, itself often guilty of this form of anachronism, always strives to disguise this fact. Postmodernist historical fiction, by contrast, flaunts it, for example in *The French Lieutenant's Woman*, where Fowles's narrator attributes to Sarah, the novel's heroine, the attitudes and psychology of a modern, that is, late-twentieth-century, woman. Here, however, the projection of a 1960s mentality back into the 1860s is realistically motivated: Sarah, we are told, represents the first glimmerings of modern sensibility in Victorian culture, the historical opening wedge of modernity; she is not anachronistic but, so to speak, progressive. No such motivation is available in the case of Elkin's *George Mills*, however, where a modern blue-collar mentality has been projected anachronistically into eleventh- and early-nineteenth-century characters. The result is a kind of double vision or split-screen effect, the present and past simultaneously in focus. This effect is if anything more pronounced in *Gravity's Rainbow*, even though the gap of time here is much shorter, decades rather than centuries. The mentality of Pynchon's characters, notably Slothrop but also lesser figures such as Roger Mexico, Seaman Bodine, or Säure Bummer, seems to flicker back and forth between the 1940s and the 1960s.

In addition to the anachronism of its heroine's sensibility, *The French Lieutenant's Woman* practices another form of self-flaunting creative anachronism in its allusions to various twentieth-century referents in a nineteenth-century context. Thus, the Cobb at Lyme is compared to a Henry Moore sculpture, a servant's dandyish taste to that of a 1960s mod; the landscape near nineteenth-century Lyme is described anachronistically as viewed from the air; a Victorian evening at home is characterized in terms of the absence of cinema and television; and so on. But this is, so to speak, innocent anachronism: it does not penetrate the fictional world, but remains at the level of the narrator's discourse, and the narrator, being our contemporary, is perfectly justified in making such allusions. Fowles, in other words, is here fore-grounding the temporal distance between the act of narration and the objects narrated, a foregrounding which is even more prominent in Barth's *LETTERS*. Addressing his Reader in letters at the beginning and end of his text, the Author juxtaposes various present times ("nows"): the present time in which, according to the fiction, the letters are being written (March 2, 1969 and September 14, 1969, respectively), the real dates of the first draft (October 30, 1973 and July 4, 1978) and final typescript (January, 1974 and October 5, 1978), and the real point in time when they are being read (about which, of course, the Author can only speculate). But Barth goes further than Fowles, not limiting himself to foregrounding the temporal distance within the authorial discourse but allowing his *characters* to share some of the benefits of their author's hindsight. Thus, for example, Lady Amherst is permitted, on August 9, 1969, to "predict" the ultimate American withdrawal from South Vietnam, still several years in the future, while A. B. Cook VI on September 10, 1969, anticipates the Arab oil boycott and "energy crisis," consequences of the 1973 Yom Kippur war. In other words, Barth, unlike Fowles, allows his own temporal perspective to penetrate his fictional world, making his charac-ters into pseudo-prophets, investing them with anachronistic knowledge of their future, which is Barth's past. Fuentes' Valerio Camillo is a pseudo-prophet in the same way, predicting what is for him the future of Spain but for us its past.[13] Similarly, Reed endows a number of his Prohibition-era charac-ters in *Mumbo Jumbo* with anachronistic foresight. One predicts the rise of a future Black leader who will "even have the red hair of a conjure man"[14] – that is, Malcolm X; another foresees the travestying of elitist white culture by "the son of a Polish immigrant . . . from some steel town in Pennsylvania"[15] – Andy Warhol. And a third predicts that Black American art of "the 50s and 60s and 70s" will surpass the Black achievements of the 1920s[16] – a prophecy which by implication includes the Black American artist Ishmael Reed him-self. In effect, Reed has enabled one of his characters to prophesy his own coming!

Historical fantasy

Prophecy, even if only anachronistic pseudo-prophecy with the benefit of authorial hindsight, brings us to the verge of historical fantasy, the post-modernist historical novelist's third strategy for foregrounding ontology in historical fiction. The strategy of integrating history and the fantastic, a flagrant violation of the realistic norms of historical fiction, was actually imposed upon John Barth from the moment when he decided to make *LETTERS* the collective sequel to *all* his previous novels. This meant that it must somehow accommodate both historical fiction, since it would be the sequel to *The Sot-Weed Factor*, and quasi-fantastic fiction, since it would also be the sequel to *Giles Goat-Boy* (1966). Thus, A. B. Cook IV, descendant of a long line of conspirators surreptitiously involved in American history, must somehow coexist in the same world with Jerome Bray, descendant of the demonic Harold Bray, self-proclaimed Grand Tutor of the University *in another world*. In a similar vein, both Grass in *The Flounder* and Coover in *The Public Burning* place historical figures in positions where they must interact with characters from another world, characters whose mode of existence is essentially fantastic – the supernatural Flounder, the quasi-mythological super-hero Uncle Sam. In both cases, such interaction is actually consummated in sexual intercourse, a kind of miscegenation between the historical and the fantastic: in *The Flounder*, between the historical Dorothea of Montau and the fantastic Flounder, in *The Public Burning* between the historical Richard Nixon and the fantastic Uncle Sam. Coover goes even further, integrating history and the fantastic within a single character, making the historical President Eisenhower the *incarnation* of Uncle Sam, and having him reveal his supernatural identity to Vice-President Nixon on the tee at Burning Tree Golf Club. Integration of the historical and the fantastic, especially integration within a single character, exacerbates the ontological hesitation which is the principle of all fantastic fiction, for here the hesitation is not between the supernatural and the *realistic* but between the supernatural and the historically *real*.

Postmodernist apocryphal history is often fantastic history at the same time. Thus, for example, one of the versions of Pynchon's secret history in *Gravity's Rainbow* involves angelic and other-worldly conspirators. Similarly, Fuentes's apocryphal history of Spain is also a fantastic history: Felipe II regresses from a human being to a wolf; Elizabeth of England uses black magic to vitalize a golem; and it is the golem who actually rules Spain from the Renaissance to our time, changing his appearance with the passage of the centuries, from Hapsburg to Bourbon to his final incarnation as Generalissimo Franco. Salman Rushdie also combines historical fantasy with secret history in *Midnight's Children*. Indian history since independence, according to this text, is supernaturally linked to the fates of the children born at the same time as the state itself, midnight on August 15, 1947. Supernatural beings, each possessing some miraculous power or talent – the power to read minds, to change shape, to pass through looking-glasses, to inspire instant infatuation in others, to perform magic, and so on – their existence is a secret; only through the telepathy of one of their number, Saleem, the novel's narrator, do the midnight children become aware of one another. As supernatural figures, they are symptomatic of the intrinsically fantastic nature of Indian reality; but more than that, they, and especially their spokesman Saleem, are microcosms of the Indian macrocosm, paralleling or mirroring public history in their private histories. "We shall be watching over your life with the closest attention," writes Jawaharlal Nehru to the infant Saleem; "it will be, in a sense, the mirror of our own."[17] This is true not "in a sense," but literally. Thus, for example, according to Rushdie's secret history of supernatural India, the true motive behind Indira Gandhi's declaration of the State of Emergency in 1976 was to flush out the midnight children and expunge their powers. This is Rushdie's version of the world: Indian history as "a struggle of secret societies" – secret and supernatural at the same time.

Here we might be moved to protest against Rushdie's falsification of history. The Emergency was not a vendetta against fantastic beings, but a real threat to Indian democracy and a source of suffering for many individual

Indians. To pretend otherwise is to lie, just as it is lying to blame technologies or angels for the Second World War, or to present the Rosenberg executions as a grotesque carnival. So moralizing critics such as John Gardner or Gerald Graff might argue, and their objections would seem to carry a good deal of weight. From this point of view, history is the record of real human action and suffering, and is not to be tampered with lightly; inventing apocryphal or fantastic or deliberately anachronistic versions of history is a betrayal of that record. This would be unassailably true, if only we could be sure that the historical record reliably captured the experience of the human beings who really suffered and enacted history. But that is the last thing we can be sure of, and one of the thrusts of postmodernist revisionist history is to call into question the reliability of official history. The postmodernists fictionalize history, but by doing so they imply that history itself may be a form of fiction.

Official history is presented as a form of fiction, for instance, in *The Public Burning*, where Coover draws our attention to the essential fictionality of public history as recorded in *Time* magazine and the *New York Times*; or in Barth's *LETTERS*, where the re-enactment of American history by a film crew seems strangely to absorb or displace the original events – a familiar experience for television-viewers. Conversely, fiction, even fantastic or apocryphal or anachronistic fiction, can compete with the official record as a vehicle of historical truth. Especially striking in this regard are the attitudes of paranoiac conspiracy-theorists like Pynchon and Reed, historians of the world's secret history, who seem intent on persuading us that their apparently crackpot accounts are closer to historical truth than those of supposedly responsible professional historians. Throughout *Mumbo Jumbo*, for example, Reed conducts a sly polemic against professional historians who will be inclined to reject his version of events as "paranoid fantasy" or "mystification." His own version, he implies, is not only serious but superior to their own rational, properly documented, orthodox versions. "Why isn't Edgar Allan Poe recognized as the principal biographer of that strange war?" he asks in *Flight to Canada*, apropos of the American Civil War:

> Fiction, you say? Where does fact begin and fiction leave off? Why does the perfectly rational, in its own time, often sound like mumbo-jumbo?[18]

Or, presumably, like *Mumbo Jumbo*.

This is "history as the novel, the novel as history," but in a considerably more radical way than what Norman Mailer intended when he made this phrase the subtitle of his subjectivized, new-journalistic account of Vietnam War protest, *The Armies of the Night* (1968). In postmodernist revisionist historical fiction, history and fiction exchange places, history becoming fictional and fiction becoming "true" history – and the real world seems to get lost in the shuffle. But of course this is precisely the question postmodernist fiction is designed to raise: real, compared to what?

PART THREE: CONSTRUCTION

In the literature of this hemisphere . . . ideal objects abound, invoked and dissolved momentarily, according to poetic necessity.

(Jorge Luis Borges, "Tlön, Uqbar, Orbis Tertius," from *The Garden of Forking Paths*, 1941)

7: WORLDS UNDER ERASURE

Here in Israel the extraordinary is run-of-the-mill. We are capable of living in a state in which certain things that have happened have not. At the same time that they have. This is The State of Israel.
    (Ronald Sukenick, *98.6*, 1975)

Of course it happened. Of course it didn't happen.
    (Thomas Pynchon, *Gravity's Rainbow*, 1973)

Everything in the stratum of presented objects is indeterminate, Roman Ingarden tells us, but some presented objects are more indeterminate than others. Some are permanently and radically indeterminate between two or more states of affairs: they "iridesce" or "opalesce." What Ingarden evidently had in mind was sentences projecting states of affairs which could be reconstructed in more than one way, the sorts of sentences handled by conventional literary criticism under the rubric of ambiguity. He almost certainly did *not* have in mind the kind of ambiguities one finds in postmodernist novels such as Clarence Major's *Reflex and Bone Structure* (1975):

> My elbows on the dressing table begin to ache.
> And someone opens the door. It's Dale who stands there, mouth open, watching us. I erase him. He's still on stage. In his glory. Cutting another notch into the totem pole of his career.
> Dale opens the door again and this time he enters.[1]

First one state of affairs is projected: "someone opens the door. It's Dale who stands there." Then that state of affairs is recalled or rescinded, "unprojected": "I erase him." Yet the "erased" state of affairs still persists, if only as a kind of optical afterimage: Dale, for the reader, was somehow *both* standing there at the door *and* still on stage at the same time. Finally the erased state of affairs is replayed: "Dale opens the door again and this time he enters." Here the "iridescence" or "opalescence" of ambiguity, the oscillation between two states of affairs, has been *slowed down* and *spread out*, distributed over several sentences and in effect analyzed into its component states, like Eadweard Muybridge's photographic analyses of continuous motion into a sequence of "stills." This allows us to examine each of these stills separately, frame by frame – Dale at the door, Dale still on stage, Dale at the door again – in the process coming to see exactly how fictional objects and events are constructed – and deconstructed – by the literary text. This process of construction, Ingarden believed, belonged permanently to the background of the literary work of art, but in the case of Major's *Reflex and Bone Structure* it has been thrust unavoidably into the foreground.

Of course, we could imagine a more conventionally ambiguous situation, something like Kurosawa's classic perspectivist film *Rashomon* (1950), in which it would be impossible to determine whether Dale had really been standing at that door at that moment or not. But this is not the kind of ambiguity we find in Major's text: here Dale both was and was not standing at that door at that moment, both stood there at that moment for the first time and stood there at a later moment *also* for the first time. In other words, the indeterminacy, the "flickering" effect, is not epistemological here, as it is in *Rashomon* and other perspectivist fictions, but ontological.

"I erase him": Major's "un-projection" of Dale recalls Jacques Derrida's practice of placing certain verbal signs *sous rature*, under erasure:

le signe ~~est~~ cette ~~chose~~ mal nommée . . . .[2]

Physically canceled, yet still legible beneath the cancelation, these signs *sous rature* continue to function in the discourse even while they are excluded from it. Derrida's purpose in using this typographical sleight-of-hand is, of course, to remind us that certain key concepts in western metaphysics – such as, in this case, *existence* and *objecthood* – continue to be indispensable to philosophical discourse even though that same discourse demonstrates their illegitimacy. They both cannot be admitted, yet cannot be excluded; so he places them *sous rature*. Of course, postmodernist fictions such as *Reflex and Bone Structure* place under erasure not signifiers of concepts in a philosophical discourse, but presented objects in a projected world; and their purpose is not, as with Derrida, that of laying bare the *aporias* of western metaphysics, but rather that of laying bare the processes by which readers, in collaboration with texts, construct fictional objects and worlds. The world of *Reflex and Bone Structure* is a world partly *sous rature*.

Or we might equally pertinently say that Major's text is a self-consuming artifact, like the seventeenth-century self-consuming artifacts that Stanley Fish has described. Here, for example, is one of Fish's paradigmatic self-consuming texts, a sentence from St Augustine which enacts on a miniature scale the typical movement of all such texts:

Illuc ergo venit ubi erat.
He came to a place where he was already.

"The first part of the sentence," Fish comments, "establishes a world of fixed and discrete objects, and then the second half . . . takes it away"[3] – takes it away with a brisk, almost audible snap which is even brisker (as Fish remarks) in the original Latin than in the English translation. Much the same snap of a world being taken away is audible in many postmodernist sentences, for instance this one from Beckett's *The Unnamable* (1952/9):

> The slopes are gentle that meet where he lies, they flatten out under him, it is not a meeting, it is not a pit, that didn't take long, soon we'll have him perched on an eminence.[4]

Here the voice of Beckett's Unnamable projects a "sliding" state of affairs, one that revises itself before our eyes from a pit to a level enclosure, and which, as the voice ironically observes, might just as easily continue sliding until the pit had been revised into an *ad hoc* hill! As in Augustine, a "world of fixed and discrete objects" is given and then taken away, with the dual effect of destabilizing the ontology of this projected world and simultaneously laying bare the process of world-construction.

There are a number of strategies through which this dual effect may be achieved. Events may be narrated and then explicitly recalled or rescinded, as in the example from *Reflex and Bone Structure*; and the same strategy of explicit "un-projection" may be applied to objects and locales, as in the example from *The Unnamable*, and even more crucially to characters. Or self-erasure may remain implicit, as when two or more – often many more – mutually-exclusive states of affairs are projected by the same text, without any of these competing states of affairs being explicitly placed *sous rature*. This violation of the law of the excluded middle becomes especially crucial when it occurs at one particularly sensitive point in the text, namely its *ending*.

Not only presented objects but, says Ingarden, entire "ontic spheres," worlds, may flicker. The worlds projected by means of these strategies of self-erasure are precisely such flickering worlds.

Something happened

Narrative self-erasure is not the monopoly of postmodernist fiction, of course. It also occurs in modernist narratives, but here it is typically framed as mental anticipations, wishes, or recollections of the characters, rather than left as an irresolvable paradox of the world *outside* the characters' minds. In other words, the canceled events of modernist fiction occur in one or other character's subjective domain or subworld, not in the projected world of the text as such. This is arguably the case, for example, in Robbe-Grillet's *Dans le labyrinthe* (1959), in which various scenarios are projected only to be canceled and replaced by other scenarios. The wandering soldier finds the door to an apartment-house ajar, enters, ends up in the apartment of a lame man; he finds the door ajar, enters, ends up in the dusty room from which this narrative initially set out and to which it regularly returns; he finds the door not ajar, is surprised when it is opened by a man half in military uniform, half in mufti, who flees from him; he finds the door not ajar, is surprised when it is opened by this same "half a soldier," who welcomes him. Each scenario except the last is abruptly negated – "No" – and replaced by the next. But the effect is ontologically less unstable than it might appear, for there is a stabilizing frame available: the mind of the wandering soldier, whose slippages among memories and anticipations explain and motivate the slow-motion "flicker" of this passage.

But no such explanatory, motivating framework is available in the case of postmodernist narratives such as Robbe-Grillet's own later text, *Projet pour une révolution à New York* (1970). As in *Dans le labyrinthe*, sequences are projected only to be abruptly negated. Laura, fleeing through the subway tunnels, discovers a room where the corpse of a murdered girl is about to be eaten by a rat, and recoils in horror: "No!" Unlike in *Dans le labyrinthe*, however, the world of the text in effect recoils with her: "Retake." This cinematic term signals the text's return to the moment before Laura escapes from the immobilized subway car, the horrific tableau of corpse and rat being placed *sous rature*. But who is responsible for this erasure? Not Laura herself, evidently: "No!" belongs to her discourse, but "Retake" almost certainly does not.

Later in the text, an indeterminate voice, pretending to some kind of authority, undertakes to explain the use of "retake" to an equally indeterminate interlocutor:

"You have used the word 'retake' two or three times in your narrative. What is its precise role?". . . .
"It seems quite clear to me. It means continue something that had been interrupted for some reason. . . ."
"What kind of reason?"
"The reason, you old phony, that you can't tell everything at the same time, so that there always comes a moment when a story breaks in half, turns back or jumps ahead, or begins splitting up; then you say 'retake' so that people can tell where they are."[5]

Obviously, this explanation explains nothing. "Retake," far from telling us where we are, leaves us hesitating between alternative, competing sequences. And the intrusion of this sourceless, mock-authoritative voice, instead of stabilizing the flickering world of this text, only further aggravates its ontological instability.

What is especially striking about the narrative sequences placed under erasure in *Projet pour une révolution* is their highly-charged, sensationalistic content: Laura face-to-face with a corpse-eating rat. And this proves to be true of many other postmodernist self-consuming artifacts, which often appeal to their readers' "lowest" instincts. Or, to put it another way, they often draw on the repertoires of peripheral or sub-literary genres – thrillers, gothic horror, pornography, cinematic or televised melodrama and farce, and so on. The aim of such sensationalism is to lure the reader into making an emotional investment in the sequence under erasure, typically by arousing his or her anxieties, fascination with the taboo, or prurient interests. Having become "involved" in the representation, the reader thus resents it when the representation is *de*-represented, erased. The reader's impulse to cling to the erased sequence heightens the tension between (desired) presence and (resented) absence, thus slowing the slow-motion flicker even further.

The use of pornographic or quasi-pornographic materials for this purpose is the clearest example. For instance, the narrator in Ronald Sukenick's novella "The Death of the Novel" (1969) narrates a sexual encounter between himself and his underage girlfriend with a view, so he claims, to increasing his story's marketability. But then, perversely, he reneges, canceling the sex-scene: "How's that? Not bad? A little sex? Okay. Now let's do a retake of that, with a little more accuracy this time."[6] Reverting to the same cinematic register to which Robbe-Grillet had had recourse, Sukenick places his sex-scene *sous rature* and substitutes a "more accurate" – that is, innocent – encounter, thus frustrating his reader in a particularly literal (perhaps even physiological) way.[7]

Steve Katz, in *The Exagggerations of Peter Prince* (1968), invites a different, although equally effective, mode of reader-engagement, not through porno-graphic titillation, but instead through pathos. His almost unbearably painful account of the accidental asphyxiation of Thwang-Nuc, Peter Prince's adopted daughter, seems certain to engage the reader emotionally. Far from identifying his or her own desires with these events, of course, the reader may very well prefer to evade or suppress them, as too painful to face directly. But it is only an apparent paradox that she or he will, nevertheless, feel a certain resentment when Katz makes one of his characters, ostensibly by way of comforting another character who is painfully moved by Thwang-Nuc's pathetic death, emphasize the unreality, the merely verbal or textual existence, of this event:

> "If you look at things long enough and hard enough they're O.K. Just go back and read that section over, sentence by sentence. There are some nice sentences in it. What more do you want? Some nice style. Some neat scenes. It's emotionally packed, but it's well written just the same. Read it some more."[8]

It does not matter that in this case, by contrast with the sex-scene from "The Death of the Novel," the reader has recoiled from the erased sequence. What matters is that she or he has been duped into a degree of emotional engage-ment, and then deprived of the event that has provoked that engagement; accordingly, the reader clings to the "lost," erased sequence as he or she might not to one less highly charged.

Something exists

Narrated events, then, can be un-narrated, placed *sous rature*; and, in much the same way, projected *existents* – locales, objects, characters, and so on – can have their existence revoked. The effect is most acute, of course, in the case of characters, since it is especially through projected people that the reader becomes involved in the fictional world. Borges, as usual, can be relied upon for a paradigmatic example. In his text "Averroës' Search" (from *A Personal Anthology*, 1968), having built up an elaborately plausible simulacrum of Moorish Spain as reflected in the consciousness of the philosopher Averroës, Borges abruptly and spectacularly withdraws its – and therefore Averroës's – reality:

He felt sleepy, he felt a bit cold. He unwound his turban and looked at himself in a metal mirror. I do not know what his eyes saw, for no historian has ever described the forms of his face. I do know that he suddenly disappeared, as if fulminated by a bolt of flameless fire, and that with him disappeared the house and the invisible fountain and the books and the manuscripts and the doves and the many raven-haired slave girls and the quivering red-haired slave girl and Farach and Abulcasim and the rose trees and perhaps even the Guadalquivir.[9]

What has happened? The author, we are told, has ceased to believe in the reality of his own character, and this sustaining belief having broken down, the character and his world flicker – "as if fulminated by a bolt of flameless fire" – out of existence.

Similarly, Beckett, in one of his short, experimental *Texts for Nothing* (#3) composed in the early 1950s, has his text's narrator invent a character for himself to play, together with a cast of supporting characters (Bibby his nanny, Vincent his crony), only to cancel them all out at the end, "de-creating" them. What occurs here in miniature is repeated on a vast scale in the trilogy of the same years. The "Unnamable" of the third volume creates and decreates *personae* for himself, called Mahood (or Basil) and Worm, and even claims to have been similarly responsible for the existence of the entire string of Beckett *personae* beginning with Murphy, and including Watt, Mercier and Camier, Molloy, Moran, and Malone.

Muriel Spark's variant on the canceled-character strategy involves a certain Mrs Hogg (in *The Comforters*, 1957) who flickers out of existence and then, unlike Borges' or Beckett's characters, flickers *back into* existence again. She vanishes whenever she is left alone or falls asleep, and rematerializes as soon as she enters the company of other people. In other words, Mrs Hogg is the witty literalization of a cliché:

She had no private life whatsoever. God knows where she went in her privacy.[10]

Steve Katz, in *The Exagggerations of Peter Prince*, has the authorial spokesman in the text complain about the ontological insubstantiality of its hero, and makes him resolve on a radical course of action:

Peter Prince, he's got no history. He's pieced apart. . . . His past erases itself like a disappearing wake. . . . I ought to grab hold of myself and finish this novel without characters: just vacancies in the environment, that's good enough.[11]

But Katz's author-surrogate has no opportunity to attempt this experiment in characterless narration, for, in a final twist of romantic irony, he is confronted by Peter Prince himself, who shifts the blame for his insubstantiality onto the author and demands to be fleshed-out more fully. If his demands are not met, he threatens to dematerialize himself, and his world with him:

The empty dishes fade away, and so does the tablecloth: the chair I am sitting on softens and slowly disappears. I have to stand up in a dark space. Peter Prince is permeated by the deep, flowing atmospheres and is tugged away in gauzy sections. "WAIT," I shout (too late, he's disappearing) and I hastily, though reluctantly, begin the description he demanded.[12]

Finally, the most spectacular instance of a "pieced apart" character in postmodernist writing must surely be Pynchon's Tyrone Slothrop. Slothrop, his self-identity monstrously compromised from the outset by behavioral conditioning in his infancy, and further eroded by his addiction to "mindless pleasures," has been sent into the occupied zone on a mission whose true purpose he will never learn, and there loses whatever scraps of identity he still possesses:

> There is . . . the story about Tyrone Slothrop, who was sent into the Zone to be present at his assembly – perhaps, heavily paranoid voices have whispered, *his time's assembly* – and there ought to be a punch line to it, but there isn't. The plan went wrong. He is being broken down instead, and scattered.[13]

By the novel's end, we are told, Slothrop has become:

> one plucked albatross. Plucked, hell – *stripped*. Scattered all over the Zone. It's doubtful if he can ever be "found" again, in the conventional sense of "positively identified and detained."[14]

At this late stage in his dissolution, his friend and fellow paranoid Seaman Bodine is:

> one of the few who can still see Slothrop as any sort of integral creature any more. Most of the others gave up long ago trying to hold him together even as a concept – "It's just got too remote" 's what they usually say. . . . Some believe that fragments of Slothrop have grown into consistent personae of their own. If so, there's no telling which of the Zone's present-day population are off-shoots of his original scattering.[15]

Like Spark's Mrs Hogg, Slothrop literalizes a cliché: just as she "has no private life," he "suffers a breakdown" or "goes to pieces" or "comes apart at the seams." But he is also a literalization in, we might say, the literal sense of the term. Structuralist poetics, in its more radical avatars, has taught us to abandon the concept of character as self-identity, as some sort of "integral creature," to regard it instead as a textual function.[16] Slothrop demonstrates this textualized concept of character: beginning as at best a marginal self, he literally becomes *literal* – a congeries of *letters*, mere words. The zone in which he is lost and scattered is not only a heterotopian projected space but, literally, a space of writing, and his disassembly "lays bare" the absorption of character by text. This is why I have called Slothrop the most spectacular postmodernist canceled character, for his example makes plainly visible what is more or less implicit in Borges' Averroës, Beckett's Unnamable, Katz's Peter Prince, and the rest: the ineluctable writtenness of character.

But characters, of course, are not the only elusive existents in the worlds projected by narrative texts. Such worlds are also "peopled" by non-human organisms, man-made artifacts, landscapes, interiors, and so on; by, in other words, objects of *description*. And all these existents, too, are like character susceptible of erasure. Here, for instance, is a self-consuming description from Christine Brooke-Rose's novel *Thru* (1975):

> She is pale and sits
> Where?
> On the campus
> Can one sit on a campus?
> She sits on a castle terrace in Spain.
> Caramba not picaresque that's as dead as the dread-letter novel.
> In Slovenia, talking to the Count
> Titles have been abolished in Slovenia
> turning her back to you. It is a warm summer evening. The benches and tables are of wood, under a trellis of vine, facing the crenellated walls that hide the view of the valley. Scrub that. The bench and tables are of wrought iron, under the palladian colonnade, facing the flight of white stone steps that lead to the wide gardens wrought-ironed beneath the moon in patterns of clipped privet.[17]

"Something," we are told, "has gone wrong with the narration owing to textual disturbances".[18] Indeed it has. Evidently, if a character like Mrs Hogg can flicker in and out of existence, so too can a setting like Brooke-Rose's campus/castle with its wooden/wrought-iron bench and tables. If sequences can be "retaken," descriptions can be "scrubbed" and projected anew.[19]

Excluded middles, forking paths

"Excluded middles," muses Pynchon's heroine Oedipa Maas, are "bad shit, to be avoided."[20] She is lamenting the absence, in her world – as indeed in our world, according to conventional logics – of any third alternative to the polarity of true and false, any mode of being between existence and nonexistence. Pynchon would go on, in *Gravity's Rainbow*, to produce a fictional world in which there *is* such a third alternative: "Of course it happened. Of course it didn't happen." But he would do so in defiance of an orthodoxy in poetics that outlaws such "in-between" modes of being in principle. The most that Umberto Eco, for example, can say for worlds in which the law of the excluded middle seems to have been abrogated is that they mount a subversive critique of world-building, although they do not constitute worlds themselves. But this description fails to capture the full ontological peculiarity of a world in which events apparently both do and do not happen, or in which the same event happens in two irreconcilably different ways.

The paradigm, once again, is the fiction of Borges, this time his well-known text, "The Garden of Forking Paths" (1941). Anticipating by some thirty years developments in structuralist narratology,[21] Borges analyzes narrative into a system of branchings. At each point in a story, the narrative agent is faced with a bifurcation, two possibilities, only one of which can be realized at a time; choosing one, he is faced with another branching; choosing again, he is faced with yet another, and so on, tracing his way through the tree-like proliferation – or, to use Borges' preferred image, the labyrinth – of the story's potential and actualized happenings. Borges in "The Garden of Forking Paths" describes a classical Chinese novel in which *all* the possible bifurcations of such a system are actualized:

> In all fiction, when a man is faced with alternatives he chooses one at the expense of the others. In the almost unfathomable Ts'ui Pen, he chooses – simultaneously – all of them. He thus creates various futures, various times which start others that will in their turn branch out and bifurcate in other times. This is the cause of the contradictions in the novel.[22]

Italo Calvino takes up Borges' notion of the labyrinth-novel in his rewriting of "The Count of Monte Cristo" (from *t zero*, 1967), where the Abbé Faria's tunnelings through the walls and floors of the Chateau d'If literalize Borges' metaphor. These tangled itineraries, in turn, are shown to be a model of the system of "forking paths" which Alexandre Dumas, with the aid of two assistants, generates as he plots his way through the original *Count of Monte Cristo*.

Borges and Calvino offer blueprints for the construction of the ideal novel of forking paths and excluded middles; they have not, of course, written any such novel themselves. For a partial approximation of such a text, we must turn to John Barth, for instance, who in "Lost in the Funhouse" (from the volume by the same name, 1969) has written a labyrinth-story or, in the terms of Barth's ironically deflated world, a funhouse-story. In this text, bifurcating, mutually-exclusive possibilities are jointly realized, juxtaposed:

> Naturally he didn't have nerve enough to ask Magda to go through the funhouse with him. With incredible nerve and to everyone's surprise he invited Magda, quietly and politely, to go through the funhouse with him.

> One possible ending would be to have Ambrose come across another lost person in the dark. They'd match their wits together against the funhouse, struggle like Ulysses past obstacle after obstacle, help and encourage each other. Or a girl. By the time they found the exit they'd be closest friends, sweethearts if it were a girl; they'd know each other's inmost souls, be bound together *by the cement of shared adventure*; then they'd emerge into the light and it would turn out that his friend was a Negro. A blind girl. President Roosevelt's son. Ambrose's former archenemy.[23]

But Barth's is an "impure" garden of forking paths – deliberately impure, no doubt. A number of the alternative "routes," as the passages quoted above suggest, are realized only in the protagonist's fantasies, in his subworld; other points of bifurcation are overlooked, the choices at these junctures having been made "silently," in the conventional way. Much more limited in its field of possibilities but, for that reason, a more perfect approximation of Borges' paradigm, is Robert Coover's story "Quenby and Ola, Swede and Carl" (from *Pricksongs and Descants*, 1969). A story of illicit sex and murderous revenge – or not, as the case may be – "Quenby and Ola" involves exactly four characters in an isolated locale, an island in a wilderness lake. Carl, a businessman on a fishing holiday, either sleeps with one of his fishing guide's women or he does not; if he sleeps with one of them, it is either Swede's wife Quenby or his daughter Ola; whichever one he sleeps with (if he actually does sleep with one of them), Swede either finds out about it or he does not; if he does find out, he either plans to kill Carl in revenge or he does not. *All* of these possibilities are realized in Coover's text. "Sometimes the pathways of this labyrinth converge," says Borges of Ts'ui Pen's novel, and in "Quenby and Ola" all the forking paths converge on the scene of Carl and Swede alone at night in a stalled motor boat, which is represented several times. This moment stands at the end of every route: either nothing has transpired between Carl and Swede's women, or Swede has not found out about what *has* transpired, or he has found out but does not intend to do anything about it – in all these cases, there is no reason to expect some dramatic turn of events in the motor boat; but if Swede possesses the right combination of knowledge and will, we can expect a murder attempt. Does Swede kill Carl, or does he not? Neither possibility is actualized, since the story breaks off at exactly this branching.

None of Coover's other variations on the garden of forking paths in *Pricksongs and Descants* can match "Quenby and Ola" for completeness and exhaustiveness. "The Elevator," "The Magic Poker," "The Babysitter" – all these texts are more complex, less homogeneous than "Quenby and Ola," and hence less perfect realizations of the forking-paths principle. "The Babysitter" in particular achieves a dizzying complexity of branching and converging pathways. Here, as in Barth's "Funhouse," additional complications are introduced through fantasized realizations of certain possible sequences, and through interference from television narratives, fictions-within-the-fiction. The last paragraph of "The Babysitter" simultaneously realizes *all* the catastrophes that stand at the end of the story's various forking paths, even though some of these endings logically exclude others (for instance, the husband can hardly have run away with the babysitter if she has been murdered in the bathtub – or is it the baby's corpse in the tub?):

> "Your children are murdered, your husband gone, a corpse in your bathtub, and your house is wrecked. I'm sorry. But what can I say?" On the TV, the news is over, they're selling aspirin. "Hell, *I* don't know," she says. "Let's see what's on the late late movie."[24]

Self-erasing narratives of the kind I have been discussing violate linear sequentiality by realizing two mutually-exclusive lines of narrative development at the same time, but this is not the only means of making linear sequences self-erasing. One can also "bend" a sequence back upon itself to form a *loop*, in which one and the same event figures as both antecedent and sequel of some other event. The presence of the same event at two different points in the sequence leaves the reader hesitating between two alternative reconstructions of the "true" sequence, in one of which event A precedes event B, while in the other event A follows event B.

A familiar example occurs in Joseph Heller's *Catch-22* (1961). Though it is hard to be certain, given this text's disturbing temporal indeterminacy, it appears that Snowden's death over Avignon, the crucial event in Yossarian's "pilgrim's progress," happens both before and after the Great Big Siege of

Bologna. In Robbe-Grillet's *La Maison de rendez-vous* (1965), the murder of Edouard Manneret functions much as Snowden's death does in *Catch-22*, floating free of any temporal moorings and introducing inconsistencies into the narrative sequence. Thus, Johnson hears of Manneret's murder from the police (and must have known about it already, since he merely "feigns astonishment" at the news), yet pays a call on him later that same night; so Manneret dies both before and after Johnson's visit. Similarly, Kim discovers Manneret's corpse, then later (having in the meantime remembered, anomalously, that she herself is the one who has killed him!) enters a room where Manneret is waiting for her. This time, however, even the elusive narrator feels compelled to acknowledge that something has gone wrong owing to textual disturbances: "If Manneret has already just been murdered, this scene takes place earlier, of course,"[25] he unhelpfully informs us. As one of Cortázar's characters says of a comparable loop structure in his *62: Modelo para armar* (1968), this constitutes "an absolute violation of time."[26]

The sense of a (non-)ending

Endings constitute a special case of self-erasing sequences, since they occupy one of the most salient positions in any text's structure. Conventionally, one distinguishes between endings that are *closed*, as in Victorian novels with their compulsory tying-up of loose ends in death and marriage, and those that are *open*, as in many modernist novels. But what are we to say about texts that seem both open and closed, somehow poised between the two, because they are either *multiple* or *circular*?

"One beginning and one ending," the narrator of Flann O'Brien's *At Swim-Two-Birds* (1939) tells us

> was a thing I did not agree with. A good book may have three openings entirely dissimilar and inter-related only in the prescience of the author, or for that matter one hundred times as many endings.[27]

As a matter of fact, this text has three endings but *four* beginnings, including the passage quoted above. It is important to note, however, that they are interrelated *not* "only in the prescience of the author," but in the mind of the character–narrator, a dilettante novelist who writes novels to illustrate his own aesthetic theories (such as the theory that a good book may have three openings). In other words, this multiplication of beginnings and endings occurs not in the "real" world of this novel, but in the subjective subworld or domain of the character–narrator.

"True" multiple-ending texts (as distinct from the subjectivized variant in *At Swim-Two-Birds*) are obviously related to the forking-path narratives in which mutually-exclusive possibilities have been jointly realized. Undoubtedly the best-known example is John Fowles's *The French Lieutenant's Woman* (1964). This novel, like the one written by Flann O'Brien's narrator, actually contains *three* alternative endings. One of these, however, comes three-quarters of the way through the book, and is framed as an imaginary subjective scenario, the tidy ending, in the style of Victorian fiction, that

Fowles' protagonist Charles wishes for; it belongs, in other words, to Charles's subworld, not to the world of the text as such. But the other two endings, coming at the true close of the text, do both belong to this novel's "real" world, and have the same ontological status. They are mutually exclusive: in one, Charles and Sarah are reconciled through their daughter; in the other, Charles loses Sarah for good. This is, almost literally, a garden of forking paths: the author intervenes at the beginning of Chapter 61, after the first ending, and returns us to the point in the sequence at which the bifurcation occurred, leading us down the alternative branching instead of the one initially chosen. And the result is that Fowles's world flickers, opalesces, at precisely the point where we conventionally expect either maximum clarity and definition (a closed ending) or total opacity (an open ending).

Fowles' double ending represents a minimal structure of non-ending, although even this minimum is quite sufficient to destabilize the ontology of the projected world. Other postmodernist writers have multiplied the alternatives without, however, improving upon Fowles' strategy in any essential way. Thus, for example, B. S. Johnson, in what he ironically calls a "magnanimous gesture," offers us "a choice of endings" to his story "Broad Thoughts from a Home" (1973):

> *Group One: The Religious.* (a) The quickest conversion since St. Paul precipitates Samuel into the joint bosoms of Miss Deane and Mother Church. (b) A more thorough conversion throws Samuel to the Jesuits. (c) A personally delivered thunderbolt reduces Samuel to a small but constituent quality of impure chemicals.
> *Group Two: The Mundane.* (a) Samuel rapes Miss Deane in a state of unwonted elation. (b) Miss Deane rapes Samuel in a state of unwonted absentmindedness. (c) Robert rapes both in a state of unwonted aplomb (whatever that may mean).
> *Group Three: The Impossible.* The next post contains an urgent recall to England for (a) Samuel (b) Robert (c) both; on account of (i) death (ii) birth (iii) love (iv) work.
> Thank you.[28]

This sudden proliferation of mutually-exclusive options – I count eighteen in all – probably approaches the limit of the number of endings that could practically be actualized in a given text. Other writers have gestured towards far higher numbers of endings, but these gestures are like those of Borges or Calvino toward the novel of forking paths. Thus, Richard Brautigan's *A Confederate General from Big Sur* (1964) has, so we are told, 186,000 endings per second, though of course Brautigan does not attempt to actualize them; while both Donald Barthelme in "Views of My Father Weeping" (1970) and Kurt Vonnegut in *Breakfast of Champions* (1973) gesture toward endlessness by closing their texts with a terse "Etc."

There is, of course, one other possible structure of textual non-ending: circularity. Borges's scholar-victim in "The Garden of Forking Paths," before he had discovered the principle of Ts'ui Pen's bifurcating novel, could only imagine one way in which a text could be infinite:

I could not imagine any other than a cyclic volume, circular. A volume whose last page would be the same as the first and so have the possibility of continuing indefinitely.[29]

Joyce's *Finnegans Wake* (1939) is just such a text with its tail in its mouth, the unfinished sentence on its last page resuming on its first page, and so "continuing indefinitely." Other variants on the ouroboros-structure include Julio Cortázar's *Hopscotch* (1963/7), Gabriel Josipovici's "Mobius the Stripper" (1974), and John Barth's minimalist Mobius-strip narrative "Frame-Tale" (from *Lost in the Funhouse*). Barth's in fact is minimal enough to be quoted in its entirety; it runs:

Once upon a time there was a story that began
once upon a time there was a story that began[30]

and so on and so on.

Finally, Barth in "Bellerophoniad" (from *Chimera*, 1972) adds a further twist of complexity to the ouroboros-structure. Here the closing sentence breaks off abruptly, lacking its final word and full stop:

It's no *Bellerophoniad*. It's a

But the completion of this fragment is not to be found in this text's opening sentence, as in the case of *Finnegans Wake*. Rather, the missing word is supplied by the book's title:

It's no *Bellerophoniad*. It's a *Chimera*.[31]

One might suppose that such a loop essentially repeated the one in *Finnegans Wake*, merely carrying us back to the title-page rather than to the opening words of the text proper. But this is not so, for, strictly speaking, the title does not belong to the text; it *names* the text, and therefore occupies the level of metalanguage relative to the object-language of the text itself. Thus the incomplete closing sentence of *Chimera* does not shape the text into a circle, but a *spiral*, returning it to its beginning while at the same time ascending to a higher level, that of metalanguage.

Etc.

8: CHINESE-BOX WORLDS

Achilles: That's quite a bit to swallow. I never imagined there could be a world above mine before – and now you're hinting that there could even be one above that. It's like walking up a familiar staircase, and just keeping on going further up after you've reached the top – or what you'd always taken to be on the top!
Crab: Or waking up from what you took to be real life, and finding out it too was just a dream. That could happen over and over again, no telling when it would stop.
(Douglas R. Hofstadter, *Gödel, Escher, Bach*, 1979)

Suppose it were decided to film a novel of forking paths – John Fowles's *The French Lieutenant's Woman* (1964), let's say. How would one go about it? One might choose to preserve the self-contradictory structure of the original, with its violation of the law of the excluded middle, producing something like Resnais's and Robbe-Grillet's *L'Année dernière à Marienbad* (1961) – a movie of forking paths. Or one might choose to do what Harold Pinter and Karel Reisz actually did when they made their film of *The French Lieutenant's Woman*, and transform one type of ontological structure into a different but related type with greater chance of being grasped by the average film-goer. Pinter and Reisz recast the double ending of Fowles's novel as a film-within-the-film, locating the unhappy ending (the hero loses the heroine for good) at the level of the film's "real world," the happy ending (hero and heroine reconciled) at the level of the film-within-the-film. This ingenious transformation suggests something like a functional equivalence between strategies of self-erasure or self-contradiction and strategies involving recursive structures – nesting or embedding, as in a set of Chinese boxes or Russian *babushka* dolls. Both types of strategy have the effect of interrupting and complicating the ontological "horizon" of the fiction, multiplying its worlds, and laying bare the process of world-construction.

A recursive structure results when you perform the same operation over and over again, each time operating on the product of the previous operation.

For example, take a film, which projects a fictional world; within that world, place actors and a film crew, who make a film which in turn projects its *own* fictional world; then within *that* world place another film crew, who make another film, and so on. This, as Douglas Hofstadter has demonstrated, is a basic structure of thought, occurring in mathematics, computer software and, of course, natural language. In Hofstadter's exemplary recursive dialogue, "Little Harmonic Labyrinth" (from *Gödel, Escher, Bach*), Achilles and the Tortoise distract themselves from a tense predicament by reading a story in which two characters called Achilles and the Tortoise enter an Escher print, in which they read a story in which two characters called Achilles and the Tortoise are lost in a labyrinth.[1] We can describe this recursive structure most easily in terms of the metalanguage of narrative levels which Gérard Genette has taught us to use.[2] Hofstadter's dialogue projects a primary world, or *diegesis*, to which Achilles and the Tortoise belong. Within that world they read a story which projects a *hypo*diegetic world, one level "down" from their own. The characters of *that* world, in turn, enter the hypo-hypodiegetic world of the Escher print; and so on, an additional "hypo" being prefixed for each level as we descend "deeper" into what Hofstadter calls the "stack" of narrative levels.

Each change of narrative level in a recursive structure also involves a change of ontological level, a change of world. These embedded or nested worlds may be more or less continuous with the world of the primary diegesis, as in such Chinese-box novels as *Wuthering Heights*, *Lord Jim*, or *Absalom, Absalom!*; or they may be subtly different, as in the play-within-the-play of *Hamlet*, or even radically different, as in Hofstadter's dialogue. In other words, although there is always an ontological discontinuity between the primary diegesis and hypodiegetic worlds, this discontinuity need not always be foregrounded. Indeed, in many realist and modernist novels, such as *Wuthering Heights* or *Lord Jim* or *Absalom, Absalom!*, it is rather the epistemological dimension of this structure which is foregrounded, each narrative level functioning as a link in a chain of narrative transmission. Here recursive structure serves as a tool for exploring issues of narrative authority, reliability and unreliability, the circulation of knowledge, and so forth.

So if recursive structure is to function in a postmodernist poetics of ontology, strategies obviously must be brought to bear on it which foreground its ontological dimension. One such strategy, the simplest of all, involves *frequency*: interrupting the primary diegesis not once or twice but *often* with secondary, hypodiegetic worlds, representations within the representation. *Hamlet*, with its single interruption by the play-within-the-play, is unproblematic in its ontological structure; the relatively frequent interruptions of the primary diegesis by the film-within-the-film in *The French Lieutenant's Woman* make it somewhat more problematic; while still more problematic are such postmodernist novels as Claude Simon's *Triptyque* (1973), Gilbert Sorrentino's *Mulligan Stew* (1979), or Italo Calvino's *If on a winter's night a traveller* (1979), where the primary diegesis is interrupted so often, by nested representations in such diverse media (novels-within-the-novel, films-within-the-novel, still-photographs-within-the-novel, and so on), that the fiction's ontological "horizon" is effectively lost.

Other such foregrounding strategies are a good deal more complex, involving logical paradoxes of various kinds. Recursive structures may raise the specter of a vertiginous infinite regress. Or they may dupe the reader into mistaking a representation at one narrative level for a representation at a lower or (more typically) higher level, producing an effect of *trompe-l'œil*. Or they may be subjected to various transgressions of the logic of narrative levels, short-circuiting the recursive structure. Or, finally, a representation may be embedded within itself, transforming a recursive structure into a structure *en abyme*. The consequence of all these disquieting puzzles and paradoxes is to foreground the ontological dimensions of the Chinese box of fiction.

Toward infinite regress

Among the forms of textual infinity proposed in "The Garden of Forking Paths" (1941), apart from infinite bifurcation and infinite circularity, Borges also mentions infinite regress, exemplified by the night of the *Arabian Nights' Entertainment* when Scheherazade begins to narrate her *own* story which, if continued, would eventually bring her to the night when she began to narrate her own story, and so on, *ad infinitum*.[3] The specter of infinite regress haunts every recursive structure in which narrative worlds have been "stacked" beyond a certain depth of embedding. Some recursive structures, such as those in modernist texts like *Lord Jim*, evade this disturbing possibility; others court it, including many postmodernist texts.

How deep does a recursive structure need to go before the tug of infinite regress begins to be felt? Certainly we feel it in John Barth's *tour-de-force* of recursively nested narrative, "Menelaiad" (from *Lost in the Funhouse*, 1968), in which Menelaus narrates how he once narrated to himself how he told Telemachus and Peisistratus how he told Helen how he told Proteus how he told Eidothea (Proteus's daughter) how he reminded Helen of what Helen herself had said to Menelaus himself on their wedding night – a Chinese-box structure totaling seven narrative levels. But do we already begin to feel the possibility of infinite regress in a recursive structure of only three levels, such as the chapter "Wind Die. You Die. We Die" from William Burroughs's *Exterminator!* (1973), where a man in a waiting-room reads a magazine story about a man reading a magazine story about a man reading a magazine story? If the specter of infinite regress does get evoked here, it is not so much by the depth of the recursive structure as by the vigor and explicitness of its foregrounding. Burroughs allows one of his magazine-readers to reflect upon the multi-leveled ontology in which he himself is sandwiched:

> Quite an idea. Story of someone reading a story of someone reading a story. I had the odd sensation that I myself would wind up in the story and that someone would read about me reading the story in a waiting room somewhere.[4]

Where a modernist text might pass over its recursive structures in silence, these postmodernist texts flaunt theirs. Our attention having thus been focused on recursiveness *for its own sake*, we begin, like Borges, to speculate: why stop the recursive operation of nesting worlds within worlds at any particular level of embedding? why stop at all, ever?

Infinity can also be approached, or at least evoked, by repeated *upward* jumps of level as well as by *downward* jumps. Thus, for example, the fictional author in Barth's "Life-Story" (also from *Lost in the Funhouse*), who is writing about an author who is writing about an author, and so on, also suspects – quite rightly – that he himself is a character in someone else's fictional text. But why stop there? If there is a *meta*-author occupying a *higher* level than his own, just as there is a hypodiegetic author occupying a level below his, then why not a meta-meta-author on a meta-meta-level, and so on, to infinity?[5] Caught between two infinities, two series of recursive nestings regressing toward two vanishing-points, Barth's fictional author breaks down, abandoning his project and beginning again with what he hopes will be a simpler structure. This, in fact, is a general pattern in postmodernist multilevel texts: complexity increasing to the point where levels collapse, as if of their own weight, into a single level of diegesis. It also happens, for instance, in Raymond Federman's *Double or Nothing* (1971). Here the "intramural setup" of the text initially involves four narrative levels – protagonist, narrator, recorder, and "fourth person" (i.e. author) – but as the text proceeds these levels begin to lose their initial clarity of definition, and the four distinct roles in the narrative structure merge into a single quasi-autobiographical figure. Setting up an elaborate hierarchy of levels, only to allow it to break down before the reader's eyes, is, of course, one means of foregrounding the ontological dimension of recursive structure. There are other variants on this strategy, to which I shall return shortly.

Trompe-l'œil

Douglas Hofstadter has shown that the human mind is capable of handling recursive structures quite readily and confidently, and that it does so all the time. "It is not too uncommon," he tells us,

> to go down three levels in real [radio] news reports, and surprisingly enough, we scarcely have any awareness of the suspension. It is all kept track of quite easily by our subconscious minds. Probably the reason it is so easy is that each level is extremely different in flavor from each other level. If they were all similar, we would get confused in no time flat.[6]

No doubt this is true, so far as everyday recursive structures and their processing are concerned. What is striking about many postmodernist texts is the way they *court* confusion of levels, going out of their way to *suppress* the "difference in flavor" that, as Hofstadter says, we depend upon for keeping levels distinct in our minds. Postmodernist texts, in other words, tend to encourage *trompe-l'œil*, deliberately misleading the reader into regarding an embedded, secondary world as the primary, diegetic world. Typically, such deliberate "mystification" is followed by "demystification," in which the true ontological status of the supposed "reality" is revealed and the entire ontological structure of the text consequently laid bare. In short, *trompe-l'œil* functions in the postmodernist context as another device for foregrounding the ontological dimension.

Jean Ricardou has called this the strategy of "variable reality," that is, the strategy whereby a supposedly "real" representation is revealed to have been merely "virtual" – an illusion or secondary representation, a representation within the representation – or vice versa, a supposedly virtual representation is shown to have been "really real" after all.[7] An example of variable reality is the *in medias res* beginning of Pynchon's *Gravity's Rainbow* (1973): a nightmarish evacuation of a big city, from the viewpoint of one of the evacuees. "Nightmarish" is the operative word here: the episode is dream-like, but not so dream-like that it couldn't pass for real; yet it proves retroactively to have been a dream of Pirate Prentice's, a nested representation, one level "down" from reality. Now, this is certainly a disorienting way to begin a novel; but even more disturbing is the way *Gravity's Rainbow* ends. For the *trompe-l'œil* strategy of variable reality, of pushing the representation back into a secondary plane, is repeated on the novel's last page, but this time on a global scale. The entire world of *Gravity's Rainbow* is retroactively revealed to have been the world of a movie-within-the-novel, hypodiegetic rather than diegetic:

> The screen is a dim page spread before us, white and silent. The film has broken, or a projector bulb has burned out. It was difficult even for us, old fans who've always been at the movies (haven't we?) to tell which before the darkness swept in.[8]

"The screen is a dim page" – or is it, the page is a dim screen? Either way, the difficulty is that the nested world of *Gravity's Rainbow* has the same "flavor" (as Hofstadter would say) as diegetic, first-order reality. Can the reader really be expected to mentally reprocess the entire fictional world, dropping it all down one level in his mind? Is it even possible for a reader to accomplish such a "re-vision," or has *trompe-l'œil* triumphed over demystification, for once?

Other examples of variable reality occur in Claude Simon's *Les Corps conducteurs* (1971) and *Tryptique*, Federman's *Double or Nothing*, John Fowles's *Mantissa* (1982), and throughout William Burroughs' fiction. Many of these examples involve erotic or luridly melodramatic or horrifically violent materials. The function of such materials in recursive structures is equivalent to their function in self-erasing structures: here, as there, they intensify ontological instability, titillating or horrifying the reader (it works equally well either way) so that she or he will resist having to "surrender" the reality of these materials when they are erased or, in the case of recursive structures, dropped down one narrative level.

A notorious example is the Orgasm Death Gimmick from Burroughs's *Naked Lunch* (1959). The Gimmick, appearing in a blue-movie-within-the-novel, involves sex-murder by hanging – one of Burroughs's nastier obsessions – followed by cannibalism. While this episode may not be pornographic, concludes David Lodge about the Orgasm Death Gimmick, neither is it what Burroughs himself claims it is, namely a satire on capital punishment. Lodge argues that the representation is simply too unstable in this text generally for the reader either to respond appropriately to pornographic solicitation, or to discover the norms necessary for satire. "It would seem to be a general rule," he writes, "that where one kind of aesthetic presentation is embedded in another, the 'reality' of the embedded form is weaker than that of the framing form,"[9] thus corroborating Hofstadter's intuition about the different "flavors" of different levels in a recursive structure. However:

> The context in which the passage under discussion is embedded (both the local context and the whole book) is no more "realistic" than the passage itself: indeed *it is in many ways less so*. That is to say, although the events reported in this passage are "impossible," the style in which they are reported is clear, lucid and for the most part of the kind appropriate to descriptions of actuality. . . . when we come to the Orgasm Death Gimmick, no norms have been established by which its nauseating grotesquerie can be measured and interpreted in the way intended by Burroughs.[10]

In other words, the realistic representation of such hair-raising material at the embedded level of a movie-within-the-novel has the effect of disorienting the reader and undermining the ontological status of the primary diegesis. Now, insofar as disorientation is undesirable both in pornography and satire, Lodge is right to consider Burroughs a poor pornographer and worse satirist; nevertheless, he is a superior postmodernist.

In addition to these strategies for soliciting the reader's involvement in "unreal," hypodiegetic worlds, there are other devices designed to encourage him or her to mistake nested representations for "realities." Among the simplest is the device of the missing end-frame: dropping down to an embedded narrative level without returning to the primary diegesis at the end. Hofstadter illustrates this in his "Little Harmonic Labyrinth": Achilles and the Torotoise go down three "stories," but only come back up two; the apparent resolution of their adventures is actually a suspension, since events on the level of the "Real" – the diegesis – remain in a kind of limbo, stranded one level *above* the level of the text's ending. It requires an attentive reader to notice this, however, for, as Hofstadter observes, "When you pop out of a movie-within-a-movie you feel for a moment as if you had reached the real world, though you are still one level from the top."[11]

Beckett, as we saw in Chapter 1 (see p. 12), does this in *Malone Dies* (1951/6), where the text actually ends one level down from the world in which Malone presumably dies. The same deception is practiced on a more local scale by Robbe-Grillet in *Projet pour une révolution à New York* (1970). His elegant sleight-of-hand involves simply omitting the end-quotes from a character's quoted discourse – *literally* a missing end-frame! Robbe-Grillet thus makes it impossible for the reader to determine where, or even *if*, a nested narrative ends. In effect, the text never rejoins the primary, diegetic level; or, to put it differently, the distinction between diegesis and hypodiegesis can no longer be safely maintained.

Another *trompe-l'œil* device violates the implicit contract with the reader even more outrageously. In this device, a nested "still" representation is transformed before our eyes into an "animated" sequence with every appearance of belonging to first-order reality. Undoubtedly the best-known example of this type of transparent deception is the etching of the "Defeat of Reichenfels" near the beginning of Robbe-Grillet's *Dans le labyrinthe* (1959). Here a still representation of a bar-room scene is described in implausibly fine and verisimilar detail, gradually acquiring movement and "liveliness" to the point that it becomes an apparently independent episode:

> The contrast between the three soldiers and the crowd is further accentu-ated by a precision of line, a clarity in rendering, much more evident in their case than in that of other individuals the same distance from the viewer. The artist has shown them with as much concern for detail and almost as much sharpness of outline as if they were sitting in the foreground. But the composition is so involved that this is not apparent at first glance. Particu-larly the soldier shown full face has been portrayed with a wealth of detail that seems quite out of proportion to the indifference it expresses. . . .
>
> He has finished his drink some time ago. He does not look as if he were thinking of leaving. Yet, around him, the cafe has emptied. The light is dim now, the bartender having turned out most of the lamps before leaving the room himself.
>
> The soldier, his eyes wide open, continues to stare into the half-darkness a few yards in front of him, where the child is standing, also motionless and stiff, his arms at his side. . . .
>
> It is the child who speaks first. He says: "Are you asleep?"[12]

At this point the text seems, impossibly, to have rejoined the diegetic level that it left when it began describing the details of the etching.

This pattern recurs in Robbe-Grillet's *La Maison de rendez-vous* (1965), where, for example, a magazine-cover illustration in the hands of a Chinese street-sweeper develops into an apparently "real" scene at Lady Ava's luxurious villa; in Burroughs' *Cities of the Red Night* (1981), where the etching "The Hanging of Captain Strobe" becomes animated and develops into an action sequence; and throughout Simon's *Les Corps conducteurs*. Even more spectacular, perhaps, are the *trompe-l'œil* effects in Robbe-Grillet's *Projet pour une révolution*. Here the girl Laura deceives a voyeur by holding a lurid book-jacket in front of the keyhole through which he is peeping – literally *trompe-l'œil*. When, much later in the text, the voyeur returns with others to break into the house, they interrupt the scene on the book-jacket, which proves not to be a nested representation but a "real" event – seen, however, not directly but reflected in a mirror, which supposedly accounts for its slight air of unreality!

As in other types of *trompe-l'œil*, here too demystification often follows deliberate mystification: dynamic episodes which have evolved illicitly from static representations often collapse back into "stills," thus abruptly reminding the reader that he or she has been at the hypodiegetic level all along. This effect parallels the "freeze-frame" or "stop-action" device of film and television. Thus, for example, the action of *Dans le labyrinthe* which has developed from "The Defeat of Reichenfels" freezes into an etching once again:

The soldier hesitates to leave the busy cafe where he has come to rest for a moment. It is the rain he is staring at through the large window with its pleated curtains and its three billiard balls on the other side of the glass. The child is also watching the rain, sitting on the floor close to the window so that he can see through the thin material. It begins to rain much harder. The umbrella in its black silk sheath is leaning on the coat rack near the furlined overcoat. But in the drawing there are so many other garments hanging on top of each other that it is difficult to make out much of anything in the jumble. Just under the picture is the chest with its three drawers.[13]

Similar stop-action or freeze-frame effects occur in *La Maison de rendez-vous*, *Projet pour une révolution*, Simon's *Corps conducteurs*, and elsewhere. The ultimate result, in every case, is to foreground the ontological dimension of the recursive structure.

Strange loops, or metalepsis

Actually, all the examples of illicit animation or its converse, freeze-frame, which I have been discussing, involve, in addition to the *trompe-l'œil* effect, a further, even stranger and more disorienting transgression of narrative logic. The nature of this transgression can best be indicated by another example from Robbe-Grillet, this time from *Topologie d'une cité fantôme* (1976). Here we encounter a description of a stage performance in which one of the actors lays down a Tarot card on which is depicted a tower. So we are already two levels down from diegetic reality when the device of illicit animation comes into play: from the top of this doubly-embedded tower a young mother with two children surveys the landscape, then, as the action scene continues to unfold, all three descend the spiral staircase within the tower until they emerge onto the very stage where the Tarot card had been dealt. Thus we are literally back where we started from, but at the wrong narrative level.[14] This is precisely the sort of violation of the hierarchy of narrative levels that occurs whenever a nested representation slips from still to animation, or vice versa. What makes this instance from *Topologie d'une cité fantôme* particularly exemplary, even emblematic, is the literally *spiral* shape of the characters' descent to their starting-place.

Douglas Hofstadter prefers to call this sort of spiral configuration a "Strange Loop." "The 'Strange Loop' phenomenon," he writes, "occurs whenever, by moving upwards (or downwards) through the levels of some hierarchical system, we unexpectedly find ourselves right back where we started."[15] A system in which a Strange Loop occurs he calls a "Tangled Hierarchy": "A Tangled Hierarchy occurs when what you presume are clean hierarchical levels take you by surprise and fold back in a hierarchy-violating way."[16] *Gödel, Escher, Bach* is full of examples of Strange Loops and Tangled Hierarchies, including, for instance, Escher's lithograph *Print Gallery* (1956), whose Strange Loop Hofstadter describes as follows:

What we see is a picture gallery where a young man is standing, looking at a picture of a ship in the harbor of a small town, perhaps a Maltese town, to guess from the architecture, with its small turrets, occasional cupolas, and flat stone roofs, upon one of which sits a boy, relaxing in the heat, while two floors below him a woman – perhaps his mother – gazes out of the window from her apartment which sits directly above a picture gallery where a young man is standing, looking at a picture of a ship in the harbor of a small town, perhaps a Maltese town – What!? We are back on the same level as we began, though all logic dictates that we cannot be.[17]

The closest verbal analogue to Escher's disturbing lithograph is a short text by Julio Cortázar called "Continuity of Parks" (from *End of the Game*, 1978): a man reads a novel in which a killer, approaching through a park, enters a house in order to murder his lover's husband – the man reading the novel! The "continuity" in this text is the paradoxical continuity between the nested narrative and the primary narrative, violating and thus foregrounding the hierarchy of ontological levels. Gérard Genette cites this text as a paradigmatic instance of what he calls *metalepsis*, the violation of narrative levels – in short, Hofstadter's Strange Loops or Tangled Hierarchies.

Postmodernist examples could be multiplied, all of them having in common the foregrounding through metalepsis of the ontological dimension of recursive embedding. They are of varying degrees of complexity. Simplest are metalepses like those in "Continuity of Parks" or Robbe-Grillet's *Maison de rendez-vous*, where for example, the fat man narrates his "classic story of white-slave traffic," which includes a party-scene at Lady Ava's, at which the fat man himself is narrating this very story. These metalepses involve only a single "jump" of level; by contrast, those in Simon's *Tryptique* tend to be more complex, involving several jumps in the same Strange Loop. For example, in the novel's closing passage, we begin with a group of boys examining individual frames of a strip of movie film; the frames they are examining develop into an animated sequence in which a fat man completes a jigsaw puzzle depicting the village in which the boys live. This already constitutes a Strange Loop; but next comes a further twist: at the moment of his completing the puzzle, the film in which the fat man appears comes to an end, and proves to be *not* still frames in the hands of a group of boys but a film being projected onto a screen. The audience exits from the theater into the street of an urban scene which (final twist) had appeared earlier in the text on movie ads posted in the boys' village!

Like M. C. Escher's famous lithograph of *Drawing Hands* (1948), in which a left hand draws a right hand while at the same time the right draws the left,[18] Christine Brooke-Rose's *Thru* (1975) exemplifies what Hofstadter (borrowing from the computer researcher Warren McCulloch) calls "heterarchy." A heterarchy is a multi-level structure in which there is no single "highest level." This means, in the case of a literary text like *Thru*, that it is impossible to determine who is the author of whom, or, to put it slightly differently, which narrative level is hierarchically superior, which subordinate. Authors and narrators abound – Armel, Larissa, their respective students, Jacques le Fataliste's Master (brazenly filched from Diderot), possibly a non-personified "third-person narrator" as well – but it proves impossible to reconstruct a stable hierarchical relationship among them all. "It is clear," we are told:

that Larissa is producing a text. But which text? It looks mightily as if she were producing this one and not, as previously appeared, Armel, or Armel disguised as narrator or the narrator I disguised as Armel. That's not very clear.[19]

No, it certainly is not very clear, and it never gets any clearer, either. The Strangeness of these Loops is irreducible. The specter of infinite regress haunts the entire enterprise: "It follows therefore that if Larissa invents Armel inventing Larissa, Armel also invents Larissa inventing Armel"[20] – and so on.

Characters in search of an author

Who will untangle these Tangled Hierarchies? A theater booking-clerk, in Robert Pinget's novel *Mahu* (1952), forces a certain Julia, wife of a policeman, to change her seat reservations. Why? Because Julia and her husband are hypodiegetic characters, invented by the story-telling character Mahu, and the original seating arrangements would have placed them beside "real" characters who "don't belong to the same spiritual zone" as the policeman and the policeman's wife.[21] Thus, thanks to the foresight of a booking-clerk, an embarrassing metaleptic paradox is narrowly avoided.

Well, of course it has not been avoided at all. What this comic parable from *Mahu* so wittily foregrounds is the function of characters in the short-circuiting of narrative levels. Characters often serve as agents or "carriers" of metalepsis, disturbers of the ontological hierarchy of levels through their awareness of the recursive structures in which they find themselves. This metaleptic function of character has especially been exploited in twentieth-century drama, paradigmatically in Pirandello's *Six Characters in Search of an Author* (1921), but also in plays by Brecht, Beckett, Jean Genet, Tom Stoppard, Peter Handke and others. Metalepsis appears so early in twentieth-century drama, and attains such precocious sophistication by comparison with prose fiction, for reasons which should be fairly obvious. The fundamental ontological boundary in theater is a literal, physical threshold, equally visible to the audience and (if they are permitted to recognize it) the characters: namely, the footlights, the edge of the stage. As theater develops self-consciousness in the modernist period, this ontological threshold becomes an obvious resource for aesthetic exploitation, much more so than the equivalent boundaries (between narrative levels, for instance) in prose texts, which must be made visible, palpable, before they can be exploited. Hence the theatrical motif of characters in search of an author.

But, of course, characters in postmodernist narrative fictions, too, can become aware of their own fictionality – characters such as Julia the police-man's wife, or the magazine-reader in Burroughs' *Exterminator!*, or the fictional author in Barth's "Life-Story." The *degree* of a character's awareness of his situation varies from case to case. Some, confronted with the evidence of their own fictionality, fail to draw the obvious conclusion; they hear their master's voice – sometimes literally – but without recognizing it. Such

characters become victims of romantic irony, the disregarded evidence functioning as a form of sly wink to the reader, and consequently as a means of
foregrounding the ontological boundary between reader and character.
Mobius in Gabriel Josipovici's story "Mobius the Stripper" (1974) hears voices
but does not realize that they belong to his author, whose own story unfolds
literally parallel to Mobius's, on the lower half of the same pages. Nabokov's
character Hugh Person, too, hears such voices. "All his life," we are told in
Transparent Things (1972), he "had experienced the curious sensation . . . of
there existing behind him – at his shoulder, as it were – a larger, incredibly
wiser, calmer and stronger stranger, morally better than he."[22] Disembodied
voices heard in the corridors of the Institute in Alasdair Gray's *Lanark* (1981)
echo fragments from the text of *Lanark* itself, although none of the characters
recognizes them. Later, however, Lanark will have an interview with someone who claims to be his author, and will be shown irrefutable proof of his
own fictionality: a manuscript page on which the very interview in progress at
that moment is inscribed. And John Barth's hero in *Giles Goat-Boy* (1966)
actually encounters a woman who is reading the novel *Giles Goat-Boy*, who is
in fact reading *this very scene* from the novel – but it fails to alert him to the
truth of his situation.

Other postmodernist characters, however, hear their master's voice and
recognize it for what it is. The classic example of such self-consciousness is
Caroline Rose, heroine of Muriel Spark's *The Comforters* (1957), who like
Josipovici's Mobius hears voices, and even a typewriter at work, but cannot
convince herself that she is merely undergoing a nervous breakdown:

> "But the typewriter and the voices – it is as if a writer on another plane of
> existence was writing a story about us." As soon as she had said these
> words, Caroline knew that she had hit on the truth.[23]

Far from filling her with fatalistic despair at her puppet-like condition,
however, this revelation only stiffens Caroline's resolve to resist, to interfere
somehow in the progress of the novel:

> I won't be involved in this fictional plot if I can help it. In fact, I'd like to spoil
> it. If I had my way I'd hold up the action of the novel. It's a duty.[24]

Ultimately she learns that the only certain way to resist being mastered by the
fiction that contains her is to master it in turn, by herself becoming the author
of the text whose composition she has overheard:

> She was aware that the book in which she was involved was still in prog-
> ress . . . . By now, she possessed a large number of notes, transcribed from
> the voices, and these she studied carefully. Her sense of being written into
> the novel was painful. Of her constant influence on its course she remained
> unaware and now she was impatient for the story to come to an end,
> knowing that the narrative could never become coherent to her until
> she was at last outside it, and at the same time consummately inside
> it.[25]

In other words, *The Comforters* amounts to a postmodernist parodic version of
Proust, tracing its heroine's apprenticeship to the point where she is literally

able to write the very text in which she figures as a character. But where Proust's *Recherche* is circular, Spark's is spiral, a meta-*Recherche*.

"Her sense of being written into the novel was painful," writes Muriel Spark of Caroline Rose, and most postmodernist characters have this painful sense without being able to resolve it as satisfactorily as Caroline Rose does. Much more typical of such characters' metaleptic awareness of their own fictionality is the humiliation and resentment felt by Steve Katz's Peter Prince. The gaze which he directs beyond the footlights toward his author is full of helpless rage: Peter Prince "knew he was going to die, no doubt about it, and he tossed my way such an immense glare of hate that if I wasn't sure of what was happening I might have turned away in shame."[26] The connection between awareness of fictionality and awareness of death in this passage is highly suggestive, for a character's knowledge of his own fictionality often functions as a kind of master-trope for determinism – cultural, historical, psychological determinism, but especially the inevitability of death. It functions this way, of course, in Beckett's *Waiting for Godot* and Stoppard's *Rosencrantz and Guildenstern Are Dead*, where being the puppet of playwright and director is a metaphor for being the puppet of fate, history, the human condition, and also in García Márquez's *One Hundred Years of Solitude* (1967). Here Aureliano, last of his line, reads the gypsy Melquíades's prophetic narrative of the destiny of the Buendías down to the very page on which the moment of his reading of this page is itself prefigured. The specter of infinite regress – Scheherezade beginning to tell her own story – is forestalled, however, by the instantaneous destruction of the manuscript and its reader, which is simultaneously the end of the book *One Hundred Years of Solitude*.

But postmodernist characters, as carriers of metalepsis and disturbers of hierarchy, do not all stop short at the footlights. Some step across to a different ontological level – not, indeed, "up" to the level of their real-world authors, a possibility closed to them, although some, such as Beckett's Unnamable, have striven to achieve this; but "down" to a hypodiegetic level, a world within their world. Thus, in a story by (of all people) Woody Allen, Kugelmass, professor of humanities at City College of New York, enlists a magician's aid to descend into the world of Flaubert's novel *Madame Bovary*, where he seduces Emma and returns with her to his own world. A parable of over-reaching desire, "The Kugelmass Episode" (1980) ends unhappily, with Kugelmass stranded at the hypodiegetic level, one "story" down from his "real" world – not, unfortunately, in *Madame Bovary*, but in the world of an old textbook, *Remedial Spanish*, where irregular verbs pursue him across a barren landscape![27] A happier ending awaits Donald Barthelme's Daumier, who, like Allen's Kugelmass, enters a hypodiegetic world – the world of his own fantasies, not of someone else's novel – and brings back the au pair girl Celeste to live with him in the "real" world (in "Daumier," from *SADNESS*, 1972). But undoubtedly the most spectacular example of a character who, as Barthelme puts it, "Motors from One Sphere to Another Sphere,"[28] occurs in Raymond Federman's *Take It or Leave It* (1976). Dissatisfied with the narrator's performance, his narratees – his audience – delegate an observer to join the protagonist at *his* narrative level, thus bypassing the hapless narrator altogether. The protagonist, naturally, is astonished:

How the hell did you manage to pass from the level of the present to the level of the past? From outside to inside this very personal recitation? Doesn't make sense! Normally such transfers are not permitted. They go against the logic of traditional narrative techniques![29]

"Don't worry about the logic," the observer counsels him. Abruptly, this "visitor from above" is withdrawn and replaced by a French-speaking delegate better qualified to interview the francophone protagonist. But this aggravated violation of narrative hierarchy begets further violations of a different kind: the new visitor from above seduces the protagonist and is sodomized by him![30] Sodomy between a fictional character and a member of his "real" audience – this must constitute the ultimate in metaleptic transgressions. The transgression is repeated later in *Take It or Leave It*, with variations, when a literary critic familiar with the works of Raymond Federman flags down the protagonist's Buick Special, reads to him from a dissertation on Federman, reviews *Double or Nothing* and *Take It or Leave It* – and picks the protagonist's pocket![31] No doubt it is precisely this sort of criminal "fraternization" between characters from different "spiritual zones" that Pinget's booking-clerk sought to forestall.

Abysmal fictions

Douglas Hofstadter, discussing the problematic notions of copying and "sameness" at different levels of a recursive structure, mentions the phenomenon of "an object's parts being copies of the object itself."[32] His example is Escher's woodcut, *Fish and Scales* (1959), in which each scale of two large fish is itself a tiny fish exactly duplicating the larger fish of which it constitutes a part. More familiar, perhaps, is the picture which used to appear on Quaker Oats packages, showing a Quaker holding a Quaker Oats package on which there is a picture of a Quaker holding a Quaker Oats package, and so on – infinite regress again. Unfortunately, there really is no term in English for Hofstadter's phenomenon, so we are left with a term from French: *mise-en-abyme*. *Mise-en-abyme* is one of the most potent devices in the postmodernist repertoire for foregrounding the ontological dimension of recursive structures.

The term itself was adapted from the language of heraldry by André Gide, who drew attention to this phenomenon in a well-known entry in his journals; since then, the concept has undergone a process of development and sophistication in French poetics.[33] A true *mise-en-abyme* is determined by three criteria: first, it is a nested or embedded representation, occupying a narrative level inferior to that of the primary, diegetic narrative world; secondly, this nested representation *resembles* (copies, says Hofstadter) something at the level of the primary, diegetic world; and thirdly, this "something" that it resembles must constitute some salient and continuous aspect of the primary world, salient and continuous enough that we are willing to say the nested representation *reproduces* or *duplicates* the primary representation as a whole. Such a salient and continuous aspect might be, for instance, the story at the primary level; or its narrative situation (narrator, narratee, act of narration, and so on); or the style or poetics of the primary narrative text.[34] By these criteria, not every part of a narrative world which resembles or copies the narrative world as a whole, not every *icon* of the primary narrative world, will qualify as a true *mise-en-abyme*. Thus, for example, the city of Rouen may be an icon of *Madame Bovary* as a whole, Dilsey may be an icon of *The Sound and the Fury* as a whole, and the weaving machine in Roussel's *Impressions d'Afrique* (1910) may be an icon of that text as a whole, but none of these meets the criteria of *mise-en-abyme* because none belongs to an inferior narrative level, a world within the world: all of them belong to the primary, diegetic narrative world.[35]

Mise-en-abyme is not, it need hardly be said, exclusive to postmodernist writing but, on the contrary, may be found in all periods, in all genres and literary modes. Nevertheless, it should be clear why postmodernist writing has exploited and developed it so extensively: *mise-en-abyme* is another form of short-circuit, another disruption of the logic of narrative hierarchy, every bit as disquieting as a character stepping across the ontological threshold to a different narrative level. The effect of *mise-en-abyme*, Gabriel Josipovici writes, "is to rob events of their solidity,"[36] and the effect of *this* is to foreground ontological structure.

So, for instance, in Donald Barthelme's *Snow White* (1967), the dwarves read a novel by a certain Dampfboot, which they describe in the following terms:

> It was hard to read, dry, breadlike pages that turned, and then fell . . . . Fragments kept flying off the screen into the audience, fragments of rain and ethics. . . . "sense" is not to be obtained by reading between the lines (for there is nothing there, in those white spaces) but by reading the lines themselves – looking at them and so arriving at a feeling not of satisfaction exactly, that is too much to expect, but of having read them, of having "completed" them.[37]

There is no difficulty in recognizing the iconic relationship here between the nested text and *Snow White* itself. Not only does Dampfboot's novel double Barthelme's – in its fragmentation, its deliberate superficiality, and so on – but this description of it in effect contains instructions to the reader for reading *Snow White*. If one multiplies the number of such iconic doublings, but without increasing the complexity of the iconic relationship in any one of them, the result will be something like Italo Calvino's *If on a winter's night a traveller*, with its ten embedded novels, all of them echoing aspects of the surrounding diegetic story. Strictly speaking, none of these ten constitutes a true novel *en abyme*, since what they double is local aspects of the story, not continuous aspects, as called for by the criteria of *mise-en-abyme*. But there are two nested texts which do meet the criteria fully, though neither is actually presented but, like Dampfboot's, merely described. First, there is Ermes Marana's novel, designed to keep a sultana permanently distracted so she will not dabble in revolution, and clearly modeled on that paradoxical night of the *Thousand and One Nights* that Borges likes to invoke:

Marana proposes to the Sultan a stratagem prompted by the literary tradition of the Orient: he will break off his translation at the moment of greatest suspense and will start translating another novel, inserting it into the first through some rudimentary expedient; for example, a character in the first novel opens a book and starts reading. The second novel will also break off to yield to a third, which will not proceed very far before opening into a fourth, and so on . . . here is a trap-novel designed by the treacherous translator with beginnings of novels that remain suspended . . . just as the revolt remains suspended.[38]

If on a winter's night is also, of course, a "trap-novel," in which novels are begun only to break off at the moment of maximum suspense; however, as we have already observed, it does not employ the device of multiply-recursive embedding that Marana plans to use, but descends no deeper at any point than the hypodiegetic level, one "story" down from the real world. So, although this nested text accurately duplicates certain pertinent aspects of the text in which it is nested, it distorts others. A more perfect duplicate is the novel which Silas Flannery plans to write:

> I have had the idea of writing a novel composed only of beginnings of novels. The protagonist could be a Reader who is continually interrupted. The Reader buys the new novel A by the author Z. But it is a defective copy, he can't go beyond the beginning. . . . He returns to the bookshop to have the volume exchanged.[39]

This novel is *If on a winter's night a traveller*, embedded *en abyme* within itself.

These are relatively unproblematical instances of postmodernist *mise-en-abyme* – if any instances of so uncanny a structure can truly be called unproblematic. Such instances are actually rather rare. It is much more typical, as Lucien Dällenbach has observed in the case of the French *nouveau nouveau roman*, to find *mise-en-abyme* in contexts so paradox-ridden that they threaten to submerge the structure *en abyme* entirely. Examples of this would include such *bricolage*-texts as Robbe-Grillet's *Project for a Revolution in New York*, Claude Simon's *Les Corps conducteurs*, or Michel Butor's *Mobile* (1962). All three of these texts are composites, scrapbooks or patchworks of "found objects" – generic clichés in Robbe-Grillet's case, actual verbal *objets trouvés* in the case of Simon and Butor.[40] While it is true, as contemporary critical theory has taught us, that *every* text is in fact an intertextual space where the materials of other texts are brought into a new relation, this intertextuality is particularly heightened and foregrounded in the *nouveau nouveau roman*. Accordingly, a *mise-en-abyme* of such texts, if it were to constitute as perfect an iconic double as, say, Dampfboot's novel does of *Snow White*, or Silas Flannery's of *If on a winter's night a traveller*, would also have to be composite, a patchwork-within-the-patchwork. But this immediately involves us in a conflict with the basic criteria of *mise-en-abyme*: for a *mise-en-abyme* must, by definition, occupy an inferior narrative level; yet a composite *mise-en-abyme*, embracing several nested representations – the individual patches in its patchwork – must occupy a level *higher* than any of its component parts, that is, it must belong to the *diegetic* level. To put it differently: if the "found objects" come from an inferior narrative level, then the intertextual space within which they are related must be located on the next highest level – the diegesis. A paradox: only an imperfect *mise-en-abyme* can constitute a perfect *mise-en-abyme* of a composite text!

Thus, what most perfectly duplicates the structure of Robbe-Grillet's *Project for a Revolution* is not any single nested representation, but rather the description of Laura's reading-habits. Laura, we are told, reads several thrillers simultaneously, ignoring the order of the chapters, skipping key episodes, even losing pages or entire signatures from the books. If one were to read as Laura does, the result would be a reading-experience rather close to the experience of reading *Project for a Revolution* straight through in the normal fashion. In other words, Laura's bizarre style of reading captures *en abyme* Robbe-Grillet's abuse of thriller conventions, his disruption of linear development and suspense, and so on. But while the thrillers that Laura reads are nested texts, texts-within-the-text, her own behavior, the means of *relating* these texts and thus of constituting the *mise-en-abyme*, of course occupies the diegetic plane. So is this or is this not a true *mise-en-abyme*? Similarly, in *Les Corps conducteurs* the closest analogue to the *bricolage*-structure of the text itself is to be found in a board fence covered with layers of tattered, superimposed political posters, a fortuitous collage of teasing verbal fragments in which no single word is completely legible. Here the idea of an intertextual space is made literal: these textual fragments only function as a *mise-en-abyme* of *Les Corps conducteurs* when they are brought together on the physical space of the board fence. But the board fence itself, of course, belongs to the diegesis – so, again, is this truly a *mise-en-abyme*, or not? The case of Butor's *Mobile* is less troublesome in this respect, although complicated enough in its own way. Among the texts juxtaposed in this *bricolage* of materials from an American tour, Butor includes passages from a brochure describing the quilts in the Shelburne Museum, Vermont. These quilts, literally patchworks, obviously duplicate the structure of *Mobile* itself – an analogy which Butor makes explicit: "This 'Mobile' is composed somewhat like a quilt."[41] But this is not the only double of *Mobile* placed *en abyme* within the text itself; another emerges in the brochure for Freedomland, a patriotic amusement-park shaped like the United States:

> Now you and your family live the fun, the adventure, the drama of America's past, present and future! Now for the first time anywhere, journey across a continent – across 200 years – to enjoy the entertainment thrill as big as America itself! . . . Many natural wonders have been transplanted to Freedomland. There are scale-size forests, a rebuilt Rocky Mountains in perspective, a miniature Great Lake, the panorama of the Great Western Plains.[42]

Now *Mobile*, too, uses its own spaces (typographical aids, the space of the page) to project a scale model, "in perspective," of the United States – a somewhat displaced model, but a model nonetheless. So Freedomland, like the Shelburne Museum quilts, functions as a *mise-en-abyme*. But as in the case of Calvino's *If on a winter's night*, one of these doubles is more accurate, less a distortion than the other, although the source of the disparity here is not

structural but ideological. The Shelburne quilts not only duplicate the structure of *Mobile*, but also represent synecdochically values that this text implicitly endorses; while Freedomland, although an equally adequate duplicate
from the structural point of view, represents values that the text implicitly
denounces and satirizes.

Which reel?[43]

Postmodernist fiction shares with classic modernist fiction an affinity for
cinema (and more recently for television), drawing upon it for models and
raw materials. There are radical differences, however, in the uses to which
modernism and postmodernism have put the movies. For modernist fiction,
the movies served primarily as a source for new techniques of
representation.[44] Such modernist cinematic techniques as cinemontage do
persist in postmodernist fiction, of course, but they are no longer the most
important or conspicuous function of the cinema model. Instead of serving as
a repertoire of representational techniques, the movies and television appear
in postmodernist writing as an ontological level: a world-within-the-world,
often one in competition with the primary diegetic world of the text, or a
plane interposed between the level of verbal representation and the level of
the "real." Postmodernist fiction at its most mimetic holds the mirror up to
everyday life in advanced industrial societies, where reality is pervaded by
the "miniature escape fantasies" of television and the movies. The plural
ontology of television-dominated everyday life appears, for instance, in
Robert Coover's "The Babysitter" (from *Pricksongs and Descants*, 1969) and
Walter Abish's "Ardor/Awe/Atrocity" (from *In The Future Perfect*, 1977); here
the ubiquitous television set, a world within the world, further destabilizes an
already fluid and unstable fictional reality.

In a television-oriented culture like the one that postmodernist writing so
often reflects, TV and the movies constitute a privileged source for the sort of
conceits that threaten to overwhelm the primary, literal reality (see pp.
133–47). After all, if the culture as a whole seems to hover between reality
and televised fictions, what could be more appropriate than for the texts of
that culture to hover between literal reality and a cinematic or television
metaphor? Pynchon, for instance, uses this strategy of suspension throughout *Gravity's Rainbow*, often turning to cinema for his metaphorical vehicles.
Pynchon's movie metaphors are developed so concretely and at such length
that we begin to lose sight of the literal reality of which they are supposedly
the vehicle:

> Of course Cherrycoke is c ld. He laughs too often. Not aimlessly either, but
> *directed at* something h · nks everyone else can see too. All of us watching
> some wry newsreel,   beam from the projector falling milky-white,
> thickening with sm ..t   m briers and cheroots, Abdullas and Woodbines
> . . . the lit profiles of m. lary personnel and young ladies are the edges of
> clouds: the manly crepe of an overseas cap knifing forward into the
> darkened cinema, the shiny rounding of a silk leg tossed lazily toe-in
> between two seats in the row ahead, the keen-shadowed turbans of velvet

and feathering eyelashes beneath. Among these nights' faint and lusting couples, Ronald Cherrycoke's laughing and bearing his loneliness, brittle, easily crazed, oozing gum from the cracks, a strange mac of most unstable plastic.[45]

The distinction between literal reality and metaphorical vehicle becomes increasingly indeterminate, until we are left wondering whether the movie reality is only a trope after all, or belongs to the "real" world of this fiction. This scene in the cinema, we need to remind ourselves, is only an elaborate conceit for Ronald Cherrycoke's peculiar laughter; or is it? Which reel?

Cinematic discourse pervades the style and imagery of *Gravity's Rainbow* from beginning to end.[46] For one transition from a bedroom scene to a conversation over breakfast, "bridge music" is specified; elsewhere, the narrative acquires a voice-over parodying that of an old-fashioned travelogue. In other words, the extended cinematic trope has here been applied *to the text itself*: the text has become the metaphorical tenor, the movies its vehicle; movie metaphors substitute for the language of novelistic narration and description. This occurs in other postmodernist texts as well. "Nobody from Bombay should be without a basic film vocabulary," Salman Rushdie's narrator remarks in *Midnight's Children*,[47] and accordingly film vocabulary is used in various places throughout this text as a mode of notation for textual strategies: "we cut to a long-shot," "cutting from two-shot of lovers to this extreme close-up," "zooming out slowly into long-shot," and so on. Similar film notation occurs throughout Robbe-Grillet's *Projet pour une révolution* ("Retake," "Cut"), and provides cinema-style closure for Ishmael Reed's *Mumbo Jumbo* (1972): "Freeze frame." William Burroughs not only uses movie discourse to capture various cinematic strategies in his texts ("Fadeout," "Cut"), but even goes so far as to compose entire episodes in the format of a screenplay or shooting-script (e.g. in *The Wild Boys*, 1971, and *Exterminator!* 1973). In effect, the cinematic techniques which postmodernist writing inherited from the modernists are here laid bare: background structure, thrust into the foreground by self-reflective cinematic notations, becomes a distinct ontological level.

Cinematic discourse can be interpreted as I have just interpreted it, as a series of metaphors for textual strategies; but it can also be read as the sign of a narrative level interposed between the text and the "real." By this reading, texts such as *Gravity's Rainbow*, *Projet pour une révolution* or *The Wild Boys* do not directly represent a reality, but rather represent a *movie* which in turn represents a reality. This reading is clearly justified in *Gravity's Rainbow*, where the presence of the interposed level of the film is revealed on the last page. And it is justified, too, throughout Burroughs's writings, where many episodes, and not only those in the format of a shooting-script, are presented as movies-within-the-novel; this is notoriously the case with the Orgasm Death Gimmick and other blue movies in Burroughs' fictions. Burroughs makes explicit what can only be inferred from other postmodernist cinematic writing, namely the *thematic* function of the interposed ontological level of the film. Reality in Burroughs is a film shot and directed by others; we are actors in the movie, our lives scripted and fixed on celluloid:

Present time is a film and if you are *on set* in present time you don't feel present time because you are *in it*. . . . How many of you people can live without film coverage? How many of you can forget you were ever a cop a priest a writer leave everything you ever thought and did and said behind and walk right out of the film? There is no place else to go. The theater is closed.[48]

In other words, the ontological level of the movies, interposed between reality and its textual representation, functions as a global metaphor for Burroughs' master-theme of *control*.

How can one free oneself from this control? How can one escape from the pre-scripted reality film? Burroughs represents characters as stepping out of the ontological level of the movies, using "film grenades" to break through to unmediated reality (*The Wild Boys*), "ripping through the film barrier,"[49] even storming the Reality Studio where the reality film is made (*The Soft Machine*, 1961/6). If the film is a master-trope for control, then escape can only be through *metalepsis*: breaching the ontological boundary, walking out of the ontological level of film to some higher (or lower) level.

Introduced as one level in the text's ontological structure, the movies thus serve as the background for spectacular metalepses, violations of the ontological hierarchy which foreground postmodernism's ontological themes (including the theme of control). Such metalepses occur throughout *Gravity's Rainbow*: cinematic images of copulation lead to the conception of two real girls; an Allied propaganda film apparently generates a real corps of Black African rocket troops; and, in a final, apocalyptic metalepsis, the rocket launched within the film-within-the-novel hangs poised above the theater in which the film itself is being viewed.

The Chinese-box structure of *Don Quixote*, Borges has said, implied that we, too, are fictional characters, and that our reality is as much a fiction as Quixote's is; hence the continuing fascination of this text for generations of readers. Pynchon seems to imply much the same thing when he implicates us in his fictional world on the last page of *Gravity's Rainbow*: "old fans who've always been at the movies (haven't we?)." *At* the movies – or should that be *in* the movies, we wonder queasily.

PART FOUR: WORDS

Language . . . constructs immense edifices of symbolic representations that appear to tower over the reality of everyday life like gigantic presences from another world.

(Peter L. Berger and Thomas Luckmann, *The Social Construction of Reality*, 1966)

9: TROPOLOGICAL WORLDS

The marvelous obscurity of Rilke
Where what begin as metaphors all turn
To autonomous imaginative realities all pursuing
Their infinitely complicated ways on ampler pinions
Than sailed yon azure deep.
(Hugh MacDiarmid, "The Progress of Poetry", from *Stony Limits*, 1934)

Metaphorical expressions, according to Benjamin Hrushovski, belong simultaneously to two frames of reference. Within one of these frames, the expression has its literal meaning; within the other it functions figuratively. Only the second of these frames of reference actually exists in the fictional world of the text (what Hrushovski calls its *field* of reference). The frame within which the expression functions literally is *nonexistent* from the point of view of the text's world, absent where the other frame is present. Hrushovski takes as an example the notorious "patient etherised upon a table" with which Eliot's "J. Alfred Prufrock" opens. The expression "patient etherised upon a table" refers literally within the frame of reference of a hospital operating-room; but of course the frame "hospital" does not exist within the world of this poem – indeed, it has been "denied existence" at this point, says Hrushovski. What *does* exist is the frame of reference "evening," and within this frame the expression can only refer metaphorically. The interaction between the two frames permits the transfer of semantic materials from one to the other, specifically the attribute of being "spread out" which is explicitly transferred from the patient to the evening by the actual wording, but also such implicit, connotative attributes as "passivity," "illness," and so on.[1]

So metaphor arises from the tension between a presence and an absence, an "existent" and a "nonexistent." The absence or nonexistence of the secondary frame of reference, however, is not necessarily absolute. Secondary frames, such as the absent "hospital" of "Prufrock," may be co-opted or expropriated, so to speak, from the world of existents, the fictional world of the text; or, alternatively, they may begin as nonexistents relative to the fictional world but subsequently enter that world as full-fledged existents. The first of these alternatives occurs, as Hrushovski observes, in romantic nature-poetry exhibiting the "pathetic fallacy," where objects or phenomena in the literal scene are seized upon as metaphorical vehicles for the tenors of the poet's inner states. It also occurs on a grand scale in Proust, as Gérard Genette has shown:[2] metonymic contiguities in the world of the *Recherche* furnish many of Proust's metaphorical comparisons. The second of these alternatives has been described by the Russian formalists under the name of "realization of metaphor": events, objects, situations initially introduced as metaphors, literal only within a nonexistent and secondary frame of reference, eventually develop into realities within the fictional world. Rilke, who supplies many of Hrushovski's examples, is notable for his practice of this "poetics of shifting from language to world,"[3] or, as Hugh MacDiarmid puts it, of the sort of obscurity "Where what begin as metaphors all turn / To autonomous imaginative realities."

Hesitation revisited

Behind Hrushovski's account of metaphor lies the phenomenological poetics of Roman Ingarden. Ingarden emphasizes the opalescence of metaphor:[4] metaphorical objects – a patient etherised upon a table – both exist and do not exist. They are at one and the same time present, in the sense that the reader may partially concretize (visualize, "realize") them, and absent, in the sense that they are excluded from the presented world, "denied existence." A metaphor "may hover between the 'style' and the 'World' of a poem," says Hrushovski.[5] In other words, metaphor by its very nature foregrounds the ontological dimension of the text. Devices such as "realization of metaphor," by rescuing metaphorical objects from the limbo of nonexistence and reintroducing them as existents in the presented world of the text, further foreground this ontological dimension, in effect heightening the opalescence of metaphor. In this respect, the modernist practitioners of "realization of metaphor," such as Rilke, deserve to be thought of as precursors of postmodernist poetics, carrying us to the brink of a poetics of ontology, and perhaps over it.

Postmodernist writing seeks to foreground the ontological *duality* of metaphor, its participation in two frames of reference with different ontological statuses. This it accomplishes by aggravating metaphor's inherent ontological tensions, thereby slowing still further the already slow flicker between presence and absence. All metaphor *hesitates* between a literal function (in a secondary frame of reference) and a metaphorical function (in a "real" frame of reference); postmodernist texts often *prolong* this hesitation as a means of foregrounding ontological structure. Such prolonged hesitation between the literal and the metaphorical is typical, for instance, of Gabriel

García Márquez's novels *One Hundred Years of Solitude* (1967) and *The Autumn of the Patriarch* (1975). Consider Father Nicanor's fund-raising efforts in *One Hundred Years*:

> He went everywhere begging alms with a copper dish. They gave him a large amount, but he wanted more, because the church had to have a bell that would raise the drowned up to the surface of the water. He pleaded so much that he lost his voice. His bones began to fill with sounds.[6]

"His bones began to fill with sounds": in almost any context this would be interpreted as a metaphorical expression for Father Nicanor's obsessive involvement in alms-begging – and in the bell for which he is collecting the alms! In almost any context, that is, *except* that of *One Hundred Years*, where a strong possibility exists that this is no metaphor but literal "fact." For *One Hundred Years* is, of course, a fantastic text, in which, as Todorov says, tropes may be literalized. Elsewhere in the text, for example, an infatuated lover's bones are found to be *literally* impregnated with the perfume of the women he adores; and the episode in question, in which Father Nicanor's bones are said to fill with sounds, climaxes with a miracle of levitation – a *literal* miracle, not a figure of speech. In other words, the global context makes it highly likely that here we are required to construct a frame of reference which would pre-emptively literalize the potential metaphor of "His bones began to fill with sounds." In fact, however, the *local* context seems to resist the literal reading, inclining us to accept the metaphorical reading after all. The point is that there is no way of processing this expression without registering the two possibilities and the tug-of-war between them – without, in other words, *hesitating* between the literal and the metaphorical.

Compare this excerpt from the monologue of a young whore in *Autumn of the Patriarch*:

> he used bread to soak up my first adolescent sauce, he would put things there before eating them, he gave them to me to eat, he put asparagus stalks into me to eat them marinated with the brine of my inner humors, delicious, he told me, you taste like a port, he dreamed about eating my kidneys boiled in their own ammonia stew, with the salt of your armpits, he dreamed, with your warm urine, he sliced me up from head to toe, he seasoned me with rock salt, hot pepper and laurel leaves and left me to boil on a hot fire in the incandescent fleeting mallow sunsets of our love with no future, he ate me from head to toe with the drive and the generosity of an old man which I never found again in so many hasty and greedy men who tried to make love to me without managing to for the rest of my life without him.[7]

This passage seems unmistakably to modulate from literal sexual extravagances to metaphor: love-making like cannibalism. Yet here, too, as in the case of Father Nicanor's sound-filled bones, we hesitate, remembering that *Autumn of the Patriarch* is a text in which it is possible for a rebellious Minister of Defense literally to be served up, roasted and garnished, to his fellow generals for dinner. If such a "realization of metaphor" is possible in the earlier context, why not here as well? Once again, local context militates against the literal reading – after all, the speaker does mention subsequent (unsatisfactory) sexual experiences, which she could hardly have had if she had actually been ingested by the dictator! But if, in the final analysis, we settle for the metaphorical reading, we do not do so without first having considered the literal alternative.

These examples would seem to suggest that when García Márquez's language hovers between trope and literal, the resolution will always be on the side of the trope. But García Márquez is also capable of turning the tables on us. Thus, for example, when in *One Hundred Years* Amaranta Ursula returns to Macondo from Europe, she is described as "leading her husband by a silk rope tied around his neck."[8] The metaphorical reading is irresistible here – particularly, of course, for English speakers, for whom it inevitably conjures up the idiom, "tied to his (wife's, mother's) apron-strings." Our surprise and disorientation are accordingly intense when we learn that this is a "realized metaphor," a literal event in the world of the novel:

> Gaston understood that she would not get married unless he took her to live in Macondo. He agreed to it, as he agreed later on to the leash, because he thought it was passing fancy that could be overcome in time.[9]

García Márquez prolongs hesitation between the literal and the metaphorical by manipulating contextual pressures – on the one hand, the fantastic norms of the global context, tugging us toward a literal reading in terms of "realized metaphor"; on the other hand, the local context which (sometimes) tugs in the opposite direction, toward a metaphorical reading. But what about texts which lack the opportunity to establish such global contextual norms to counter-balance local context, or in which such norms have yet to be established? Here, for example, is a self-contained chapter from Richard Brautigan's *The Tokyo–Montana Express* (1980), entitled "Pleasures of the Swamp":

> The pleasures of the swamp just keep happening to me, oozing down through my waking hours, alligatoring my perceptions of reality and teaching me that stagnant water has its own intelligence and can be as brilliant as a Nobel Prize winner if you deal with it on its own terms and don't try to make it into a Himalayan skyline.
> Dangerous snakes?
> I use them for silverware. They can turn a dull meal into an exciting experience. A hamburger steak can become a matter of life and death.
> Mosquitoes?
> They're just bloodthirsty flying air conditioners. After you lose your blood egotism, they are no problem.
> Quicksand?
> I think of quicksand as a telephone call to a lover. We have a nice conversation about secret weather and agree to meet next week at a coffee shop that resembles the pleasures of the swamp.[10]

Insistently but elusively figurative, this passage unmistakably involves two interacting frames of reference (as the final sentence confirms): "swamp" and "coffee shop." But which is literal, which figurative? The opposing thrusts toward literal swamp, figurative coffee shop, and toward figurative swamp, literal coffee shop, seem perfectly balanced. ("Nobel Prize winner" and "Himalayan skyline" introduce additional frames, more unequivocally metaphorical.) Brautigan has promoted this strategy of irresolution to the constitutive principle of the text in *Trout Fishing in America* (1967). Here "trout fishing," like "swamp" in the passage I have quoted, vacillates between literal and figurative functions throughout the text.[11]

Compare the strategy of Leonard Michaels's story "Mildred" (from *Going Places*, 1969). A visit to Miller and Mildred by their somewhat sinister friends Max and Sleek ends with a conversation about wombs and, bizarrely, an examination of Mildred's:

> He whispered, "The womb is resilient. Always recovers." Max said, "Made of steel." "Of course," said Sleek, "chicks are tough." Mildred agreed, sat up, showed us her womb. Max took it, squeezed, passed it to Sleek. He suppressed a laugh, then glanced at me.
>
> "Squeeze, squeeze," I said.
>
> He said, "Tough number. Like steel."
>
> I said it looked edible. Sleek stared at Mildred. She got up and took her womb to the stove. I had a bite. Max munched and let his eyelids fall to show his pleasure. Sleek took a sharp little bite and made a smacking noise in his mouth. I felt embarrassed, happy. Mildred seemed happy, seeing us eat.[12]

How are we to read this passage, as metaphor or "realized metaphor"? On the one hand, it seems possible to understand this passage analogously to the way we came to understand the young whore's monologue from *Autumn of the Patriarch*. There the literal frame of reference "love-making" was related to the metaphorical frame "cannibalism"; here, analogously, the literal frame "men discussing a woman in her presence" could be seen as relating to the metaphorical frame "handling and eating her womb," with appropriate transfers of semantic material from one frame to the other. Alternatively, however, we could read this scene as fantastic, exemplifying Todorov's notion of the supernatural as literalized trope.[13] There is even a third possibility: the four characters have just dosed themselves with recreational drugs, so this examination and consumption of the womb could be a joint hallucination. (This reading, however, instead of accentuating actually neutralizes the ontological tension, shifting the problem into an epistemological key, so to speak.) As in the case of Brautigan, this strategy of hesitation between the literal and the figurative is recurrent in Michaels's writing. It dominates, for example, the stories "Sticks and Stones" and "Fingers and Toes" (both from *Going Places*).

Hypertrophy

Hesitation, whether ultimately resolved or unresolved and unresolvable, is one strategy for foregrounding the ontological structure of metaphor; but it is not the only strategy. Instead of poising an expression between "style" and

"World" one can, for example, openly display its metaphoricity but then so extend and elaborate the metaphorical frame of reference that it approaches the status of an independent fictional world of its own, an autonomous (or at any rate quasi-autonomous) imaginative reality. The great precursor here is Proust, who notoriously begins with a relatively simple metaphor or explicit analogy – an opera box like a tank of water (near the beginning of *The Guermantes Way*), homosexual courtship like a bee pollinating a flower (in the opening pages of *Cities of the Plain*) – and develops from it an elaborate metaphorical system in which the two frames of reference are congruent at a maximum number of points: a world of nymphs, sea-monsters, and undersea flora and fauna unfolds parallel to the world of aristocrats at the opera, an entire botanical-biological realm develops parallel to the realm of homo-erotic behavior. This development may extend over several pages of text. Of course, Proust is careful to "ground" his hypertrophied metaphorical developments, motivating them at every point to prevent his reader from mistaking the "minor" world of the metaphor for the "major" world of the novel.

Postmodernist writers are not always so considerate. Their metaphorical miniature worlds tend to acquire an internal consistency and "liveliness" of their own; gathering momentum, they may even lose touch with the ground of their literal frame of reference and "take off." An example of metaphors that very nearly take off from their ground is Donald Barthelme's one-sentence story "Sentence" (from *City Life*, 1970):

> the sentence falls out of the mind that holds it (temporarily) in some kind of an embrace, not necessarily an ardent one, but more perhaps the kind of embrace enjoyed (or endured) by a wife who has just waked up and is on her way to the bathroom in the morning to wash her hair, and is bumped into by her husband, who has been lounging at the breakfast table reading the newspaper,[14]

and so on for another dozen or so lines, by which time this little domestic scene has developed an independent reality of its own, no longer congruent at every point with the literal frame (the sentence itself), and the sentence really *has* "fallen out of the mind."[15] Having lost his primary world (and his reader!) in this way, Barthelme starts over again with a new metaphor:

> there is another way of describing the situation too, which is to say that the sentence crawls through the mind like something someone says to you while you're listening very hard to the FM radio,

and so on, specifying in the course of the next page or so of text[16] exactly what "you" are listening to, "your" state of mind at the time etc. Again, as the metaphorical frame of reference comes to dominate the foreground, and the literal frame retreats into the background, the metaphor threatens to take off.

Are readers really liable to confuse such hypertrophied metaphor with literal reality? Perhaps not in the case of Barthelme's "Sentence," but consider what happens in Marjorie Perloff's reading of a prose text by John Ashbery, "The New Spirit" from his paradoxically-titled *Three Poems* (1972).[17] The passage from "The New Spirit" begins this way:

> At this point an event of such glamor and such radiance occurred that you forgot the name all over again. It could be compared to arriving in an unknown city at night, intoxicated by the strange lighting and the ambiguities of the streets. The person sitting next to you turned to you,

and so on for the remainder of the page. As the metaphorical frame of reference swells and complicates, the language of the passage becomes increasingly abstract, making it easy to forget that the concrete scene upon which this abstract language has been brought to bear is not itself *ultimately* concrete, but an elaborate figure; the literal frame of reference, all but lost in the shuffle, remains the unspecified glamorous event with which the passage opened, and not the scene in the railway carriage. Perloff, in her reading, in effect suppresses the sign of figurativeness ("could be compared to") and treats this scene in the railway carriage itself as the Proustian "privileged moment" in question[18] – when, in fact, it is part of Ashbery's characteristic elusiveness and indirection (as well as a mark of his postmodernism) that the literal "privileged moment," whatever it might have been, is *absent*; what is present here is no more than a metaphorical analogue for that moment, and technically *does not exist*.

At very nearly the limit of hypertrophy, perhaps, we find the metaphors of Pynchon's *Gravity's Rainbow* (1973), grossly distended tropes that develop coherent, finely-detailed internal worlds which threaten to swamp the literal world of the novel, and *from* which any return to the literal world of the novel tends to be problematical:

> Living inside the System is like riding across the country in a bus driven by a maniac bent on suicide . . . though he's amiable enough, keeps cracking jokes back through the loud-speaker, "Good morning folks, this is Heidelberg here we're coming into now, you know the old refrain, 'I lost my heart in Heidelberg,' well I have a friend who lost both his *ears* here! Don't get me wrong, it's really a nice town, the people are warm and wonderful – when they're not dueling. Seriously though, they treat you just fine, they don't just give you the key to the city, they give you the bung-starter!" u.s.w. On you roll, across a countryside whose light is forever changing – castles, heaps of rock, moons of different shapes and colors come and go. There are stops at odd hours of the mornings, for reasons that are not announced: you get out to stretch in lime-lit courtyards where the old men sit around the table under enormous eucalyptus trees you can smell in the night, shuffling the ancient decks oily and worn, throwing down swords and cups and trumps major in the tremor of light while behind them the bus is idling, waiting – *passengers will now reclaim their seats* and much as you'd like to stay, right here, learn the game, find your old age around this quiet table, it's no use: he is waiting beside the door of the bus in his pressed uniform, Lord of the Night he is checking your tickets, your ID and travel papers, and it's the wands of enterprise that dominate tonight . . . as he nods you by, you catch a glimpse of his face, his insane, committed eyes, and you remember then, for a terrible few heartbeats, that of course it will end for you all in blood, in shock, without dignity – but there is meanwhile this trip to be on . . . over your own seat, where there ought to be an advertising

plaque, is instead a quote from Rilke: "Once, only once . . ." One of Their favorite slogans.[19]

Pynchon's trope is also a second-order trope. "Living inside the System" is not only like taking this sinister bus-tour; it is also like losing oneself *inside* apparently limitlessly inflatable, hypertrophied figures such as this one! Strikingly, Pynchon brings his monster metaphor to rest, as on a resolving chord, with an allusion to Rilke, whose tropological worlds, poised between the literal and the figurative, were forerunners of Pynchon's own.

Postmodernist allegory

Metaphor, one might think, could hardly be more hypertrophied than this monstrous specimen from Pynchon; but in fact it can, although it loses the name of metaphor in the process. Imagine, for example, taking one of Barthelme's hypertrophied metaphors – a sentence like a vague embrace, a sentence like being distracted while listening to the radio – and inflating it still further, like a balloon, to the point where it became contiguous with the limits of the text. Or, better still, take the balloon itself as your trope: a text like a balloon. This has the advantage of functioning on two levels, like Pynchon's trope for living inside the System: not only is a text like a balloon, but the trope "a text like a balloon" itself behaves like a balloon, inflating to the limits of the text. Then (to continue our trope) you have only to cast loose the moorings, allowing the balloon to float free, that is, suppress the explicit markers of the metaphor (such as "a text is like . . ."). The result is a text-length trope which preserves the two-level ontological structure of metaphor (literal frame of reference, metaphorical frame of reference), but in which, instead of being announced explicitly, the two-level structure remains implicit, disseminated throughout the text. In this particular instance, the actual result is Barthelme's text "The Balloon" (from *Unspeakable Practices, Unnatural Acts*, 1968), in which a gigantic balloon, mysteriously inflated over Manhattan, invites interpretations by New Yorkers and the reader alike. The result, in other words, is an allegory.

"We seem in the last quarter of the twentieth century to have reentered an allegorical age," writes Maureen Quilligan.[20] This is due partly to our renewed capacity to recognize and appreciate allegory; through the efforts of critics and theorists such as Edwin Honig, Angus Fletcher, Paul DeMan, and Quilligan herself,[21] the romantic prejudice against allegory has been lifted, and it has once again become possible to call a work allegorical without being pejorative. But the critical rehabilitation of allegory is only part of the story; even more important, as Quilligan is right to point out, is the resurgence of the practice of allegory in our time. Exhibit A in Quilligan's case for contemporary allegory is *Gravity's Rainbow*, but she might just as easily have selected any of a number of postmodernist narratives which are wholly or partly allegorical, including John Barth's *Giles Goat-Boy* (1966), Jerzy Kosinski's *Being There* (1971), Ishmael Reed's *Mumbo Jumbo* (1972), Barthelme's *The Dead Father* (1974) and of course "The Balloon," Günter Grass' *The Flounder* (1977), Robert

Coover's *The Public Burning* (1977), Salman Rushdie's *Midnight's Children* (1981), as well as any text by William Burroughs. Her explanation of this resurgence, both of critical insight and allegorical practice, focuses on the "linguistic turn" of twentieth-century thought, involving the recovery of a "medieval" or "suprarealist" view of language as possessing, at least potentially, a sacralizing power. No doubt this is true, but the revival of allegory in postmodernist writing can also be related to postmodernism's ontological poetics. The fictional world of an allegorical narrative is a tropological world, a world within a trope. Its ontological structure is *dual*, two-level, one level (or frame) that of the trope – the balloon, say, in Barthelme's story – the other that of the literal – the balloon's meaning of "text" (or perhaps "work of art" in general). In terms of Hrushovski's model of the ontology of metaphor, allegory is metaphor's *inverse*: where in a metaphor the metaphorical frame of reference is absent, the literal frame present, in allegory it is the literal frame of reference that is missing and must be supplied by the reader – only the metaphorical frame is given. Like metaphor, however, allegory offers itself as a tool for exploring ontological structure and foregrounding ontological themes; so in a sense we should hardly be surprised at the contemporary resurgence of allegory.

Nevertheless, allegory is not universally recognized as being compatible with postmodernist writing, not even by the postmodernist practitioners themselves. Robbe-Grillet, for example, saw fit to prefix the following disclaimer to his novel *Dans le labyrinthe* (1959):

> the reality in question is a strictly material one; that is, it is subject to no allegorical interpretation. The reader is therefore requested to see in it only the objects, actions, words, and events which are described, without attempting to give them either more or less meaning than in his own life, or his own death.[22]

Such disclaimers, of course, are notoriously not to be trusted. In fact, *Dans le labyrinthe* is unmistakably allegorical, although allegorical in the postmodernist manner. Insofar as Robbe-Grillet is serious in his rejection of an allegorical reading, this must derive from an overly narrow sense of the possibilities of allegory – the sort of narrowness that prevailed prior to the recent upsurge of critical and theoretical interest. Or, to put it differently, Robbe-Grillet's disclaimer probably contains an implicit recognition of the elusiveness of postmodernist allegory, relative to what we usually think of as the unequivocalness of traditional allegories.

This elusiveness is an inheritance from the founding texts of postmodernist allegorical practice (from which *Dans le labyrinthe* clearly descends): Kafka in his novels and stories, Beckett in his narratives and plays, Joyce in *Finnegans Wake* (1939). Kafka's texts seem to promise allegorical meaning, soliciting an allegorical interpretation from the reader, yet withholding any indication of *specific* allegorical content. Everything is *potentially* allegorical, but nothing is *actually* an allegory; the trope seems to lack a specific literal level or frame of reference. Each vision of the Castle, for instance, seems to charge it with potential abstract meaning, eliciting in the reader a drive to specify that meaning – God? the Old Law? Authority? History? Culture? and so on – and eliciting the same drive in K., whose own interpretations offer a very poor model to the reader, sliding as they do from possibility to possibility without ever settling on a determinate meaning. Beckett's invitations to allegorical reading typically take the form of punning names – Mr Knott, Youdi, Macmann, Hamm – names that cry out to be treated as clues around which to assemble one or several allegorical meanings, theological allegories for the most part. Of course the supremely theological pun, the temptation to allegorize that no one has been quite able to resist, is "Godot," which brings out (designedly, no doubt) the worst in literary critics – brings out, that is, what Keats would have called the "irritable reaching after fact & reason" that issues in univocal theological or archetypal readings of *Waiting for Godot* (1952).[23] In *Finnegans Wake*, finally, nothing is literal, everything is tropological. Every expression belongs simultaneously to several frames of reference, none of them identifiable as the basic world of the text, relative to which the other frames are metaphorical; instead, there is a perpetual jostling and jockeying for position among a plurality of simultaneously present (and therefore simultaneously absent) worlds.

Finnegans Wake, then, like *The Castle* or *Waiting for Godot*, invites us to read allegorically but refuses to satisfy our drive. These are overdetermined allegories: they have *too many* interpretations, more than can possibly be integrated in a univocal reading. The result of overdetermination is indeterminacy; and this indeterminacy has profound ontological consequences, for it sets in motion a game of musical chairs involving the literal frame of reference. If the Castle, say, or Knott's house, or Godot, or Anna Livia Plurabelle have no allegorical meaning, then they belong unproblematically to the literal frame of reference; if, however, they *do* possess allegorical meaning, then it is that meaning which constitutes the literal level, while they themselves function as tropes: the Castle *is* authority, Knott's house *is* the universe, Godot *is* God, Anna Livia *is* the River Liffey. In each of these equations, the second term is "realer" than the first. But if there are *several* distinguishable allegorical meanings, then the literal level circulates among them, so to speak, never coming to rest, each level in turn functioning as literal relative to the others. In short, indeterminate allegory is a means of inducing an ontological oscillation, the same hesitation or "slow flicker" that characterizes other types of tropological world.

But if Kafka, Beckett and Joyce do establish the dominant mode of postmodernist allegory, as I have said, then why is it that certain postmodernist allegorists, instead of exploiting indeterminate allegory to destabilize ontological structure, seem to have opted for relatively transparent, univocal allegorical narratives, offering apparently no obstruction to interpretation? Variations on the venerable mode of psychomachia, these allegories typically involve the confrontation of warring principles, semantic oppositions personified; Manichaean allegories, we might call them. Where ancient psychomachias characteristically pitted personified Good against personified Evil, however, the postmodernist versions tend to prefer the Nietzschean opposition between the Apollonian and Dionysian principles, rational order vs. mindless pleasures. "Mindless pleasures," of course, was Pynchon's original title for the novel finally published as *Gravity's Rainbow*, undoubtedly the most highly visible specimen of Manichaean allegory – or, as Pynchon would perhaps call it, paranoid allegory, the allegory of conspiracy and counterconspiracy, force and counterforce. More than one critic has noted how Pynchon's world falls into a pattern of polar oppositions – the Elect vs. the Preterite, the zero vs. one, fathers vs. sons, white vs. non-white, gravity vs. the rainbow, even Beethoven vs. Rossini – where the first pole of the opposition corresponds to Apollonian order and repression, the second to Dionysian anarchy and the pleasure-principle.[24]

"Check out Ishmael Reed," Pynchon advises us. "He knows more about it than you'll ever find here."[25] And when we do check out Ishmael Reed, specifically *Mumbo Jumbo* (1972), we find another psychomachia between Apollonian and Dionysian principles, this time in the form of a millennial struggle between antagonistic secret societies, the Atonists and the Osirians. A similar struggle is enacted throughout William Burroughs's writings. Here, again, the opposition is between the principle of control and the various avatars of the life-force that resist control. Control is allegorized in a number of ways: as power-mad bureaucrats, as junk, as parasitic viruses, and ultimately as the Word itself.[26] Since popular subliterary genres have often favored Manichaean world-views, it is perhaps unsurprising that Burroughs should seize on the form of the cops-and-robbers story – Nova Mob vs. Nova Police – as the vehicle for his allegory. Similarly, Angela Carter has adapted the inherent Manichaeanism of gothic horror fiction to her own uses in *The Infernal Desire Machines of Dr Hoffman* (1972). Carter's allegory is particularly interesting because in it the Apollonian vs. Dionysian struggle has specifically ontological overtones: the Apollonian authority-figure, the Minister of Determination, is a relentless empiricist bent on preserving the integrity of reality against Dr Hoffman, Dionysian agent of fantasy and pleasure.

Allegory against itself

These Manichaean allegories, it would appear, coincide rather closely with the "unenlightened" view of allegory as the direct translation of abstract concepts into a transparently-motivated narrative. If such transparency were the norm of postmodernist allegory, then Robbe-Grillet would be right to issue his disclaimer, in order to avoid any confusion between this determinate type of allegory and his own altogether more elusive, more problematical – more Kafkaesque – mode. But are these Manichaean allegories – Pynchon's, Reed's, Burroughs's, Carter's – really so determinate after all?

We have already seen how, as Lodge argues, Burroughs's fiction fails to function adequately as satire because of the radical instability of his fictional worlds (see pp. 116–17). The same could be said of Burroughs's allegory: if the intention was to produce an unequivocal allegory of the struggle between the control principle and principles of liberty and pleasure, then Burroughs has failed, for the instability of his world blocks our efforts to establish an integrated allegorical interpretation. As in Kafka or Beckett or Joyce, the literal level is elusive: is "virus" a metaphor for control, or a literal threat in a futuristic (or not-so-futuristic) world of death-dealing technologies, or both? Burroughs' fiction, from one perspective, is "really about" drug addiction and the evils of propaganda and the mass media, in a fairly literalistic, indeed didactic, way, and control has only the status of a metaphor; from another perspective, control is literal, while junk and language are tropes. The hierarchy is reversible and re-reversible.

Ishmael Reed's superficially univocal Manichaean allegory similarly breaks down under closer scrutiny, though for different reasons. In the case of *Mumbo Jumbo*, Reed has gone to considerable lengths to persuade us that the confrontation of Atonists and Osirians is not allegorical but literal historical fact. He even resorts to the apparatus of "straight" historical research – footnotes, a bibliography (which certainly looks authentic) – as well as sly pre-emptive ripostes to the anticipated objections of professional historians. In other words, Reed deliberately complicates his otherwise transparent and symmetrical Manichaean allegory by introducing a distracting *additional* ontological tension, that between the historical and the fictional.

Carter, too, deliberately spoils her lucid allegory of fantasy vs. reality, and in a particularly visible way. Having posed the allegorical conflict in terms of a struggle between two men, the Minister and Dr Hoffman, Carter reveals through her hero Desiderio that each deuteragonist in fact possesses the characteristics that ought to belong, according to the logic of the allegory, to the other: in the empiricist Minister, Desiderio discerns an unruly Faustian impulse, a strain of imaginative overreaching (all in the service of everyday reality, of course), while Hoffman, he discovers, is really a colorless empiricist, a Gradgrind. In short, what had been posed as a polar opposition proves to be a complex and paradoxical interpenetration. This is Pynchon's strategy as well. Each of the terms in his series of polar opposites proves to contain elements or traces of its opposed term. Thus, for example, Pynchon's musical Manichaeanism, pitting the Beethoven-aesthetic of death ("All you feel like listening to Beethoven is going out and invading Poland. Ode to Joy indeed",[27] against the Rossini-aesthetic of pleasure, breaks down as soon as the figure of Webern is introduced. Webern unmistakably belongs to the great line of Beethoven, "standing at the far end of what'd been going on since Bach, an expansion of music's polymorphous perversity till all notes were truly equal at last," yet he is linked, through his accidental death at the hands of the Americans – "Senseless, accidental if you believe in accidents"[28] – with other sympathetic, doomed Preterite figures. So the Apollonian Webern is also implicated in the Dionysian side of the confrontation. The symmetries are systematically undone, the polar opposites allowed to "bleed" into one another.

In all these cases, it looks as though Manichaean allegory is in fact only another lure, an invitation to the unwary reader to interpret in terms of a univocal allegorical meaning. The trap is sprung the moment the reader recognizes the inconsistencies and incoherences of the allegory: determinate meaning dissolves into indeterminacy, the two-level ontological hierarchy of metaphorical and literal begins to oscillate, to opalesce. One might even suspect an element of parody. Are these Manichaean allegories really mock-allegories after all? Suspicion deepens into near-certainty when one encounters, late in *Gravity's Rainbow*, Paranoia personified as "a girl all in silver lamé, a loud brassy dame" who, after a dramatic entrance, performs a couple of Broadway-musical numbers with a chorus-line of Blacks dressed in sailor-suits: "She is the allegorical figure of Paranoia (a grand old dame, a little wacky but pure heart)."[29]

As a flagrant parody of conventional personification allegory, this perhaps outstrips anything in Burroughs or Reed or Carter, but it is matched by other postmodernist allegorists. Mock-allegory, indeed, is a characteristic mode of postmodernist writing. Robert Coover, for example, easily exceeds the flagrancy of Pynchon's parody. His *The Public Burning*, a massive parody of Cold-War Manichaean ideology and rhetoric, pits the allegorical figure of Uncle Sam, aided and abetted by such highly nonallegorical figures as Richard Nixon, against The Phantom – none other than the "spectre of Communism," Marx's and Engel's metaphor inflated into a personification. John Barth, too, parodies Cold-War Manichaeanism in *Giles Goat-Boy*, in which east and west are allegorized as feuding campuses of a university. The transparency and mechanical symmetry of the allegory alerts us to the parodic intention. As in Angela Carter, conceptual oppositions are embodied in sets of paired characters, antagonists in the narrative action: the opposition of chaos vs. order is personified in the pair of Maurice Stoker and Lucky Rexford, mind vs. body in Eierkopf and Croaker, innocence vs. experience in Peter Greene and Kenneth Sear, and so on. Having established this mechanical oppositional structure, Barth proceeds to invalidate it, not by insinuating into each term traces of its dialectical opposite, as Carter and Pynchon do, but rather by reflecting explicitly on the entire mechanism of opposition. Giles, Barth's hero, undergoes three successive "revelations": the first affirms opposition; the second denies it, substituting a paradoxical and suprarational merger of opposites; the third, in a dialectical synthesis of the first two, simultaneously affirms and denies both alternatives, opposition and unification alike. In this vertiginous play of same and different, the psychomachia is utterly swept away.

Parody, of course, is a form of self-reflection and self-critique, a genre's way of thinking critically about itself. Parody of allegory, then, is allegory reflecting upon allegory. With this turn of the screw of self-consciousness, postmodernist allegory would appear to have distanced itself from what we are still apt to think of as the "naïveté" of traditional allegories (*Everyman*, *Pilgrim's Progress*). Not so, if Maureen Quilligan is to be believed. According to her, all allegory, at all periods, is self-reflective because it is generated from the tensions between different meanings of polysemous words – systematic punning, in short. One meaning of such a word (e.g. *just* in passus 16 of *Piers Plowman*, *error* in Book I of *The Faerie Queene*, *letter* in *The Scarlet Letter*) sets in motion the allegorical narrative, opening the way for the development of the fictional world; the other refers to realities beyond that world. Regularly, however, the "other" meaning reasserts itself, and the tropological world collapses. As Quilligan puts it, allegory has a "tendency to slide tortuously back and forth between literal and metaphorical understandings of words, and therefore to focus on the problematical tensions between them."[30] This is also an *ontological* tension: allegory projects a world and erases it in the same gesture, inducing a flicker between presence and absence of this world, between tropological reality and "literal" reality – literal in the *literal* sense of "words on the page." For what this flicker foregrounds above all is the *textuality* of the text. If you ask what is the "realest" level of an allegorical text, the answer – upon which allegory, according to Quilligan, never ceases to insist – can only be the words on the page in front of you.

This is certainly true of Quilligan's prime postmodernist example, *Gravity's Rainbow*. Pynchon's characters persist in behaving as though their world were a text – which of course, literally, it is – and they its readers. Säure Bummer reads reefers, Miklos Thanatz reads whip-scars, Pfc. Eddie Pensiero reads shivers, Ronald Cherrycoke reads personal effects (cravat, fountain-pen, pince-nez), Igor Blobadjian of the New Turkic Alphabet G Committee learns how to read molecular structure. Mr Pointsman interprets the Book (Pavlov, not Holy Writ); Katje interprets Osbie Feel's cryptic movie scenario. Enzian the Rocket-Kabbalist regards the bombed-out German landscape as a text, while Slothrop, scion of "word-smitten Puritans", sees a normal day-in-the-life (reluctantly) in much the same way:

> He gets back to the Casino just as big globular raindrops, thick as honey, begin to splat into giant asterisks on the pavement, inviting him to look down at the bottom of the text of the day, where footnotes will explain all. He isn't about to look. Nobody ever said a day has to be juggled into any kind of sense at day's end. He just runs.[31]

Again and again postmodernist allegorical worlds collapse into "literal" texts in just this way, "simply evaporate" as Quilligan says, inducing a sense of "vertigo" in the reader.[32] On a miniature scale, this is what happens in Barthelme's "Sentence," where the tropological worlds of a sleepy early-morning embrace or of listening to FM radio simply evaporate, leaving us with the only thing that was "literally" there all along – the sentence itself. This vertigo-inducing collapse of world into word occurs on the largest scale of all in *Finnegans Wake*, where the fictional world is perpetually evaporating, perpetually sliding back and forth between trope and "literal." Whatever else Anna Livia Plurabelle might be – a woman of Dublin, the River Liffey, Everywoman, Irish History – she is also a sequence of printed letters and (sub-vocalized) sounds, letters and sounds that, disseminated throughout the text, are susceptible of unlimited manipulations. Anna Livia "appears" or "manifests" herself (it is hard to know what term to use) in various alternative versions of her name, or in phrases that echo her name –

Anna Lynchya Pourable
anny livving plusquebelle
Appia Lippia Pluviabilla
allaniuvia pulchrabelled;

or in a more fragmentary form, the syllables of her name distributed throughout words and phrases that no longer bear much resemblance to it –

Alla tingaling pealabells
Allalivial, allalluvial
Avelaval;

or, finally, in the initial letters of three-word phrases, reduced to her own initials A.L.P. –

Annshee lispes privily
ambling limfy peepingpartner
annie lawry promises
addle liddle phifie
Amy Licks Porter
ancients link with presents,

and so on. Anna Livia is made out of text – letters, words, connected discourse; she *is* text. So too are all other fictional characters, of course, even those in the most realistic of novels. The difference between realistic novels and *Finnegans Wake* is that *Finnegans Wake* never permits us to forget this fact. "The stage setting of an allegory begins," writes Maureen Quilligan,

as it might in any fiction, but at some point in the play of the narrative the action fades, as if the lights were to go off behind the scrim, so that the audience is left facing the curtain on which are printed the author's words.[33]

10: STYLED WORLDS

The poet struggles to keep his words from saying something, although, like the carrot, they want to go to seed.
> (William H. Gass, "Carrots, Noses, Snow, Rose, Roses," 1978)

The reader will see that what I am driving at is that these words that he is reading – are words.
> (Gilbert Sorrentino, *Imaginative Qualities of Actual Things*, 1971)

The action fades, the lights go off behind the scrim, and we are left facing the words on the page: this happens again and again in postmodernist writing, and not only when tropological worlds collapse. It also happens whenever our attention is distracted from the projected world and made to fix on its linguistic medium.

Sound-formations and small-scale semantic units, Ingarden tells us, constitute the lowest ontological strata of the literary work, the foundations upon which the higher strata of presented objects and their projected world are erected. To call attention to the lowest strata at the expense of the highest is to drive a wedge into the ontological structure of the literary work, splitting it into "words" and "world." The differing ontological statuses of words and world are brought into sharp focus, the words being made to appear more "real," more present, than the world they project. In a sense, this is only a kind of optical illusion, for words, no less than projected worlds, are intentional objects of the reader's consciousness, and as such are no more real or present than the higher strata of the literary work. But it is a potent illusion, and one that blocks and reverses our normal habit of effacing the level of words as we reconstruct the world of the text. For once, it is the world that seems, at least momentarily, to have been effaced. Thus the foregrounding of the linguistic medium induces a kind of ontological flicker, or, as Marjorie Perloff puts it, a "tension between reference and compositional game, between a pointing system and a self-ordering system."[1]

The foregrounding of style is hardly new with postmodernism, of course. It is already characteristic of the earliest modernist writing – Flaubert, Henry James. Flaubert in particular is responsible for introducing what Jonathan Culler has called a "labor theory of value," whereby the aesthetic value of verbal art is to be measured in terms of the amount of work that has gone into the production of the linguistic surface.[2]

The unit of measure, we might say, the sign of value, is the *mot juste* – or rather, the effort we perceive as having been invested in the search for *le mot juste*. This valuing of a highly-finished surface inevitably has the effect of interfering with the "vertical" relation between word and projected world (Ingarden's lower and higher strata respectively), substituting in its place a "horizontal" relation among verbal elements on the same level. "The more obscure a discourse appears," writes Allon White (referring to Henry James), "the more its formal features are foregrounded, and the more significance shifts away from the (ever more remote) denotation of the discourse to its formal, verbal connotations. . . . This transference is one of the grounding processes of modernism."[3]

Foregrounded style in modernist fiction is pulled in two different directions, toward, on the one hand, an epistemological function, and on the other hand toward an "autotelic" function – free-standing style to be valued in and for itself. In the first of these tendencies, style is foregrounded only to serve as a representation of a character's consciousness in its interaction with the world, or – if style cannot plausibly be attributed to the character's consciousness, as in the "Cyclops" chapter of *Ulysses* or Virginia Woolf's *The Waves* – then it serves as a kind of surrogate or displaced consciousness, diffused throughout the text, in *its* interaction with the world. This is "style as vision."[4] Alternatively, style in modernist fiction tends to shake itself free from content, implicitly repudiating its mimetic commitments. The model here is the *livre sur rien* which Flaubert never quite managed to write, a content-free collection of sentences "whose polished surfaces might aspire to the condition of sculpture."[5]

No book in the modernist period is a better candidate for the label *livre sur rien* than Gertrude Stein's *Tender Buttons* (1914). Here Stein treats words "as counters, as seemingly empty, although interestingly shaped, containers that gained significance only by means of their relationship with other words on the page."[6] Words approach the status of objects in their own right, tangible *things*, through a process of reification that involves the disruption of syntax and the foregrounding of nonsemantic relations:

BUTTER
Boom in boom in, butter. Leave a grain and show it, show it. I spy.
   It is a need it is a need that a flower a state flower. It is a need that a state rubber. It is a need that a state rubber is sweet and sight and a swelled stretch. It is a need. It is a need that state rubber.
   Wood a supply. Clean little keep a strange, estrange on it.
   Make a little white, no and not with pit, pit on in within.[7]

In the absence of a controlling syntax, it is repetition that does the work of making the text cohere – repetition not only of words and whole phrases (boom in, show it, it is a need, flower, state, rubber, little, pit) but also of sounds: there are rhymes, masculine and feminine (I/spy, butter/flower/ rubber, it/pit, in/within), assonances (butter/rubber, leave/need/sweet/clean/ keep, grain/state, it/little/pit/in/within), consonances (state/sweet/slight/ swelled/stretch/strange/estrange), and so on. The sequence develops through repetition-with-variation, for instance from *a flower* to *a state flower* to *a state rubber* to *state rubber*. One consequence of such repetition is the "leveling" of words, grammatical form-words and full lexical words appearing as equals from the point of view of their participation in various patterns. Rhythm contributes to this effect, the recurrent heavy spondees (I spy, state flower, state rubber, swelled stretch) hobbling the flow of the prose rhythms and tending to distribute stress equally among the words, setting each word apart from its fellows. Words, freed from syntactical constraints, become grammatically ambiguous, changing functions before our eyes like Gombrich's famous visual paradox, the duck-rabbit: *flower* vacillates between noun and verb, as does *state*; *rubber* functions both as a noun and as a slightly distorted verb phrase (*rub her*). Semantics, too, comes unstuck, puns proliferate. One pun is made explicit in the text – *a strange, estrange* – which should sensitize us to the presence of others: *boom in* and *booming, rubber* and *rub her, wood* and *would*. So words do enter into semantic as well as nonsemantic relations, but "illicit," punning ones. The connections here are all horizontal, it would seem, word to word, rather than vertical, word to world.

Nevertheless, I think Wendy Steiner is being extreme when she claims that Stein, in texts like *Tender Buttons*, cripples the world-projecting potential of language.[8] Stein could not, Steiner argues, build up "synthetic" representations from minimal mimetic units, as her friends the Cubist painters could, because words freed of controlling syntax do not signify at all. The result is less like the synthetic cubism of Picasso or Juan Gris than it is like the radically nonmimetic painting of the later abstract expressionists. But after all these words *do* have a context which mobilizes some, at least, of their semantic material: the context, namely, of the title "Butter." This cue, it would seem, authorizes us to seek out butter-oriented connotations of these words. Thus, "sweet and sight and a swelled stretch" can be seen to refer to various objective qualities of butter, "rubber" can be interpreted as a visual and tactile metaphorical substitute for butter, "flower" can be interpreted as a pun on a word often associated with butter in cooking – "flour" – and so on. *Tender Buttons*, writes William H. Gass, "is above all a book of kits like those from which harpsichords or paper planes or model bottle boats are fashioned, with intricacy no objection, patience a demand, unreadable plans a pleasure."[9]

Even in so radical a case as *Tender Buttons*, then, syntactical disruption and nonsemantic patterning do not completely block the reconstruction of fragments of a world. This is because words, unlike paint, are not abstract "counters," things, no matter how we manipulate them; inevitably they belong to associational fields, carry semantic charge, *mean*. Sentences, Culler is careful to say, can only *aspire* to the condition of sculpture – the implication is that they cannot attain it. Words, says Gass in my epigraph, "want to go to seed." Indeed, if this were not the case, the foregrounding of style would be of no use in the repertoire of ontological poetics, for the objective is not to efface the world once and for all but to "lay bare" (by exacerbating it) the tension between word and world, to induce an ontological flicker – between, say, "Butter" as an abstract formal pattern, repetition-with-variation, and "Butter" as a portrait of butter.

If Gertrude Stein has not written the *livre sur rien*, she has certainly gone further in that direction than Joyce or Woolf, further than any other modernist, to the point where it seems more satisfying to think of her not as an early modernist but a precocious postmodernist. The next step beyond *Tender Buttons* brings us to the postmodernist texts *sur rien* – the *exercises de style* of Raymond Queneau (1947), Flann O'Brien (*At Swim-Two-Birds*, 1939), Guillermo Cabrera Infante (*Tres tristes tigres*, 1965), and Gilbert Sorrentino (*Mulligan Stew*, 1979), the "free prose"[10] of Samuel Beckett's later writings, John Ashbery's prose-poems, and the fictions of Kenneth Patchen, William Burroughs, Donald Barthelme, Walter Abish, Ronald Sukenick, Steve Katz, George Chambers, Richard Brautigan, and others.

Kitty-litter, litanies, back-broke sentences

The postmodernist *livre sur rien* is not, of course, completely *sur rien*, any more than *Tender Buttons* was. Inevitably, it casts a shadow, as Roland Barthes once said:[11] it projects a world, however partial or incoherent. The aim of such a text is not to prevent the reconstruction of a world – which, in any case, it could not do – but only to throw up obstacles to the reconstruction process, making it more difficult and thus more conspicuous, more perceptible. To accomplish this, it has at its disposal a repertoire of stylistic strategies, including lexical exhibitionism, the catalogue, and "back-broke" and invertebrate sentences.

Lexical exhibitionism involves introducing words which are by their very nature highly conspicuous, self-foregrounding as it were: rare, pedantic, archaic, neologistic, technical, foreign words. Words, in short, which many readers will need to look up, and which they may not be able to find outside of the *OED* – or even inside it, for that matter. Here is a rather startling example from Guy Davenport:

> Kaatje lay back. Adriaan sliddered to the divergence of her thighs and sank his tongue into the consilient melt, roving his hands from thicket to breasts. Cunningly he set off the systolic chill of wild honeycomb convulsed by a crowding of light.
> She squealed and gasped as he pushed past the slick vexillaries and shot the full shaft into the deep recondite let, *geheel in al*. He rode his strokes with glutinous pull and thrust, a charm thronging lascivious and opulent in the pitching glans, a thick tremor gathering in his scrotum.
> . . . . he put her on the bed with a pillow under her butt. The full reach of his instroke tamped hydranths papillary and marine in her myxoid deep. The outslide of the suction stroke slithered past supple muscling in wanton throes. He mired his plunges with animal urgency, she kept pace with bucking hips.
> Bruno mounted again as soon as he had tugged free.

> Winded and codshotten, Adriaan sat on the floor by the bed watching the nannippus prance of Bruno's hips, Kaatje's arched back and jumping breasts, pritchkemp and cocket. The sensibilia they ravened was as weightless as essence itself.[12]

The center of consciousness in Davenport's text is one Adriaan van Hovendaal, polymath philosopher, so there is a more or less plausible source for this language. Van Hovendaal would certainly have to be polymath, and polyglot, to produce such words; he seems, in particular, to command a range of botanical and biological vocabularies (e.g. vexillaries, hydranths, papillary, myxoid). A spectacular lexical performance, it is made all the more spectacular by superimposed patterns of assonance and consonance, as in tongue-twisting sentences like, "The outslide of the suction stroke slithered past supple muscling in wanton throes."

Davenport's writing here is, of course, exhibitionistic in two different senses, sexually as well as lexically – at the level of world as well as at the level of words. Words compete for our attention with narrative contents that are, to say the least, arresting, and it is not clear which level wins out in the end. By selecting from unexpected stylistic registers, and by foregrounding lexical extravagance through purely formal patterning, Davenport induces a divided attention in the reader, forcing him or her to focus simultaneously on two centers of interest, foregrounded style and sexual content. In short, Davenport, like William Burroughs in the Orgasm Death Gimmick, is a poor pornographer but a good postmodernist. The principle is the same as in Burroughs's Gimmick (described in Chapter 8, pp. 116–17) using highly-charged content to intensify ontological tensions, here the tension between the text continuum (the level of style) and the level of the projected world.

Says William Gass:

> If you take really bowel-turning material, from the point of view of its pragmatic importance in the world, and surround it like kitty litter with stuff that is there purely for play, then you get an electric line between the two poles clothes would turn white simply hanging on. The electricity of Elizabethan drama is total. They are talking always of life and death matters, but they are standing there playing with their mouths.[13]

This intense polarization between "bowel-turning material" and the "kitty litter" of an exhibitionistic style is a basic strategy of Gass's own fiction, as well as the fiction of Guy Davenport, Vladimir Nabokov, and Gass's friend Stanley Elkin. Elkin vexes moralistic critics by "playing with his mouth" in the context of illness, death, and almost unbearable pathos (e.g. in *George Mills*, 1982, or *The Magic Kingdom*, 1985). Nabokov, like Davenport, exploits scandalous sexual content – pedophilia in *Lolita*, homosexuality in *Pale Fire*, incest in *Ada*, and so on – while maintaining a linguistic surface of word-games, multilingual puns, and lexical rarities.

But rarities are not the only vocabulary items that can be "exhibited"; so too can lexical stupidities and trivialities, the debased coinage of language. "Filling" or "stuff," one of Barthelme's seven dwarfs calls it, enunciating an aesthetics of "those aspects of language that may be seen as a model of the trash phenomenon," language that possesses "a 'sludge' quality."[14] The precursor here is Joyce, the first part of whose "Nausicaa" chapter exhibits middle-class feminine clichés and verbal found objects on a par with Barthelme's sludge. Joyce, however, has taken pains to integrate this fore-grounded antistyle within his projected world, providing a verisimilar verbal source (Gertie McDowell) to motivate the lexical stupidities. Barthelme, by contrast, seems in texts like *Snow White* (1967), *The Dead Father* (1975), or "For I'm the Boy Whose Only Joy is Loving You" and "The Big Broadcast of 1938" (both from *Come Back, Dr Caligari*, 1964) to encourage this sludgey discourse to achieve self-sufficiency, a kind of free-standing monumentality, all but disconnecting it from its supposed sources. Other postmodernist writers who have exhibited such linguistic sludge in their fiction are Richard Brautigan, Steve Katz, Ronald Sukenick, and even Kurt Vonnegut.

As Gertrude Stein demonstrated, in order to detach the stratum of words from the stratum of world, it is first necessary to disengage words from the syntax that controls the projection of worlds. Words disengaged from syntax – this could be a definition of the catalogue structure, a recurrent device of postmodernist style. From the ontological point of view, catalogues are paradoxical. On the one hand, they can appear to assert the full presence of a world, as they do in the Biblical psalms or the poetry of Smart, Whitman, Ginsberg and other rhapsodists. Such catalogues seem to project a crowded world, one so inexhaustibly rich in objects that it defies our abilities to master it through syntax; the best we can do is to begin naming its many parts, without any hope of ever finishing. Yet at the same time, the decon-textualization of words through the catalogue structure can have the opposite effect, that of evacuating language of presence, leaving only a shell behind – a word-list, a mere exhibition of words. Both tendencies are represented in *Ulysses*: on the one hand, the assemblages of the "Ithaca" chapter, projecting a world dense with things; on the other hand, the lists of comic names in the "Cyclops" chapter, transparently linguistic improvisations.

Catalogues in postmodernist fiction seem inevitably to gravitate toward the word-list pole, even if they begin as assemblages of objects. This mechanism can be observed in the hypertrophied lists of titles and names in Gilbert Sorrentino's *Mulligan Stew*, the mock-Homeric catalogues of Barthelme's *The Dead Father*, or the list of everything that is not nothing in the latter's "Nothing: A Preliminary Account" (from *Amateurs*, 1974). "The only form of discourse of which I approve," declares a character in Barthelme's "The Indian Uprising" (1978),

> is the litany. I believe our masters and teachers as well as plain citizens should confine themselves to what can safely be said. Thus when I hear the words *pewter, snake, tea, Fad #6 sherry, serviette, fenestration, crown, blue* coming from the mouth of some public official, or some raw youth, I am not disappointed. . . . Some people," Miss R. said, "run to conceits or wisdom but I hold to the hard, brown, nutlike word. I might point out that there is enough aesthetic excitement here to satisfy anyone but a dammed fool."[15]

But of course, *pace* Miss R., the hard, brown nutlike word is not the only linguistic object that may be manipulated to produce this peculiarly postmodernist aesthetic excitement. The sentence, too, can be made a source of such excitement. Characteristic of postmodernist writing is what might be called the device of deliberate nonfluency: the construction of sentences so awkward (to the point of ungrammaticality) that it is the sentence-structure itself that fixes the attention, distracting us from whatever content that structure might carry. Here, once again, Flaubert is the great precursor. Superfluous commas that disturb the rhythmical flow, deliberate anti-climaxes, elaborate constructions disproportionate to their trivial content – these are the features of the Flaubertian sentence, the means by which Flaubert sought to neutralize content and create a kind of monumental language. The result, as Culler has shown, is free-floating irony: these queer sentences *must*, we feel, signal an ironic intention, but it is impossible to determine what exactly is being ironized, or to reconstruct the ironist's position. Such sentences in effect disengage themselves from their discourse-context without having to be physically isolated in a "litany."[16]

Joyce has left us quite a number of deliberately non-fluent sentences, especially in the "Eumaeus" chapter of *Ulysses*. So, too, of course, has Gertrude Stein: e.g. "A dog which you have never had before has sighed" (from *How to Write*, 1931).[17] Donald Barthelme has even proposed an aesthetics of what he calls "back-broke sentences":

> I look for a particular kind of sentence, perhaps more often the awkward than the beautiful. A back-broke sentence is interesting. Any sentence that begins with the phrase, "It is not clear that . . ." is clearly clumsy but preparing itself for greatness of a kind. A way of backing into a story – of getting past the reader's hardwon armor.[18]

The back-broke sentence, like lexical exhibitionism and the catalogue structure, is a recurrent feature of postmodernist writing. Here is a brief anthology:[19]

> 1 The fact would seem to be, if in my situation one may speak of facts, not only that I shall have to speak of things of which I cannot speak, but also, which is even more interesting, but also that I, which is if possible even more interesting, that I shall have to, I forget, no matter.
>
> 2 And you can never touch a girl in the same way more than once, twice, or another number of times however much you may wish to hold, wrap, or otherwise fix her hand, or look, or some other quality, or incident, known to you previously.
>
> 3 Having acquired in exchange for an old house that had been theirs, his and hers, a radio or more properly radio *station*, Bloomsbury could now play "The Star-Spangled Banner," which he had always admired immoderately, on account of its finality, as often as he liked.
>
> 4 "The score?" The score is that nothing is happening in my heart, not even the action so familiar, you know, and one has to exercise those muscles to keep their tone.
>
> 5 The police are on their way now, over the fear-inducing back roads, many of them mountainous, that are known to be nerve-shattering even to the strongest nerves.

Sentences 1 and 2 are spectacular examples of the type of sentence that, in

Culler's words, "appears to fritter itself away."[20] Entropic sentences, they seem to run out of steam before our eyes, the first stumbling, in typical Beckett fashion, from one inarticulacy to the next, to the very brink of silence, while the second loses itself (and us) in a proliferation of unhelpful and confusing (pseudo-) logical alternatives, a miniature garden of forking paths. Sentences 3 and 4 are classic back-broke sentences; indeed, the opening phrase of sentence 4 ("The score is that nothing is happening") echoes Barthelme's example of a sentence that is "preparing itself for greatness of a kind." The back-brokenness of 4 is reinforced by the inexplicable intensifier ("*so* familiar"), and the indecisive vacillation of tone between colloquial "you know" (a phrase positioned so as to do maximum damage to the sentence's rhythm) and formal "one has to." Sentence 3 fulfills another of Barthelme's prescriptions: the opening sentence of a story, it "gets past the reader's hardwon armor" by holding its content in abeyance, using delaying tactics to suspend its main clause and then suspending its suspensions by introducing pointless elaborations ("theirs, his and hers," "a radio or more properly radio *station*") and even a gratuitous rhyme (immoderately/finality). Sentence 5 would seem to be on a par with the others; in fact, however, it represents a somewhat different phenomenon, since it emanates from a fictional author who appears to be undergoing a nervous breakdown. In other words, this is motivated solecism: the back-brokenness of this sentence must be read as a *symptom* of the author-character's condition, and thus has more in common with, say, the motivated stupidities of "Nausicaa" than with the other specimens in my little anthology.

"The ambition to write 'un livre sur rien,'" Culler tells us:

> can be realized only if readers can be cajoled into sucking the apparent content out of the sentences and leaving only that empty form which asks to be filled but makes one chary of actually filling it.[21]

The postmodernist sentences which I have quoted (and many others like them) do just that, inviting us to relieve them of their meaning and then defying us to put meaning back into them again. Only a sucker would take up the challenge: these sentences make suckers of their readers.

Back-broke sentences, taken to their ultimate extreme, yield what might be called *invertebrate* sentences, rambling, apparently interminable, shape-shifting constructions, of which Barthelme's "Sentence" (discussed on p. 139) is exemplary. Over nine pages long, Barthelme's one-sentence text intermittently projects scenes and anecdotes, then reabsorbs them into its own constantly-changing surface; the sentence

> has a festering conscience of its own, which persuades it to follow its star, and to move with all deliberate speed from one place to another, without losing any of the "riders" it may have picked up just by being there, on the page, and turning this way and that, to see what is over there, under that oddly-shaped tree, or over there, reflected in the rain barrel of the imagination.[22]

As a "man-made object," the sentence concludes about itself, it deserves "to be treasured for its weakness."[23] Here there is no question of content – the sentence is its own content. Its only *raison d'être* is self-exhibition. Comparable shape-shifting, invertebrate sentences occur in Beckett's *The Unnamable* and Gabriel García Márquez's *The Autumn of the Patriarch* (1975), as well as other places; the modernist precursors are Proust and Faulkner. These are "incestuous sentences," writes William Gass,

> sentences which follow their own turnings inward out of sight like the whorls of a shell, and which we follow warily, as Alice after that rabbit, nervous and white.[24]

These are the sentences, concludes Gass, which "we should like to love – the ones which love us and themselves as well." The sentence from which these phrases have been lifted is itself dozens of lines long, a specimen of what it describes – incestuous, lovable. More than merely a particularly conspicuous example of stylistic exhibitionism, it is, as Gass's allusion to Alice and the White Rabbit suggests, a kind of Wonderland – a heterotopian space, a zone.

Letters

Such stylistic strategies as lexical exhibitionism, the catalogue, and back-broke and invertebrate sentences strew obstacles in the path that leads from text continuum to reconstructed world, making the process of reconstruction more difficult, hence more highly visible. But this does not yet mark the limit of postmodernist radical stylization. It is possible to heighten still further the visibility of the reconstructive process by taking the words of the text continuum literally, *à la lettre*.

This is what Richard Brautigan does when, in *The Tokyo–Montana Express* (1980), he designates Osaka as the "orange Capital of the Orient." The real-world Osaka, so far as I can discover, has nothing in particular to do with oranges; nevertheless, Brautigan's motive for associating Osaka with oranges is transparent – transparent in the sense that it depends on the signifiers of the signs in question, on the word in the most literal sense. Osaka is the Orange Capital of the Orient simply because Osaka, Orange and Orient all begin with the letter "O." There is, moreover, an iconic relationship involved: at the level of the written (printed) word, the letter "O" resembles an orange. Here formal features of the verbal signifier – alliteration, even letter-shape – have been given the power to generate signifieds; the word transparently determines the make-up of Brautigan's world.

In a sense, of course, the words of the text continuum *always* determine the reconstructed world of the text, for it is on the basis of the text's verbal signs that we reconstruct its world. But this determination of world by word is normally kept in the background, below the threshold of perceptibility, allowing us to efface the text continuum in favor of a world which we may think of as free-standing, independent of the text's language, or even as itself *determining* the text's language – the reverse of the true state of affairs. Texts like Brautigan's, however, foreground the determination of world by word, visibly placing the world at the mercy of the word, indeed at the mercy of the *letter*.

A world at the mercy of the alphabet: this is the principle of the "abecedary," the familiar mnemonic device for children learning their alphabet:

A was an archer,
who shot at a frog;
B was a butcher,
and had a great dog.
C was a captain,

and so on, down to the letter Z. A rudimentary fiction, this abecedary, like others of its kind, in effect projects piecemeal a (very partial) fictional world: a cast of "characters," each one identified by profession and associated (somewhat arbitrarily, through the exigencies of rhyme) with some creature, inanimate object, or quality. An effective tool for ordering words, and therefore for ordering a world, alphabetization has sometimes been used to impose arbitrary order on postmodernist texts. This is especially characteristic of texts in the tradition of Menippean satire, hybrid fictional-nonfictional, discursive-narrative texts which are often made up of discontinuous, heterogeneous fragments. Such fragments may be assembled into a transparently arbitrary order by assigning each fragment a chapter-heading or key-word and alphabetizing them. This is the ordering principle, for instance, of Gilbert Sorrentino's *Splendide-Hôtel* (1973), Roland Barthes's *Le Plaisir du texte* (1973) and *Fragments d'un discours amoureux* (1977), and Kenneth Gangemi's *The Volcanoes from Puebla* (1979). "One must find some structure," Sorrentino comments, "even if it is the haphazard one of the alphabet."[25] He is being disingenuous; alphabetical order has not been fixed on in these texts *faute de mieux*, but precisely in order to flaunt their haphazardness.

John Barth goes a step further in this same direction in his novel-in-letters called, appropriately, *LETTERS* (1979). Here Barth uses the seven letters of his title to determine the overall structure of his text, somewhat as Sorrentino, Barthes, and Gangemi do when they surrender the ordering of their texts to the arbitrariness of the alphabet. But where they exploit alphabetical order, Barth uses the *shapes* of the letters. He superimposes the seven capital letters L, E, T, T, E, R, S on the calendars for the months March through September, 1969; the dates covered by the letter-forms determine *when* the letters making up this epistolary novel are written. This scheme also determines *who* writes, for each of Barth's seven correspondents writes only on one particular day of the week: thus, Lady Amherst writes only on Saturdays, Todd Andrews only on Fridays, Jacob Horner on Thursdays, and so on. So, for instance, the shape of the letter L, superimposed on the calendar for March, 1969, determines that The Author writes letters on the four consecutive Sundays of the month, namely the 2nd, 9th, 16th, and 23rd; Ambrose Mensch writes on Monday the 3rd; Jerome Bray writes on Tuesday the 4th; A. B. Cook writes on Wednesday the 5th; Jacob Horner writes on Thursday the 6th; Todd Andrews writes on Friday the 7th; and Lady Amherst writes on Saturday the 8th; and so on for the other six months, and the other six letters, that make up *LETTERS*.[26]

Thus *LETTERS* is a "world of letters" in several punning senses. An epistolary novel, or novel-in-letters, it is also *about* the world of letters in the sense of the institutions of literature and the literary life, as well as, of course, being conspicuously *determined* by letters. But if it constitutes a world of letters in this latter, literalistic sense, it does so only in its gross architectonic structure; the details of its world are apparently free, not visibly determined by constraints at the level of the text continuum. For a world in which even the details of space, time, description, narration, plot, and character are subject to the determination of letters, we need to turn to a text such as Walter Abish's *Alphabetical Africa* (1974),[27] or, even more elusive and disturbing, his "Ardor/Awe/Atrocity" (from *In the Future Perfect*, 1977).

"Ardor/Awe/Atrocity" appears at first glance to be another variant on the abecedary, something like Sorrentino's *Splendide-Hôtel* or Gangemi's *Volcanoes from Puebla*. Each of its twenty-six short fragments is headed by three words beginning with the same letter of the alphabet, from "Ardor/Awe/Atrocity" and "Buoyant/Bob/Body" to "You/Yelled/Youthfulness" and "Zoo/Zodiac/Zero." But the similarity with alphabetically-ordered texts ends here, for these headings are not key-words, and in fact bear no discernible relation to the textual fragments they introduce; the juxtaposition, it appears, is wholly arbitrary. Furthermore, each head-word has been assigned a superscript number, from 1 to 78: thus, "Ardor[1]/Awe[2]/Atrocity[3]," "Buoyant[4]/Bob[5]/Body[6]," and so on. Whenever the head-words appear anywhere in the text itself, they carry this same superscript number. The result is a sort of cross-referencing system, each recurrence of a given word being referred through its superscript number to every other occurrence of the same word, both in the body of the text and in the heading.

But what purpose does this cross-referencing system have? None whatsoever, except to foreground certain verbal repetitions. Thus the reader is constantly being distracted from the level of world to the level of words by means of a transparently pointless and empty formalism. The syntactical flow is disturbed, the projected world undermined, collapsing time and again, then reconstituting itself only to collapse once more; it flickers. The reader becomes schizoid, his or her attention divided between the level of world and the level of words. And this ontological tension is further exacerbated by the nature of this text's content. "Ardor/Awe/Atrocity" represents a woman's increasing and ultimately fatal involvement in sadomasochistic sexual practices. The juxtaposition between this highly-charged sexual material and the coolly arbitrary formal pattern is intensely strange and disorienting:[28]

> The wall-to-wall rug in the room is an off-white,[68] the tiles in the bathroom are white,[68] so is the washbasin, the bathroom ceiling, and the Venetian blinds. Knees[31] are for supporting the body[6] in a crouching position[48] as the man who is holding her by the waist thrusts[58] himself into her again and again. Both she and the man are committed to complete silence. Each is immersed in his own watchfulness as the bodies[6] acquire greater and greater independence, disregarding the instructions they keep receiving from their separate centers of communication, their minds.

Here once again, in other words, we have "bowel-turning material" surrounded with "kitty litter," "stuff that is there purely for play," as William

Gass says. The result, as in the case of Guy Davenport's lexical exhibitionism, is electrical: we are arrested by the contents of this text – whether attracted or repelled makes no difference – and simultaneously alienated, distanced, by its transparently arbitrary form. Ontological instability is the consequence: the world flickers between presence and absence, between reconstructed reality and words on the page. In all these abecedarian texts, *Alphabetical Africa* and *LETTERS* as well as, more acutely, "Ardor/Awe/Atrocity," ontological structure becomes a foreground source of tension and disorientation; it cannot be taken for granted.

Machines

An alphabet is a machine for generating texts and their worlds. This is so in the trivial sense that all the words of a text are made from the letters of the alphabet; but it becomes true in a more substantial way when the alphabet is allowed to determine the order of the text, as in *Splendide-Hôtel* or *LETTERS*, or even the details of its world, as in *Alphabetical Africa*. In these cases, part of the "freedom" of fiction has been ceded to the automatic unfolding of a pre-established scheme. Whenever such an automatic, pre-established scheme is in place, it serves to foreground fiction's determination "from below," the way in which the world of fiction depends upon the words of a text.

If abecedarian texts such as *LETTERS* or *Alphabetical Africa* are in this sense "automatic," machine-generated, how much more so are the strange text-machines of Raymond Roussel, *Impressions d'Afrique* (1910) and *Locus Solus* (1914). Full of bizarre, apparently fantastic inventions and spectacles, and grossly implausible turns of events, Roussel's worlds are nevertheless not the fruit of a surrealist imagination (although the surrealists later "adopted" him as one of their own). Rather, they are end-products of a system for generating fictional objects and narratives from latent, pretextual puns and word-games.[29] Roussel's procedure involved taking a standard French idiom or expression, or a line of verse by a "classic" author, and manipulating it in such a way as to preserve homonymy (more or less) while radically altering the meaning. Thus, for example, beginning with a couplet from Victor Hugo,

Oh revers oh leçon quand l'enfant de cet homme
Eut reçu pour hochet la couronne de Rome,

Roussel reinterprets the second line as

Ursule brochet lac Huronne drome[30]

– roughly equivalent in sound to the original, but wildly different in meaning. Next he constructs a fragment of a world in which the state of affairs projected by this reinterpreted line could occur. In this case, he improvises a spurious American Indian legend involving a certain Ursula who magically restores four transformed malefactors to their original shapes. This is how Roussel's worlds have been generated – piecemeal, each part constructed to motivate or realize the state of affairs projected by a particular pun. Roussel's procedure demonstrates with maximum purity the "play of the signifier" – worlds determined "from below," by word-play.

There are certain difficulties with this procedure as a means of foregrounding the relation between text continuum and reconstructed world, however. For one thing, if Roussel's texts are supposed to demonstrate the play of the signifier, shouldn't the reader be enabled to play along, so to speak? Unlike the alphabetically-ordered texts of Barth or Abish, Roussel's machinery for textual generation is not transparent but opaque, inaccessible to the reader. Indeed, we would not even suspect that these texts had been generated mechanically had Roussel not described his procedures in his posthumously-published pamphlet, *Comment j'ai écrit certains de mes livres* (1935). Even here, only a handful of Roussel's many puns are explicated; the rest are irretrievable. What good is an opaque machine, if the object is to render visible the world-making process? Writes Linda Hutcheon:

> If linguistic play is going to activate the productive labour involved in reading, it presumably has to be textually immanent, and in some way evident: cryptograms are different from anagrams. . . . Roussel's texts do *not* point, however, to their linguistic pre-textual generators.[31]

Furthermore, it is often difficult to distinguish overdetermined, machine-generated texts like Roussel's from what ought to be their diametric opposite, underdetermined, aleatory texts. Both types of procedure produce much the same effect, perceptually, Christopher Butler has argued. Whether overdetermined, like the integral serialism of Pierre Boulez, or underdetermined, like the aleatory music of John Cage, the effect on the reader is one of "alloverness," a flood of stimuli all of equal importance, lacking hierarchy or syntax.[32] Ultimately, the underlying machinery of Roussel generates text which, at least in places, is barely distinguishable from many passages in William Burroughs' fiction. But these passages from Burroughs have, we know, been generated by aleatory procedures: pre-existing texts have been physically cut up, scrambled, and randomly reassembled, or two texts have been folded together at random to produce a new, hybrid text.[33] But if Roussel's overdetermined texts are perceptually identical with the sorts of textual accidents courted by Burroughs, then how can they serve to foreground fiction's determination "from below"?

In fact, these are both pseudoproblems, it seems to me. If the object of such texts, machine-generated and aleatory alike, is to expose the dependency of the reconstructed world on the text continuum, then, despite what Hutcheon says, a cryptogram *will* serve as well as an anagram. The reader need not be able to retrace the operations of Roussel's text-generating puns, for instance, in all their details, as Hutcheon seems to assume; he or she only needs to be aware of the fact that such a procedure has been used. The machine does not have to be fully visible in order for the foregrounding to work; it only has to be conspicuously present, conspicuously *in place*. And this is as true of aleatory procedures as it is of mechanical procedures: as long as we are aware that Burroughs has cut up and folded in other texts in order to generate the text we are reading, then the foregrounding works much as it does in the case of overdetermined text-machines. The perceptual similarity of the end-product is not as important, from the point of view of an ontological poetics, as our knowledge of how these texts have been generated. From this point of view, chance-generated and machine-generated texts are functionally equivalent.

And there is no question that both Roussel and Burroughs keep us aware of how their texts have been generated. In the case of Roussel, there is the evidence of his "instruction-manual," *Comment j'ai écrit*, which, as Foucault has argued, is the key and organizing center of his entire *oeuvre*.[34] But even if one is inclined to view the appeal to an ancillary text as in some way illegitimate, Roussel, like Burroughs, has made a point of announcing his pretextual text-generating procedures in the texts themselves. Both Roussel's and Burroughs's texts incorporate representations or scale-models of their own procedures, some of them constituting structures *en abyme* in the strict sense, others not. Hence, in Roussel, the proliferation of zany machines preprogrammed to produce works of art, the *tableaux vivants* purporting to show, for instance, "Handel composing the theme of his oratorio, *Vesper*, by a mechanical process" (in *Impressions d'Afrique*). Hence, in Burroughs, the many episodes in which the protagonist cuts up or splices together or folds in a text or a tape or a film, even the Mayan Codices, as a means of disrupting the authority of those with the power of control over minds, and opening up new possibilities. Hence, above all, the "writing machine" incorporated *en abyme* in the text of Burroughs's *The Ticket That Exploded* (1962):

> A writing machine that shifts one half one text and half the other through a page frame on conveyor belts – (The proportion of half one text half the other is important corresponding as it does to the two halves of the human organism) Shakespeare, Rimbaud, etc. permutating through page frames in constantly changing juxtaposition – the machine spits out books and plays and poems – The spectators are invited to feed into the machine any pages of their own text in fifty-fifty juxtaposition with any author of their choice and provided with the result in a few minutes.[35]

The writing machine lays bare the way in which the world of *The Ticket That Exploded* has been generated "from below" by Burroughs's aleatory procedures. More than that, it lays bare the way in which *every* text really is, as Umberto Eco says, *"a machine for producing possible worlds."*[36]

11: WORLDS OF DISCOURSE

The novel is the expression of a Galilean perception of language, one that denies the absolutism of a single and unitary language – that is, that refuses to acknowledge its own language as the sole verbal and semantic center of the ideological universe.

(Mixail Baxtin, "Discourse in the novel," 1934–5)

The litany, or catalogue, is the only form of discourse of which Donald Barthelme's Miss R. approves. But is the sort of litany she has in mind really a form of discourse at all, or is it rather a subversion of discourse, an anti-discourse? Here is Miss R.'s own example of an "approved" discourse:[1]

pewter
snake
tea
Fad #6 sherry
serviette
fenestration
crown
blue.

Such a catalogue, we know, functions to disengage words from syntax, thus hindering the reconstruction of the projected world, and foregrounding the ontological difference between the stratum of words and the stratum of worlds. But it also has another function, for it forces us to reflect on the principles of selection and order that could have produced such a hetero-geneous assemblage. Is this a word-list, and if so, what governed the selection of these words, and their arrangement in this particular order? Not alphabetization, or any of the other familiar ways of ordering a list of words. Or is it a collection of objects, and if so, why these particular objects? Miss R. herself is of little help in elucidating the underlying principles of her dis-course: "I run to liquids and colors,"[2] she says, but these categories account for no more than half the items.

The problem becomes more acute, and our disorientation even stronger, when a catalogue of Miss R.'s sort appears in a context which claims to be representational – for instance, when such a catalogue purports to describe a barricade thrown up against the marauding Indians:

> I analyzed the composition of the barricade nearest me and found two ashtrays, ceramic, one dark brown and one dark brown with an orange blur at the lip; a tin frying pan; two-litre bottles of red wine; three-quarter-litre bottles of Black & White, aquavit, cognac, vodka, gin, Fad #6 sherry; a hollow-core door in birch veneer on black wrought-iron legs; a blanket, red-orange with faint blue stripes; a red pillow and a blue pillow; a woven straw wastebasket; two glass jars for flowers; corkscrews and can openers; two plates and two cups, ceramic, dark brown; a yellow-and-purple poster; a Yugoslavian carved flute, wood, dark brown; and other items.[3]

This assemblage does not cohere either as discourse or as representation; order is conspicuous by its absence. No principle of selection can be proposed that would account for the make-up of this barricade – not even the principle of selecting items that could not plausibly be used in barricade-construction, since the catalogue does include a "hollow-core door," which might plausibly serve in a barricade. But not in *this* barricade.

"The thing we apprehend in one great leap," writes Michel Foucault:

> the thing that, by means of the fable, is demonstrated as the exotic charm of another system of thought, is the limitation of our own, the stark impossibility of thinking *that*.[4]

He is referring to the heterogeneous Chinese encyclopedia of Borges' fable, but he might as well be talking about the impossible litanies of Barthelme's "The Indian Uprising" (1978). What we learn from Barthelme's litanies is the stark impossibility of thinking *that* – of thinking the order of things that could have generated such an assemblage. Reflecting on the impossibility of such an order, we come also to reflect on the ideas of order which *are* possible for us to think. The form of discourse of which Miss R. approves is, in this sense, the "other" of our own familiar discourses, and reflecting on this unthinkable "other" makes us freshly aware of our own discourses, and of discursive ordering in general.

So perhaps we should say that Miss R.'s sort of litany is not a "form of discourse" at all, but rather a *heterotopia*, the disorder that is made up of fragments of a number of incommensurable orders. Like the heterotopian space of the zone, where incommensurable spaces are juxtaposed or super-imposed, here discursive orders mingle promiscuously without gelling into any sort of overarching "super-order." In fact, the world of "The Indian Uprising," in which these assemblages appear, is itself a heterotopia. From moment to moment in the world of this text we undergo disorienting shifts among what Barthelme calls "situations" – in effect, shifts from one world to another:

> Once I caught Kenneth's coat going down the stairs by itself but the coat was a trap and inside a Comanche who made a thrust with his short, ugly knife at my leg which buckled and tossed me over the balustrade through a

window and into another situation. Not believing that your body brilliant as it was and your fat, liquid spirit distinguished and angry as it was were stable quantities to which one could return on wires more than once, twice, or another number of times I said: "See the table?"[5]

Abruptly, without the least motivation, we, along with Barthelme's protagonist, are literally precipitated into a different world. And this other world in which we find ourselves is characterized by a different mode or genre of discourse; it *is*, in effect, this other mode of discourse, and the shift we have undergone is a shift between different discursive orders, different worlds of discourse.

Thus the heterotopian form of discourse, or antidiscourse, of which Miss R. approves, actually mirrors the global structure of "The Indian Uprising": it functions as a scale-model of that global structure, a *mise-en-abyme*. Conversely, "The Indian Uprising," in the global structure of its projected world, literalizes or realizes the uneasy juxtaposition of discourses that characterizes Miss R.'s litanies, turning incommensurable *discourse* into incommensurable *worlds*, and a discursive heterotopia into an ontological heterotopia. At both levels, that of global structure and that of structure *en abyme*, "The Indian Uprising" confronts us with the unthinkable "other" of our own familiar discourses, and forces us to reflect on the discursive order of things.

Discourse in the novel

Postmodernist fictions such as Donald Barthelme's "The Indian Uprising" are fictions *about* the order of things, discourses which reflect upon the worlds of discourse. As such, they participate in that very general tendency in the intellectual life of our time toward viewing reality as *constructed* in and through our languages, discourses, and semiotic systems. Especially identified with Wittgenstein and linguistic philosophy, and more recently with Michel Foucault, this intellectual tendency is by now widely diffused throughout the so-called "human sciences."[6] Not everyone has been able to sympathize with postmodernist fiction's role in this project of unmasking the constructed nature of reality, however. There is in some quarters considerable nostalgia for fiction in which the emphasis falls upon the order of *things* rather than upon the *order* of things – for, in other words, a mimetic fiction purporting to give direct access to extralinguistic and extratextual reality, and for a criticism willing to acknowledge the legitimacy of this claim, instead of suspiciously deconstructing it.

Among those who exhibit this nostalgia for unproblematic mimesis, Robert Alter is one of the most enlightened and most persuasive. "The attack on mimesis ultimately depends," Alter writes, "on defining experience out of existence,"[7] and so he sets about defending real-world experience from its deconstructors. The word *tiger*, as everyone has known since Saussure, is a sign which acquires its meaning from the system of relations among the other signifiers and signifieds of the language; it is only conventionally and arbitrarily related, Alter concedes, to "the real striped beast in the jungle." *Tiger*, the word, may of course function in a text such as, for instance, Jorge

Luis Borges' "El otro tigre." But this certainly does not mean that the *real* tiger has been textualized. The ontological status of the real tiger is unaffected by the textualization of the word *tiger*: "We are free to decenter, deconstruct, decode, re-encode a tiger in a text, but even the hardiest structuralist would not step inside the cage with the real beast, whose fangs and claws, after all, are more than a semiotic pattern." And certain texts, "El otro tigre" among them, aspire to evoke the direct experience of that irreducibly real, irreducibly extra-textual tiger. These are the texts which we describe as mimetic.

Alter's witty parable of the tiger makes a strong, commonsensical case for mimesis and the *pre*constructed nature of reality, but not an unanswerable one. The best answer might be formulated in terms of the by-now widely familiar poetics of the Russian literary theorist, Mixail Baxtin. In effect, Baxtin reminds us of how little the novel has historically been concerned with real-world experience on the order of Alter's irreducibly real tiger, and how much it has been concerned with *human* and *social* reality – reality that is first and foremost linguistic and discursive, reality experienced in and through discourse. In Baxtin's view, the function of the novel, throughout its history, has been to represent *that* reality in all its polyphonic complexity, and not the tigerish reality which Alter is so intent on defending. Its purpose has been, we might say, to represent not the tiger but "the tiger" – "tiger" as a sign in human semiotic systems, one which changes as it passes from discourse to discourse, from speaker to speaker, becoming a miniature arena in which the dialogues between different voices and discourses are acted out. A mimetic theory of fiction, Baxtin's theory is nevertheless unlikely to satisfy the nostalgia for unproblematic mimesis, for what the novel mimes, according to Baxtin, is social discourses, the vehicles of human social experience.[8]

From the Baxtinian point of view, then, postmodernist fictions about the discursive order of things, such as Barthelme's "The Indian Uprising," only carry a step further the reflection upon discourse which has been characteristic of the novel throughout its history, merely giving an extra turn to the screw of discursive self-consciousness. Or perhaps, bearing in mind our reading of Barthelme's text, we ought to say that postmodernist fiction literalizes or realizes what in Baxtin is only a metaphor: the metaphor of "worlds" of discourse. Behind each discourse in the novel, as indeed behind each discourse in social life, we can, according to Baxtin, discern the ideological position or world-view which animates it and from which it emanates:

> Every language in the novel is a point of view, a socio-ideological conceptual system of real social groups and their embodied representatives . . . any point of view on the world fundamental to the novel must be a concrete, socially embodied point of view, not an abstract, purely semantic position; it must, consequently, have its own language with which it is organically united. A novel is constructed not on abstract differences in meaning nor on merely narrative collisions, but on concrete social speech diversity.[9]

Baxtin slips easily from the abstractions of "socio-ideological conceptual system" and "socially embodied point of view" to the convenient metaphor of "worlds":

Actual social life and historical becoming create within an abstractly unitary national language a multitude of concrete worlds, a multitude of bounded verbal-ideological and social belief systems.[10]

Baxtin himself comes close to literalizing his own metaphor when, in the passage I have cited as my epigraph, he speaks of the novel's "Galilean perception of language" – Galilean as in Galileo, that is. Unlike the Ptolemaic, geocentric model of the universe which preceded him, and which he helped to unseat, Galileo perceived the universe as comprising a plurality of worlds. Similarly, the polyphonic novel, unlike monological genres, acknowledges and embraces a plurality of discourses and the ideologies and world-views associated with them. This is still metaphor, of course, but metaphor barely a step away from its literalization in the interplanetary motifs of science-fiction – or postmodernist fiction.[11] To speak of "world-views," and the juxtaposition or confrontation of world-views, is to speak in epistemological terms; to take the metaphor literally, projecting worlds which are the realizations of discursive world-views, is to convert an epistemological motif into an ontological one.

Baxtin has shown us how dialogue among discourses is a staple of all polyphonic novels. Postmodernist fiction, by heightening the polyphonic structure and sharpening the dialogue in various ways, foregrounds the ontological dimension of the confrontation among discourses, thus achieving a polyphony of *worlds*.

Heteroglossia

"A novel is constructed," Baxtin tells us, "not on abstract differences in meaning nor on merely narrative collisions, but on concrete social speech diversity." The "concreteness" of this diversity of discourse is secured by using different repertoires of stylistic features, correlating with different situations or uses of language – what M. A. K. Halliday would call *registers*.[12] The interweaving of different registers in the text of the novel produces the effect of *heteroglossia*, plurality of discourse; and it is this concrete heteroglossia which serves as the vehicle for the confrontation and dialogue among world-views and ideologies in the novel, its orchestrated *polyphony* of voices.

It is important to distinguish between the formal and stylistic heteroglossia of a text and its ideological polyphony, for heteroglossic texts are not inevitably polyphonic. Thus, for example, "classic" modernist texts such as *The Waste Land* or Dos Passos's *U.S.A.* trilogy are genuinely heteroglossic, juxtaposing and interweaving a variety of languages, styles, registers, genres, and intertextual citations; yet their heteroglossic form is held in check by a unifying monological perspective.[13] Resisting the "pluralization" of worlds which is implicit in heteroglossia, modernist texts integrate the multiple worlds of discourse into a single ontological plane, a unified projected world. Or rather they *strive toward* such an integration and unification; for heteroglossia is not easily kept under control, and tends to exert a centrifugal counterpressure on the text. Eliot's notorious notes to *The Waste Land* attest to the strength of this counterpressure. By drawing attention in his notes to the presence of his poem's unifying mythic structure, Eliot seems to be trying to buttress it, to assert unity in the face of the text's dis-integrative tendencies. Paradoxically, the notes actually tend to have the opposite effect, further complicating the already complicated form of the poem by introducing another genre of discourse – that of scholarly footnotes – and aggravating the text's dis-integration by foregrounding the problem of its *boundaries* (do the notes stand inside or outside the text proper? what *is* the "text proper"?). Polyphony, in other words, is *inadvertent* in modernist writing, an unintended side-effect of heteroglossia. Postmodernism erects this advertence into a positive principle; the side-effect is shifted to the center. Instead of resisting centrifugal tendencies, postmodernist fiction seeks to enhance them. Heteroglossia is used here as an opening wedge, a means of breaking up the unified projected world into a polyphony of worlds of discourse.

How heteroglossic diversity serves as an opening wedge for polyphony is suggested by Donald Barthelme in a comic parable from *Snow White* (1967). Here Jane writes a letter to a certain unfortunate Mr Quistgaard, drawing his attention to the discontinuity between the "universe of discourse" he occupies and her own:

> You and I, Mr. Quistgaard, are not in the same universe of discourse. You may not have been aware of it previously, but the fact of the matter is, that we are not. We exist in different universes of discourse. . . . It may never have crossed your mind to think that other universes of discourse distinct from your own existed, with people in them, discoursing. You may have, in a commonsense way, regarded your own u. of d. as a plenum, filled to the brim with discourse. You may have felt that what already existed was a sufficiency. People like you often do.[14]

Jane threatens to introduce discourse from her own "universe of discourse" into Quistgaard's universe, thus disrupting, in effect "pluralizing," his monological world:

> At any moment I can pierce your plenum with a single telephone call, simply by dialing 989-7777. You are correct, Mr. Quistgaard, in seeing this as a threatening situation. The moment I inject discourse from my u. of d. into your u. of d., the yourness of yours is diluted. The more I inject, the more you dilute. Soon you will be presiding over an empty plenum, or rather, since that is a contradiction in terms, over a former plenum, in terms of yourness. You are, essentially, in my power. I suggest an unlisted number.[15]

There is a striking analogy between this "injection" of alien discourse into a closed, homogeneous world of discourse, and the fantastic motif of "another world's intrusion into this one." Much as the other-worldly spirits penetrate and seize the middle-class house in Cortázar's fantastic story, "House Taken Over" (from *End of the Game*, 1978), or Dr Hoffman threatens to overwhelm the City with unreality in Angela Carter's *The Infernal Desire Machines of Dr Hoffman* (1972), so here Jane threatens to penetrate and overwhelm Mr Quistgaard's monological world of discourse.

This is only a parable, but in fact the strategy of "injecting" a specialized register of language into a homogeneous discourse-world, as a means of inducing polyphony, is typical of postmodernist fiction. Barthelme himself uses this strategy in texts like "The Police Band" (1968), where the highly incongruous specialized register of jazz breaks in upon the world of police discourse, with disorienting effect:

> What are our duties? we asked at the interview.
> Your duties are to wail, the Commissioner said.[16]

This same strategy also underlies William Gass's story "Icicles" (1968), where the closed discourse-world of a real-estate agency is uncannily disrupted by the injection of discourse from, of all things, the highly specialized register of flower arrangement.[17]

More radical than this intrusion of one specialized register into the world of another is the strategy of antilanguage. An antilanguage is the specialized discourse of a deviant social group – either deviant in the usual negative sense (e.g. criminal and prison subcultures) or what we might call prestigiously deviant (e.g. military elites, religious mystics, perhaps even poets). Just as the group's behavior deviates from social norms, so analogously its language deviates from the standard. Antilanguage is developed through systematic transformation of the standard language, especially through such lexical processes as relexicalization (adaptation of a standard word to special, nonstandard use within the group) and overlexicalization (proliferation of synonyms or near-synonyms for concepts especially important to the group). Thus, an antilanguage is inherently *dialogic*, in Baxtin's sense of the term, conducting an implicit polemic against the standard language and its world-view. It creates in effect an "anti-world-view," a counterreality of its own that is dialectically related to "straight" or "official" reality.[18]

Roger Fowler has described the function of the criminal antilanguage in William Burroughs's *Naked Lunch* (1959). Here, Fowler argues, the implicit dialogue between language and antilanguage, reality and counterreality, generates a true polyphony and not, as in modernist writing (or in Fowler's other example, Anthony Burgess's *A Clockwork Orange*), a polyphony that ultimately flattens out into monologue:

> If *Naked Lunch* is successfully polyphonic, it is not so merely because it includes a large number of distinct social voices. It is so because each of these voices embodies a significant ideological position . . . and because these ideologies related to one another, and to an implicit norm ideology, dialectically.[19]

Among the devices that Burroughs uses to foreground the language/ antilanguage dialectic in *Naked Lunch*, Fowler observes, is that of glossing specialized counterculture vocabulary, translating it into the language of the "straight" world:

> (Note: Grass is English thief slang for inform.)
> (Note: People is New Orleans slang for narcotic fuzz.)
> (Note: Yen pox is the ash of smoked opium.)
> (Note: Make in the sense of dig or size up.)[20]

The effect of such glossing is not, as the text seems to pretend, helpful, but on the contrary aggressive, alienating:

> it draws attention to the limitations of readers' knowledge; suggests that the narrator knows that the reader's knowledge is limited, that the reader is an outsider.[21]

Another of Burroughs's foregrounding devices may be illustrated from *The Ticket That Exploded* (1962) – namely, quick-cutting back and forth between passages of antilanguage and a specialized register of "straight" language:

> (desperately effete negation of societal values fecundate with orifices perspective and the ambivalent smugness of unavowed totalitarianism.)
>
> I knew why he was standing there. He didn't have the ready to fill his script. He was waiting for somebody he could touch.
>
> (foundering in disproportionate exasperation he doesn't even achieve the irrelevant honesty of hysteria but rather an uneasy somnolence counterpointed by the infantile exposure of fragmentary suburban genitalia.)
>
> "Need bread for your script, man?"[22]

The ready, script, touch, bread – these belong to the "shop talk" of the underworld, specifically, in this case, the junkie underworld. The "straight" register parodied here is what Burroughs calls "prose abstracted to a point where no image track occurs" – that is, intellectual prose, in this case the review of a book that sounds suspiciously like Burroughs' own. Thus, the implicit dialectic between "straight" reality and criminal counterreality is brought into the open: on the one side, the antilanguage of the junkie world projected by Burroughs' book; on the other, the language which the official culture uses to talk *about* that book and its world.

Interestingly, Burroughs stages this confrontation between language and antilanguage without violating the mimetic framework of the episode. The quick-cutting is motivated by the fictional situation: Inspector Lee, while waiting for a junkie suspect to arrive at the chemist's for his fix, browses through an issue of *Encounter* at a newsstand. There are other texts, however, in which the confrontation between worlds of discourse occurs outside of any motivating context, in a representational void; where the only worlds we are able to reconstruct are the worlds *of* discourses, and not any fictional world that might plausibly contain them. This is the case, for instance, with Donald Barthelme's collage texts, including "The Viennese Opera Ball" (1964), "A Picture History of the War" (1968), "The Rise of Capitalism" (1972), "Aria" (1981), and of course "The Indian Uprising." Of these the earliest, "The Viennese Opera Ball," is in some ways the most radical, for here the mimetic framework that might serve to motivate the clash of discourses realistically has been reduced to the absolute minimum – namely, to the phrase "the Viennese Opera Ball" itself. Punctuating the collage of disparate genres and registers – obstetrics, anthropology, etiquette, marriage manual, magazine genres (*Glamour, Fortune*), encyclopedia entries, botany, arts foundation report, index to a book on Dostoyevski, specifications for an electrical generator, sentences quoted from Hemingway's "The Short Happy Life of

Francis Macomber" – this recurrent phrase indicates, though only residually, the presence of a fictional situation.

In "A Picture History of the War," by contrast, identifiable fictional characters have been projected into the foreground of the collage text: Kellerman and his father, the general. General Kellerman is unmistakably a preliminary sketch for the Dead Father, a quasi-allegorical authority-figure representing a conservative and univocal culture. This Father-figure with a capital "F" acts out the conflict between a monological world-view and the multiple-world universe of Barthelme's polyphonic text. "Why does language subvert me," the general exclaims:

> subvert my seniority, my medals, my oldness, whenever it gets a chance? What does language have against me – me that has been good to it, respecting its little peculiarities and nicilosities, for sixty years?[23]

(Reaching for our dictionaries to look up "nicilosities," we may well wonder what Barthelme's language has against *us*.) Through his parable of General Kellerman, Barthelme directs our attention to the subversive potential of polyphony, its relativizing and leveling effect, its undermining of stable, univocal ontology.

Barthelme juxtaposes discourses along a *horizontal* axis. That is, segments from different discourses are spliced end-to-end in "The Viennese Opera Ball" or "A Picture History of the War," and the ontological tension between incommensurable discourse-worlds develops, so to speak, *across the seams* between adjacent segments. It is also possible, however, to construct a *vertical* collage. In this case, two or more discourse-worlds coexist within the same segment. Extrapolated to the dimensions of a six-hundred-page text, this strategy of "internal dialogism"[24] becomes the structural principle of Joyce's *Finnegans Wake*. Here each segment belongs to two or more discourses at the same time; the result is a layering of discourses, a *lamination*:

> Is it not that we are commanding from fullback, woman permitting, a profusely fine birdseye view from beauhind this park? Finn his park has been much the admiration of all the stranger ones, grekish and romanos, who arrive to here. The straight road down the centre (see relief map) bisexes the park which is said to be the largest of his kind in the world. On the right prominence confronts you the handsome vinesregent's lodge while, turning to the other supreme piece of cheeks, exactly opposite, you are confounded by the equally handsome chief sacristary's residence. Around is a little amiably tufted and man is cheered when he bewonders through the boskage how the nature in all frisko is enlivened by gentlemen's seats . . . . The black and blue marks athwart the weald, which now barely is so stripped, indicate the presence of sylvious beltings. Therewithal shady rides lend themselves out to rustic cavalries. In younder valley, too, stays mountain sprite. Any pretty dears are to be caught inside but it is a bad pities of the plain. A scarlet pimparnell now mules the mound where anciently first murders were wanted to take root.[25]

Leaving aside the many local effects of internal dialogism, we can discern in this passage two superimposed discourses: at one level, the register of a tourist's guidebook (a book rather than a tour-guide's discourse, because of "see relief map"); at another level, a sexual discourse, transforming the topography of Phoenix Park ("Finn his park") into the topography of the male body, with special emphasis on the buttocks (*beauhind, cheeks, gentlemen's seats*). The park, as well as being the body, is also apparently the site of sexual activity – sadomasochistic activity? (note *black and blue marks, weald, beltings*). In any case, the "pretty dears" that may be caught in the park at the level of the sexual discourse do double duty as decorative animals at the level of the guidebook discourse. The relation between the two discourses invites allegorization: we might say that just as the park's foliage and topography hides sexual goings-on, so the "innocent" discourse of the guidebook hides the language of sexuality.[26]

Notoriously, Joyce builds up his vertical collage not merely from the registers and discourses of the English language, but from other national languages as well. *Finnegans Wake* is a multilingual text in the strict sense, nearly every phrase yielding a bi- or tri- or even quadri-lingual pun. According-ing to Baxtin, radical heteroglossia emerges in cultures which embrace several languages, cosmopolitan cultures in which the various national languages are mutually aware of one another. This is the source of the "Galilean perception of language" which finds its expression in the novel. Thus the polyphonic novel develops first in the cosmopolitan and polyglot Hellenistic culture, then emerges again in the equally cosmopolitan and polyglot Renaissance. Joyce, by superimposing several national languages in his multilingual text, thus reconstructs the original conditions for the novel's emergence, returning the novel to its historical roots in heteroglossia.

Carnival

In Donald Barthelme's "Kierkegaard Unfair to Schlegel" (1970), one of the interlocutors explains how the government stands "in an ironic relation to itself." The point of an army is deterrence, and the essence of deterrence is credibility; yet the government sells off surplus army uniforms to kids, thus undermining its own credibility, for these kids in army-surplus uniforms constitute "this vast clown army . . . parodying the real army."

> And they mix periods, you know, you get parody British grenadiers and parody World War I types and parody Sierra Maestra types. So you have all these kids walking around wearing these filthy uniforms with wound stripes, hash marks, Silver Stars, but also ostrich feathers, Day-Glo vests, amulets containing powdered rhinoceros horn . . . You have this splendid clown army in the streets standing over against the real one. And of course the clown army constitutes a very serious attack on all the ideas which support the real army including the basic notion of having an army at all.[27]

It is hard not to see in this account a reflection on Barthelme's own collage texts, such as "The Indian Uprising," "The Viennese Opera Ball," and "A Picture History of the War." Like these texts, the clown army is a collage of second-hand ("found") materials. Like them, too, it is subversive of monological authority. In a sense, these kids' mock-military costumes are fragments of discourses, and assembling them into an army is analogous to producing a polyphonic text. Barthelme, in other words, has in this little parable of the "splendid clown army" reconstructed the historical connection between polyphony of discourses and discourse-worlds, and popular carnival.

That connection has been argued most influentially, of course, by Mixail Baxtin.[28] Baxtin traced the polyphonic character of the novel back to its historical roots in popular carnival practices and the various verbal genres associated with carnival. In particular, carnival practices have been transmitted through the genre of the Menippean satire, which initially developed in direct contact with popular carnival, and which has been reconstituted at intervals throughout the course of literary history as the dialectical response to the consolidation of "official," monological literary genres.[29] "Carnivalized" genres such as Menippean satire are in this sense official literature's dialectical antithesis and parodic double. Postmodernist fiction is the heir of Menippean satire and its most recent historical avatar.

Baxtin has made it possible to characterize the formal features of carnivalized literature. Where the traditional genres of official literature are stylistically homogeneous, carnivalized literature is heterogeneous and flagrantly "indecorous," interweaving disparate styles and registers. Where the official genres are typically unitary, both generically and ontologically, projecting a single fictional world, carnivalized literature interrupts the text's ontological "horizon" with a multiplicity of inserted genres – letters, essays, theatrical dialogues, novels-within-the-novel, and so on. Carnivalized literature, in other words, is characterized by stylistic heteroglossia and recursive structure – features we are already familiar with in postmodernist fiction.

In addition, Baxtin has associated the formal heterogeneity of carnivalized literature with a repertoire of *topoi* at the level of the projected world – characteristic plot-types, character-types, locales, and motifs – which both motivate and mirror the text's formal heterogeneity. The typical plot of carnivalized narrative is that of a picaresque adventure-story in which the *pícaro* seeks not social and economic advancement, or not only that, but answers to "ultimate questions." This philosophical pursuit of ultimate questions leads the *pícaro* to the very limits of his world, or even beyond them. He visits heaven, hell, or other planets, and engages in "threshold dialogues" with inhabitants of those worlds. Testing the limits of human experience, he experiments with extreme states of mind and body – hallucination, madness, sexual excess – and deliberately violates social norms through scandalous or criminal behavior. Yet the quest of the *pícaro* is animated throughout by a visionary or Utopian hunger for a more perfect social order. Besides these *topoi*, which are essentially those of Menippean satire, carnivalized literature has also absorbed directly from popular carnival practices their characteristic grotesque imagery of the human body: the inversion of the hierarchy of "upper" and "lower" parts of the body, the transgression of the body's limits through grotesque excesses of ingestion, defecation and copulation, the dismemberment or "explosion" of the body, and so on.

Clearly, this repertoire of Menippean and carnivalesque *topoi* overlaps at certain points with the repertoires of the fantastic and science fiction genres, and thus with the postmodernist adaptations of fantastic literature and science fiction. But in fact the overlap is more general than that: these characteristic *topoi* of carnivalized literature are also characteristic *topoi* of postmodernist fiction.

The *topos* of philosophical picaresque persists in postmodernist adventure-stories, where the postmodernist *pícaro* – Kenneth Patchen's Albion Moonlight, Pynchon's Tyrone Slothrop, Alasdair Gray's Lanark, the nameless protagonists of Sukenick's *Out* and Federman's *Take It or Leave It* (1976), and so on – sets out in pursuit of ultimate questions across the paradoxical spaces of the zone. This quest takes the *pícaro* to other planets in William Burroughs' novels of the Nova Conspiracy, and to heaven, hell, or purgatory in Flann O'Brien's *The Third Policeman* (1940/67), Christine Brooke-Rose's *Such* (1966), Pynchon's *Gravity's Rainbow* (1973), R. M. Koster's *The Dissertation* (1975), Stanley Elkin's *The Living End* (1979) and Alasdair Gray's *Lanark* (1981). The limits of sexual excess and drug abuse are tested in the novels of Burroughs, Pynchon, and Robbe-Grillet, and in Leonard Cohen's *Beautiful Losers* (1966). The topos of scandal is exemplified by Burroughs' outrageous prankster-figure A.J., and by the episodes of Roger Mexico urinating on a conference of company directors in *Gravity's Rainbow*, Miles Faber copulating on the steps of a college library in Anthony Burgess's *M/F* (1971), and, the epitome of scandal, Vice-President Richard Nixon dropping his trousers before a Times Square crowd in Coover's *The Public Burning* (1977). A Utopian element colors many postmodernist fictions, including Richard Brautigan's *In Watermelon Sugar* (1968), Monique Wittig's *Les Guérillères* (1969), Sukenick's *98.6* (1975), Grass's *The Flounder* (1977), and Guy Davenport's "The Dawn in Erewhon" (1974) and "Au Tombeau de Charles Fourier" (1979).

Grotesque imagery of the human body, a direct inheritance from carnival practices, is also highly typical of postmodernist fiction. The postmodernist motifs of the inverted and exploded body can be traced back through such early-twentieth-century precursors of postmodernism as Alfred Jarry, in his *Ubu* plays (1896, 1900, 1944), and Witold Gombrowicz in *Ferdydurke* (1937). The postmodernist apotheosis of the lower body can be seen in Burroughs' *Naked Lunch* (1959), where Dr Benway tells a gruesome story of a talking anus that gradually takes control of its "host's" entire body; in Joe Orton's *Head to Toe* (written, 1961; published, 1971), with its penis the size of a mountain and its voyage up the alimentary tract; and in Juan Goytisolo's *Reivindicacion del Conde Don Julián* (1970), where we are given a guided tour of a Spanish virgin's vagina. Comic dismemberment occurs in Flann O'Brien's *At Swim-Two-Birds* (1939), Brigid Brophy's *In Transit* (1969), Steve Katz's *Moving Parts* (1977), and Salman Rushdie's *Midnight's Children* (1981). Feats of gluttony and even cannibalism are celebrated in García Márquez's *Autumn of the Patriarch* (1975), Grass's *The Flounder*, and Pynchon's *Gravity's Rainbow*, defecation in *The Flounder* and *Midnight's Children*, and copulation almost everywhere.

Examples could be multiplied, demonstrating how postmodernist fiction has reconstituted both the formal and the topical or motival repertoires of carnivalized literature. In fact, it has gone even further than that toward recovering its carnival roots. According to Baxtin, the further the novel grows away from its origins in carnivalesque genres, the more tenuous its link with popular carnival, to the point where the modern novel is no more than a drastically reduced form of carnivalized literature. Carnival continues to be the implicit "connecting principle" which motivates the coexistence of these disparate carnivalesque *topoi*, but carnival as such, the *model* for carnivalized literature, has been lost, eroded away.[30] Postmodernist fiction compensates for this loss of the carnival context by incorporating carnival, or some surrogate for carnival, at the level of its projected world. In the absence of a *real* carnival context, it constructs fictional carnivals.

Inevitably, postmodernist representations of carnival often take the form of some reduced or residual version of carnival, rather than the full-fledged popular carnival such as Baxtin describes. The festive dinner or wild party is one such reduced version, as in Grass's *The Flounder* or Pynchon's *Gravity's Rainbow*, texts constructed around recurrences of this quasi-carnival *topos*, or even, in its most radically reduced form, in Barthelme's "The Viennese Opera Ball." Communal dancing functions as another surrogate for carnival in Wittig's *Les Guérillères* and Ishmael Reed's *Mumbo Jumbo* (1972), and so does the regatta in Guy Davenport's carnivalesque text, "Christ Preaching at the Henley Regatta" (1981).

Representations of circuses, fairs, sideshows, and amusement parks often function as residual indicators of the carnival context in postmodernist fiction. John Barth's story "Lost in the Funhouse" (1968) is typical of this *topos* of reduced carnival. Traveling shows frequently function in postmodernist fantastic texts as agents of disruption, vehicles for insinuating the supernatural or paranormal into "normal" reality. Postmodernist examples include Bulgakov's *The Master and Margarita* (1928–40), Ishmael Reed's *Yellow Back Radio Broke-Down* (1969), and Angela Carter's *The Infernal Desire Machines of Dr Hoffman* (1972).[31]

If such reduced and displaced forms of carnival are the most typical, nevertheless full-fledged popular carnivals do sometimes occur in the worlds of postmodernist fiction, and when they do they tend to serve as summations or all-embracing frameworks for the text's various carnivalesque motifs. This is the case with the Schweinheldfest in *Gravity's Rainbow*, the festival of Senta Euphorbia in Burgess's *M/F*, and, an inverted carnival, the public executions of the Rosenbergs in Coover's *The Public Burning*. Essential to popular carnival are parodies of official ceremonies, such as we find in the mock-coronation and dethronement of the carnival king in Jarry's *Ubu Roi*, the carnivalesque funerals in Goytisolo's *Conde Julián* and García Márquez's "Los funerales de la Mama Grande" (1962) and *Autumn of the Patriarch*, the mock-trials in Fuentes's *Cambio de piel* (1967) and Grass's *The Flounder*, and the grotesque circus wedding in Burgess's *M/F*. The apotheosis of postmodernist carnival occurs in Carlos Fuentes's *Terra nostra*, where the end of the world takes the form of a monstrous Parisian carnival. A hyperbolic transformation of the medieval carnivals studied by Baxtin, Fuentes's apocalyptic carnival juxtaposes mass murder (human sacrifice at St-Sulpice) with mass births on the quais of the Seine. At the center of this dance of death and rebirth we find the card-party, a reduced form of carnival, at which characters from a range of

Latin-American postmodernist novels play poker, constituting a carnivalesque intertextuality that sums up the Latin-American literary "boom" much as the carnival outside on the streets sums up the entire history of the western world.

At the point where representations of carnival converge with carnivalized literature's Utopian themes we find the postmodernist *topos* of revolution. This is not political or social revolution, however, so much as it is ludic and sexual revolution, revolution *as* carnival; its real-world models are the May Events in Paris and the Prague Spring. Dionysian outbursts of energy, anarchic and iconoclastic, such carnivalesque revolutions break out, for instance, in Burroughs's *Naked Lunch* and *The Wild Boys*, Brigid Brophy's *In Transit*, Leonard Cohen's *Beautiful Losers*, Pynchon's *Gravity's Rainbow*, and of course in Barthelme's "The Indian Uprising," our starting-point.

Agents of disorder, of heterogeneity, polyphony, the promiscuous mingling of discourses – that is what all these Dionysian revolutionaries are:

> They say they foster disorder in all its forms. Confusion troubles violent debates disarray upsets disturbances incoherencies irregularities divergences complications disagreements discords clashes polemics discussions contentions brawls disputes conflicts routs débâcles cataclysms disturbances quarrels agitation turbulence conflagrations chaos anarchy.

This passage comes from Monique Wittig's *Les Guérillères*.[32] Here the revolutionaries are women, and the object of their revolution is not just to overthrow men but to topple the entire culture that men have created, including male-dominated material culture. Thus, at one point they assemble all the tools used in all the trades and manufacturing processes of our culture – an immense catalogue of things, from "distaffs looms rollers shuttles combs" through "machine-tools spinners bobbin-winders staplers assembly-lines," not neglecting such domestic tools as "stewpans sauce pans plates stoves . . . vacuum-cleaners washing-machines brushes." Then:

> They heap them on to an immense pyre to which they set fire, blowing up everything that will not burn. Then, starting to dance round it, they clap their hands, they shout obscene phrases, they cut their hair or let it down. When the fire has burnt down, when they are sated with setting off explosions, they collect the debris, the objects that are not consumed, those that have not melted down, those that have not disintegrated. They cover them with blue green red paint to reassemble them in grotesque grandiose abracadabrant compositions to which they give names.[33]

These assemblages, "grotesque grandiose abracadabrant compositions," are of course structures *en abyme*, scale-models of *Les Guérillères* itself, and of other postmodernist polyphonic texts as well. Like the antidiscursive litanies of Barthelme's "The Indian Uprising," they are the result of "exploding" a discursive order. Like the "splendid clown army" of "Kierkegaard Unfair to Schlegel," they subvert monological (masculine) authority, and demonstrate again the connection between postmodernist carnival and the polyphony of worlds.

PART FIVE: GROUNDINGS

Reading . . . is always this: there is a thing that is there, a thing made of writing, a solid, material object, which cannot be changed, and through this thing we measure ourselves against something else that is not present, something else that belongs to the immaterial, invisible world, because it can only be thought, imagined, or because it was once and is no longer, past, lost, unattainable, in the land of the dead.

(Italo Calvino, *If on a winter's night a traveller*, 1979)

12: WORLDS ON PAPER

"Everything you have experienced and are experiencing . . . is made of one thing."

"Atoms," said Lanark.

"No. Print. Some worlds are made of atoms but yours is made of tiny marks marching in neat lines, like armies of insects, across pages and pages and pages of white paper."

(Alasdair Gray, *Lanark*, 1981)

Had the Cambridge undergraduates Christopher Isherwood and Edward Upward actually completed their projected cycle of tales about the imaginary village of Mortmere, they might have figured among the precursors of the postmodernist fantastic. As it is, all that exists of their project is Upward's story "The Railway Accident" (1928, published 1949) and Isherwood's account, in *Lions and Shadow* (1941), of some of the other unwritten or uncompleted stories – which does, indeed, read like postmodernist reviews of nonexistent books by Borges or Nabokov or Lem. But Mortmere's precocious postmodernism does not appear only in the fictional world which Isherwood and Upward imagined for their stories; it extends even to the physical *book* in which the stories were to be printed. This book, Isherwood reports, was to have been illustrated with oil paintings, brasses, and carvings. It was to incorporate fireworks displays, recorded music, even appropriate odors, and would contain gifts for friends and booby-traps for enemies.

Isherwood and Upward never got any further than fantasizing about such a book, of course. But postmodernist books resembling their projected Mortmere book – although using considerably less luxurious materials – do in fact exist. William Gass's *Willie Masters' Lonesome Wife* (1968), for example, is printed on blue, green, red and glossy white paper. Like the hypothetical Mortmere book, it intrudes upon its readers' real-world existence, not by means of mood-music or booby-traps, but through the black-and-white photographs of a female nude which accompany the text, and which are clearly designed to stimulate sexual interest or tension of one kind or another in the reader. Moreover, Gass's book exploits typography and page layout, physical elements of the printed book which Isherwood and Upward had neglected to take into account. Certain pages of *Lonesome Wife* are "concrete prose," shaped into icons of their own contents (an eye, a Christmas tree); others contain abstract typographical shapes which appear to have no illustrative or mimetic function. On still other pages the text is split into two or even three parallel texts, forcing the reader to decide on some arbitrary order of reading, since *simultaneous* reading of two or more texts at once is, strictly speaking, impossible.

"We badly need a new way of thinking about novels that acknowledges their technological reality," Ronald Sukenick writes. Books like *Willie Masters' Lonesome Wife* promote such a new way of thinking through their conspicuous manipulation of the "technological," that is, physical, material elements of the printed book. Sukenick goes on:

> We have to learn how to look at fiction as lines of print on a page and we have to ask whether it is always the best arrangement to have a solid block of print from one margin to the other running down the page from top to bottom, except for an occasional paragraph indentation. We have to learn to think about a novel as a concrete structure rather than an allegory, existing in the realm of experience rather than of discursive meaning.[1]

To think this way about a book is to think about its *ontology*, its modes of being, in the plural. The novel as "concrete structure" exists, says Sukenick, in the "realm of experience," which he opposes to the realm of "discursive meaning." Using parallel language, Italo Calvino, in my epigraph, establishes an opposition between "a thing that is there, a thing made of writing, a solid, material object" on the one hand, and "something else that belongs to the immaterial, invisible world" on the other. They are both talking about an ontological opposition, marking a basic ontological boundary, the one between the real-world object, the book which shares our world with us, and the fictional objects and world which the text projects.

Ingarden tells us that all the ontological strata of the literary work of art ultimately rest on the material book and its typography, which guarantee their continuing existence. The material book, in other words, although in a sense it does not belong to the text's ontological structure, nevertheless constitutes a kind of ontological subbasement or foundation, without which the structure could not stand. A major ontological "cut" divides the book as real, material object from the text as intentional object. Books like *Willie Masters' Lonesome Wife* foreground this cut. The reality of the fictional character, the wife whose monologue we are supposed to be reading (hearing?), is constantly being jeopardized and undermined by the book's insistence on its *own* reality: its distractingly colored pages and distorted typography, its provocative and apparently irrelevant illustrations, its parallel texts which force the reader to improvise an order of reading, and so on. The wife's reality is dissipated whenever the book's reality is foregrounded – and vice versa. We might almost speak of a *struggle* between antagonistic realities, inducing an ontological flicker, the fiction's reality and the book's coming into focus by turns, first one, then the other. And this flicker seems to induce other ontological disturbances, for instance the wife's tendency to slip back and forth between *literal* fiction and *allegory* (see Chapter 9, pp. 140–7). Or perhaps we should say that here one ontological instability functions as "objective correlative" of the others: the struggle between material book and fictional world is the outward-and-visible-sign of the other "flickering" ontological structures in *Lonesome Wife*.

By the same argument, Isherwood's and Upwards's Mortmere book, had it ever been produced, might have been more than just undergraduate dandyism run wild. Like the real postmodernist books which have followed it, its technological structure might have served as the objective correlative of Mortmere's unstable and flickering reality.

"A spatial displacement of words"

The invention of printing embedded the word in *space*, as Father Ong has observed.[2] While a manuscript could still be regarded as the record of an oral performance, which unfolds in time, a book was a *thing*, and its material qualities and physical dimensions inevitably interacted with the word. Far from exploiting this interaction, however, fiction in the realist tradition has sought to suppress or neutralize it; realist fiction, says Sukenick, "tends to deny its technological reality."[3] It does so by conventionalizing space right out of existence. Nothing must interfere with fiction's representation of reality, so the physical dimensions of the book must be rendered functionally invisible. Thus we get that "solid block of print from one margin to another running down the page from top to bottom, except for an occasional paragraph indentation" of which Sukenick speaks. So familiar and predictable is this format that it has come to seem like a "second nature"; it is, as the Prague structuralists would have said, fully "automatized." Indeed, the functional invisibility of space in prose fiction is what distinguishes prose from verse, with its conventions of the unjustified right margin and stanza breaks. *Spacing* is the sign of verse; prose, the unmarked member of the pair, is identified by its *spacelessness*.

Against this background convention of the page of solid print as "second nature," the introduction of blank space has the effect of foregrounding the presence and materiality of the book, and of disrupting the reality of the projected world. Spacing, we might say, allows the book to show through the fiction. "Espaçons. L'art de ce texte, c'est l'air qu'il fait circuler entre ses paravents." So writes Jacques Derrida in *Glas* (1974), a book whose materiality cannot be ignored, and which uses this foregrounded materiality as leverage against metaphysics.[4] "The art of this text," in short, is postmodernist art, the art of an ontological poetics. In the same spirit, Raymond Federman opens his novel *Take It or Leave It* (1976) with a "Pretext" ("to be inserted anywhere in the text") subtitled "a spatial displacement of words." The spatial displacement of words in postmodernist writing produces other displacements: of the conventions of prose fiction; of the ontological structure of novels.

Critics have often described postmodernist writing as *discontinuous*,[5] but have not always recognized the connection between this semantic and narrative discontinuity and its physical "objective correlative," the *spacing* of the text. Postmodernist texts are typically spaced-out, literally as well as figuratively. Extremely short chapters, or short paragraphs separated by wide bands of white space, have become the norm. Indeed, so familiar has this new convention of segmentation become that we are apt to forget what an effect it has on our reception of texts by, for instance, Brautigan, Barthelme, or Vonnegut.[6] A trivial, superficial convention, one might think, of no real significance; but, depending upon the context in which it appears, spacing can be motivated as an act of subversion – and not just subversion of literary norms, either. Or so, at least, Monique Wittig claims at the end of her spaced-out text, *Les Guérillères* (1979):

LACUNAE LACUNAE
AGAINST TEXTS
AGAINST MEANING
WHICH IS TO WRITE VIOLENCE
OUTSIDE THE TEXT
IN ANOTHER WRITING
THREATENING MENACING
MARGINS SPACES INTERVALS
WITHOUT PAUSE
ACTION OVERTHROW[7]

Here spacing is the objective correlative not just of a destabilized fictional ontology, but also of carnivalesque revolution (see Chapter 11, pp. 171–5).

The physical discontinuity and spaciness of postmodernist texts is often further highlighted by the use of titles or headlines, in a more prominent typeface, at the head of each short chapter or isolated paragraph. Such headlines tend to corroborate what the spacing already implies, namely that each short segment constitutes an independent unit, a miniature text in its own right, thus in effect completing the physical disintegration of the text that spacing begins. An example is Gass's story "In the Heart of the Heart of the Country" (1968), which is fragmented into short "chapters" each with its own boldface title ("A Place," "Weather," "My House," "A Person," and so forth).[8] The title of Gass's story seems to allude to the opening paragraph of the "Aeolus" chapter of Joyce's *Ulysses*, which bears the headline, "In the Heart of the Hibernian Metropolis." The allusion is appropriate, since "Aeolus," with its newspaper-style headlines, parodying the layout of a newspaper page, is among the modernist precursors of postmodernist writing's characteristically spacey layout.

The spacing-with-headline format, so widespread in postmodernist writing, economically foregrounds the printed book's most basic physical components, namely paper and print. It foregrounds the materiality of paper through spacing, that is, through the contrast between blank space and text; and it foregrounds the materiality of print through its juxtaposition of different type-faces (boldface headline vs. text). Hyperbolic extensions or expansions of both components are possible. Entire passages or blocks of text may be printed in boldface or upper-case type, as in Wittig's *Les Guérillères* (see the passage reproduced above) or Barthelme's *Snow White* (1968) or

"Brain Damage" (1970); or, instead of alternating between two type-faces or type-sizes, the text may use several, as in *Willie Masters' Lonesome Wife*, Michel Butor's *Mobile* (1962), Raymond Federman's *Take It or Leave It* or Alasdair Gray's *1982, Janine* (1984). Similarly, the amount of blank space intervening between blocks of print may be expanded from a more or less narrow band to entire blank pages, as in Cabrera Infante's *Tres tristes tigres* (1965), Sukenick's *Long Talking Bad Conditions Blues* (1979), and Gray's *1982, Janine*.[9] Colored pages inserted among pages of print have an analogous effect of foregrounding the materiality of the page: the black page in *Tres tristes tigres*, the blue pages in Eugene Wildman's *Montezuma's Ball* (1970) and Federman's *Double or Nothing* (1971). In an ultimate hyperbolic transformation of this strategy, the text may simply "disappear" into blank space, ending with a sequence of empty pages. This is the case with pages 173 through 184 of *Montezuma's Ball*, the closing pages of two of the monologues in B. S. Johnson's *House Mother Normal* (1971), and the final eleven pages of Ronald Sukenick's *Out* (1973). In the latter two texts, the proportion of blankness to print increases systematically from chapter to chapter. Each of Johnson's nine aged monologuists is more senile than the previous one, their mental blankness being represented by increasingly larger gaps in the text. Similarly, Sukenick's protagonist becomes progressively more vacuous as the text unfolds. White space here imitates both this internal vacuity and the "wide-open spaces" of the American West, climaxing at the moment when the protagonist, having reached a maximum dispersal of his personality, embarks upon the void of the Pacific Ocean. Clearly, in both these texts (unlike Wildman's), white space serves a mimetic or iconic function.

The spacing-with-headline format, as well as its development in progressively spaced-out texts such as *House Mother Normal* and *Out*, only exploits *horizontal* space: in effect, blank horizontals have been substituted for the expected horizontal lines of print. Horizontal space can be foregrounded in other ways, too, for instance by tampering with the margins. Thus, in Federman's *Take It or Leave It* or Butor's *Mobile*, margins of variable width are used, while in Christine Brooke-Rose's *Thru* (1975), the text is sometimes justified only at the left margin, like poetry, sometimes only at the right, and sometimes at both margins. But of course a page has other axes beside the horizontal, and in principle space on these axes could also be exploited to foreground the materiality of the book – perhaps to even greater effect, since vertical and diagonal space is even more heavily camouflaged and neutralized in conventional formats than the horizontal axis. Type could be arranged diagonally across the page, for example, as in *Thru*, or the "Pretext" of Federman's *Take It or Leave It*, or on certain pages of his *Double or Nothing*. Or the text could read *upward* vertically or diagonally, or could be printed around a square or circle; examples can be found, again, in *Thru* and *Double or Nothing*. The text could even be printed upside-down or sideways, so that, in order to read it, the reader literally has to manipulate the book, turning it sideways or completely around; this is what he or she is forced to do when attempting to read Chapter 11 of *1982, Janine*. As an extreme case of such strategies, Steve Katz in *The Exagggerations of Peter Prince* (1986) and Federman in *Double or Nothing* superimpose on the same page a text that can be read in the normal orientation and a text that must be read with the book turned sideways or upside-down.

In all these cases, the reader, as Jerome Klinkowitz says of *Double or Nothing* in particular,

> is forced to concentrate on the actual writing, or – better yet – typing; it's impossible to fall through the words into the suspension of disbelief in the story itself.[10]

In other words, the spacing-out of the text, along whatever axis or combination of axes, induces an ontological hesitation or oscillation between the fictional world and the real-world object – the material book.

Concrete prose

The shaped typography of Federman, Katz, Butor, Brooke-Rose, Gass, and others obviously bears a close resemblance to concrete poetry; indeed, we might call this mode of writing "concrete prose" or "concrete fiction." Like concrete poetry, many pieces of concrete prose are literally "verbal icons," imitating through their shapes the shapes of objects or processes in the real world. The model for this type of concrete prose can be found in the *calligrammes* of Apollinaire, where the text is shaped into a visual representation of an appropriate object. Other pieces mime not objects or processes, but rather invisible *concepts*; here the iconic relation between the shaped text and the "thing" imitated is metaphorical or allegorical, and depends upon the reader's interpretation. In general, however, contemporary concrete prose, like contemporary concrete poetry, tends, as Dick Higgins observes,

> to be far less mimetic. The visual element is often purely expressive and improvised, in the manner of an abstract expressionist painting. Or it is clean and geometrical.[11]

The model for this "abstract expressionist" prose is not Apollinaire but rather Stéphane Mallarmé, in the noniconic passages of his famous shaped text, "Un coup de dés jamais n'abolira le hasard" (1897). Although iconic shaped texts also foreground the materiality of the book and the ontological tension between the book as object and the world of the text, abstract shaped texts such as "Un coup de dés" do so particularly single-mindedly. Such texts illustrate or imitate nothing, except their own existence. Their sole function is to focus attention on the ontological "cut": on the one side of the cut, the world projected by the words; on the other side, the physical reality of inkshapes on paper.

Federman in *Double or Nothing* has invented a different typographical format for each page of his text. Thus it is full of examples of "concrete prose" of all types, but especially of iconic designs: the narrator's room is imitated by four "walls" of upper-case words; the act of entering the subway by typography that descends and rises diagonally across the page; the view up a girl's skirt by the word "triangular" arranged in a triangle; and so on.[12] Brooke-Rose's *Thru* contains verbal icons of two classrooms. One of these is a traditional classroom of writing-desks arranged in rows (words arranged in a rectangular grid); the other, a large lecture theater where "you lecture on a raised dais in an amphibian theatre to a sea of floating faces rising in waves upward and away" (*Figure 1*):[13]

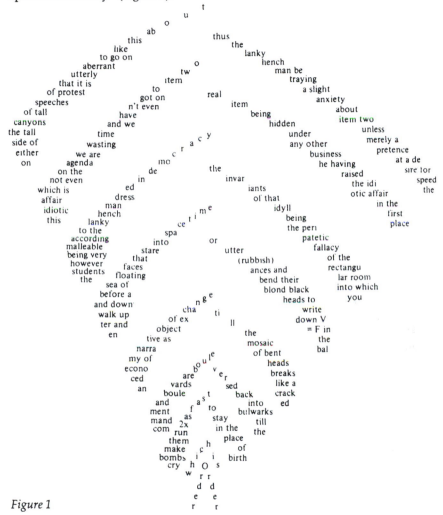

Figure 1

Several passages from Sukenick's *Long Talking Bad Conditions Blues* (1979) are icons of objects or processes, including the blank page mentioned above (an iconic representation of a blizzard!) and a passage whose spacing imitates a certain urban landscape (*Figure 2*).[14]

There are, as the text itself informs us, "certain clear physical correspondences" between the gaping holes in this passage and the holes in the half-razed cityscape it describes. But that does not exhaust its iconic functions. The passage continues: "the odd gaps in consciousness concerning

there were certain clear physical correspondences here to
the new conditions for example the frequent gaping holes   these
were areas that had been razed some years ago in strategic parts of
the city at a time when ambitious civic projects had been planned
and commissioned   whole blocks had been demolished popu-
lations relocated then between demolition and construction the
original plans had been found inadequate or wrongheaded or too
expensive or unpropitious for the times   these gaping holes as
they were generically called had gradually become part of the
normal landscape the politicians were constantly proposing new
schemes for them which were clearly unworkable   the citizens
referred to them with affectionate irony and they had even become
proverbial as in the saying necessary as a gaping hole or fraught with
gaping holes

Figure 2

the new conditions and the curious lacunae in the conditions themselves
were visibly manifest in these civic ellipses and confused stalemates." In
other words, the gaps in the text do not just mime the gaps in the city; rather,
both the textual gaps *and* the razed areas of the city are icons of the "bad
conditions" themselves. Similarly with Brooke-Rose's pattern of broken arcs:
this shape imitates the physical appearance of an amphitheater, but it also
imitates "faculty meetings where faculties never meet even on an imagined
curve even as an audiovisual illusion of a coherent structure diminishing in
size."[15] Thus, in both cases, shaped typography functions as the *allegory of a
concept*, as well as icon of an object or process.

Other conceptual icons may be found in Sukenick's *Out*, where, as I
observed earlier, the book's increasingly spaced-out format imitates a
psychological and metaphysical condition as well as the geographical spaces
of the American West; and Butor's *Mobile*, whose shaped page-spaces are
icons of no *particular* geographical space, but rather of the *idea* of American
space. Thus, conceptual icons lend a kind of concreteness and palpability to
complex or diffuse or highly abstract ideas, such as Sukenick's elusive "bad
conditions" or Butor's American space. They can also serve to capture the
unutterable, as in Federman's concrete-prose ideograms of the holocaust in
Take It or Leave It. The dilemma is by now a familiar one, though no less
intractable for being so familiar: how is a writer who has survived the
holocaust to write about the mass death that he himself so narrowly escaped?
One of Federman's solutions is *not* to write about it at all, but to let the blank
spaces in the text – or the X's or zeroes or other typographical icons – speak for
him (see *Figure 3*).[16]

It is the gaps that convey the meaning here, in a way that the shattered words
juif, cremation, lampshade, Auschwitz, responsabilité, and so on, could never
have done had they been completed and integrated into some syntactical

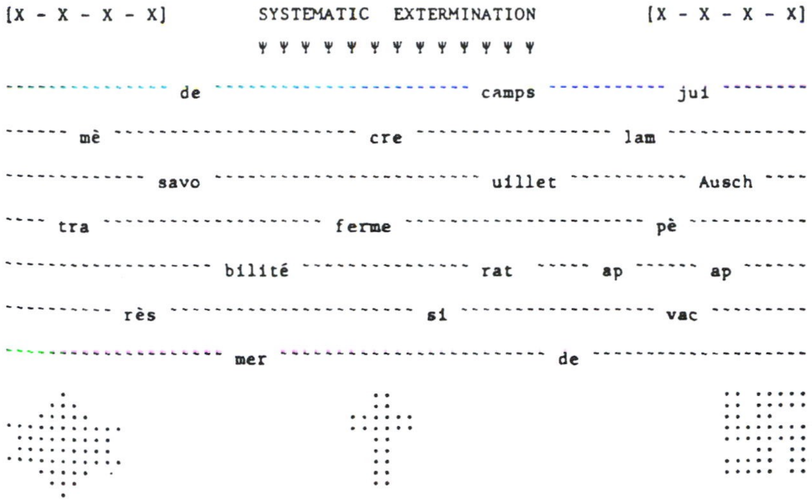

[X - X - X - X]   SYSTEMATIC   EXTERMINATION   [X - X - X - X]

                         Y Y Y Y Y Y Y Y Y Y Y Y Y Y

---------------- de ----------------------- cAmps ------------ juÍ --------

------- mè --------------------------- cre ------------------ lam ------------

------------- savo --------------------------- uillet ----------- Ausch ----

----- tra ------------------- ferme -------------------------- pè -----------

-------------------- bilité --------------- rat ----- ap ------ ap ------

----------- rès ----------------------- si ---------------------- vac --------

------------------------ mer ------------------------- de --------------------

Figure 3

continuity. Visually, the effect is that of a tombstone (a defaced tombstone?). This shaped passage, it seems to me, serves to prove (if proof were needed) that concrete prose can be a good deal more than just a trivial joke.

Dick Higgins has spoken of "abstract expressionist" and "clean and geometrical" types of concrete poetry. These types may also be found in concrete prose. Examples of the geometrical type include the square, circular, and chiasmic arrangements of words in Brooke-Rose's *Thru*, as well as the zig-zags, hourglass shapes, rectangular slots, and so on, in Federman's *Double or Nothing*. Both these texts also contain various irregular, free-form, "purely expressive and improvised" typographical forms: the crossword-puzzle formats of certain pages of *Thru*, where words must be read vertically as well as horizontally, from bottom to top as well as from top to bottom; or Federman's "twisted disgression" in *Double or Nothing* (see *Figure 4*).[17]

In such abstract expressionist designs, even more than the geometrical or iconic types, we are made to experience the ineluctable *materiality* of the book; consequently, these fictional worlds, momentarily eclipsed by the real-world object, are forced to flicker in and out of existence.

Illustration and anti-illustration

An iconic shaped text in effect illustrates itself: its shape illustrates its content. Since postmodernist writing exploits, as I have shown, the printed text's potential for self-illustration, as a means of foregrounding the materiality of the book, it would be surprising if it did not also exploit in the same way the book's potential for incorporating drawings and photographs. And of course postmodernist writing *does* exploit the possibilities of illustration. A number of postmodernist books are illustrated, either with photographs, or with drawings lifted or collaged from other sources, or, more rarely, with drawings by the authors themselves.[18] In a sense, of course, the use of illustration

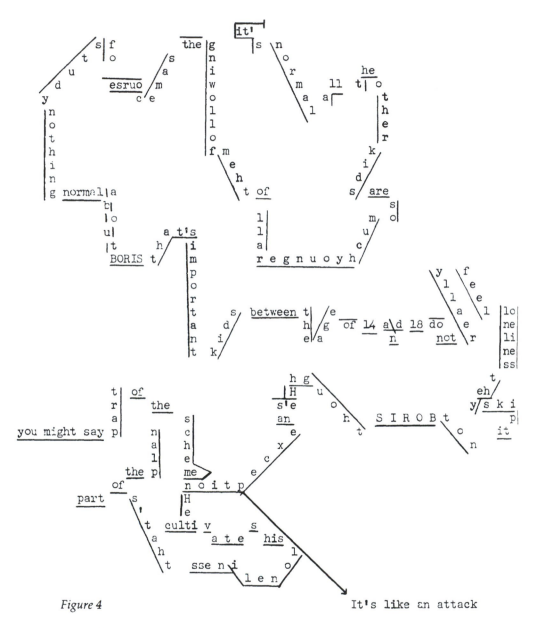

Figure 4   It's like an attack

is hardly innovative; after all, most nineteenth-century realist novels were illustrated texts. But the reappearance of illustration as a major resource in postmodernist writing does indicate once again the extent of postmodernism's divergence from modernist poetics. By the modernist period, illustration had been demoted from its place in the serious novel, displaced downward and outward in the literary system until its last strongholds were popular magazine fiction and children's literature. When illustration re-emerged late in the modernist period, it did so in new and unprecedented forms: as surrealist collage-novels, and as photographic illustration.

Collage-novels such as those of Max Ernst (e.g. *Une semaine de bonté*, 1934) constitute in effect extended jokes at the expense of illustration. What many earlier novelists had feared has here come to pass: the illustrations have completely supplanted the verbal text. But at the same time the illustrations have lost their narrative logic and coherence through the artist's collaging together of visual *non sequiturs* (animal-heads in place of human faces, and so on). This is a parody of the conventions of illustration – anti-illustration. The parodic element is especially evident when Ernst uses complete full-page illustrations from sensationalistic nineteenth-century novels as the base onto which he superimposes other visual materials. Disrupted in this way, these pictures no longer tell the coherent story they once told; or rather, what they now "tell" is the discourse of the unconscious.

So the collage-novel is a kind of double-edged revenge of the visual illustration against the verbal text, the illustration destroying itself in the process, the only clear winner being the unconscious, which here finds its "voice." Photographic illustration, too, can be a form of revenge of the visual against the verbal. As practiced by late-modernist writers, it focuses certain of modernism's epistemological anxieties. The classic example is *Let Us Now Praise Famous Men* (1941), in which the successful collaboration of the photographer Walker Evans and the writer James Agee should not blind us to the tension between the competing claims of self-consciously "objective" photography and self-consciously "subjective" writing. Despite Agee's insistence on the ultimate truthfulness of subjective impression, he is transparently anxious about the camera and its implicit claims to a superior truthfulness. This anxiety takes the strange form of laborious prose descriptions, or indeed redescriptions, of objects that Evans has already captured photographically: the furnishings of a tenant farmer's house, graves in a rural cemetery. Inevitably this is self-defeating. Agee might just as well be describing the photograph as the reality behind it; indeed, he refers us to the photograph for corroboration of his own verbal account. In short, Agee's verbal text is constantly in danger of becoming merely extended *captions* to Evans's photographs – and Agee knows it.

But the writer need not succumb to Agee's epistemological anxieties about the photography, as witness André Breton's *Nadja* (1928). Breton said that the purpose of the photographs in *Nadja* was to eliminate the necessity for description, which suggests the kind of anxious dependence of verbal text on its photographic illustrations that we find in *Let Us Now Praise Famous Men*. But in fact many of the photographs in *Nadja* represent objects that would not have been described in any case: sites where events pointedly *did not* occur, people who *do not* figure in the narrative (who are only mentioned in a footnote, for instance). What do these photographs illustrate? Nothing; they are anti-illustrations. Once again, as in the case of Ernst's collage-novels, we detect an element of parody and derision in Breton's use of photography.

Postmodernist illustration is typically anti-illustration; it has learned more from the surrealists' playfulness and parody than it has from Agee's anxious earnestness. For example, Richard Brautigan in *Trout Fishing in America* (1967) seems to flirt with the idea that his text is only a kind of extended caption for the photograph on its cover. But when he jokes about "returning" to the book's cover, his joke has point, for this "return" is ambiguous: on the one hand, his fictional characters return to it in the sense of revisiting the site depicted in the photograph; on the other hand, the *reader* returns to the cover by physically *closing the book* and re-examining its cover-photo. In other words, Brautigan's playful manipulation of the conventions of cover-illustration serves to foreground the ontological opposition between the fictional world and the material book.

Postmodernist anti-illustration typically functions to foreground ontological structure, although not always in the same way that *Trout Fishing in America* does. In many postmodernist texts, the absence of any apparent relation between the illustration and the verbal text turns these visual materials into pure demonstrations of the *visuality*, and therefore the three-dimensionality and materiality, of the book. In this respect they function analogously to the "abstract expressionist" type of concrete poetry or prose, such as Federman's "twisted disgression." Other postmodernist illustrations, especially those that derive from surrealist collage practices (for example, Guy Davenport's illustrated text "Au Tombeau de Charles Fourier," 1979, or Donald Barthelme's "Brain Damage," 1970), are integrated into the structure of the verbal text as *other modes of discourse* – visual discourses. Thus they contribute to and serve to heighten the polyphonic structure of these texts; through their surrealist *non sequiturs*, they bring worlds of discourse, visual and verbal, into collision.

The schizoid text

In what order do we "read" mixed visual-verbal texts like "Brain Damage"? First the verbal text, then the visual, or vice-versa? Or do we glance back and forth, interrupting our reading of the verbal text to re-examine the drawings? Clearly, there is no fixed order of reading in such dual-medium texts, as there is in a purely verbal text, where we must read the first sentence before the second and the second before the third, or risk losing the meaning. And this is true not only of "Brain Damage" and other texts in which the illustrations are *non sequiturs* relative to the verbal text, but also of texts such as Reed's *Mumbo Jumbo* or Gass' *Lonesome Wife* in which the illustrations are obliquely or diffusely related to the verbal text. In short, dual-medium texts approach the condition of *simultaneity*: ideally their visual and verbal components should be "read" simultaneously. But this is not the only form of simultaneity in postmodernist writing.

As long ago as 1945, Joseph Frank in his seminal essay on "Spatial form in modern literature" (reprinted in an expanded form in *The Widening Gyre*, 1963) demonstrated how the aspiration toward simultaneity animated modernist writing. In texts like *Ulysses*, Proust's *A la Recherche du temps perdu*, or Djuna Barnes' *Nightwood*, understanding was less a process unfolding in time than the reconstruction by the reader of a pattern in space, drawing on elements widely separated in the text. Of course, given the temporality of the reading process, true simultaneity is unachievable in a verbal medium, as Frank's critics were quick to point out. But Frank himself never said that it was achievable, only that the modernist writers approached it as nearly as possible in view of the limitations inherent in their medium.[19]

Frank's essay can be seen as a statement of modernist orthodoxy on the issue of spatial form. From the modernist point of view, Joyce, Proust and Barnes had gone about as far as one could possibly go in the direction of simultaneity; they marked out the limits. But of course one *could* go further in that direction – only, however, by rediscovering the possibilities implied by such texts as Mallarmé's "Un coup de dés," which Frank (and he was not alone) dismissed as a "fascinating historical curiosity," the "necessary limit" of spatial form.[20] Beyond this "necessary limit" lay the postmodernist *split text*, two or more texts arranged in parallel, to be read simultaneously – to the degree that that is possible.

Various formats have been devised for running two or more texts in parallel. Different texts have been printed on alternate pages of a book, or even on alternate *lines*.[21] By far the most successful split-text formats, however, have been modeled either on the scholarly gloss or the newspaper page.

There are, of course, two familiar formats for glossing a text: the text with marginal gloss, the text with footnotes. Literary precursors which spring to mind include, in the case of marginal gloss, Coleridge's *Rime of the Ancient Mariner*, and, in the case of the footnoted text, *The Waste Land*.[22] Whenever a text is split into text proper and gloss, whether marginal or in footnotes, questions arise about the relation between the two parallel texts. According to the conventions of scholarly and scriptural commentary, of course, the gloss ought to be accessory or supplemental to the text proper; in practice, however, the postmodernists often flout this convention. For instance, the poem "Pale Fire," in Nabokov's novel by that name, dwindles to insignificance alongside its manic annotator's grossly swollen end-note commentary, which is in any case largely irrelevant to the poem. Elsewhere, the weight of relative importance is more evenly distributed between text proper and gloss, the main text functioning less as a mere pretext and more like an equal partner. This is the case, for example, in Flann O'Brien's *The Third Policeman* (1940/67) and R. M. Koster's *The Dissertation* (1975). Our attention and involvement are more evenly divided, in the first of these examples, between the narrator's fantastic adventures in the main text and the life and opinions of the crackpot scientist DeSelby in the footnotes; in the second example, between the biography of Léon Fuertes in the main text and his biographer's forays into the Other World in the footnotes.

Split texts like Koster's and Flann O'Brien's approximate simultaneity more closely than does *Pale Fire* (1962), for in reading *Pale Fire* we tend to opt for the gloss over the main text, while the more symmetrical distribution of interest and importance in *The Third Policeman* and *The Dissertation* encourages us to try to follow both texts simultaneously. This, of course, is impossible, strictly speaking. Even with Koster and Flann O'Brien we are forced to choose which to read first, main text or footnotes; we must improvise an order – jump from main text to gloss whenever we encounter a footnote? Or read forward through the main text to a certain point, then backtrack to read all the footnotes? Or the other way around, first all the footnotes to a certain point, then the main text? This is precisely how the various formats for glossing a text – in the margins, in footnotes, or even interlinearly – foreground the materiality of the book. Reading these quasi-simultaneous texts involves, at the very least, the reader's eye skipping across the page, from center to margin or from top to bottom; and in some cases, such as *Pale Fire* or *The Dissertation*, it even involves flipping from the main text in the front of the text to the commentary at the end, and back again. We are forced to manipulate the book as a physical object, thus never losing sight of the ontological "cut" between the projected world and the material book. This can be annoying, as any reader of books with footnotes printed at the end can attest; but even annoyance can become a device of foregrounding.

Tod Andrews, John Barth's narrator in his late-modernist first novel, *The Floating Opera* (1956), hesitating between two possible openings for one of his chapters, experiments with a two-column text, but abandons the experiment after a mere six lines for fear of alienating his readers. This consideration has evidently not deterred the many postmodernist writers who have laid out their texts in imitation of a newspaper page, running two or more parallel texts in vertical columns, presumably to be read simultaneously.[23] Vertical columns is not the only option, of course; it is also possible to run parallel texts in horizontal blocks across the upper and lower parts of the page, as in Gabriel Josipovici's "Mobius the Stripper" (1974) or Gass's *Willie Masters' Lonesome Wife*. The questions that arise with multiple-column texts are essentially identical to those raised by glossed or footnoted texts: where should we begin? In what order should the parallel columns or blocks be read? The consequences, too, are much the same: the reader, forced to *improvise* an order of reading, since none is unequivocally imposed on him or her as would be the case in a conventional prose format, remains constantly aware of the spatiality and materiality of the page and the book. This awareness tends to eclipse, if only sporadically, the projected fictional world.

We can observe these consequences in one of the more spectacular examples of a double-column text, Jacques Derrida's *Glas* (1974). Derrida describes the format of *Glas*:

> Deux colonnes inégales . . . dont chaque – enveloppe ou gaine, incalculablement renverse, retourne, remplace, remarque, recoupe l'autre.[24]

The two parallel columns are "inégales" in a number of ways. The right-hand column, containing an essay on Jean Genet, is more spaced-out than the left, and printed in a larger type-size; the effect is that the left-hand column, devoted to Hegel, is distinctly denser, blacker. Each of the two columns may in turn fission into a main text with marginal gloss in smaller type, the double-column text in effect becoming three or occasionally even four columns wide. Alternatively, extended quotation from documents may be introduced into either column, and when this occurs the quoted extract is heavily indented relative to the margins of the column; the result is an increase in white space, giving the page a "spacey" appearance. In what order is this strange, fluctuating text to be read? The complete left-hand essay first, then the right-hand one, or vice-versa? Or page by page? Or some combination of these reading patterns? And should we expect to find some relationship between the two columns, as the passage I cited above seems to promise? Are the two columns in some sense analogous, mutually illuminating? Are the juxtapositions deliberate or merely random? Obviously, *Glas* projects no fictional world, as double-column fictions like *In Transit* (1969) or *Peter Prince* or "Mobius the Stripper" do, so no ontological tension is generated here between projected world and real-world book. But the spatial form of *Glas* does foreground the materiality of the printed book by contrast with the elusive presence/absence of the authors who supposedly "stand behind" the printed word – not only Hegel and Genet, but Derrida himself.

There are other means of confronting the reader with a choice among alternative orders of reading, besides the glossed text and the double-column text. The simplest of these, surprisingly, has been little used: namely, numbering the divisions of the text (books, chapters) out of order. This strategy gives the reader two alternatives, either to read the text in the order indicated by the numbering, or to read it in the order in which it is actually printed. I am aware of only one text that exploits this possibility: Alasdair Gray's *Lanark*, which begins with Book 3, followed by the Prologue, then Books 1 and 2, then Book 4, interrupted about two-thirds of the way through by the Epilogue. In fact, the out-of-order numbering of *Lanark* is not designed to give the reader a real choice among alternatives, but merely "lays bare" this novel's *in medias res* structure. "I want *Lanark* to be read in one order but eventually thought of in another," the "author" tells his character in the Epilogue: "It's an old device. Homer, Vergil, Milton and Scott Fitzgerald used it."[25] So after all the misnumbering of *Lanark* is not as radical a violation of conventional format as it might at first appear. Nevertheless, it does foreground the order of reading.

Not as strongly, however, as certain other innovative texts which really do offer the reader a choice among alternative orders of reading, notably Cortázar's *Hopscotch* (*Rayuela*, 1963) and B. S. Johnson's *The Unfortunates* (1969). *Hopscotch*, the better known of the two, invites the reader to choose between two alternative orders, either the normal order of reading, beginning with Chapter 1 and finishing with Chapter 56, or an order beginning with Chapter 73 and "hopscotching" through the text. Johnson multiplies alternatives by presenting his text in the form of 27 stapled gatherings contained in a box rather than between covers. One of these gatherings is marked "First," another "Last," but all the others are free to fall into any order that the reader determines. Both of these striking formats require the reader to manipulate the text physically. If, in the case of *Hopscotch*, he or she opts for the "hopscotch" order, this entails flipping pages in pursuit of the next chapter in the irregular but fixed order. In the case of *The Unfortunates*, the reader must literally handle the gatherings, shuffle them, stack them. Such manipulations certainly serve to keep the materiality of the book in the forefront of the reader's consciousness.[26]

Model kits

Novels like *Hopscotch* and *The Unfortunates* appear to give us the opportunity to build our own texts and, to an extent, our own fictional worlds. In this sense they are like model kits.[27] Now, as Umberto Eco tells us, *every* text is in some sense a model kit, or, as he puts it, a *"machine for producing possible worlds."*[28] Some, however, are more transparently machine-like than others. Among the most transparent are texts which generate worlds by arbitrarily or mechanically manipulating words, texts such as Roussel's *Locus Solus* (1914) and *Impressions d'Afrique* (1910), Abish's *Alphabetical Africa* (1974) and "Ardor/Awe/Atrocity" (1977), Barth's *LETTERS* (1979), (see Chapter 10, "Styled worlds.") Here the machine produces word-patterns and meaning goes along for the ride. Words, however, are not the only elements capable of being manipulated in this way; paper and print, elements of the "technological structure" of the book, can be used in the same way, and with the same consequences.

Spacing, I have said, is conventionally associated with verse, and just as verse form – rhyme-schemes, or the repetition of end-words in a sestina – imposes constraints on the projected world, so spacing by itself can impose comparable constraints. The analogy between spacing and rhyme-scheme is particularly exact in the case of Guy Davenport's "Au Tombeau de Charles Fourier." Davenport's text is divided into 30 numbered sections or chapters, each chapter in turn being divided by white space into nine paragraphs, each paragraph comprising exactly four lines of type. These mechanically regular paragraphs do not behave like conventional paragraphs, however, for they do not correspond to shifts in topic or content; rather, such shifts typically occur *within* Davenport's paragraphs, and the same topic often continues from one paragraph to the next. In short, these paragraphs are semantically *enjambed*, in the same way that lines of verse may be syntactically enjambed. The effect is rather like that of a cookie-cutter punching out identical shapes regardless of the material upon which it is being imposed; or, if a more elevated comparison is called for, it is rather like the effect of a Pindaric ode, whose content-units spill over the formal divisions between stanzas. The cookie-cutter falters only in the final section of "Au Tombeau," which is defective, containing only two paragraphs, the last of them three rather than four lines long. By a deliberate irony, it is in these defective final lines that the text reflects on its own regularity of spacing. Here Davenport quotes Gertrude Stein's account, in *The Autobiography of Alice B. Toklas*, of the victory parade in Paris at the end of the First World War: "Pershing and his officer carrying the flag behind him were perhaps the most perfectly spaced."[29]

Perfection of spacing also imposes artificial constraints on the world of Raymond Federman's *The Voice in the Closet* (1979), but to more profound effect. This is an astonishing example of a split text, for here the two parallel texts are (theoretically) identical, but in different languages, one in English, the other in French. Federman had already experimented with this possibility in the double-column page of *Double or Nothing*, the right-hand column of which was an English translation of the French text in the parallel left-hand column. In *The Voice in the Closet*, this format has been expanded into two parallel twenty-page texts, bound back-to-back within the same covers. In other words, each text is printed upside-down and backwards relative to the other. This means that, in order to compare the two texts, the reader must flip the book over and turn it upside-down – an arrangement which guarantees the reader's continuing awareness of *The Voice in the Closet* as physical object.

Even more extraordinary, however, is the fact that each of these texts follows a rigorous typographical format: each page of the English text forms a perfect square of print, each French page a perfect rectangle. "Boxes of words," says the author's surrogate self in *The Twofold Vibration* (1982), describing *The Voice in the Closet*, "words abandoned to deliberate chaos and yet boxed into an inescapable form."[30] These "boxes" have been composed in obedience to strict and arbitrary rules: no extra spacing between words to make the lines come out even; no hyphenation of words at the ends of lines. To achieve a straight margin, in other words, the writer must have been forced to experiment with various rewordings until he found one that worked, changing his text to accommodate it to his tyrannical format:

> think of the madness of sketching all these possible words into an appropriate form, the desire and the need to add more, the excitement of chance too, but also think of the cool restraint, the control, the necessary calculation, to the point of counting the number of letters in words to justify their presence, or their elimination, think of the extreme reserve and the cunning, ah yes the cunning that such a game presupposes.[31]

This format is literally a Procrustean bed on which to stretch a world, requiring the writer to lop, stretch, substitute – and in two languages! And the result, as in analogous cases such as Abish's "Ardor/Awe/Atrocity," is acute tension between the transparently artificial format and the highly-charged content "trapped" within that format.

For the quadrangular formats are "verbal icons" of the closet in which the autobiographical protagonist eluded the Nazis who deported the rest of his family to their deaths. The closet shape, in one sense, *generates* the world of this text, just as, in an analogous sense, the closet experience generated the writer Federman and everything that he has written. The closet-shaped text is transparently a machine for producing worlds, a model kit:

> If you read the text carefully . . . you'll see appear before you on the shattered white space the people drawn by the black words, flattened and disseminated on the surface of the paper inside the black inkblood, that was the challenge, never to speak the reality of the event but to render it concrete into the blackness of the words.[32]

Compare the world-generating machines designed by Sukenick in his texts *Out* and *Long Talking Bad Conditions Blues*, described earlier in this chapter. Here, however, it is not a single spatial format that generates the world of the text, as in *The Voice in the Closet*, but the succession of changing formats: the long expiration of breath or "dying fall" of *Out*, as increasingly larger swatches of white space shoulder the print aside; the systole and diastole of *Long Talking Bad Conditions Blues*, dictating the gradual deterioration and then amelioration of "conditions" (material, social, psychological) in this world. These are machines made of changing configurations of white space. But white space is not the only element of a book's "technological structure" from which world-generating machines may be constructed. Illustrations, too, can be manipulated to this end. Consider, for example, Italo Calvino's well-known text, *The Castle of Crossed Destinies* (1969; expanded, 1973). At first glance this appears to be a collection of stories within a traditional frame-tale structure, illustrated with reproductions of cards from two different Tarot packs. The layout is distinctive and intriguing, the illustrations running along the margins of the verbal text, giving the impression of a marginal gloss, literally a parallel visual text keyed to the verbal text. But first impressions are misleading; in fact, the relationship of illustration to text is precisely the reverse – the verbal text actually glosses the images from the Tarot pack, rather than the other way around. The relation is more nearly that of a verbal caption to the photograph it accompanies. So, at least, the frame-tale alleges, and this account is apparently confirmed by the author in a note which closes the book. First the Tarot cards were laid out in various arrangements – fictionally by the characters in the frame-tale, but really by the author; then the written narratives were composed at the instigation of the cards, with the purpose of motivating and explaining their images and their sequence:

> This book is made first of pictures – the tarot playing cards – and secondly of written words. Through the sequence of the pictures stories are told, which the written word tries to reconstruct and interpret.[33]

In short, the illustrations propose, the writer merely disposes, transcribing the stories which the pictures seem to suggest. "A machine for constructing stories," the author calls this format.[34] A machine whose workings are clearly visible – as visible as those of Davenport's, Federman's and Sukenick's world-making machines. Indeed, the workings of *all* postmodernist world-making machines are visible, in one way or another, to one degree or another; this, precisely, is what makes them postmodernist.

13: AUTHORS: DEAD AND POSTHUMOUS

I think you will agree that I am alive in every part of this book; turn back
twenty, thirty, one hundred pages – *I am back there*. That is why I hate the
story; characters are not snakes that they must shed their skins on every
page – there can only be one action: what a man is. When you have
understood this, you will be through with novels.
(Kenneth Patchen, *The Journal of Albion Moonlight*, 1941)

Dead, but still with us, still with us, but dead.
(Donald Barthelme, *The Dead Father*, 1975)

After twelve chapters of flirting with real-world historical fact, the narrator of
John Fowles's *The French Lieutenant's Woman* (1969) abruptly confronts us with
an irrefutable fact of a different kind: "This story I am telling is all imagination. These characters I create never existed outside my own mind."[1] With
this gesture, the illusory reality of the fictional world is destroyed, and in its
place we are offered, if not *the* real world, at least *a* real world. For what is
ultimately real in the ontological structure of *The French Lieutenant's Woman*, if
not the author's performance in creating that world? The author occupies an
ontological level superior to his world; by breaking the frame around his
world, the author foregrounds his own superior reality. The metafictional
gesture of frame-breaking is, in other words, a form of superrealism.[2]

Frame-breaking is a risky business. Intended to establish an absolute level
of reality, it paradoxically *relativizes* reality; intended to provide an ontologically stable foothold, it only destabilizes ontology further. For the metafictional gesture of sacrificing an illusory reality to a higher, "realer" reality, that
of the author, sets a precedent: why should this gesture not be *repeatable*?
What prevents the author's reality from being treated in its turn as an illusion
to be shattered? Nothing whatsoever, and so the supposedly absolute reality
of the author becomes just another level of fiction, and the *real* world retreats
to a further remove. Or to put it differently, to reveal the author's position
within the ontological structure is only to introduce the author *into the fiction*;

far from abolishing the frame, this gesture merely *widens* it to include the author as a fictional character. These consequences of frame-breaking are clear from *The French Lieutenant's Woman*. In Chapter 13, the voice of the "author" intrudes upon his fiction to declare its fictionality; in Chapter 61, the "author" *enters* his world in the person of an interfering "impresario" whose physical features caricature those of the real John Fowles. The cycle of metafictional frame-breaking is repeated twice, once at the level of the fictional world, once at the level of the author, who now is revealed as himself a fiction.

In an effort to stabilize this dizzying upward spiral of fictions, metafictions, meta-metafictions, and so on to infinite regress, various postmodernist writers have tried introducing into their texts what appears to be the one irreducibly real reality in their performance as writers – namely, the act of writing itself. Thus arises the postmodernist *topos* of the writer at his desk, or what Ronald Sukenick has called "the truth of the page":

> The truth of the page is that there's a writer sitting there writing the page . . . . If the writer is conceived, both by himself and by the reader, as "someone sitting there writing the page," illusionism becomes impossible . . . the reader is prevented from being hypnotized by the illusion of that make-believe so effective in the hands of the nineteenth-century novelists but which by now has become a passive, escapist habit of response to a creative work – instead he is forced to recognize the reality of the reading situation as the writer points to the reality of the writing situation, and the work, instead of allowing him to escape the truth of his own life, keeps returning him to it but, one hopes, with his own imagination activated and revitalized.[3]

The truth of the page is asserted in Sukenick's own texts *Up* (1968) and "The Death of the Novel" (1969), as well as, for instance, in Steve Katz's *The Exagggerations of Peter Prince* (1969); but its *locus classicus* is Samuel Beckett's *Texts for Nothing* of the early 1950s.

Here we seem to be in touch with the real world at last, for what could be more undeniably real than the actual conditions under which the writer has produced the text we are reading? No element of illusionism seems to have been interposed. Yet ambiguities arise. Does not the mere introduction of the scene of writing into a text involve a degree, perhaps a very large degree, of fictionalization? Is the image of the writer at his desk essentially any less fictional than, say, Fowles' caricature of the writer as impresario? "Someone sitting there writing the page" is always, despite what Sukenick says, only a fictional reconstruction after all. And this reconstruction of the act of writing depends upon *what has been written* – on the text that we read. In this sense, the writing itself is "more real" than the act of writing that presumably gave rise to it!

Where, then, does the level of the irreducibly "real" world lie? The harder we look for it, the more elusive and mirage-like it becomes. Behind the "truth of the page" – the reality of the writer at his desk – lies the superior reality of the writing itself; but behind the reality of the writing must lie the superior reality of the *act* of writing that has produced it! An uncomfortable circularity, and one that hinges on the strangely amphibious ontological status, the presence/absence, of the author. The author is no newcomer to our ontological poetics of postmodernist writing, s/he has been with us all along, more or less surreptitiously. Whenever some element of ontological structure or some ontological boundary is foregrounded, the author's role and activity is inevitably foregrounded along with it. Who else could be held responsible for the practice of foregrounding, who else could be credited with the *intention to foreground*, if not her or him? Clearly, it is time that we approached this paradox head-on – or as nearly head-on as possible, given its elusiveness.

The dead author

"Exit Author" – if one were looking for a slogan or motto for modernist writing, this surely would be among the candidates. Coined by the critic Joseph Warren Beach in 1932, it memorably captures what various modernist innovators – Flaubert, James, Joyce – had been saying all along about their own and others' practice: that the visible, intrusive authorial persona of Thackeray, Balzac, Trollope had been superseded; that henceforth the author would be invisible and unobtrusive, above or behind but not *in* his creation. The modernists sought to remove the traces of their presence from the surface of their writing, and to this end exploited or developed various forms of ostensibly "narratorless" texts – texts based in large part on direct dialogue exchanges (Hemingway, Ivy Compton-Burnett) or on free indirect discourse (early Joyce, Woolf, Dos Passos). Or they effaced their own subjectivities behind the surrogate subjectivity of a first-person narrator or interior monologuist (Conrad, Faulkner, Joyce in *Ulysses*, Woolf in *The Waves*). Paradoxically, the more they sought to efface themselves, the more they made their presence conspicuous. Strategies of self-effacement, while ostensibly obliterating surface traces of the author, in fact call attention to the author as *strategist*. This is true even of the limit-case of self-effacement, montage texts like the "Newsreels" of Dos Passos' *U.S.A.*, where the apparent absence of a controlling authorial voice provokes the reader to *reconstruct* a position for the missing author to occupy, in effect an *image* of the author. Self-effacement, it turns out, is a form of self-advertisement.

Postmodernist fiction has brought the author back to the surface. Free once again, as we have seen, to break in upon the fictional world, as in Chapter 13 of *The French Lieutenant's Woman*, the postmodernist author is even free to confront us with the image of himself or herself in the act of producing the text, as in Beckett's *Texts for Nothing*, Sukenick's *Up*, or Katz's *Exagggerations of Peter Prince*. But if modernist self-effacement is a form of self-advertisement, then, by the logic of paradox, self-advertisement is conversely a form of self-effacement. Thus, the postmodernist slogan, successor to modernism's "Exit Author," is "The Death of the Author." Roland Barthes, in an essay with this slogan for its title (1968), writes that "the text is henceforth made and read in such a way that at all its levels the author is absent."[4] Writing is no longer an expression emanating from a unified source or origin, but rather "a multi-dimensional space in which a variety of writings, none of them original, blend and clash," "a tissue of quotations drawn from the innumerable centers of culture."[5] The writer does not *originate* his discourse, but mixes already extant discourses.

The most memorable parable of the death of the author is Jorge Luis Borges' "Borges and I" (1957).[6] This text begins as a pastiche of a typical romantic attitude, the sense of a division between the authentic self and an inauthentic role or mask. The innovation here, and the source of paradox, is Borges' identification of inauthenticity with the self that emerges in and through *writing*, the written persona from which the authentic self claims to be in constant retreat:

> Years ago I tried to free myself from him, and I went from the mythologies of the city suburbs to games with time and infinity, but now those games belong to Borges, and I will have to think up something else. Thus is my life a flight, and I lose everything, and everything belongs to oblivion or to him.[7]

But if the protest against the inauthentic written self is itself made in and through writing, then from whom does this protest originate? Who speaks? "I don't know which one of the two of us is writing this page." The writer vanishes, eclipsed by "his" writing: he "dies" by projecting himself into writing, just as one day he will die biologically: "I am destined to perish, definitively, and only some instant of me may live on in him." "Writing," says Barthes,

> is that neutral, composite, oblique space where our subject slips away, the negative where all identity is lost, starting with the very identity of the body writing.[8]

Michel Foucault has questioned the "Death of the Author" concept, but in such a way as to affirm it in the end. "What is an author?" he asks (1969), and answers that whatever it (he, she) is, it is not dead, or if it *is* dead, it has *always* been dead. Contemporary notions of the death of the author, such as those that are implicit in Borges and explicit in Barthes, actually *preserve* the author in a displaced form. The unity formerly supposed to be guaranteed by the author has been displaced to the *oeuvre*, as if that concept were unproblematical; the *oeuvre* is only the author in disguise. The authority formerly invested in the author has been displaced to a hypostatized writing where, again, the author persists under the camouflage of "transcendental anonymity."[9]

How, then, are we to begin rethinking the concept of author without lapsing either into a naïve theory of presence or an equally naïve theory of absence? Foucault answers, by discarding the notion of author as *entity*, and beginning to think of the author as a *function* in texts and in the culture at large, a function that varies from period to period and from one social order to another. From this perspective, the author appears as an *institution*, governed by the institutions which in a particular society regulate the circulation of discourses (e.g. copyright laws); as a *construct* of the reading-process, rather than a textual given; as *plural* rather than unitary. The object of this rethinking, Foucault insists, is not to re-establish the theme of an originating subject, but to grasp the subject's points of insertion, modes of functioning, and systems of dependencies . . . it is a matter of depriving the subject (or its substitute) of its role as originator, and of analysing the subject as a variable and complex function of discourse.[10]

In other words, Foucault's theory of the author-function *incorporates* the death of the author but is not reducible to it. If the author is absent, he is not *newly* absent; he has been absent in different modes throughout history – or, it would be equally true to say, *present* in different modes. But if Foucault's thinking is not reducible to the slogan "Death of the author," it nevertheless is symptomatic of the same change of consciousness that produced that slogan. As Barthes remarks, writing has no doubt *always* involved the eclipse of the subject writing, but the degree of *awareness* of this fact has varied. Our period has "rediscovered" the death of the author; and it is this rediscovery that permits Foucault to conceive of the author as a function.

What is strange and disorienting about the postmodernist author is that even when s/he appears to know that s/he is only a function, s/he chooses to behave, if only sporadically, like a subject, a presence. This is strikingly true of the writings of Raymond Federman. Here authority and subjectivity are dispersed among a plurality of selves, in a way apparently quite compatible with the contemporary awareness of authorial eclipse and displacement. Thus, in *Double or Nothing* (1971), the authorial role is distributed among figures located at different levels of a recursive Chinese-box structure: a protagonist who acts and suffers, a narrator who tells his story, a "recorder" who relays the narrative and takes responsibility for the typographical arrangement of the text on the page, and a fourth figure – the "author"? – who regulates the relations among the other three. In *Take It or Leave It* (1976), the narrative subject is initially divided between the protagonist and a "second-hand teller" who relays the protagonist's story to an audience. But these figures fission as the text unfolds, the protagonist into a narrating self (or "first-hand teller") and narrated self, the second-hand teller into Hombre de la Pluma, whose biography, a thinly-disguised version of Federman's own, is introduced by way of a text-within-the-text. In *The Twofold Vibration* (1982) the subject is dispersed into four figures, not, as in *Double or Nothing*, located at different ontological levels, but all located at the same level, the roles of character, narrator, and author circulating among them. Finally, and most radically of all, *The Voice in the Closet* (1979) dramatizes the paradoxical relation between writer and written self which is the theme of "Borges and I." Here the writing rebels against its writer, against Federman himself, succeeding finally in ridding the text of his presence, liberating itself, but into an anarchic and unreadable "free play" of language from which it recovers only in the last line.

Disintegrated and disseminated in these various ways, the author in Federman's texts nevertheless *reassembles himself*, asserting his unitary identity against the centrifugal force of the text. The four-tier structure of *Double or Nothing* ultimately collapses into a single surrogate self, a compound protagonist–narrator–"recorder"–author, while in *Take It or Leave It* the protagonist and second-hand teller tend to fuse, over the teller's strenuous (and therefore suspect) protests. In *The Twofold Vibration*, too, the four subjects converge, losing their separate identities. And in *The Voice in the Closet*, the writer, expelled from the writing, returns in its closing line. The author, supposedly absent from the text "at all its levels," nevertheless manages to assert his presence at some of them, at least. After all, even the parable "Borges and I" is equivocal about which self is finally responsible for the text. The paradox cuts both ways: if the authentic self cannot write without becoming the written self, the written self cannot protest its authenticity without becoming, in some sense, the authentic self!

This oscillation between authorial presence and absence characterizes the postmodernist author. Fully aware that the author has been declared dead, the postmodernist text nevertheless insists on authorial presence, although not consistently. The author flickers in and out of existence at different levels of the ontological structure and at different points in the unfolding text. Neither fully present nor completely absent, s/he plays hide-and-seek with us throughout the text, which projects an illusion of authorial presence only to withdraw it abruptly, filling the void left by this withdrawal with surrogate subjectivity once again. Like Barthelme's Dead Father, the author, it appears, is *"dead, but still with us, still with us, but dead."*

It should be obvious by now why postmodernist texts have opened themselves once again to intrusions by the authorial persona. This ontologically amphibious figure, alternately present and absent, embodies the same action of ontological vacillation or "flicker" that we have observed in other elements of postmodernist poetics. The author, in short, is another tool for the exploration and exploitation of ontology. S/he functions at two theoretically distinct levels of ontological structure: as the vehicle of autobiographical *fact* within the projected fictional world; and as the *maker* of that world, visibly occupying an ontological level superior to it.

Auto-bio-graphy

Steve Katz's *The Exagggerations of Peter Prince* includes an episode in which Peter Prince, touring in Italy, encounters an eccentric Danish sculptor named Nilsen, his wife and circle of friends. The episode is rather conventionally novelistic, except for two oddities: first, it is placed under erasure, literally crossed out; secondly, interleaved among the canceled pages of this episode are uncanceled passages in which Katz reveals the autobiographical basis for Peter Prince's fictional encounter, its "origins" in his own experience. Thus, we learn that Katz himself really took the tour that Peter Prince is said to have taken, that Nilsen's real name was Sorensen, and so on. This is puzzling: why fictionalize autobiography at all if you are going to "defictionalize" it on the facing page? why invent a fictional name for a real person if you are going to reveal the real name behind the substitution? in general, why confront autobiographical fiction and "straight" autobiography in this way?

Ronald Sukenick sheds some light on Katz's rationale:

> The use of the self in such books as Steve Katz's *Exagggerations of Peter Prince* and my own *Up* was quite contrary to the doctrine of self-expression. We were not writing autobiography or confession – we were at times using those forms as ways of incorporating our experience into fiction at the same level as any other data.[11]

Note Sukenick's emphasis: he does *not* say, "at the same level as any other *fiction*." That would have been demonstrably untrue. Autobiography claims a different ontological status from "pure" fiction, and a *stronger* one. Even if we acknowledge (as of course we must) the fictional element in all autobiography, nevertheless the relative ontological strength of autobiography is clearly perceived whenever fiction and autobiography are confronted, as they literally are on facing pages of *Exagggerations of Peter Prince*. Fiction is fatally compromised; it is the autobiographical fiction, not the "straight" autobiography, that seems redundant here. But this relative strength also belongs to other forms of real-world data – facts from almanacs, encyclopedias, science, historical research. Sukenick is correct in locating autobiographical fact "at the same level as any other data." Autobiography functions in texts like Katz's *Exagggerations* as a distinct ontological level, a world to be juxtaposed with the fictional world, and thus as a tool for foregrounding ontological boundaries and tensions.

In the tape transcripts incorporated in "The Death of the Novel," Sukenick's interlocutor is Lynn Sukenick, at that time his real-life wife. Having played her part, she "exits" from the fictional world:

> Becoming real again, she returns to, as she puts it, her own interests. What I need is a bunch of friends who would be willing to become my characters for a whole story. Maybe I can hire some. Somebody ought to start a character rental service.[12]

Although Sukenick never actually co-opts his friends for the duration of any of his texts, he does assemble a number of them for the party in the closing pages of *Up*. Lynn is in attendance, mingling with her husband's invented, purely fictional girlfriends; so, too, are several other real-life friends, including the novelist Steve Katz. Characters from wholly separate ontological spheres rub shoulders. The effect is analogous to that of co-opting fictional characters from other writers' novels (as in Sorrentino's *Imaginative Qualities of Actual Things*, 1971, or Fuentes's *Terra nostra*, 1975) or inserting real-world historical figures into fictional situations (as in Max Apple's stories or Coover's *The Public Burning*, 1977). In short, throwing a fictional party for one's real-life friends is another case of transworld identity between real and fictional entities. This is a particularly heightened form of ontological boundary-violation: like travelers to or from other worlds in science fiction, these "visitors" from the world of autobiography function as synecdoches of their place of origin, in effect carrying their reality into the midst of the fictional world and setting off a whole series of disruptive ontological repercussions.

Transworld identity between fictional characters and real-world friends is disruptive enough by itself, but it becomes even more disorienting when the friend *confirms* that he has been co-opted into fiction. Steve Katz, we are told during the end-of-the-novel party in *Up*, is "here briefly on a special guest appearance from his own novel . . . take a bow Steve."[13] Katz mentions this guest appearance in his *own* novel, *The Exagggerations of Peter Prince*, even blaming the delays in his narrative on his prior obligation to Sukenick: "it's probably some little insignificant thing he's going to have me do," gripes Katz, with some justification, as it turns out.[14] In a similar vein of paradox, Federman's narrator in *Take It or Leave It* (1976) temporarily "steps out" of his own fictional world to lend Sukenick a hand, leaving responsibility for the narrative with its protagonist, who of course makes a hash of it:

> What? Oh you guys want to know where I was? Why I left my post . . . why I deserted the recitation? Deserted! You guys exaggerate. I had to go to the bathroom. No . . . I'm kidding. I went to see a friend. Buddy of mine, Ronnie. Ronald Sukenick. You know UP and OUT and 98.6 – Fiction Collective. He was having problems with his story. Wanted me to help a bit. I was only gone a short time.[15]

The claim to have left one fictional world in order to work in (or, in Federman's case, help with) another fiction gives the illusion of *corroborating* the transworld identity. The analogy here is with *retour de personnage*, in which the recurrence of a fictional character in another text by the same author gives the illusion of corroborating the character's "real" existence, as in Balzac or Faulkner. What is not perfectly clear is whether we should consider the present case as one of transworld identity between a real-world person and a fictional character, or between fictional characters in two different texts – the "Steve Katz" who appears in Sukenick's *Up*, on the one hand, and the "Steve Katz" who appears in Katz's own *Exagggerations of Peter Prince*, on the other. Or perhaps this is a *triangular* identity, involving two fictional Katzes and a real one . . . .

Katz once told an interviewer:

> Though I love to create the illusionist's space, I also enjoy disrupting those illusions, so there's no attachment to them. To accomplish that end I have employed Steve Katz to patrol my books.[16]

If co-opting one's friends is a heightened form of transworld identity and consequently of ontological foregrounding, then co-opting *oneself* is an even more heightened form of it. The author as a character in his own fiction signals the paradoxical interpenetration of two realms that are mutually inaccessible, or ought to be. Steve Katz is not the only author who has been employed to patrol his own books. After all, it is a character named "Ronnie Sukenick" who throws the party in *Up*. Sukenick also appears as a character in several of the texts in *The Death of the Novel*, and in the novels *Out* (1973) and *98.6* (1975). Similarly, Gabriel García Márquez appears near the end of *One Hundred Years of Solitude* (1967) as the bosom friend of the youngest Aureliano Buendía; Salman Rushdie plays a tiny walk-on role as an older schoolmate of the narrator in his own novel *Midnight's Children* (1981); Max Apple steps into a prize-fight ring with Norman Mailer in Apple's story "Inside Norman Mailer" (from *The Oranging of America*, 1976); and Kurt Vonnegut, Jr, appears as Billy Pilgrim's fellow prisoner-of-war in *Slaughterhouse-Five* (1969), suffering diarrhoea in Billy's presence and glimpsing Dresden for the first time over Billy's shoulder:

> That was I. That was me. That was the author of this book.[17]

But who is this "I" or "me" who shares the world of the fictional characters? Roland Barthes reminds us of what happens to the author when he (she) inserts or inscribes himself in his text:

> It is not that the Author may not "come back" in the Text, in his text, but he then does so as a "guest." If he is a novelist, he is inscribed in the novel like one of his characters, figured in the carpet; no longer privileged, paternal, aletheological, his inscription is ludic. He becomes, as it were, a paper-author: his life is no longer the origin of his fictions but a fiction contributing to his work . . . . The word "bio-graphy" re-acquires a strong, etymological sense, at the same time as the sincerity of the enunciation . . . becomes a false problem: the *I* which writes the text, it too, is never more than a paper-*I*.[18]

The paper-author, the author as a guest in his own text: these paradoxes are dramatized especially strikingly in Sukenick's *Out*. Here the author as character makes a highly foregrounded entrance and exit, not, like Lynn Sukenick in *Up* and "The Death of the Novel," merely crossing from one ontological realm to another and then casually "returning to her own interests." The character named "Ron Sukenick" enters this text by filling the void left by its protagonist's departure – literally, for he appears first as a zombie, the reanimated corpse of the character who called himself "Rex." Eventually "Ron Sukenick" takes over the responsibility for narrating his own story, and the text becomes a first-person narrative for several episodes. But at the beginning of Chapter 4 the author in his role *as author*, not as character, requisitions the first-person pronoun for metafictional purposes. When the protagonist reappears, he is no longer "Ron Sukenick' but "Roland Sycamore." What has become of the Sukenick character? The author explains:

> Roland Sycamore you don't know this yet peeled off from the Sukenick character after the karate fight and the latter is no longer a character at all but the real me if that's possible I'm getting out of this novel[19]

So the character "Ron Sukenick" has exited from the fictional world to become Sukenick the author. Who, then, was performing as author while Sukenick existed at the fictional level, *inside* the world of the text? (The same puzzle is posed when Federman's narrator temporarily absconds from *Take It or Leave It*.) And where does this surrogate, "Roland Sycamore," come from? If he had "peeled off" from the Sukenick character, does this mean he is in some sense part of Sukenick's subjectivity? But in what sense? Sukenick as author is "the real me if that's possible" – a formulation which recalls "Borges and I," for surely, as long as this Sukenick intrudes upon the text in the role of author, he is not the "real me" but still a paper-author, still inscribed, still a fictional character. And now this paper-author, too, we are told, departs; and it is true that there are no more overt authorial intrusions or metafictional gestures for the remainder of the text. "Exit Author" – but in a way that Joseph Warren Beach certainly never anticipated.

Roman-à-clef

Transworld identity between real-world persons and fictional characters depends upon identity of proper names; this is part of its definition. What fixes our attention on the ontological boundary is the appearance of a real-world proper name in a fictional context. "Steve Katz," "Ronnie Suke-nick," "Gabriel García Márquez" – or "Howard Johnson," "Norman Mailer," "Richard Nixon" – attached to a fictional character: this is the source of the ontological scandal. There is, however, a form of autobiographical fiction which preserves much of the ontological force of transworld identity but *without* reproducing real-world proper names – namely, *roman-à-clef*. Here proper names have been suppressed or "changed to protect the innocent" (actually, of course, to protect the guilty, that is, the potentially libellous author). Transworld identity between real-world persons and fictional char-acters has been deliberately *occluded*, requiring of the reader an act of decoding or decrypting. An element of *roman-à-clef* or lightly camouflaged autobiography characterizes much modernist writing – Proust, D. H. Law-rence, Joyce's *A Portrait of the Artist as a Young Man* and *Ulysses*. It would be surprising if the postmodernists did not in some way exploit the ontological potential of *roman-à-clef*, and of course they do exploit it. A good example is Gilbert Sorrentino's *Imaginative Qualities of Actual Things*, whose characters, the author insists, are modeled on real-world persons. If we recognize their "originals," the characterizations will make sense; if not, not:

> All these people are follow-the-dot pictures – all harsh angles that the mind alone can apprehend because we have already seen their natural counter-parts. I'm saying that if you know Leo, you'll see him plain. If not, you'll see what I let you see.[20]

The tone here is aggressive, even insulting: *roman-à-clef* as provocation to the reader. Is this fiction for the initiated, in-crowd fiction? The author claims to have known his "characters" personally, indeed to be in touch with some of them at the very moment he is writing about them: he reports receiving a phone-call from the real "Leo Kaufman,"[21] a letter from the real "Anton Harley"[22]; he shows the episode of April Detective's extramarital sexual escapades to her husband Dick, who laughs them off as fiction.[23] Yet at the same time the author insists on the transparent fictionality and arbitrariness of his fictional world, continually calling our attention to his own role as inventor and puppet-master. If this is in-crowd fiction, its satisfactions for those "in the know" are transitory; the biographical revelations promised one moment are rescinded the next:

> I don't know anything about Guy's character . . . Guy's character. What is that? I don't even know who he is. There is, in fact, no Guy Lewis. This is a novel. He used to have a different name, anyway. . . . Right now, under

that old name, he is living in Santa Fe with Lena, on welfare and writing imitations of Chandler.[24]

So is "Guy Lewis" modeled on a real-world person, or is he purely a fictional improvisation of the author's? Logically he cannot be *both*. Swerving from one position to another, from assertion of fictionality to denial of fictionality, the author effectively destabilizes the ontological status of his characters. The *roman-à-clef* element unmistakably functions here as a means of intensifying ontological flicker.

The author as character plays a relatively marginal role in *Imaginative Qualities of Actual Things*, observing the other characters from a position within their world but not interfering very substantially in their lives; he attends their parties and openings, reads their books, views their paintings. Elsewhere, the author as character moves to the center, becoming the hero of the *roman-à-clef*. *Roman-à-clef* as more or less camouflaged autobiography: an example is Richard Brautigan's fiction, which, except for his genre parodies, is all fairly transparently autobiographical, despite the change of proper name and the occasional disclaimers.[25]

Raymond Federman, too, makes his novels the vehicles of autobiography, but subjects it to the centrifugal force of the text. As we have seen, the authorial subject in a Federman text is distributed among several figures, which fission and converge as the text unfolds. Federman's life-story in effect *circulates* among these figures, attaching itself successively or simultaneously to one or more of them. The story itself is always the same, although it has never been told in its entirety and must be pieced together from scattered, partial versions: it involves the fortuitous preservation of a French-Jewish boy, Federman himself, from the Nazi death-camps, his emigration to the United States after the war, his ordeal in the "lower depths" of Detroit, his involvement with jazz, his army service, his education thanks to the GI Bill of Rights, his career as academic and writer. Dispersed throughout Federman's textual structures, this highly-charged story obviously functions much as the *roman-à-clef* element of *Imaginative Qualities of Actual Things* does, intensifying the ontological flicker. Federman's autobiography plays hide-and-seek with the reader throughout his writings.

Autobiography plays hide-and-seek with us even more elusively in Nabokov's writings. All of Nabokov's English-language novels are in some sense *romans-à-clef* – the question is, in what sense, exactly? As with Gilbert Sorrentino, we seem to glimpse personal revelations, but about the author himself rather than others; however, again as in the case of Sorrentino, this appearance of self-exposure is caught up in an ontological game, and we may well wonder whether what we have glimpsed is the "real" Nabokov or whether, as seems more likely, the "real" Nabokov maintains a safe distance from his texts. Certain elements of Nabokov's autobiography seem to have been acquired even by Humbert Humbert of *Lolita* (1955), and much more of it by Kinbote of *Pale Fire* (1966). Indeed, Kinbote at the end of that text threatens to metamorphose into a figure who could only be Nabokov himself:

I may assume other disguises, other forms, but I shall try to exist. I may turn up yet, on another campus, as an old, happy, healthy, heterosexual

Russian, a writer in exile, sans fame, sans future, sans audience, sans anything but his art.[26]

Baron R. of *Transparent Things* (1972) is another caricature of Nabokov, this time in the role of a writer notorious, like Nabokov himself, for his "luxurious and bastard style" – and also notorious for writing scandalous *romans-à-clef*! The most elaborate displacement of autobiography, however, occurs in *Ada* (1969), whose alternative reality is designed so as to consolidate in a single time and place the various phases of Nabokov's career (see pp. 19, 47). All the elements of our own world seem to exist in this parallel world, but differently combined, and this includes Nabokov's own writings, which have been detached from Nabokov or his quasi-autobiographical surrogate Van Veen and disseminated throughout the fictional world, turning up in the unlikeliest contexts : *Lolita*, for instance, appears here as a town in Texas and a type of skirt, *Pale Fire* as the name of a racehorse, and so on.

This strategy of displacement is carried to its logical extreme in *Look at the Harlequins* (1974), the memoirs of a Russian *émigré* novelist whose autobiography somewhat obliquely resembles Nabokov's own, but which also incorporates material displaced from Nabokov's fiction rather than from his life; thus, for example, the protagonist Vadim's relationship with his daughter Bel distantly echoes Humbert's fictional relationship with his Lolita. The most teasing displacements occur in Vadim's bibliography. The novels listed as "Other Books by the Narrator" obviously correspond to Nabokov's own, although the titles and dates have been slightly scrambled and, as we learn in the course of this text, their contents have been recombined. Thus, *See under Real* (1939, or is it 1940?) corresponds to *The Real Life of Sebastian Knight* (1941), but incorporates certain materials from *Pale Fire*; *Dr Olga Repnin* is Pnin with the sex of the protagonist switched; *A Kingdom by the Sea* combines elements of *Ada* and *Lolita*; *Ardis* (1970) is *Ada* (1969); and so on.

But just as the inhabitants of the Antiterra of *Ada* intuit the existence of a corresponding Terra – our world – so Vadim in *Look at the Harlequins* begins to suspect the existence somewhere of another writer who is his "original" – to suspect, in short, that he is a character in a *roman-à-clef*:

> I now confess that I was bothered . . . by a dream feeling that my life was the non-identical twin, a parody, an inferior variant of another man's life, somewhere on this or another earth. A demon, I felt, was forcing me to impersonate that other man, that other writer who was and would always be incomparably greater, healthier, and crueler than your obedient servant.[27]

This uncanny, schizoid feeling is aggravated by other people's "mistakes" – that of the publisher Oksman, who confuses Vadim's titles with Nabokov's, that of a Soviet literary functionary who accuses Vadim of having written Nabokov's *Lolita*, and so on. Vadim's' "delusions" lead finally to a breakdown, in the throes of which he imagines that his "real" name is something other than what he has always supposed:

> Yes, I definitely felt my family name began with an *N* and bore an odious resemblance to the surname or pseudonym of a presumably notorious

(Notorov? No) Bulgarian, or Babylonian, or, maybe, Betelgeusian writer with whom scatter-brained *émigrés* from some other galaxy constantly confused me; but whether it was something on the lines of Nebesnyy or Nabedrin or Nablidze (Nablidze? Funny) I simply could not tell. I preferred not to overtax my willpower (go away, Naborcroft) and so gave up trying.[28]

Here the ontological barrier between *roman-à-clef* and autobiography totters but does not finally fall. The *roman-à-clef* convention is laid bare, yet at the same time the "real" Nabokov remains as elusive for the reader as for his fictional double.

In *Ada*, as we have seen, Nabokov's bibliography is displaced and disseminated throughout the text, appearing in camouflage, as it were, "under" other words. Nabokov's precursor in this, as in much else, is Joyce, who similarly concealed the titles of his other writings "under" the words of *Finnegans Wake*. Thus, for example, all the titles of the *Dubliners* stories appear in more or less distorted form in the space of two pages of the text:[29] "The Sisters" appears as *Sistersen*, "An Encounter" as *wrongcountered*, "Araby" as *arrahbejibbers*, "Eveline" (which opens in the evening) as *eveling*, "After the Race" as *after the grace*, "Two Gallants" as *two gallonts*, and so on. On another page we find all of the chapter-titles from Book II of *Ulysses*, submitted to comparable transformations. And not only the books' titles but also their publishing histories and the circumstances of their composition appear here in various degrees of disguise – in short, Joyce's entire autobiography has been distributed among several of the "characters" (if that's the word for them) of *Finnegans Wake* – Earwicker the father, Shaun the son, but especially the other son, Shem the Penman or Sheames de la Plume, that is, James the writer. "His" chapter is I.vii, where he is described as follows:

> this Esuan Menchavik and the first till last alshemist wrote over every square inch of the only foolscap available, his own body, till by its corrosive sublimation one continuous present tense integument slowly unfolded all marryvoising moodmoulded cyclewheeling history (thereby, he said, reflecting from his own individual person life unlivable, trans-accidentated through the slow fires of consciousness into a dividual chaos, perilous, potent, common to allflesh, human only, mortal)[30]

This "continuous present tense integument" and "dividual chaos" must be *Finnegans Wake* itself; and the paper upon which it is written, according to this passage, is Shem's own body. So Shem is not only the author of *Finnegans Wake*, he is identical with the text itself. Joyce's earlier books were, I noted above, *romans-à-clef* to some degree. But there the "key" turned easily in the lock: Joyce "is" Stephen Dedalus, the artist as a young man, or he is divided between Stephen and Bloom. In *Finnegans Wake*, however, he is not merely distributed among the characters but disseminated among the *words* of the text; like Shem the Penman, he is the substance of the text. Here autobiographical fact constitutes an ontological level not within or alongside the fictional world, but within or "under" the words themselves.

Authority

"These days, often," William Gass says, "the novelist resumes the guise of God."[31] The analogy between the author and God is, as we already know, an old one. Nevertheless, the postmodernist writers seem to be obsessed with it – obsessed enough, at any rate, to be willing to sacrifice novelistic illusion for the sake of asserting their "authority" in the most basic sense, their mastery over the fictional world, their ontological superiority as authors. In short, romantic irony has returned, and is once again a source of aesthetic interest and excitement.

The postmodernist author arrogates to himself the powers that gods have always claimed: omnipotence, omniscience. Here, for instance, is Kurt Vonnegut, Jr, flexing his authorial muscle and playing God with his fictional world:

> I was on a par with the Creator of the Universe. . . . I shrunk the Universe to a ball exactly one light-year in diameter. I had it explode. I had it disperse itself again.
>
> Ask me a question, any question. It is one half-second old, but that half-second has lasted one quintillion years so far. Who created it? Nobody created it. It has always been here.[32]

In this same text, *Breakfast of Champions* (1973), the author flaunts his omnipotence by manipulating characters and events like a puppet-master, working his characters' "controls."[33] He flaunts his godlike omniscience by quoting bust, waist, and hip measurements for every female character, and penis length and diameter for every male character. Other authors who lay bare their roles as puppet-masters in a comparable way include Robert Coover in "The Magic Poker" (from *Pricksongs and Descants*, 1969), Gilbert Sorrentino in *Imaginative Qualities of Actual Things*, Nabokov in *Transparent Things* (1972), and Clarence Major in *Reflex and Bone Structure* (1975). Of these, Nabokov is the most discreet, preferring a more muted rhetoric of mastery, never obviously bullying his characters in the way that Vonnegut sometimes does; while Coover is the most assertively godlike (or rather Prosperolike, since the world and characters of "The Magic Poker" echo *The Tempest*).[34]

One of the most astonishing demonstrations of authority, however, is Stanley Elkin's hybrid essay/short story, "Plot" (1980). Elkin leans toward Nabokovian discreetness rather than Vonnegut's or Coover's muscle-flexing; nevertheless he begins by asserting his ontological superiority and control in no uncertain terms:

> Suppose we do this. Suppose we take for our situation a bank robbery, and suppose, to remain within clear, clean lines, we decide it shall be a one man job.[35]

In this way Elkin unfolds his story (and here "his" indicates proprietorial, not just grammatical, possession): the bank-robber takes a pregnant woman hostage, kills her, stops at a highway rest area to dispose of the body, kills a picnicking husband and wife, steals their car. A hair-raising story, all the more hair-raising for being narrated in a flat, all but toneless style, and within a framework which constantly foregrounds its hypothetical status (recall the use of highly-charged materials in recursive and self-erasing structures, and in "styled worlds"). At this point Elkin stops and returns to his initial situation:

> Now suppose we do this. Suppose, for the sake of argument, that we introduce stream-of-consciousness into our tale, that we finesse, as one erases a tape, whatever minimal body of ideas we had permitted the bank robber in our initial account and substitute other, even nobler ones.[36]

Elkin now retells his story, leaving the external action unchanged but interpolating flash-backs, scenes presumably stored in the bank-robber's memory – wildly inappropriate flash-backs, however, so that the result is a travesty of a story, "as though we had transplanted Steve Canyon's brains onto Popeye's neck."[37] The moral of Elkin's demonstration is, of course, the inseparability of plot and character, a principle of poetics from Aristotle through Henry James and beyond; but in the process he also demonstrates the freedom of the author.

Elkin's essay on "Plot" focuses our attention on the status of *character* in a text with a godlike author; so do Vonnegut, Nabokov, Coover, Sorrentino, and Major, for that matter. In "Worlds under erasure" (pp. 103–6), I argued that since the reader's involvement in the fictional world is normally channeled through its characters, the cancelation or de-creation of a character has particularly disorienting consequences. The same is true of the *creation* of a character when it is performed before our eyes. The effect is twofold: on the one hand, the ontological instability and tentativeness of the fictional world is demonstrated; on the other hand, the ontological superiority of the author is dramatized. "Aestho-autogamy," Flann O'Brien calls this, and his novel *At Swim-Two-Birds* (1939) provides the comic paradigm for the conspicuous creation of character in the "birth" of John Furriskey:

> There was nothing unusual in the appearance of Mr. John Furriskey but actually he had one distinction that is rarely encountered – he was born at the age of twenty-five and entered the world with a memory but without a personal experience to account for it. His teeth were well-formed but stained by tobacco, with two molars filled and a cavity threatened in the left canine. His knowledge of physics was moderate and extended to Boyle's Law and the Parallelogram of Forces.[38]

Furriskey's distinction may be rarely encountered *outside* of fiction, but of course *in* fiction it is a common occurrence: creation *ab ovo et initio* is not only an acceptable fictional practice, but the *normal* practice. The only difference is that it is not normally laid bare as it is in *At Swim-Two-Birds*.

A more elaborate example of this same phenomenon is "my paredros," the non-existent character in Julio Cortázar's *62: A Model Kit* (1968). A collective fiction, "my paredros" is created again and again before our eyes, brought into a kind of being whenever some member of the group of friends in Cortázar's novel requires him (her?) for the performance of some function in the discourse:

> my paredros was a routine in the sense that among us there was always something we called my paredros, a term introduced by Calac and which we used without the slightest feeling of a joke because the quality of paredros alluded . . . to an associated entity, a kind of buddy or substitute or babysitter for the exceptional, and, by extension, a delegating of what was one's own to that momentary alien dignity without losing anything of ours underneath it all.[39]

In other words, "my paredros" is a playful ontological extension of what Roman Jakobson called *shifters*,[40] those elements of language, especially pronouns and other deictics, which have no determinate meaning outside of a particular instance of discourse, their meaning changing (shifting) as the discourse passes from participant to participant. Anyone can say *I* or *you*, and each person who says them means a different *I* (the present speaker) and a different *you* (the present addressee), depending upon the situation. Similarly, anyone can say "my paredros," and each person who says it means something different by it: "my paredros" can mean "Calac's paredros" or "Juan's paredros" or "Polanco's paredros," depending upon whether it is Calac or Juan or Polanco who speaks. "My paredros" has no substance; it is merely an empty slot, filled differently each time it occurs – a long shadow cast by a pronoun. Yet this shadow comes gradually to acquire a kind of substance:

> There were even times when we felt that my paredros was a kind of existence on the margin of us all, that we were us *and* him . . . on the strength of giving him the word, of referring to him in our letters and our gatherings, of mixing him into our lives, we came to act as if he no longer were any one of us successively, as if at certain privileged times he emerged by himself, looking at us from outside.[41]

This is precisely what happens in the course of the novel *62*. As the group itself disintegrates, suffering a series of disasters, "my paredros" does indeed "emerge by himself"; he is last seen, on the novel's closing pages, standing *alone* by the exit gate of the Montparnasse station, smoking a cigarette. A collective fiction, a purely discursive entity, has achieved independent existence and entered the fictional world!

The conspicuous creation of "my paredros" dramatizes the author's freedom and ontological superiority, but only by analogy: in the same way that the characters invent "my paredros," so their author has invented them; their "authority" parallels, and perhaps parodies, his own. For a *direct* demonstration, rather than one that relies upon analogy, we must look to Federman's *Take It or Leave It*, and the generation by "aestho-autogamy" of a character called Robert Moinous. Equipped with the attributes of a conventional novelistic character – a physical description, a background, certain tastes and attitudes, and so on – Moinous is nevertheless a transparent improvisation, created before our eyes. "A kind of gratuitous apparition," Federman's narrator calls him: "he's just an afterthought. Unpremeditated. Free. . . . He just happened on the spot!"[42] Thus Moinous is brought into being, an exercise of the author's "freedom of speech" – of his ontological freedom. His disappearance is equally extraordinary. Moinous's death is anticipated in a proleptic scene, a flash-forward: he will be killed in a bar brawl in San Francisco, and the novel's protagonist, at the end of his cross-country journey, will be on hand to identify the body in the morgue. But this journey never actually materializes: it is canceled, its reality revoked. But what, then, becomes of Moinous? Is he murdered, as predicted, or does his death fall into the same ontological limbo that has engulfed the journey itself? Moinous is "revived" in a subsequent novel, *The Twofold Vibration*, where a deliberately implausible story is invented to explain his recovery from apparent death. But in any case this retroactive "revival" does not solve the ontological puzzle of Moinous's state of suspended animation, his death under erasure, at the end of *Take It or Leave It*. Like his conspicuous creation, this conspicuous suspension above all demonstrates the author's ontological superiority and "authority," attributes copied from those of the deity.

Short-circuit

"Enter the Author," reads the stage direction in the dialogue "Six-Part Ricercar" from Douglas Hofstadter's *Gödel, Escher, Bach*; and so the author penetrates his own fictional world, introduces himself to his characters ("please call me Doug"), and explains to them their roles *as* characters in the book *Gödel, Escher, Bach*. The level of the fictional world and the ontological level occupied by the author as maker of the fictional world collapse together; the result is something like a short-circuit of the ontological structure. Logically, such a short-circuit is impossible; but in fact it happens all the time, or at least *appears* to happen. We have already seen a number of examples – from Sukenick, Katz, Vonnegut, Sorrentino – where the author enters the fictional world and confronts his characters *in his role of author*. It constitutes a *topos* of postmodernist writing: the *topos* of the face-to-face interview between the author and his character. Although it also occurs in earlier periods – notably, in the modernist period, in Miguel de Unamuno's *Niebla* (1914) – the interview *topos* has become especially widespread in postmodernism, amounting almost to a postmodernist cliché.

The interview *topos* can take forms that are relatively muted or forms that are more assertive and pronounced. In its muted forms, the author may share a train compartment with his character, without ever actually addressing him, as in Chapter 55 of Fowles's *The French Lieutenant's Woman*; or he may deposit a book he has written with the librarian who happens to be narrating the *present* book, again without revealing his "authority" over his character, as Richard Brautigan does in *The Abortion* (1971). Most delicate and discreet of all in his dealings with his characters is the Author in John Barth's *LETTERS* (1979). Here the interaction between the Author and his characters is always indirect, conducted by letters or (in one case) over the telephone, never reaching the point of a face-to-face interview (although the Author does claim to have met some of his characters face-to-face in the past). Although the ontological structure of *LETTERS* has been short-circuited from the outset, the actual moment when the spark leaps the gap, so to speak, is avoided. This avoidance of a face-to-face confrontation gives rise, in the case of one character, Lady Amherst, to a good deal of comic choreography, as she traces her author to his home in upstate New York, only to find that he is not at home – literally absent!

This coy choreography of avoidance had already been dropped, however, in "Dunyazadiad," from *Chimera* (1972), where the author intrudes upon his characters in person. A recognizable caricature of the real-world John Barth, he penetrates the world of Scheherazade and her sister, to whom he describes his own impasse as a middle-aged writer with writer's block, and for whose benefit he recounts stories from the *Thousand and One Nights*, which Scheherazade will in turn narrate to Shahryar. This is not just a temporal short-circuit or endless loop, like those that so fascinate science-fiction writers of time-travel stories, but an ontological short-circuit as well, for the world that "John Barth" penetrates is the world that he is in the process of inventing. Comparable short-circuits occur at the party near the end of *Up*, when "Sukenick" criticizes one of his characters for his lack of verisimilitude ("You're what I call a bad character"),[43] or when Peter Prince confronts "Steve Katz" in *The Exagggerations of Peter Prince*; or when, in the "Epilogue" of Alasdair Gray's *Lanark* (1981), Lanark has a distressing interview with his author (here called "Nastler," a transparent distortion of "Alasdair"). Nastler cites as a precedent for this sort of interview Vonnegut's *Breakfast of Champions*, certainly one of the most conspicuous postmodernist examples. In this text, the fictional character Kilgore Trout begins to suspect that the stranger in dark glasses who is present in the same cocktail lounge with him is in fact his author. As Vonnegut explains, "Trout was the only character I ever created who had enough imagination to suspect that he might be the creation of another human being."[44] Later Trout's suspicions are confirmed when his author intercepts him and forces him to hear a strange message:

> "I am approaching my fiftieth birthday, Mr. Trout," I said. "I am cleansing and renewing myself for the very different sorts of years to come. Under similar spiritual conditions, Count Tolstoi freed his serfs. Thomas Jefferson freed his slaves. I am going to set at liberty all the literary characters who have served me so loyally during my writing career. . . . Arise, Mr. Trout, you are free, you are *free*."[45]

The paradox, of course, is that by setting him free, Vonnegut reveals his character's *un*freedom. This is a paradigmatic postmodernist moment of ontological short-circuit.

John Fowles adds a mind-boggling additional complication to the interview *topos* in *Mantissa* (1982). The complication here is that both parties to this interview – the writer Miles Green and his Muse, Erato – claim to be the author of the other party, Green insisting that Erato is a character in his writings, Erato countering that all his inventions come ultimately from her. Or rather, Erato sometimes claims this, at other times complaining of her unfree state as a character:

> "I have absolutely no rights. The sexual exploitation's nothing beside the ontological one. You can kill me off in five lines if you want to. Throw me in the wastepaper basket, never think of me again."[46]

Both attempt to demonstrate control of the fictional world by taking a turn at generating *ex nihilos* secondary characters and bits of decor, and then de-creating them. Who is the master or mistress of whom? Which is ontological superior, which inferior? which stands above the fictional world, which within it? which is inscribed, which the inscriber? The paradoxes multiply, until in a final section the entire confrontation is revealed to have been scripted in advance, a game or performance in which *both* collaborate. They are co-authors, then. But a question remains: who has produced the passage in which the two discuss the preceding scripted activity? This seems to stand outside the "authority" of either of them, or of both together. "An unwritable non-text," Erato calls it,[47] and logically she is right: *neither* can have been responsible for this scene, so someone else must be, namely, John Fowles, who is, of course, ultimately responsible for *both* of them and everything they do, say, write.

Mantissa thus foregrounds a fact which we have already run into more than once: the inscribed author is always a fiction, a "paper-author" as Barthes says, "figured in the carpet." As soon as the author writes himself into the text, he fictionalizes himself, creating a fictional character bearing the name "Steve Katz" or "John Barth" or (with a slight distortion) "Nastler," who is formally transworld-identical with himself, while the author himself with-draws to a further remove from the world of the text. The autobiographical character who is also a godlike author *is* impossible after all: ontological short-circuits never really occur, texts merely *pretend* that they do. The penetration of the author into his fictional world is always, as Umberto Eco has put it, *trompe-l'œil*: this "author" is as fictional as any other character. The ontological barrier between an author and the interior of his fictional world is absolute, impenetrable. It is the ceiling which retreats from Beckett's Unnam-able even as he stretches towards it (see p. 13). No one can ever really reach through it, either from below, like Beckett's character-in-search-of-an-author, or from above, like the authors-in-search-of-characters of so many postmod-ernist fictions.

PART SIX: HOW I LEARNED TO STOP WORRYING AND LOVE POSTMODERNISM

Brain damage caused by art. I could describe it better if I weren't afflicted with it.

(Donald Barthelme, "Brain Damage," from *City Life*, 1970).

14: LOVE AND DEATH IN THE POSTMODERNIST NOVEL

> since my college studies,
> When the thought was made available to me,
> I have never been able to make any sort of really reasonable connection
> Between Love and Death
>
> (Ron Padgett, "When I Think More of My Own Future Than of Myself," 1968)

If certain critics had their way, postmodernist novels and short stories would come with a warning label along the lines of the warnings on cigarette packs and advertisements:

> Warning: The Surgeon General (or whoever) Has Determined That Reading Postmodernist Fiction Is Dangerous to Your Health.

Postmodernist fiction, if critics such as John Gardner, Gerald Graff, and Charles Newman are to be believed,[1] is morally bad art, and tends to corrupt its readers. It does so by denying external, objective reality. There was a time when denying the reality of the outside world could be seen as a bold gesture of resistance, a refusal to acquiesce in a coercive "bourgeois" order of things. But that time has passed, and nowadays everything in our culture tends to deny reality and promote unreality, in the interests of maintaining high levels of consumption. It is no longer official reality which is coercive, but official *unreality*; and postmodernist fiction, instead of resisting this coercive unreality, acquiesces in it, or even *celebrates* it.

This means, ironically enough, that postmodernist fiction, for all its anti-realism, actually continues to be mimetic. Unfortunately, it has chosen to imitate the *wrong thing*, and it imitates it passively and uncritically:

> Where reality has become unreal, literature qualifies as our guide to reality by de-realizing itself . . . . In a paradoxical and fugitive way, mimetic theory remains alive. Literature holds the mirror up to unreality. . . . its conventions of reflexivity and anti-realism are themselves mimetic of the

kind of unreal reality that modern reality has become. But "unreality" in this sense is not a fiction but the element in which we live.[2]

Postmodernist fiction, Gerald Graff tells us, manifests "a consciousness so estranged from objective reality that it does not even recognize its estrangement as such."[3] And, Charles Newman adds, "The vaunted fragmentation of art is no longer an aesthetic choice; it is simply a cultural aspect of the economic and social fabric."[4] According to this view, postmodernist fiction has become just another part of the problem, rather than part of the solution.

These are serious charges, and need to be answered. They are all the more serious for having come from critics sophisticated enough to know *not* to identify reality simplistically with the conventions of nineteenth-century realism. It is too late in the day, even for those who are most nostalgic for unproblematic mimesis, to recommend a return to the fiction of Austen, Balzac, Tolstoy, George Eliot. Everyone knows now that the conventions of nineteenth-century fiction were just that, conventions, and not a transparent window on reality, and that there are other, equally legitimate means of getting access to the real besides Victorian realism.

Or rather, these critics are sophisticated enough not to *openly* recommend a return to the nineteenth century. However, the more one probes their critical assumptions, the more it appears that Victorian realism is, after all, the norm against which they have measured postmodernist fiction and found it wanting. Both Graff and Gardner, for example, generously allow the legitimacy of fantastic and nonrealistic methods. But there is a catch. Graff writes:

> The critical problem – not always attended to by contemporary critics – is to discriminate between anti-realistic works that provide some true understanding of non-reality and those which are merely symptoms of it.[5]

In practice, this turns out to mean that the only acceptable antirealistic writing is antirealism that implies a nostalgia for a lost order and coherence – for instance, in Borges, Gide or Musil – or antirealism in the service of social satire – for instance, in Barthelme. In other words, writing is acceptably antirealistic only if it stands in some fairly explicit and direct relation to a form of realism. Where this relation becomes more distant or oblique, as in science fiction, Graff withholds his imprimatur.[6]

Similarly, Gardner grants a certain legitimacy to art that is not realistic. Fabulous art, he tells us, can be morally as good as realistic art, as long as it stands by its (fantastic) premises and proceeds honestly from them.[7] Obviously such a stipulation has to be made, otherwise Gardner would be in the position of having to condemn all of the world's life-affirming fabulous art – not least of all his *own* fabulous fictions, such as his celebrated first novel *Grendel* (1971). But this justification of the fabulous is in fact something of a ruse. Like Henry James, whose argument in "The art of fiction" (1884) he echoes, Gardner parades his willingness to grant the artist his or her *donnée*, refusing to judge a realistic *donnée* as necessarily superior to a nonrealistic one. Yet in fact the case has been prejudged, for Gardner, like James before him, requires that fiction should project the "air of reality," the "illusion of life" – that it should possess the values of Victorian realism, in short. In other words, by all means let us grant the artist his *donnée*, whatever it may be, provided he does not break the illusion or disturb the air of reality. This is the one thing that Gardner requires of all fiction, realistic or fabulous: that it not break the illusion. Fiction should unfold "like a dream in the reader's mind"; reading it,

> We have the queer experience of falling through the print on the page into something like a dream, an imaginary world so real and convincing that when we happen to be jerked out of it by a call from the kitchen or a knock at the door, we stare for an instant in befuddlement at the familiar room where we sat down, half an hour ago, with our book.[8]

This underlying and unexamined principle – an *aesthetic* principle, not an ethical one – explains, it seems to me, Gardner's and Graff's negative evaluations of postmodernist fiction. For postmodernist fiction, as I have shown at length, is above all illusion-breaking art; it systematically disturbs the air of reality by foregrounding the ontological structure of texts and of fictional worlds. It foregrounds precisely what Gardner insists must stay in the background if fiction is to be moral. This is the difference between experiencing fiction as a dream unfolding in the mind, and experiencing it as the moment of wakening from the dream into reality, or the moment of slipping from reality into dream; or the experience of being aware that you are dreaming in the midst of the dream itself, *while* you are dreaming it.

But to point out these critics' aesthetic *parti pris* is not really to answer the charge of "estrangement from objective reality" that they have brought against postmodernism. To answer it, one would have to show that postmodernist fiction does in fact imitate something other than the "unreal reality that modern reality has become." Of course, given the semiotic nature of language and readers' will to meaning, postmodernist texts, even experiments toward the *livre sur rien*, cannot help but be *about* something. "Aboutness" lingers even in the most radically anti-mimetic texts, if only as a kind of optical after-image. Indeed, as Graff has convincingly argued, the less realistic the text, the more insistent, paradoxically, its "aboutness":

> Modern experimental texts . . . having renounced story and narrative, depend much more heavily on the reader's ability to locate thematic propositions capable of giving their disjunctive, fragmentary, and refractory details some exemplary meaning and coherence. Lacking a continuous story (or argument), images and motifs can have little unity or relevance to one another apart from the abstract concepts they illustrate.[9]

The problem (or one of the problems) is that the range of concepts that such texts could "illustrate" has come to be so limited. In fact, it has come to be limited to one theme only, if Graff is right, namely the theme of "unreal reality," and within that theme the only range of variation is between (good) texts that resist unreality and (bad) texts that acquiesce in it. There is no denying that "unreal reality" is a recurrent theme and object of representation in postmodernist fiction. It is the theme of postmodernism's revisionist approach to history and historical fiction, and of postmodernism's incorporation of television and cinematic representations as a level interposed between us and reality. But if this were postmodernist fiction's *only* object of representation, then Graff would be justified in wondering whether this doesn't make postmodernism as much a *symptom* of unreality as a representation of it.

In fact, the "unreality of reality" is *not* the only tune that postmodernist fiction can play, and postmodernism is not as fully the creature of the contemporary "crisis of reality" as Graff says it is. Postmodernist fiction may be antirealistic, but antirealism is not its sole object of representation. Indeed, two of the favored themes to which it returns obsessively are about as deeply colored with "traditional" literary values as anyone could wish. What could be more traditional than love and death?

Love . . .

"It has become difficult to imagine literature without love." This, the opening proposition of John Bayley's *The Characters of Love* (1960), is true in more ways than one. The representation of erotic love between fictional characters has, of course, been a staple of western fiction since at least the Middle Ages. It has even been possible to argue that at a more profound level the novel as a genre is structured according to a "romantic triangle" of desire and rivalry.[10] The author's relation to his or her characters, too, has been described as a form of love. According to John Bayley, love as the object of representation is inseparably bound up with the author's love for his or her characters: true representations of love are only possible where the author respects and takes delight in the characters' independent existence.[11] Finally, the erotic relation can also serve as a productive model for the text's relation to the reader. Narratives "seduce" their readers, in the sense that they solicit and attempt to manipulate relationship:

> All narratives are necessarily seductive, seduction being the means whereby they maintain their authority to narrate. . . . Narrative seduction . . . seems as complex and varied in its tactics as are the erotic seductions of everyday life; and its range, from active enterprise, through the "simple" invitation, to a carefully calculated "refusal," is not dissimilar to what can be observed wherever people relate sexually to one another. What is constant is the basic duplicity whereby a seductive program is condemned so that a seductive program can be pursued.[12]

Love, it appears, makes fiction go round; or at least it circulates everywhere *in* fiction.

Love as a principle of fiction is, in at least two of its senses, metaleptic. If authors love their characters, and if texts seduce their readers, then these relations involve violations of ontological boundaries. An author, by definition, occupies an ontological level superior to that of his or her character; to sustain a relation with a character (if only the sort of "hands-off" relation that Bayley has in mind) means to bridge the gap between ontological levels. Similarly, the text that seduces its reader reaches across an ontological divide to become a force to reckon with in the reader's real world. If Bayley and Ross Chambers are right, these metaleptic relations are permanent features of modern western literature; but of course, "traditional" fiction keeps them more or less in the background, out of the reach of fictional self-consciousness. By contrast, postmodernist writing systematically foregrounds them, as we have already seen. The author's relation with the characters of her or his fiction is dramatized and laid bare, whether through the visible exercise of "authority" over them (as in Coover's "The Magic Poker," 1969, Vonnegut's *Breakfast of Champions*, 1974, Nabokov's *Transparent Things*, 1972), or by interaction between author and characters at the characters' ontological level, thus "short-circuiting" the ontological hierarchy (as in Fowles's *The French Lieutenant's Woman*, 1969, or *Mantissa*, 1982, or Barth's "Dunyazadiad," from *Chimera*, 1972). More generally, love as a metaleptic relation across ontological boundaries is evoked, in a more or less displaced form, whenever characters change ontological levels, or show an awareness of the ontological hierarchy, or even when, as in the fantastic, they are made to confront the boundaries between worlds.

The changed function of metaleptic relation in postmodernist writing can be traced through the changing fortunes of the second-person pronoun: *you*. The second person is *par excellence* the sign of relation. Even more strongly than the first person, it announces the presence of a communicative circuit linking addressor and addressee. This made it a fruitful resource for earlier novels when they sought to establish an explicit rhetorical relation with their "gentle readers" or "dear readers." But *you* is shifty. Technically, of course, it is a "shifter" in Jakobson's sense, an "empty" linguistic sign whose reference changes with every change of speaker in a discourse situation: every reader is potentially *you*, the addressee of the novelistic discourse. This shiftiness of the second person was already exploited as early as Sterne's *Tristram Shandy*, with its addressees singular and plural, male and female, peer and commoner, critic and amateur. Modernist aesthetics, following the examples of Flaubert and James, all but eliminates the explicit *you*. The communicative circuit becomes oblique, narrative seduction becomes indirect rather than direct; "showing" replaces "telling," as Percy Lubbock taught us to say. Rather than engaging its reader in face-to-face discourse, modernism turns its back on the reader, and requires him or her to *infer* all the things that that turned back might signify.[13]

The second-person pronoun does occur in modernist and late-modernist contexts, but in such a way as to lose its function of direct address. Sometimes the second person substitutes for the first person pronoun, indicating that a character is "talking to himself," addressing himself or some interiorized alter ego in a kind of interior dialogue; this is the case, for instance, in the "Camera Eye" of Dos Passos's *U.S.A.* trilogy (1930, 1932, 1936), and in many parts of Carlos Fuentes's *La Muerte de Artemio Cruz* (1962). Elsewhere, *you* stands in for the third-person pronoun of the fictional character, functioning in a kind of displaced free indirect discourse, as in Michel Butor's *La Modification* (1957), Fuentes's "Aura," (1962) or the opening chapter of John Hawkes's *The Lime Twig* (1962). In none of these situations is the reader directly implicated in the reference of the second-person pronoun. Nevertheless, even in these displaced forms *you* retains a connotation of the vocative, of direct appeal to the reader, which imparts to these texts a slightly uncanny aura, as I think any reader would attest.

Postmodernist writing extends and deepens this aura of the uncanny, exploiting the relational potential of the second-person pronoun. The post-modernist second-person functions as an invitation to the reader to project himself or herself into the gap opened in the discourse by the presence of *you*. Its paradigm is the parodic questionnaire which Donald Barthelme introduced in the middle of *Snow White* (1967), and which Raymond Federman repeated with variations in *Take It or Leave It* (1976). Here, of course, the "gap" to be filled by the reader is literal:

> 14. Do you stand up when you read? (   )
>   Lie down? (   ) Sit? (   )

This poetics of the questionnaire is extended throughout the text in Italo Calvino's *If on a winter's night a traveller* (1979), most visibly in its first chapter, where the situations in which "you, Reader" might be reading Calvino's book are evoked so concretely and with such variety of options that every reader will recognize herself or himself in some part of it. Here, at least for the duration of the opening chapter, *you* is incorporated as a character in the fictional world without ceasing to be the extratextual reader at the same time:

> This book so far has been careful to leave open to the Reader who is reading the possibility of identifying himself with the Reader who is read: this is why he was not given a name, which would automatically have made him the equivalent of a Third Person, of a character . . . and so he has been kept a pronoun, in the abstract condition of pronouns, suitable for any attributes and any action.[14]

The "abstract condition" of the second-person pronoun is further explored in a short prose text by W. S. Merwin, actually called "The Second Person" (from *The Miner's Pale Children*, 1970). Merwin skillfully equivocates between language and metalanguage, and between the *you* of grammar and the *you* of an actual situation of discourse. The result is in one sense strictly truthful, but in another sense fictional, with the reader being made to act the role of a character in the fiction:

> You are the second person.
> You look around for someone else to be the second person. But there is no one else. Even if there were someone else there they could not be you. . . . The words come to you as though they were birds that knew you and had found you at last, but they do not look at you and you never saw them before.[15]

Yet if the second person is a character, she or he is not a character in the same way that a third-person character would be. Here, as in Calvino's *If on a winter's night*, the tendency to resolve the second person into a displaced third person – the solution of *La Modification* or *The Lime Twig* – is resisted, blocked:

> You make a pathetic effort to disguise yourself in all the affectations of the third person, but you know it is no use. The third person is no one. A convention.[16]

Merwin's second person uncannily straddles the ontological divide between the reader's real world and the text's fictional world.

If a metaleptic relation is to be sustained with the reader by means of the second-person pronoun throughout a long text, various contextual strategies will have to be brought to bear: the inherent "shiftiness" of *you* will have to be exploited to its utmost. This strategic shiftiness produces a kind of "hovering" or "floating" *you*, one in which equivocation is kept alive and in the foreground to the end of the text, and the reader continues to be able to project himself or herself into the discourse-situation. This hovering *you* is a feature of Pynchon's *Gravity's Rainbow* (1973). Here different contextualizations of *you* impose different readings; but in addition, many contexts incorporate evidence pointing to ambiguous or even contradictory readings, a *you* referring simultaneously to the reader and to a specific character within the fictional world:

> When are you going to see it? Pointsman sees it immediately.
>
> Is the baby smiling, or is it just gas? Which do you want it to be?
>
> She favors you, most of all. You'll never get to see her. So somebody has to tell you.
>
> None of it was real before this moment: only elaborate theater to fool you. But now the screen has gone dark, and there is absolutely no more time left. The agents are here for you at last.[17]

Pynchon exploits the shiftiness of *you* in order to keep its metaleptic potential alive until the end of the text, when in fact he has the most need of it. For here, on the text's last page, we are solicited most importunately to fill the gap in the text, projecting ourselves into the doomed theater upon which the rocket is about to fall.

Unmistakable in Pynchon's use of second-person direct address is the element of aggression: these passages insult and even threaten the reader. "Offending the Audience," the title of a play by Peter Handke (1966), might serve to describe many of these postmodernist second-person texts. The *topos* is recurrent and widespread:

> The reader! You, dogged, uninsultable, printoriented bastard, it's you I'm addressing, who else, from inside this monstrous fiction.
>
> Now that I've got you alone down here, you bastard, don't you think I'm letting you get away easily, no sir, not you brother.
>
> Ha, ha! Caught *you* with your hand in your pants! Go on, show us all what you were doing or leave the area, we don't need your kind around. There's nothing so loathsome as a sentimental surrealist.
>
> Did you ever see Christmas on Baltic or DeGraw Street? If you haven't, you haven't begun to live. Stick that cucumber sandwich up your ass.

These examples are from Barth, Gass, Pynchon, and Sorrentino;[18] many more could easily be found. So unpleasant does this aggressive stance become, that at least one postmodernist writer, Ronald Sukenick in "The Death of the

Novel" (1969), has felt it necessary to make a dramatic renunciation of the "offending the audience" *topos*, apologizing for his abuse of the readers:

> But why am I always baiting my readers? That's a nasty habit. This is not *Notes from Underground* after all. Why am I so hostile and defensive? . . . from now on I'm going to be completely open with you my friend, as wide open as the form of this performance.[19]

Surely "offending the audience" cannot be thought of as a manifestation of love? Yes, in fact it can. For one thing, as the Sukenick example makes clear, it may function as a seductive strategy, a "lovers' quarrel" deliberately staged as the prelude to a tender reconciliation. Furthermore, aggression and abuse are themselves forms of relation – negative forms, perhaps, but better than nothing when the alternative is no relation at all. This is the point of Handke's play, where the performers insult the audience as a means of breaking down the conventional theater's barriers to relation:

> We will insult you because insulting you is one way of speaking to you. . . . The distance between us will no longer be infinite.[20]

And finally, aggression may be an integral part of the erotic relation. Postmodernist representations of sadomasochism function as models of the "sadistic" relation between text and reader; here the metaleptic relation with the reader is mirrored by the text's content. This is especially clear in William Gass's *Willie Masters' Lonesome Wife* (1968), a metaleptic text in which the seductive discourse of the lonesome wife, who is identified with the text itself, periodically turns nasty and aggressive, as in the passage quoted above.

Metalepsis, the violation of ontological boundaries, is a model or mirror of love. Implicit in the postmodernist use of the second person, this analogy is actually made explicit in certain texts. Calvino ends *If on a winter's night a traveller* by having his two Readers, male and female, go to bed together; there, no longer second person singulars but a joint second person plural, they "read" each other in an erotic analogy with the way they have been read as characters. John Barth has half-seriously proposed an erotic theory of reading, whereby the author plays the masculine role, the reader the feminine role, and the text functions as their intercourse. A Genie, unmistakably a projection of Barth himself, propounds this view to Scheherazade and her sister in Barth's "Dunyazadiad" – an appropriately erotic and metaleptic context. Brigid Brophy has gone even further, speculating in *In Transit* (1969) that consciousness itself arises from love for an internalized interlocutor; and of course this theory is used to justify the many apostrophes to the reader that recur throughout Brophy's text. The ultimate *reductio ad absurdum* of this analogy between love and metalepsis occurs in Raymond Federman's *Take It or Leave It*. Here the narrator's audience delegates two of its number to enter the fictional world in order to keep track of the hero and his adventures. In a parodic dramatization of a metaleptic erotic relationship, one of these delegates seduces the hero and is sodomized by him.

When William Gass's lonesome wife reaches across the ontological divide and invites us to enter into an erotic relationship with her, what constitutes the *she* with whom we are supposed to relate? Photographs, for one thing; but

for the most part *text* – sentences, writing. The pleasure of the text, Roland
Barthes taught us, arises from the erotic charge displaced into language itself.
William Gass himself has endorsed this same view in his essay *On Being Blue*
(1975):

> the ultimate and essential displacement is to the word, and . . . the true
> sexuality in literature – sex as a positive aesthetic quality – lies not in any
> scene and subject, nor in the mere appearance of a vulgar word, not in the
> thick smear of a blue spot, but in the consequences on the page of love well
> made – made to the medium which is the writer's own, for he – for she – has
> only these little shapes and sounds to work with . . . what counts is not
> what lascivious sights your loins can tie to your thoughts like Lucky is to
> Pozzo, but love lavished on speech of any kind, regardless of content and
> intention.[21]

The sentence, in Barthelme's text entitled "Sentence" (from *City Life*, 1970),
submits to the embrace of the reader's mind in the way that a woman submits
to her husband's embrace when bumped into by him on her way to the
bathroom in the morning to wash her hair – "not necessarily an ardent"
embrace, Barthelme tells us, but an embrace nonetheless. Here the *reductio ad
absurdum* is Gilbert Sorrentino's grotesque literalization of the reader's erotic
relation to the text:

> Reminds me of that snide story I once heard about the hip politician
> discovered sexually assaulting his copy of *Lolita*. I don't believe a word of it,
> really. Not that it couldn't happen. A politician can do anything, the
> weirder the better. . . . Take the strange case of *In Cold Blood*. How about
> the man discovered fucking that book? No names please. Do you think I'm
> interested in the books people love?[22]

That we "love" the books we read (and write) is of course a mere cliché, a
dead metaphor. Postmodernist writers like Sorrentino, Barthelme, and Gass
reanimate this cliché and restore to it its full erotic connotations.

It should be clear now what I mean when I say postmodernist writing is
"about" love. I am not so much interested in its potential for representing
love between fictional characters, or for investigating the theme of love
(although of course it can do both of these things), as in its *modeling* of erotic
relations through foregrounded violations of ontological boundaries (for
instance through metaleptic uses of the second-person pronoun). Love, then,
is less an object of representation than a *meta*object, less a theme than a
*meta*theme. It characterizes not the fictional interactions *in* the text's world,
but rather the interactions *between* the text and its world on the one hand, and
the reader and his or her world on the other. And the same is true of the
second object of postmodernist representation, to which I now turn.

. . . and death

What John Bayley said about love might just as truthfully be said about death:
it is difficult to imagine literature without it. Nevertheless, the place of death

in western fiction is quite unlike the place of love. Where erotic love among characters is often represented in and for itself, occupying the foreground of the fiction, death is more typically functional: it sets stories going (paradigmatically in murder-mysteries) or, of course, brings them to an end. To put it differently, death often marks the *limits* of the representation. There are important exceptions to this, when death becomes itself the object of representation, as in the graveyard paraphernalia and "special effects" of gothic fiction, or, more substantially, in the crucial and (one might say) lovingly represented death-bed scenes of eighteenth- and nineteenth-century fiction: think of Richardson's *Clarissa*, Dickens's *Dombey and Son*, Stowe's *Uncle Tom's Cabin*, Flaubert's *Madame Bovary*. Their death-bed scenes may strike us as the least "modern," the most indigestibly "Victorian" aspects of these novels. But in fact the death-bed *topos* persists into twentieth-century modernist writing – transformed, naturally, in a typically modernist direction, turned inward, becoming death-bed monologues. The *topos* of the death-bed monologue may be traced back at least as far as Tolstoy's *Death of Ivan Ilych*; it includes, for instance, Hemingway's "Snows of Kilimanjaro," the death of Charley Anderson in Dos Passos's *The Big Money*, and Hermann Broch's *The Death of Virgil*, and extends to such late-modernist variants as Beckett's *Malone Dies* (1951/6), Fuentes' *Muerte de Artemio Cruz*, and even the death of the orbiting brain Imp Plus in Joseph McElroy's *Plus*.

The modernist and late-modernist death-bed monologue not only continues and transforms the Victorian death-scene tradition, it also revives a much older *topos* of death and fiction, that of *les hommes-récits*, story-persons. The phrase is Tzvetan Todorov's;[23] he is thinking of characters such as, classically, Scheherazade, whose existence, inside as well as outside the fictional world, depends upon their continuing to tell stories. As long as she produces narrative discourse, Scheherazade lives; at the moment her discourse falters or stops, she will die. Here, quite graphically, life has been equated with discourse, death with the end of discourse and silence. Essentially this is also the situation of the death-bed monologuists Ivan Ilych, Malone, Artemio Cruz, and the others: as long as the thread of their discourse continues to spin out, they are alive; at the moment this thread breaks, and they lapse into silence, they are dead. "Filibustering fate," Sukenick calls it,[24] thinking especially of Beckett's monologuists whose pointless but insistent chatter only serves to stave off the silence that means their nonexistence: "you must go on, I can't go on, I'll go on."

When modernist and late-modernist monologuists filibuster fate, the "archaic" equation of life with discourse, death with silence remains more or less in the background; the postmodernists bring it into the foreground. John Barth, for instance, makes this correlation time and again, obsessively, throughout *Lost in the Funhouse* (1968). The disembodied discourses of "Autobiography" and "Title" – it would be misleading to call them "narrators" or "speakers" – world-weary, suicidal, painfully self-conscious about their own status *as* discourse, know that, try as they might, they cannot utter their own annihilation, for as long as they utter *anything* they continue to exist. The only "death" for them is silence, a blank page; and sure enough, both "die," break off, in mid-sentence. Steve Katz in *The Exagggerations of Peter Prince* (1968) shamelessly manipulates probabilities and the norms of his fictional world in order to stave off his hero's death, working Peter Prince into corners where death seems inevitable and then producing some implausible *deus ex machina* or other to save him; transparently this is because the death of Peter Prince would break the thread of the narrative and silence the discourse. The title of Maggie Gee's metafictional murder-mystery *Dying,in other words* (1981) means, among other things, living in *this* discourse and dying *outside of* this discourse. Accordingly, death for each character is equated with the end of her or his story. To end the book, the author must end the entire world in which all of these stories have unfolded; so she closes with a nuclear apocalypse, in some sense the logical consequence of equating life with discourse and the end of discourse with death.[25]

When Tristram Shandy promises to be good-natured "as long as I live or write (which in my case means the same thing)" (Vol. III, Chap. iv), he is reviving and literalizing the *topos* of *les hommes-récits*. But of course his literalization goes much further than this: when in Vol. VII Death comes knocking and Tristram sets out pell-mell on his Continental travels, the implicit analogy between discourse and the evasion of death, between spinning out the thread of the discourse and headlong flight, is made concrete and explicit. Sterne's literalistic version of writing as the evasion of death is taken up again by the postmodernists, for instance by J. M. G. LeClézio in *Livre de fuites* (1969), or even more profoundly by Raymond Federman in *Double or Nothing* (1971) and *Take It or Leave It*. Federman's autobiographical heroes are refugees from death; leaving Europe behind, with its associations of war and holocaust, they flee to the New World, then continue fleeing across the continent (or they try to, at least). Their journeys are transparently analogues of Federman's own headlong, improvisatory writing, which is in turn a kind of "objective correlative" of his own life-story. Death, for Federman as for his heroes, lies *behind* him, in his past: he should have died when the Nazis deported his family to the death-camps, so the rest of his life, and his writing, constitutes a flight from this death in the past. The holocaust is never narrated in Federman's fiction; it appears only as a *blank space* – sometimes literally a blank space on the page – and the function of Federman's writing is thus to hurry *away* from the blank space and fill up pages with discourse.[26] This strategy is brought to the hero's attention by another character in Federman's *The Twofold Vibration* (1982):

> you have found a way to make your past live by pointing to its grave with your finger and of course we can't catch you at it, it's just a motion, a gesture, a clever substitution, and this way you put all your guilt on others, on us, but the fact that you choose to speak about it, even evasively, and write about it too, I suppose, is that transcendence or escape

To which the Federman character replies:

> Yes that's exactly the problem, exactly what my life is all about, transcendence or escape, you've put your finger right on it, though I would say more escaping than transcending.[27]

For Federman, as for Laurence Sterne, writing is more escape from death than transcendence. But other postmodernist writers have attempted to imagine transcendence; filibustering fate even beyond the supposedly ultimate limit of death itself, they project discourse *into* death. Here is one of the most serious functions of the fantastic in postmodernist writing, this attempt to imagine a posthumous discourse, a voice from beyond the grave. Significantly, when Federman's discourse in *The Voice in the Closet* (1979) attempts to go on *without* Federman, after imagining his death, it loses coherence and dissolves into a kind of pastiche of automatic writing, only recovering syntax in the last line with the return of the proper name "federman." But certain of Beckett's texts might properly be thought of as posthumous discourses – *The Unnamable* (1952), some of the *Texts for Nothing* (1954), *How It Is* (1961), *Company* (1980). So, too, might Robbe-Grillet's self-contradictory and self-canceling text *Dans le labyrinthe* (1959), in which the narrating "I" seems to be identical with the wandering soldier, yet seems also to survive beyond the point of the soldier's death, and in which the soldier himself seems to have survived beyond the death of a fellow-soldier who may or may not be himself. If these are posthumous discourses, they are discourses more or less in a void. Other postmodernist texts flesh out the posthumous voice more fully, surrounding it with some of the circumstantial details of an afterlife; examples include Flann O'Brien's *The Third Policeman* (1940/67), Guy Davenport's "C. Musonius Rufus" (from *Da Vinci's Bicycle*, 1979), Stanley Elkin's *The Living End* (1979), and Russell Hoban's *Pilgermann* (1983).

Such posthumous discourses are queasily double-edged in their implications. On the one hand, they claim to have successfully filibustered fate, to have transcended death; on the other hand, they are the voice *of* death itself, death personified and made articulate. This double-edgedness is already present in the ancient *topoi* of death and fiction. Discourse may be life for *les hommes-récits*, but writing is also a monument, as Shakespeare and the Renaissance never tired of saying, and the New Critics later repeated, and a monument presupposes the death of the one monumentalized. Or at least, once a monumental text has been inscribed, the author's continuing existence becomes irrelevant: "A text as such is so much a thing of the past that it carries with it necessarily an aura of accomplished death."[28] This, of course, is the by now familiar notion of the death of the author, writing as annihilation of the subject, to be found not only in Father Ong (whom I have just been quoting) but also in Derrida, Foucault, Barthes, and others (see "Authors: dead and posthumous," pp. 197–215). Its clearest, most analytical fictional manifestation occurs in the writing of Maurice Blanchot, especially, perhaps, in *L'Arrêt de mort* (1948). A metaphysical or displaced ghost-story, this text also functions as an allegory of death and writing. In it, writing figures both as the uncanny *repetition* of life and, paradoxically, as the sign of death; its narrator claims to have survived his own death, yet another character identifies him as death itself. Less equivocally, in Gee's *Dying, in other words*, the author Moira must die in order for her discourse to exist: "She was ended, the book could begin."[29] And recall "Borges and I": "I am destined to perish, definitively, and only some instant of me may live on in him. . . . Thus is my life a flight, and I lose everything, and everything belongs to oblivion, or to him."[30]

Of course, like the correlations between eros and writing, these correlations between death and writing are permanent features of *all* literature, in
all periods. But just as in the case of love, they have traditionally remained in
the background, below the threshold of fictional self-consciousness, except in
postmodernist fiction, which thrusts them into the foreground. In other
words, postmodernist fiction is *about* death in a way that other writing, of
other periods, is not. Indeed, insofar as postmodernist fiction foregrounds
ontological themes and ontological structure, we might say that it is *always*
about death. Death is the one ontological boundary that we are all certain to
experience, the only one we shall all inevitably have to cross. In a sense, every
ontological boundary is an analogue or metaphor of death; so foregrounding
ontological boundaries is a means of foregrounding death, of making death,
the unthinkable, available to the imagination, if only in a displaced way. This
is more or less obviously and trivially true of fantastic writing – ghost-stories,
including postmodernist ghost-stories like *L'Arrêt de mort* – or of postmodernist texts that actually project an "other world," such as *Ragtime* or *The
White Hotel*, or, more satisfactorily, *Gravity's Rainbow, The Hothouse by the East
River, Lanark*, and so on. But it is equally true, less obviously but also less
trivially, of all the other strategies postmodernist writing employs in order to
foreground ontological structure, from the construction of paradoxical spaces
and the use of science-fiction conventions, through self-erasure, Chinese-box
construction, and metalepsis, to all the various confrontations between trope
and literal, language and world, world and book, real and fictional, and so on.

"Death inhabits texts," as Father Ong memorably puts it, so tragic or
serious texts about death are also, as if inevitably, about texts, about themselves:

> Because writing carries within it always an element of death, the tragic
> literary work – or simply the serious written work in general, the work
> which deals with life and death honestly – often turns out to be in some way
> about itself. . . . That is to say, a work about death often modulates readily,
> if eerily, into a work about literature.[31]

I would also like to argue that the converse is true, that texts about themselves, self-reflective, self-conscious texts, are also, as if inevitably, about
death, precisely because they are about ontological differences and the
transgression of ontological boundaries. This idea is hardly original with me;
indeed, it is sufficiently widespread as to seem a truism. Gabriel Josipovici
said it one way: the shattering of the fictional illusion leaves the reader
"outside" the fictional consciousness with which he or she has been identifying, forcing the reader to give up this consciousness and, by analogy, to give
up her or his own, in a kind of dress-rehearsal for death.[32] Douglas Hofstadter
has said it another way: imagining one's own death is a kind of existential
strange loop, or what I have been calling (after Genette) a metalepsis:

> Perhaps the greatest contradiction in our lives, the hardest to handle, is the
> knowledge "There was a time when I was not alive, and there will come a
> time when I am not alive." On one level, when you "step out of yourself"
> and see yourself as "just another human being," it makes complete sense.

But on another level, perhaps a deeper level, personal non-existence makes no sense at all. All that we know is embedded inside our minds, and for all that to be absent from the universe is not comprehensible. This is a basic undeniable problem of life; perhaps it is the best metaphorical analogue of Gödel's Theorem. When you try to imagine your own nonexistence, you have to try to jump out of yourself, by mapping yourself onto someone else. You fool yourself into believing that you can import an outsider's view of yourself into you. . . . though you may imagine that you have jumped out of yourself, you never can actually do so.[33]

Or, you never can do so *except* through some medium of displacement – through metaphor or fiction. It is this possibility of *simulating* death for the use of the imagination that leads Robert Alter to conclude of the self-conscious novel (I would say, of postmodernist writing in general) that the "death of the novel" may be a less pertinent focus for discussion than "death *in* the novel."[34]

So perhaps this reputedly nonserious and irresponsible form of writing turns out to be "about" something after all, and something supremely serious, at that. Postmodernist writing models or simulates death; it produces simulacra of death through confrontations between worlds, through transgressions of ontological levels or boundaries, or through vacillation between different kinds and degrees of "reality." Thus postmodernist writing may, after all, meet John Gardner's criteria for moral fiction: "True moral fiction is a laboratory experiment too difficult and dangerous to try in the World but safe and important in the mirror image of reality in the writer's mind."[35] Certainly death must be the example *par excellence* of something "too difficult and dangerous to try in the world," which makes fictional "laboratory experiments" with death perhaps the most important and valuable of all. Postmodernist writing enables us to experiment with imagining our own deaths, to *rehearse* our own deaths. We have all but lost the *ars moriendi*; we no longer have anyone to teach us how to die well, or at least no one we can trust or take seriously. Postmodernist writing may be one of our last resources for preparing ourselves, in imagination, for the single act which we must assuredly all perform unaided, with no hope of doing it over if we get it wrong the first time.

CODA: THE SENSE OF JOYCE'S ENDINGS

Thus then the skull last place of all makes to glimmer again in lieu of going out.

(Samuel Beckett, *For to End Yet Again/Pour finir encore*, 1976)

James Joyce ends three of his four prose fictions (*A Portrait of the Artist as a Young Man* is the exception) with simulacra of death. This is most explicit in "The Dead," the story that ends *Dubliners* (1914); indeed, it is already explicit in its title. Here Gabriel Conroy, on the verge of sleep, experiences or imagines he experiences communion with the dead – specifically with Michael Furey, his wife's long-dead admirer, but also with the "vast hosts of the dead" in general. Simulation of death is further displaced from death itself in Molly Bloom's soliloquy at the end of *Ulysses* (1922), for here there is no visionary communing, only the "little death" of natural sleep. Nevertheless, Molly's bedtime discourse, leading us to the limit of waking consciousness and then falling abruptly silent as consciousness is extinguished, has much in common with the *topos* of the death-bed monologue. Finally, the end of *Finnegans Wake* (1939) represents the extinction of Anna Livia Plurabelle's consciousness in the waters of the Irish Sea – actual death, not sleep; yet it is in some ways the furthest displaced of the three representations.

There are other similarities among these three endings. Each focuses on a husband and wife, and the possibility (or actuality) of unfaithfulness on the part of one or both of the partners. Each involves a merging or confusion of personal identities – of Gabriel Conroy with Michael Furey and the hosts of the dead, of Leopold Bloom with Molly's first lover Mulvey (in Molly's memory), of Anna Livia Plurabelle with Finn MacCool, the sea. And each ends by circling back, one way or another, to its beginning. Such similarities tell us something about Joyce's sense of an ending – about, that is, a recurrent pattern which is specific to Joyce. The *differences*, however, tell us something about modernist and postmodernist fiction in general, and what distinguishes one from the other.

In "The Dead" and *Ulysses*, the simulation of death has been passed through the medium of an individual consciousness, "an ordinary mind on an ordinary day" – Gabriel Conroy's mind, Molly Bloom's mind. These texts are, in the first place, representations of minds, and only secondarily representations of the onset of sleep and, by extension, of death. The formal technique is, in one case, free indirect discourse ("The Dead"), in the other direct interior monologue (*Ulysses*). But in both cases, it is through the represented consciousness of the character that the represented world – whether immediately present, remembered, or anticipated – is filtered to us. And this world is stable and reconstructable, forming an ontologically unproblematic backdrop against which the movements of the characters' minds may be displayed.

Modernist fiction, in short.

The end of *Finnegans Wake*, too, represents an interior discourse, that of Anna Livia Plurabelle. But hers is not a consciousness like Gabriel Conroy's or Molly Bloom's, not "an ordinary mind on an ordinary day," but more like a collective consciousness – "Allgearls is wea" – or even the collective *un*conscious located in language itself. Molly Bloom's soliloquy notoriously represents the "stream of consciousness," but Anna Livia is the thing itself: the personification of the River Liffey, she literalizes the metaphor "stream of consciousness." Just as her discourse seems to sweep up all language in its stream, so it also sweeps up the projected world of this text: there is no stable world *behind* this consciousness, but only a flux of discourse in which fragments of different, incompatible realities flicker into existence and out of existence again, overwhelmed by the competing reality of language.

Postmodernist fiction, in short.

As modernist texts, "The Dead" and *Ulysses* project unified ontological planes, no more nor less than one world each. Death here, even death displaced into sleep, constitutes an absolute limit beyond which these texts do not venture. If Gabriel Conroy imagines himself approaching the world of the dead, we understand from the norms of this text that this can only be a subjective vision or delusion. But when Anna Livia Plurabelle approaches the limit of death, the norms of this text lead us to expect that she will transgress the limit and pass to some other world. For this is not the first time such a boundary has been crossed in this text; far from it. In fact, ontological boundaries are *continually* being crossed in *Finnegans Wake*: the boundary between the literal world, in which Anna Livia is a Dublin housewife, and the topological world of allegory, in which she is the personification of the River Liffey, married to the personification of the Hill of Howth; the boundary between projected reality and the level of language, in which she is the letters and syllables of her name, fractured and disseminated throughout the text; and so on. Anna Livia has slipped back and forth between worlds many times. She has, in a sense, died many times before the moment when her death is actually represented: she has "died" from language into projected reality and back again, from literal reality into allegory and back again, and so on. Death, in other words, is simulated not *once* in *Finnegans Wake*, but over and over again, whenever an ontological boundary is transgressed. We rehearse our deaths not only on the last page, when Anna Livia "passes out" into annihilation in the sea, but on *every page* of the text – indeed, in almost *every word* of the text.

So when the annihilation does finally come, and Anna Livia's discourse is silenced, we can hardly be surprised if this proves *not* to be the end of the discourse after all. Anna Livia breaks off in mid-sentence, tumbling into the silence of blank page; but of course this sentence is resumed elsewhere – on the first page of *Finnegans Wake*

A way a lone a last a loved a long the

riverrun, past Eve and Adam's, from swerve of shore to bend of bay, brings us by a commodius vicus of recirculation back to Howth Castle and Environs.[1]

Dead on the last page, this discourse is resurrected, "by a commodius vicus of recirculation" on the first. Postmodernist writing in *Finnegans Wake* models not only the ontological limit of death, but also the dream of a return.

NOTES

1: From modernist to postmodernist fiction: change of dominant

1 See Hans Bertens, "The postmodern *Weltanschauung* and its relation with modernism: an introductory survey," in Bertens and Fokkema (eds.), *Approaching Postmodernism* (Amsterdam and Philadelphia, John Benjamins, 1986), 9–52.

2 Richard Kostelanetz, "An ABC of contemporary reading," *Poetics Today* 3:3 (Summer 1982), 38.

3 John Barth, "The literature of replenishment," *Atlantic Monthly* (June 1980), 66.

4 Charles Newman, "The post-modern aura: the act of fiction in an age of inflation," *Salmagundi* 63–4 (Spring-Summer 1984), 17.

5 John Gardner, *On Moral Fiction* (New York, Basic Books, 1978), 56.

6 Christine Brooke-Rose, *A Rhetoric of the Unreal: Studies in Narrative and Structure, Especially of the Fantastic* (Cambridge, Cambridge University Press, 1981), 345.

7 Frank Kermode, "Modernisms," in *Continuities* (London, Routledge & Kegan Paul, 1968), 27. This view of the so-called postmodernist breakthrough – namely, that it never happened – is widespread. For instance, Richard Kostelanetz has insisted that "It is more apt to regard advanced art and writing today as extensions of earlier modernist developments. . . . Artworks that are currently considered 'innovative' neither close modernism nor transcend it"; "An ABC of contemporary reading," 38. Similarly, Jean-François Lyotard has written that "Postmodernism . . . is not modernism at its end but in the nascent state, and this state is constant"; "Appendix: answering the question: what is postmodernism?" in *The Postmodern Condition: A Report on Knowledge* (Minneapolis, University of Minnesota Press, 1984), 79. And Barthes once asserted that the last major break in our conception of language, text and writing dates back to the appearance of Marxism and Freudianism, "so that in a way it can be said that for the last hundred years we have been living in repetition": "From work to text," in *Image–Music–Text* (New York, Hill and Wang, 1977), 155–6.

8 A. O. Lovejoy, "On the discrimination of romanticisms," in *Essays in the History of Ideas* (Baltimore, Johns Hopkins University Press), 1948.

9 Barth, "The literature of replenishment"; Newman, "The post-modern aura"; Lyotard, *The Postmodern Condition*; Hassan, "POSTmodernISM: a paracritical bibliography," in *Paracriticisms: Seven Speculations of the Times* (Urbana, Chicago and London, University of Illinois Press, 1975), 39–59. For an overview of the varieties of postmodernism – in effect, an essay on the discrimination of postmodernisms – see Bertens, "The post-modern *Weltanschauung*," in *Approaching Postmodernism*.

10 Hassan, "POSTmodernISM," in *Paracriticisms*.

11 Charles Newman has asserted, correctly I think, that postmodernism reacts not so much against modernist practice as against the "second revolution" in criticism and pedagogy that interpreted, codified, and canonized the aesthetic innovations of the "first revolution"; "The post-modern aura," 27 and *passim*. In other words, postmod-

ernism seeks to differentiate itself from the explicit poetics of modernism, not necessarily from the modernist innovators themselves. Quite the contrary, postmodernist writers such as B. S. Johnson or Ronald Sukenick often make a point of establishing their legitimate descent from the modernist avant-garde: see Johnson, "Introduction" to *Aren't You Rather Young to be Writing Your Memoirs?* (London, Hutchinson, 1973),12 –13; Sukenick, *In Form: Digressions on the Act of Fiction* (Carbondale and Edwardsville, Southern Illinois University Press, 1985), 35, 209 and *passim*.

12   Roman Jakobson, "The dominant," in Ladislav Matejka and Krystyna Pomorska (eds), *Readings in Russian Poetics: Formalist and Structuralist Views* (Cambridge, Mass. and London, MIT Press, 1971), 105–10.

13   David Lodge, *The Modes of Modern Writing: Metaphor, Metonymy, and the Typology of Modern Literature* (Ithaca, NY, Cornell University Press, 1977), 220–45; Hassan, "POSTmodernISM," 54–8; Wollen, "Godard and counter cinema: *Vent d'Est*," in *Readings and Writings: Semiotic Counter-Strategies* (London, Verso, 1982), 79–91; Fokkema, *Literary History, Modernism, and Postmodernism* (Amsterdam and Philadelphia, John Benjamins, 1984).

14   Jakobson, "The dominant," 108.

15   Fokkema, *Literary History, Modernism, and Postmodernism*; see also his "A semiotic definition of aesthetic experience and the period code of modernism," in *Poetics Today* 3:1 (1982), 61–79.

16   William Faulkner, *Absalom, Absalom!* (Harmondsworth, Penguin, 1936) 83.

17   ibid.

18   See Arthur F. Kinney, *Faulkner's Narrative Poetics: Style as Vision* (Amherst, University of Massachusetts Press, 1978).

19   See Brian McHale, "L'Abîme américain: pour une théorie systématique de la fiction américaine, " *Littérature* 57 (1985), 48–65.

20   *A Dialectic of Centuries: Notes towards a Theory of the New Arts* (New York and Barton, Vermont, 1978), 101.

21   See Shlomith Rimmon-Kenan, "From reproduction to production: the status of narration in *Absalom, Absalom!*" in *Degrés* 16 (1978), ff.19; also Robert Dale Parker, *Faulkner and the Novelistic Imagination* (Urbana and Chicago, University of Illinois Press, 1985), 115–46.

22   This backgrounding of epistemology has already been recognized elsewhere, by Dick Higgins in his formulation of the opposition between "cognitive" and "postcognitive" art, but also by the postmodernist novelist Ron Sukenick in an interview (February 1981) conducted by Larry McCaffery. McCaffery asked whether contemporary writers no longer needed to deal with epistemological issues, as they once did, to which Sukenick replied: "Not exactly. Contemporary fiction still has to deal with the issue. . . . But it doesn't have to *focus* on it necessarily. . . . maybe this issue is already established now as something we can take for granted. . . . That's one of those issues that we don't have to concentrate on anymore. We assume that now, and are free to investigate other things"; Tom LeClair and Larry McCaffery (eds), *Anything Can Happen: Interviews with American Novelists* (Urbana, Chicago and London, University of Illinois Press, 1983), 286. The "other things" – although Sukenick does not say so – are, I would contend, the ontological issues.

23   See Jacques Derrida, *De la grammatologie* (Paris, Minuit, 1967), 31.

24   Alan Wilde, *Horizons of Assent: Modernism, Postmodernism, and the Ironic Imagination* (Baltimore and London, Johns Hopkins University Press, 1981). I claim no great advantage for my label over Wilde's – certainly it is no improvement from the point of view of elegance – except that it does manage to incorporate the notion of *cas-limite*, of teetering on the brink, that I wish to emphasize.

25   See Umberto Eco, "*Lector in Fabula*: pragmatic strategy in a metanarrative text," in *The Role of the Reader: Explorations in the Semiotics of Texts* (Bloomington and London, Indiana University Press, 1979), 200–66.

26   See Peter Rabinowitz, "Truth in fiction: a reexamination of audiences," in *Critical Inquiry* 4:1 (1977), 121–41.

27   Brooke-Rose, *A Rhetoric of the Unreal*, 369–71.

28   Baxtin, *Problems of Dostoevsky's Poetics*, trans. R. W. Rotsel (Ann Arbor, Ardis, 1973 [1929]), 157–61.

29 Thomas Pynchon, *The Crying of Lot 49* (New York, Bantam, 1972), 1.
30 ibid., 88, 92.
31 See Tony Tanner, *Thomas Pynchon* (London and New York, Methuen, 1982), 56.
32 Pynchon, *Lot 49*, 10–11.
33 ibid., 56.
34 ibid., 59.
35 ibid., 128.
36 ibid., 136–7.
37 Annie Dillard, *Living by Fiction* (New York, Harper & Row, 1982), 11.

2: Some ontologies of fiction

1 Alan Wilde, *Horizons of Assent: Modernism, Postmodernism, and the Ironic Imagination* (Baltimore and London, Johns Hopkins University Press, 1981), 173.
2 See Hans Bertens, "The postmodern *Weltanschauung* and its relation with modernism: an introductory survey," in Hans Bertens and Douwe Fokkema (eds), *Approaching Postmodernism* (Philadelphia and Amsterdam, John Benjamins, 1986).
3 Thomas Pavel, "Tragedy and the sacred: notes towards a semantic characterization of a fictional genre," *Poetics* 10:2–3 (1981), 234.
4 Philip Sidney, *Prose Works of Sir Philip Sidney*, IV, ed. Albert Feurillerat (Cambridge, Cambridge University Press, 1962), 8.
5 John Crowe Ransom, "Poetry: a note in ontology," in *The World's Body* (New York, Scribner's, 1938), 131.
6 Thomas Pavel, "Fiction and the ontological landscape," *Studies in Twentieth Century Literature* 6:1–2 (Fall-Spring 1982), 161. This is somewhat surprising coming from Pavel, given his sophisticated treatment of fiction's ontological plurality and complexity, its *internal* ontological "cuts"; see below.
7 Benjamin Hrushovski, "Fictionality and frames of reference: remarks on a theoretical framework," *Poetics Today* 5:2 (1984), 227–51.
8 John Barth, *Lost in the Funhouse* (New York, Bantam, 1969), 125.
9 William Gass, *Fiction and the Figures of Life* (New York, Vintage, 1972), 36.
10 Throughout the account that follows I am paraphrasing D. C. Muecke, *The Compass of Irony* (London, Methuen, 1969).
11 Roman Ingarden, *The Literary Work of Art* (Evanston, Northwestern University Press, 1973 [1931]), 218.
12 Gilbert Sorrentino, *Mulligan Stew* (London, Picador, 1981), 30; the ellipsis is Sorrentino's.
13 Ingarden, *The Literary Work of Art*, 254.
14 Ronald Sukenick, "Nine digressions on narrative authority," in *In Form: Digressions on the Act of Fiction* (Carbondale and Edwardsville, Southern Illinois University Press, 1985), 99.
15 See Samuel R. Delany, "About 5,750 words" [1968], in *The Jewel-Hinged Jaw: Notes on the Language of Science-Fiction* (Elizabethtown, NJ, Dragon Press, 1977), 33–49. Delany offers another informal approach to the logical status of fiction from a practitioner's (i.e. a science-fiction writer's) point of view. All the sentences in a given fictional text, he argues, are governed by the same "level of subjunctivity," and this level varies from genre to genre. Non-fiction reporting, for example, is governed by a "blanket indicative tension," such that every sentence might be prefaced by the phrase, *this happened*. A different tension informs the sentences of naturalistic fiction, where the implied phrase is, *this could have happened*. Pure fantasy writing falls under the rubric *this could not have happened*, while the level of subjunctivity in science fiction is captured by the phrase, *this has not happened (yet)*. Compare Lubomír Doležel, "Narrative worlds," in Ladislav Matejka (ed.), *Sound, Sign and Meaning: Quinquagenary of the Prague Linguistic Circle* (Ann Arbor, Department of Slavic Languages and Literatures, University of Michigan, 1976), 542–52.
16 See, for example, David Lewis, who treats fiction as similar to counterfactual reasoning, where we make one "provisional supposition" – such as, what if the President of the

United States were a woman? – then follow out its implications, altering only those facts about the world that need to be altered in order to make the supposition come true, and leaving everything else in the world untouched. The counterfactual, in other words, is developed against a fixed factual background: if we provisionally suppose that Sherlock Holmes lives at 221B Baker Street, this supposition is played out against an unchanged background of facts about the real-world London, the British Empire, physics, and so on; "Truth in fiction," *American Philosophical Review* 15:1 (January 1978), 37–46.

17 Thomas Pavel, "'Possible worlds' in literary semantics," *Journal of Aesthetics and Art Criticism* 34:2 (Winter 1975), 174–5.

18 Lubomír Doležel, "Narrative semantics," *Poetics and Theory of Literature* 1 (1976), 41–8.

19 Umberto Eco, *"Lector in Fabula*: pragmatic strategy in a metanarrative text," in *The Role of the Reader: Explorations in the Semiotics of Texts* (Bloomington and London, Indiana University Press, 1979), 234.

20 "Truth and authenticity in narrative," *Poetics Today* 1:3 (Spring 1980), 23.

21 Thomas Pavel, "Fiction and the causal theory of names," *Poetics* 8:1–2 (April 1979), 190.

22 Thomas Pavel, "Narrative domains," *Poetics Today* 1:4 (Summer 1980), 108.

23 See Thomas Pavel, "The borders of fiction," *Poetics Today* 4:1 (1983), 83–4.

24 ibid., 88.

25 Eco, *"Lector in Fabula,"* 223.

26 Jorge Luis Borges, "Tlön, Uqbar, Orbis Tertius," in *Ficciones*, trans. Alastair Reid (New York, Grove Press, 1962), 17.

27 Eco, *"Lector in Fabula,"* 229.

28 ibid., 241.

29 Pavel, "Fiction and the causal theory of names," 184.

30 Eco, *"Lector in Fabula,"* 259–60.

31 See Pavel, "Fiction and the causal theory of names," 188–9; "Tragedy and the sacred," 239; "The borders of fiction," 86–7.

32 Pavel, "Fiction and the causal theory of names," 189.

33 Pavel, "Fiction and the ontological landscape," *passim.*

34 Peter L. Berger and Thomas Luckmann, *The Social Construction of Reality: A Treatise in the Sociology of Knowledge* (Garden City, NY, Doubleday, 1966).

35 ibid., 24.

36 Stanley Cohen and Laurie Taylor, *Escape Attempts: The Theory and Practice of Resistance to Everyday Life* (Harmondsworth: Penguin, 1978 [1976]). I am indebted to Kevin McHale for bringing this valuable book to my attention.

37 ibid., 139.

38 In Tom LeClair and Larry McCaffery (eds), *Anything Can Happen: Interviews with American Novelists* (Urbana, London: University of Illinois Press, 1983), 231.

39 See Berger and Luckmann: "The transition between realities is marked by the rising and falling of the curtain. As the curtain rises, the spectator is 'transported to another world,' with its own meanings and an order that may or may not have much to do with the order of everyday life. As the curtain falls, the spectator 'returns to reality,' that is, to the paramount reality of everyday life by comparison with which the reality presented on the stage now appears tenuous and ephemeral, however vivid the presentation may have been a few moments previously"; *The Social Construction of Reality*, 24–5.

40 See Berger and Luckmann, *The Social Construction of Reality*, 88–94.

41 Eugene H. Falk, *The Poetics of Roman Ingarden* (Chapel Hill, University of North Carolina Press, 1981), 193.

42 Benjamin Hrushovski, "The Structure of Semiotic Objects: A Three-Dimensional Model," *Poetics Today* 1:1–2 (1979), 365–76; repr. in Wendy Steiner, (ed.), *The Sign in Music and Literature* (Austin, University of Texas Press, 1981).

43 For a dissenting voice on this point, see Uri Margolin, "Dispersing/voiding the subject: a narratological perspective," *Texte* 5 (1986).

3: In the zone

1   Italo Calvino, *Invisible Cities*, trans. William Weaver (New York, Harcourt Brace Jovanovich, 1978), 128.
2   Michel Foucault, *The Order of Things: An Archeology of the Human Sciences* (New York, Pantheon, 1970), xviii.
3   Thomas Pynchon, *Gravity's Rainbow* (New York, Viking, 1973), 549.
4   ibid., 668; Pynchon's ellipsis.
5   See Elrud Ibsch, "Historical changes of the function of spatial description in literary texts," *Poetics Today* 3:4 (Autumn 1982), 98–113.
6   Raymond Roussel, *Impressions of Africa*, trans. Lindy Foord and Rayner Heppenstall (Berkeley and Los Angeles, University of California Press, 1967), 19.
7   Guy Davenport, *Da Vinci's Bicycle* (Baltimore and London, Johns Hopkins University Press, 1979), 121–2.
8   Walt Whitman, "Song of Myself," xvi, in *Leaves of Grass: Comprehensive Reader's Edition*, ed. Harold W. Blodgett and Sculley Bradley (New York: New York University Press, 1965), 45.
9   Donald Barthelme, *Come Back, Dr Caligari* (Boston and Toronto, Little, Brown, 1964), 130, 137.
10   Kenneth Patchen, *The Journal of Albion Moonlight* (New York, New Directions, 1961), 56–7.
11   Ronald Sukenick, *98.6* (New York, Fiction Collective, 1975), 168, 171–2.
12   Donald Barthelme, *City Life* (New York, Quokka, 1978), 30.
13   Richard Chase, *The American Novel and Its Tradition* (Garden City, NY, Doubleday, 1957), 19.
14   See Brian Attebery, *The Fantasy Tradition in American Literature: From Irving to LeGuin* (Bloomington, Indiana UP, 1980), Ch. 5, 83–108. Attebery notes the close coincidence in time between America's first wave of disillusionment with its historical dream for itself, and Baum's invention of an alternative America that resumes that dream, but in a fantastic mode. This is the ideological dimension of the closing of the frontier: with the West henceforth a limit rather than a promise of further expansion, America is no longer the open-ended proposition it had once seemed, and so American progressive impulses turn introspective and Utopian.
15   The phrase is Pynchon's, and refers to the United States; *Gravity's Rainbow*, 711. Pynchon, of course, attests to the pertinence of Oz as a model for the zone when he places an epigraph from the movie version of *The Wizard of Oz* at the head of part three of *Gravity's Rainbow*. Underneath the title, "In the Zone," we read Dorothy's (that is, Judy Garland's) words upon arriving in Oz: "Toto, I have a feeling we're not in Kansas any more."
16   Angela Carter, *The Passion of New Eve* (London, Victor Gollancz, 1977), 167.
17   Alejo Carpentier, *Explosion in a Cathedral* (Harmondsworth, Penguin, 1971), 202–3, 203–4.
18   Walter Abish, *Alphabetical Africa* (New York, New Directions, 1974), 53.
19   ibid., 35, 63.
20   ibid., 36, 40.
21   Angela Carter, *The Infernal Desire Machines of Dr Hoffman* (London, Rupert Hart-Davis, 1972), 213.
22   How will this latest development in twentieth-century war, the permanent threat of nuclear destruction, transform our ontological landscape? It is too early to tell, but two recent postmodernist texts give some indications. Both project England as a war zone. Maggie Gee in *Dying, in other words* (Brighton, Harvester, 1981) has written a kind of "collective novel," adapting the familiar *topos* of the boarding-house whose residents represent a range of grotesque types. She transposes this *topos* into a postmodernist key by making these grotesques characters in a novel being written by another resident, who writes her own death into her novel. This paradox of the death of the author inside her own fiction is repeated at the macrocosmic level when on the closing pages of *Dying, in other words* Maggie Gee "kills off" her own world, both inside and outside her novel, by means of a nuclear attack. The space of the boarding-house which had been the locus of her novel is reduced to a zone of undifferentiated waste: "miles and miles of litter and

ice and ice and litter and chaos. . . . No speech, and no stories. The last great story was death: someone failed to tell it, or else no one wanted to hear" (213). The missile left suspended at the end of *Gravity's Rainbow* has fallen and all the world is a zone.

Russell Hoban in *Riddley Walker* (1980) appears at first glance to have constructed some kind of witty alternative reality or parallel world, like the Antiterra of Nabokov's *Ada*. Here England, or "Inland," is inhabited by nomadic tribes – an English version of Patchen's Ohio cannibals? – and all the familiar place-names are queerly skewed, Canterbury appearing as Cambry, Folkestone as Fork Stoan, Dover as Do It Over, Sandwich as Sam's Itch, and so on. A parallel world? No, the war zone, but some two thousand years after the fact: Hoban's zone is a double-exposure of the familiar England of our world and a future England reduced by nuclear war to a hunting-gathering culture out of which, after more than two millennia, it is just beginning to emerge.

23 Lubomír Doležel, "Extensional and intensional narrative worlds," *Poetics* 8:1–2 (April 1979), 196–7.
24 Robert Alter, *Partial Magic: The Novel as a Self-Conscious Genre* (Berkeley, Los Angeles, London, University of California Press, 1975), 99.
25 Flann O'Brien, *At Swim-Two-Birds* (Hardmondsworth, Penguin, 1975), 25.
26 Gilbert Sorrentino, *Imaginative Qualities of Actual Things* (New York, New Directions, 1971), 193.

4: Worlds in collision

1 Darko Suvin, *Metamorphoses of Science Fiction: On the Poetics and History of a Literary Genre* (New Haven and London, Yale University Press, 1979), 4.
2 Robert Scholes, *Structural Fabulation: An Essay on Fiction of the Future* (Notre Dame and London, Notre Dame University Press, 1975), 29, 61–2.
3 Suvin, *Metamorphoses of Science Fiction*, 71–2; Mark Rose, *Alien Encounters: Anatomy of Science Fiction* (Cambridge, Mass., and London, Harvard University Press, 1981), 26–7.
4 Jorge Luis Borges, "The Garden of Forking Paths," in *Ficciones*, trans. Anthony Kerrigan (New York, Grove Press, 1962), 100.
5 See David Porush, *The Soft Machine: Cybernetic Fiction* (New York and London, Methuen, 1985), esp. Ch. 8, "Deconstructing the machine: Beckett's *The Lost Ones*," 157–71.
6 See Hugh Kenner, "Art in a closed field," in *Learners and Discerners: A Newer Criticism*, Robert Scholes (ed.), (Charlottesville, Va., University Press of Virginia, 1964), 109–33.
7 See also Christine Brooke-Rose's postmodernist novel *Such* (1966), whose protagonist, having died in our world, enters a bizarre wonderland of death, only to be medically revived and returned, Lazarus-like, to life. He relapses into this death-world at intervals in dreams and ultimately, perhaps – the ending is ambiguous – in a second death. This is the purest sort of ontological fiction, expressly designed to juxtapose two incommensurable worlds and to foreground the boundary between them. "I draw the line as a rule between one solar system and another," Lazarus/Larry declares (London, Michael Joseph, 1966, 128), but he does so only in order to violate it, thus making the line itself palpable. The disparities between the two worlds are further accentuated by Larry's alien status in each. He is a one-man embodiment of "another world's intrusion into this one," on *both* sides of the boundary.
8 See Teresa L. Ebert, "The convergence of postmodern innovative fiction and science fiction: an encounter with Samuel R. Delany's technotopia," *Poetics Today* 1:4 (Summer 1980), 91–104.
9 Raymond Federman, *The Twofold Vibration* (Bloomington, Indiana University Press, 1982).
10 Vladimir Nabokov, *Ada, or Ardor: A Family Chronicle* (Greenwich, Conn., Fawcett Crest, 1970), 25.
11 ibid., 263–4.
12 ibid., 383.
13 ibid., 13.

14   On the realist poetics of science fiction, see Christine Brooke-Rose, "Science fiction and realistic fiction," in *A Rhetoric of the Unreal*, 72–102.
15   On similar modular or serial constructions in certain postmodernist texts, see Dina Sherzer, "Serial constructs in the nouveau roman," in *Poetics Today* 1:3 (Spring 1980), 87–106.
16   Teresa Ebert has argued (in "The convergence of postmodern innovative fiction and science fiction") that this "taming" of *Triton* is counteracted by the open-ended effect of its appendices, which include background information on future "Philosophy of Mind," "Omitted Pages," and an essay on science-fiction language. The self-reflective character of these appendices, Ebert claims, tends to destroy the integrity of the world of *Triton* and to blur its external boundaries. I suspect, however, that she has under-estimated the strength of the reading-conventions that apply to appendices and similar textual apparatus. After all, texts such as *The Lord of the Rings* or *Dune* also have elaborate appendices which are to some degree, although no doubt more restrainedly, self-reflective; but the worlds of these texts are preserved intact by the convention that instructs us to regard appendices as essentially marginal, extra-textual.
17   One difficulty: *Dhalgren*, Delany's postmodernist text (according to my reading of it), appeared in 1974, actually preceding *Triton*, his modernist text, by two years. A case of regression, then? No, I think Delany's career in the 1970s should serve to warn us against simple-mindedly "progressivist" ideas about the inevitable march of literary change, and to remind us that a *range* of literary modes – postmodernist, modernist or late-modernist, even nineteenth-century-style realist – are all simultaneously available to contemporary writers and may be selected by them at will.

5: A world next door

1   Rosemary Jackson, *Fantasy: The Literature of Subversion* (London and New York, Methuen, 1981), 46–7.
2   Tzvetan Todorov, *Introduction à la littérature fantastique* (Paris, Seuil, 1970); *The Fantastic: A Structural Approach to a Literary Genre*, trans. Richard Howard (Ithaca, Cornell University Press, 1975). Cf. Christine Brooke-Rose's discussion of Todorov's genre-theory in *A Rhetoric of the Unreal: Studies in narrative and structure, especially of the fantastic* (Cambridge, London, New York, Cambridge University Press, 1981), 55–71 and *passim*.
3   Jackson, *Fantasy*, 29. According to Jackson, "Gothic narrates . . . epistemological confusion" (97); from the earliest gothic novels through Maturin's *Melmoth the Wanderer*, Hogg's *Confessions of a Justified Sinner*, and Poe's "The Fall of the House of Usher," to latter-day British and American Gothic, the history of this genre is one of "progressive internalization" (24, 56), the conversion of external demons into problems of perception and psychology.
4   Todorov, *The Fantastic*, 72–3, 169–74.
5   ibid., 167–8.
6   Brooke-Rose has already noticed this: *A Rhetoric of the Unreal*, 67.
7   Roland Barthes, *The Pleasure of the Text*, trans. Richard Miller (New York, Hill and Wang, 1975), 32.
8   Jackson, *Fantasy*, 35–7 and *passim*.
9   cf. Lubomír Doležel's analysis of the two-world ontological structure of Kafka's *The Trial* and *The Castle*, "Intensional function, invisible worlds, and Franz Kafka," *Style* 7:3 (Spring 1983), 120–41.
10   Richard Brautigan, *In Watermelon Sugar* (New York, Dell, 1973), 39–40.
11   Quoted by Todorov, *The Fantastic*, 169.
12   Jorge Luis Borges, *Ficciones*, trans. Anthony Kerrigan (New York, Grove Press, 1962), 34.
13   Angela Carter, *The Infernal Desire Machines of Dr Hoffman* (London, Rupert Hart-Davis, 1972), 12.
14   ibid., 19.
15   ibid., 28.
16   In fantastic writing, Todorov tells us, "The supernatural often appears because we take

a figurative sense literally," *The Fantastic*, 76–7. He cites an example from Beckford's *Vathek* in which a character, to shield himself from the caliph's kicks, "huddles into a ball" – a figure of speech – but under continued kicking undergoes a fantastic metamorphosis into a *literal* ball (77–9). On the postmodernist strategy of literalized metaphor, see Chapter 9, "Tropological worlds."

17 Julio Cortázar, *Hopscotch* (New York, Signet, 1967), 326–7.
18 cf. Oliveira's meditation on the road accident and hospitalization that seem to break through the novelist Morelli's isolation: "If men like them [i.e. like Morelli] are silent, as is most likely, the others will triumph blindly, without evil intent, of course, without knowing that the consumptive over there, that injured man lying naked on that bed, are doubly alone, surrounded by beings who move about *as if behind a glass*, from a different place in time." (*Hopscotch*, 88; my italics).
19 *End of the Game and Other Stories*, trans. Paul Blackburn (New York, Harper & Row, 1978), 9.

6: Real, compared to what?

1 For instance, here is the disclaimer from Clarence Major's novel, *Reflex and Bone Structure* (New York, Fiction Collective, 1975): "This book is an extension of, not a duplication of reality. The characters and events are happening for the first time." And here is Raymond Federman's, from *Take It or Leave It* (1976): "All the characters and places in this book are real, they are made of words, therefore any resemblance with anything written (published or unpublished) is purely coincidental." See also the two contradictory disclaimers prefixed to Alain Robbe-Grillet's *La Maison de rendez-vous* (1965).
2 Jack Kennedy appears in *Gravity's Rainbow* (1973), Walter Abish's "The Istanbul Papers" (from *Minds Meet*, 1975), and R. M. Koster's *The Dissertation* (1975); Robert Kennedy in Barthelme's "Robert Kennedy Saved from Drowning" (from *Unspeakable Practices, Unnatural Acts*, 1968) and Sukenick's *98.6* (1975); Richard Nixon in Guy Davenport's "The Richard Nixon Freischütz Rag" (from *Da Vinci's Bicycle*, 1979) and Coover's *The Public Burning* (1977); Chairman Mao in "The Richard Nixon Freischütz Rag," T. Coraghessan Boyle's "Second Swimming" (from *Descent of Man*, 1979) and *The Dissertation*; Lenin in Davenport's "Tatlin!" (from *Tatlin!*, 1974); Trotsky in Leonard Michaels's "Trotsky's Garden," from *I Would Have Saved Them If I Could* (1975); Freud in Doctorow's *Ragtime* (1975), D. M. Thomas's *The White Hotel* (1981) and *The Dissertation*; Idi Amin in Boyle's "Dada" (from *Descent of Man*); Che Guevara in Russell Banks's "With Ché at the Plaza" (from *Searching for Survivors*, 1975); Sanjay Gandhi in Rushdie's *Midnight's Children* (1981); Mailer in Abish's "The Istanbul Papers," Richard Brautigan's *Sombrero Fallout* (1976) and of course Apple's "Inside Norman Mailer" (in *The Oranging of America and Other Stories*, 1976); Malcolm X in *Gravity's Rainbow*; Hess and the Duke and Duchess of Windsor in Timothy Findley's *Famous Last Words* (1981).
3 The texts in which these figures appear are as follows: Fowles, *The French Lieutenant's Woman* (1969): Rossetti, Swinburne, Ruskin; Barthelme, "Engineer-Private Paul Klee Misplaces an Aircraft Between Milbertshofen and Cambrai, March 1916" (from *SADNESS*, 1972): Klee; Reed, *Mumbo Jumbo* (1972): Harding, Mellon; Pynchon, *Gravity's Rainbow*: Rathenau, Mickey Rooney; Vonnegut, *Breakfast of Champions* (1973): Rockefeller; Davenport, "Tatlin!" and "The Aeroplanes at Brescia" (from "Tatlin!"): Chagall, Picasso, Shklovsky, Kafka, Brod, Wittgenstein; Abish, "How the Comb Gives Fresh Meaning to the Hair" (from *Minds Meet*): Proust; Michaels, "Annabella's Hat" (from *I Would Have Saved Them*): Byron; Reed, *Flight to Canada* (1976): Lincoln; Elkin, *The Living End* (1980): Ilie Nastase; Alasdair Gray, "Logopandocy" (from *Unlikely Stories, Mostly*, 1983): Milton; Robert Nye, "The Whole Story" (from *The Facts of Life and Other Fictions*, 1983): Stein, Joyce, Lawrence, Yeats (among others); Findley, *Famous Last Words*: Ezra Pound; Max Apple, "Walt and Will" (from *Free Agents*, 1984): Walt Disney.
    I have not even attempted to tabulate the great number of historical characters who populate *Ragtime*, *The Public Burning*, *The Flounder*, *Terra nostra*, *LETTERS*, or T. Coraghessan Boyle's *Water Music* (1982).

4 See the account of Hrushovski's model of fields of reference in Chapter 2, "Some ontologies of fiction."
5 Itamar Even-Zohar, "Constraints on realeme insertability in narrative," *Poetics Today* 1: 3 (Spring 1980), 65–74.
6 Thomas Pavel, "Ontological issues in poetics: speech acts and fictional worlds," *Journal of Aesthetics and Art Criticism* 40:2 (Winter 1981), 175.
7 Ishmael Reed, *Mumbo Jumbo* (New York, Bantam, 1973), 19–20.
8 Carlos Fuentes, *Terra nostra* (Harmondsworth, Penguin, 1978), 644.
9 ibid., 644–5.
10 ibid., 647.
11 ibid., 646.
12 Reed, *Mumbo Jumbo*, 70.
13 Fuentes, *Terra nostra*, 646–7.
14 Reed, *Mumbo Jumbo*, 43.
15 ibid., 127.
16 ibid., 149.
17 Salman Rushdie, *Midnight's Children* (London, Pan Books, 1982), 122.
18 Ishmael Reed, *Flight to Canada* (New York, Avon, 1977), 18.

7: Worlds under erasure

1 Clarence Major, *Reflex and Bone Structure* (New York, Fiction Collective, 1975), 20.
2 Jacques Derrida, *De la grammatologie* (Paris, Minuit, 1967), 31.
3 Stanley Fish, *Self-Consuming Artifacts: The Experience of Seventeenth-Century Literature* (Berkeley and Los Angeles, University of California Press, 1972), 41.
4 Samuel Beckett, *The Unnamable*, in *The Beckett Trilogy* (London, Pan Books, 1979), 330.
5 Alain Robbe-Grillet, *Project for a Revolution in New York*, trans. Richard Howard (London, Calder & Boyars, 1973), 131–2.
6 Ronald Sukenick, "The Death of the Novel," in *The Death of the Novel and Other Stories* (New York, Dial Press, 1969), 51.
7 See also the episode of Franz Pölkler's supposed incest with his supposed daughter Elsa, which Pynchon uses to titillate or disgust us (or both), only to "undo" the event that has so engaged our interest, retroactively canceling it out; *Gravity's Rainbow* (New York, Viking, 1973), 420–1. I have analyzed this confidence trick of Pynchon's in "Modernist reading, post-modern text: the case of *Gravity's Rainbow*," *Poetics Today* 1:1–2 (1979), 92–3.
8 Steve Katz, *The Exagggerations of Peter Prince* (New York, Holt, Rinehart & Winston, 1968), 96.
9 Jorge Luis Borges, "Averroës' Search" in *A Personal Anthology*, trans. Anthony Kerrigan (London, Jonathan Cape, 1968), 109.
10 Muriel Spark, *The Comforters* (London, Macmillan, [1957] 1974), 117.
11 Katz, *The Exagggerations of Peter Prince*, 162.
12 ibid., 164–5.
13 Thomas Pynchon, *Gravity's Rainbow* (New York, Viking, 1973), 738.
14 ibid., 712.
15 ibid., 740, 742.
16 See e.g. Joel Weinsheimer, "Theory of character: *Emma*," *Poetics Today* 1:1–2 (1979). "In semiotic criticism," writes Weinsheimer, "characters dissolve and only text remains" (208).
17 Christine Brooke-Rose, *Thru* (London, Hamish Hamilton, 1975), 114.
18 ibid., 115.
19 cf. Alain Robbe-Grillet, "Time and description in fiction today," in *For a New Novel: Essays on Fiction*, trans. Richard Howard (New York, Grove Press, 1965): "such description particularly seems to be inventing its object when it suddenly contradicts, repeats, corrects itself, bifurcates, etc. Yet we begin to glimpse something, and we suppose that this something will now become clearer. But the lines of the drawing accumulate, grow heavier, cancel one another out, shift, so that the image is jeopar-

dized as it is created. A few paragraphs more and, when the description comes to an end, we realize that it has left nothing behind it: it has instituted a double movement of creation and destruction which, moreover, we also find in the book on all levels and in particular in its total structure – whence the *disappointment* inherent in many works of today" (147–8).

20 Thomas Pynchon, *The Crying of Lot 49* (New York, Bantam, 1972), 136.
21 See e.g. Claude Bremond, *Logique du récit* (Paris, Seuil, 1973).
22 Jorge Luis Borges, "The Garden of Forking Paths," in *Ficciones*, trans. Anthony Kerrigan (New York, Grove Press, 1962), 98.
23 John Barth, "Lost in the Funhouse," in *Lost in the Funhouse: Fiction for Print, Tape, Live Voice* (New York, Bantam, 1969), 86, 83.
24 Robert Coover, "The Babysitter," in *Pricksongs and Descants* (New York, New American Library, 1969), 239.
25 Alain Robbe-Grillet, *La Maison de rendez-vous*, trans. Richard Howard (New York, Grove Press, 1967), 130.
26 Julio Cortázar, *62: A Model Kit*, trans. Gregory Rabassa (London, Marion Boyars, 1976), 185.
27 Flann O'Brien, *At Swim-Two-Birds* (Harmondsworth, Penguin, 1967), 9.
28 B. S. Johnson, "Broad Thoughts from a Home," in *Aren't You Rather Young to be Writing Your Memoirs?* (London, Hutchinson, 1973), 110.
29 Borges, "The Garden of Forking Paths," in *Ficciones*, 97.
30 Barth, "Frame-Tale," in *Lost in the Funhouse*.
31 John Barth, *Chimera* (New York, Random House, 1972), 308.

8: Chinese-box worlds

1 Douglas R. Hofstadter, "Little Harmonic Labyrinth," in *Gödel, Escher, Bach: An Eternal Golden Braid* (Harmondsworth, Penguin, 1980), 103–26.
2 Gérard Genette, "Discours du récit," in *Figures III* (Paris, Seuil, 1972), esp. 238–43. Actually, the use of the prefix "hypo-" to designate embedded narrative levels follows a recommendation of Mieke Bal's; Genette prefers to use "meta-," for which, however, both Bal and I have other uses; see Bal, *Narratologie* (Paris, Klincksieck, 1977). Genette defends his terminological preferences in *Nouveau discours du récit* (Paris, Seuil, 1983).
3 The example of Scheherazade's infinite regress – or rather, *potential* infinite regress – recurs in Borges's essay, "Partial Enchantments of the *Quixote*" (from *Other Inquisitions 1937–1952* translated by Ruth L. C. Simms (Austin and London: University of Texas Press, 1964), 43–6, where it is coupled with examples from the Ramayana and, of course, *Don Quixote* Part Two.
4 William Burroughs, *Exterminator!* (New York, Grove Press, 1973), 41. Actually, by my calculation, Burroughs is mistaken here. *This* magazine-reader has *not* read a "story of someone reading a story of someone reading a story": he has only read a "story of someone reading a story." In other words, this reader claims to be aware of more levels of embedding than Burroughs has provided for! These words should have been attributed to the *next* reader, the one located one "story" (level) *above* the present one.
5 cf. the dialogue "Little Harmonic Labyrinth," *Gödel, Escher, Bach*, 110–15, where Hofstadter also includes an example of recursive meta-levels, a genie who depends for his authority upon a meta-genie, who in turn depends upon a meta-meta-genie, and so on, to GOD – not the divinity, but an infinitely recursive acronym which may be expanded as "GOD Over Djinn, Over Djinn, Over Djinn," and so on for as long as one has the patience to continue.
6 Hofstadter, *Gödel, Escher, Bach*, 128.
7 Jean Ricardou, "Réalités variables, variantes réelles," in *Problèmes du nouveau roman* (Paris, Seuil, 1967), 23–43.
8 Thomas Pynchon, *Gravity's Rainbow* (New York, Viking, 1973), 760.
9 David Lodge, *The Modes of Modern Writing: Metaphor, Metonymy, and the Typology of Modern Literature* (London, Edward Arnold, 1977), 37.
10 ibid., 37–8.

11 Hofstadter, *Gödel, Escher, Bach*, 184.
12 Alain Robbe-Grillet, *In the Labyrinth*, in *Two Novels by Robbe-Grillet*, trans. Richard Howard (New York, Grove Press, 1965), 152–3. See Christine Brooke-Rose's admirable account of *Dans le labyrinthe*, "The real as unreal: Robbe-Grillet," in *A Rhetoric of the Unreal* (Cambridge, London, New York, Cambridge University Press, 1981), 291–310.
13 Robbe-Grillet, *In the Labyrinth*, in *Two Novels by Robbe-Grillet*, 271.
14 See Ann Jefferson's description of this perplexing passage, in *The Nouveau Roman and the Poetics of Fiction* (Cambridge and London, Cambridge University Press, 1980), 203–6.
15 Hofstadter, *Gödel, Escher, Bach*, 10.
16 ibid., 691.
17 ibid., 715.
18 The comparison between Escher's "Drawing Hands" and Brooke-Rose's *Thru* is made by Shlomith Rimmon-Kenan in her "Ambiguity and narrative levels: Christine Brooke-Rose's *Thru*," *Poetics Today* 3:1 (Winter 1982), 21–32.
19 Christine Brooke-Rose, *Thru* (London, Hamish Hamilton, 1975), 66.
20 ibid., 108.
21 Robert Pinget, *Mahu, or, The Material*, trans. Alan Sheridan-Smith (London, Calder & Boyars, 1966), 68.
22 Vladimir Nabokov, *Transparent Things* (Harmondsworth, Penguin, 1975), 101.
23 Muriel Spark, *The Comforters* (London, Macmillan, 1974), 66.
24 ibid., 117.
25 ibid., 206.
26 Steve Katz, *The Exagggerations of Peter Prince* (New York, Holt, Rinehart & Winston, 1968), 257.
27 "The Kugelmass Episode" appears in Woody Allen's *Side Effects* (New York, Random House, 1980), 41–55. It has been briefly discussed by Genette, *Nouveau discours du récit*, p. 59 fn. 1; but it was not Genette who first drew my attention to it, but my friend Bob Parker.
28 Donald Barthelme, "Daumier," in *SADNESS* (New York, Bantam, 1974), 178.
29 Raymond Federman, *Take It or Leave It* (New York, Fiction Collective, 1976), Ch. xvii.
30 ibid., Ch. xviii.
31 ibid., Ch. xxi.
32 Hofstadter, *Gödel, Escher, Bach*, 146.
33 See especially Jean Ricardou, "L'histoire dans l'histoire," in *Problèmes du nouveau roman*, 173–6; Lucien Dällenbach, *Le Récit spéculaire: Essai sur la mise en abyme* (Paris, Seuil, 1977); and Mieke Bal, "Mise en abyme et iconicité," *Littérature* 29 (1978), 116–28.
34 Ross Chambers has recently drawn a helpful distinction between *narrational* embedding, in which the primary narrative act is doubled by a secondary narrative act embedded within it, and *figural* embedding, in which some figure – in both senses: a personage, but also a trope – doubles the narrative in which it appears. An example of the first of these is the narrator's story-telling relationship with Madame de Rochefide which duplicates the narrative situation of Balzac's story "Sarrasine"; an example of the second is the stuffed parrot, an anti-model of art, in Flaubert's "Un Coeur simple." Narrational embedding will always qualify as *mise-en-abyme*, figural embedding only sometimes. See Chambers, *Story and Situation: Narrative Seduction and the Power of Fiction* (Minneapolis, University of Minnesota Press, 1984), 33–4.
35 See, for the *Madame Bovary* example, Mieke Bal, *Narratologie*; for the *Sound and the Fury* example, Arthur F. Kinney, *Faulkner's Narrative Poetics: Style as Vision* (Amherst, University of Massachusetts Press, 1978), 155; for the Roussel example, Dällenbach, *Le Récit spéculaire*, 127.
36 Gabriel Josipovici, *The World and the Book: A Study of Modern Fiction* (London, Macmillan, 1971), 299. Josipovici's term for *mise-en-abyme* is "demonic analogy," alluding to a phrase from Mallarmé about "le démon de l'analogie."
37 Donald Barthelme, *Snow White* (New York, Bantam, 1968), 105–6.
38 Italo Calvino, *If on a winter's night a traveller*, trans. William Weaver (New York and London, Harcourt Brace Jovanovich, 1981), 125.
39 ibid., 197.
40 On *Les Corps conducteurs*, see Wladimir Krysinski, *Carrefours de signes: Essais sur le roman moderne* (The Hague, Paris, Mouton, 1981), 295–309.

41 Michel Butor, *Mobile: Study for a Representation of the United States*, trans. Richard Howard (New York, Simon & Schuster, 1963), 28.
42 ibid., 187–9.
43 I have lifted this joke from a radio-play by the comedy group Firesign Theater, *Don't Crush That Dwarf, Hand Me the Pliers* (1970). "This is no movie. This is real," says one character from a television movie, to which the reply, inevitably, is, "Which reel?" Violation of the boundaries between TV and the real world is a staple of the Firesign Theater's ontological jokes in *Don't Crush That Dwarf*.
44 See Claude-Edmonde Magny, *L'Age du roman américaine* (1948; repr. Paris, Seuil, 1968), still the classic account of how the representational techniques of American modernist fiction were modeled on the movies.
45 Thomas Pynchon, *Gravity's Rainbow* (New York, Viking, 1973), 150, Pynchon's ellipses.
46 On uses of cinema in *Gravity's Rainbow*, see the excellent Chapter 3 of David Cowart's *Thomas Pynchon: The Art of Allusion* (Carbondale and Edwardsville, Southern Illinois University Press, 1980).
47 Salman Rushdie, *Midnight's Children* (London, Pan, 1982), 33.
48 William Burroughs, *Exterminator!* (New York, Viking, 1973), 165, 167. cf. Cowart on Pynchon: "He intimates . . . that life imitates film, because film *creates* reality in its own image. Film, therefore, ranks higher in the ontological scale than ordinary everyday reality; conversely, ordinary everyday reality must itself be essentially immaterial, no more substantial than the flickering images on a movie screen" (*Thomas Pynchon: The Art of Allusion*, 36).
49 Burroughs, *Exterminator!*, 143.

9: Tropological worlds

1   Benjamin Hrushovski, "Poetic metaphor and frame of reference," *Poetics Today* 5:1 (1984), 5–43.
2   Gérard Genette, "Métonymie chez Proust," *Figures III* (Paris, Seuil, 1972), 41–63.
3   Hrushovski, "Poetic metaphor and frames of reference," 30.
4   See Eugene Falk, *The Poetics of Roman Ingarden* (Chapel Hill, University of North Carolina Press, 1971), 142.
5   Hrushovski, "Poetic metaphor and frames of reference," 7.
6   Gabriel García Márquez, *One Hundred Years of Solitude*, trans. Gregory Rabassa (Harmondsworth, Penguin, 1972), 81.
7   Gabriel García Márquez, *The Autumn of the Patriarch*, trans. Gregory Rabassa (New York, Avon, 1977), 206–7.
8   Márquez, *One Hundred Years of Solitude*, 347.
9   ibid., 351.
10 Richard Brautigan, *The Tokyo–Montana Express* (New York, Dell, 1981), 246–7.
11 See David Lodge, *The Modes of Modern Writing: Metaphor, Metonymy, and the Typology of Modern Literature* (London, Edward Arnold, 1977), 235–9.
12 Leonard Michaels, "Mildred," in *Going Places* (New York, Dell, 1970), 118.
13 Tzvetan Todorov, *The Fantastic: A Structural Approach to a Literary Genre*, trans. Richard Howard (Ithaca, Cornell University Press, 1975), 76–7. See Chapter 5, "A world next door."
14 Donald Barthelme, *City Life* (New York, Pocket Books, 1978), 109.
15 ibid., 109–10.
16 ibid., 110–11.
17 Marjorie Perloff, "'Fragments of a buried life'; John Ashbery's dream songs," in David Lehman (ed.), *Beyond Amazement: New Essays on John Ashbery* (Ithaca and London, Cornell University Press, 1980), 66–86. The Ashbery passage in question comes from "The New Spirit," in *Three Poems* (Harmondsworth, Penguin, 1977), 37.
18 Perloff, "John Ashbery's dream songs," in *Beyond Amazement*, 79–81.
19 Thomas Pynchon, *Gravity's Rainbow* (New York, Viking, 1973), 412–13.
20 Maureen Quilligan, *The Language of Allegory: Defining the Genre* (Ithaca and London, Cornell University Press, 1979), 155.

21   Edwin Honig, *Dark Conceit: The Making of Allegory* (New York, Oxford University Press, 1959); Angus Fletcher, *Allegory: The Theory of a Symbolic Mode* (Ithaca, Cornell University Press, 1964); Paul DeMan, "The rhetoric of temporality," in Charles Singleton (ed.), *Interpretation: Theory and Practice* (Baltimore, Johns Hopkins University Press, 1969).

22   Alain Robbe-Grillet, *In the Labyrinth*, in *Two Novels by Robbe-Grillet*, trans. Richard Howard (New York, Grove Press, 1965).

23   On *Godot* as a kind of litmus test of "negative capability" on the critic's part, see Reuven Tsur, "Two critical attitudes: quest for certitude and negative capability," *College English* 36:7 (March 1975).

24   See e.g. David Leverenz, "On trying to read *Gravity's Rainbow*," in George Levine and David Leverenz (eds), *Mindful Pleasures: Essays on Thomas Pynchon* (Boston, Little, Brown, 1976); Lawrence Wolfley, "Repression's rainbow: the presence of Norman O. Brown in Pynchon's big novel," *PMLA* 92 (October 1978), 873–89; Douglas Fowler, *A Reader's Guide to "Gravity's Rainbow"* (Ann Arbor, Ardis, 1980).

25   Pynchon, *Gravity's Rainbow*, 588.

26   See especially *The Ticket That Exploded* (1962), where the allegory of control is spelled out with an explicitness unmatched elsewhere in the Burroughs canon; cf. Eric Mottram, *William Burroughs: The Algebra of Need* (London, Marion Boyars, 1977).

27   Pynchon, *Gravity's Rainbow*, 440.

28   ibid.

29   ibid., 657.

30   Quilligan, *The Language of Allegory*, 67.

31   Pynchon, *Gravity's Rainbow*, 204.

32   Quilligan, *The Language of Allegory*, 68.

33   ibid., 253.

10: Styled worlds

1   Marjorie Perloff, *The Poetics of Indeterminacy: Rimbaud to Cage* (Princeton, NJ, Princeton University Press, 1981), 72.

2   Jonathan Culler, *Flaubert: The Uses of Uncertainty* (London, Paul Elek, 1974), 12–13.

3   Allon White, *The Uses of Obscurity: The Fiction of Early Modernism* (London, Routledge & Kegan Paul, 1981), 149.

4   I have borrowed the phrase "style as vision" from the subtitle of Arthur F. Kinney's *Faulkner's Narrative Poetics* (Amherst, Mass, University of Massachusetts Press, 1978). The distinction between style as representation of character-consciousness and style as a displaced "textual" consciousness corresponds roughly to Kinney's distinction between "narrative consciousness" and "constitutive consciousness"; see 86–118.

5   Culler, *Flaubert*, 15.

6   Richard Bridgman, *The Colloquial Style in America* (New York, Oxford University Press, 1966), 189.

7   Gertrude Stein, *Tender Buttons*, in *Selected Writings of Gertrude Stein*, ed. Carl van Vechten (New York, Random House, 1972), 491. On Stein's reification of words, see Wendy Steiner, *Exact Resemblance to Exact Resemblance: The Literary Portraiture of Gertrude Stein* (New Haven and London, Yale University Press, 1978), 59–60 and *passim*.

8   Steiner, *Exact Resemblance to Exact Resemblance*, 154–6.

9   William H. Gass, "Gertrude Stein and the geography of the sentence," in *The World Within the Word* (New York, Knopf, 1978), 97. Aside from the "domestic" frame of reference explicitly announced by the titles, Gass discerns two latent frames of reference in *Tender Buttons* in general, two subtexts: sex and writing. In "Butter," both these subtexts, the sexual and the scriptural, emerge in the word "rubber," which hides the sexual phrase "rub her" and at the same time refers to a writing implement, a rubber eraser. And after all, a "rubber" (in the sense of an eraser) does come in handy if you are writing and need to expunge something – say, certain illicit sexual materials.

10   The term is Northrop Frye's, but its application to postmodernist prose is due to Marjorie Perloff, *The Poetics of Indeterminacy*, 42–3 and *passim*.

11   Roland Barthes, *The Pleasure of the Text*, trans. Richard Miller (New York, Hill & Wang, 1975), 32.
12   Guy Davenport, "The Dawn in Erewhon," from *Tatlin!* (Baltimore and London, Johns Hopkins University Press, 1982), 242–3.
13   William Gass, in Tom LeClair and Larry McCaffery (eds), *Anything Can Happen: Interviews with American Novelists* (Urbana, Chicago, London, University of Illinois Press, 1983), 160.
14   Donald Barthelme, *Snow White* (New York, Bantam, 1968), 96–7.
15   Donald Barthelme, "The Indian Uprising," in *Unspeakable Practices, Unnatural Acts* (New York, Pocket Books, 1978), 16.
16   Culler, *Flaubert*, 75–6, 199–206.
17   See Fredric Jameson's discussion of this sentence in "Metacommentary," *PMLA* 86:1 (Jan. 1971), 9.
18   Donald Barthelme in LeClair and McCaffery (eds), *Anything Can Happen*, 34.
19   These sentences come from: Samuel Beckett, *The Unnamable*, in *The Beckett Trilogy* (London, Pan Books, 1979), 267; Donald Barthelme, "The Indian Uprising," in *Unspeakable Practices, Unnatural Acts*, 17; Barthelme, "The Big Broadcast of 1938," in *Come Back, Dr Caligari* (Boston and Toronto, Little, Brown, 1964), 67; Steve Katz, *Creamy and Delicious: Eat My Words (In Other Words)* (New York, Random House, 1970), 38; Gilbert Sorrentino, *Mulligan Stew* (London, Pan Books, 1981), 294–5.
20   Culler, *Flaubert*, 76.
21   ibid., 199.
22   Donald Barthelme, in *City Life* (New York, Pocket Books, 1978), 112.
23   ibid., 118.
24   William Gass, *On Being Blue: A Philosophical Inquiry* (Boston, David R. Godine, 1976), 57–8.
25   Gilbert Sorrentino, *Splendide-Hôtel* (New York, New Directions, 1973), 14.
26   On *LETTERS*, see Theo D'haen, *Text to Reader: Fowles, Barth, Cortazar and Boon* (Amsterdam and Philadelphia, John Benjamins, 1983).
27   See Chapter 3, "In the zone." cf. also Carl D. Malmgren, "Alphabetical Space in *Alphabetical Africa*," in *Fictional Space in the Modernist and Postmodernist American Novel* (Lewisburg, Pa., Bucknell University Press, 1984), 173–6.
28   Walter Abish, "Ardor/Awe/Atrocity," in *In the Future Perfect* (New York, New Directions, 1977), 44.
29   The classic treatment of Roussel is Michel Foucault, *Raymond Roussel* (Paris, Gallimard, 1963); to my knowledge, it has yet to be bettered.
30   Roussel, *Comment j'ai écrit certains de mes livres* (Paris, Alphonse Lemerre, 1935), 20–1.
31   Linda Hutcheon, *Narcissistic Narrative: The Metafictional Paradox* (New York and London, Methuen, 1984), 122–3.
32   Christopher Butler, *After the Wake: An Essay on the Contemporary Avant-Garde* (Oxford, Oxford University Press, 1980), 147–8 and *passim*.
33   For descriptions of these techniques, see Eric Mottram, *William Burroughs: The Algebra of Need* (London, Marion Boyars, 1977), 37–40. Cf. also Butler, *After the Wake*, 103–5.
34   See Foucault, *Raymond Roussel*, 81–5.
35   William Burroughs, *The Ticket That Exploded* (New York, Grove Press, 1968), 65.
36   Umberto Eco, "*Lector in Fabula*: pragmatic strategy in a metanarrative text," in *The Role of the Reader: Explorations in the Semiotics of Texts* (Bloomington and London, Indiana University Press, 1979), 246.

11: Worlds of discourse

1   Donald Barthelme, "The Indian Uprising," in *Unspeakable Practices, Unnatural Acts* (New York, Pocket Books, 1978), 16.
2   ibid.
3   ibid., 11–12.
4   Michel Foucault, *The Order of Things: An Archeology of the Human Sciences* (New York, Pantheon Books, 1970), xv.

5 Barthelme, "The Indian Uprising," in *Unspeakable Practices, Unnatural Acts*, 14–15.
6 See e.g. Benjamin Lee Whorf, *Language, Thought and Reality: Selected Writings of Benjamin Lee Whorf*, ed. John B. Carroll (Cambridge, Mass, MIT Press, 1956); Peter Berger and Thomas Luckmann, *The Social Construction of Reality: A Treatise in the Sociology of Knowledge* (Garden City, NY, Doubleday, 1966); M. A. K. Halliday, *Language as Social Semiotic: The Social Interpretation of Language and Meaning* (London, Edward Arnold, 1978). For a synthesis of many of these tendencies – including Whorfian linguistics, Hallidayan social semiotics, Berger's and Luckmann's sociology of knowledge, as well as Foucauldian "archeology" and various Marxist and neo-Marxist tendencies – with a direct pertinence to literary studies, see the work of the East Anglia group (now dispersed): Gunther Kress and Robert Hodge, *Language as Ideology* (London, Routledge & Kegan Paul, 1979); Roger Fowler, Robert Hodge, Gareth Jones, Gunther Kress, and Tony Trew, *Language and Control* (London, Routledge & Kegan Paul, 1979); and Roger Fowler, *Literature as Social Discourse: The Practice of Linguistic Criticism* (London, Batsford, 1981).
7 Robert Alter, "Mimesis and the motive for fiction," *TriQuarterly* 42 (Spring 1978), 233.
8 This is not to say that Baxtin is a naïve representationalist when it comes to the representation of discourse, as others are when it comes to the representation of "things." Novels, in his view, do not merely reproduce specimens of real-world language; rather they create the "image of a language," which may not reproduce the actual features of a linguistic variety in a way that would satisfy, say, a dialectologist, but which is *functionally equivalent* to the real-world discourse in a particular novelistic context; see Baxtin, "Discourse in the novel," in *The Dialogic Imagination*, ed. and trans. Caryl Emerson and Michael Holquist (Austin and London, University of Texas Press, 1981), 336 and *passim*. For a case-study of how novels create the "image of a language," see my "Speaking as a child in U.SA.: A problem in the mimesis of speech," *Language and Style* 17:4 (Fall 1984), 321–70.
9 Baxtin, "Discourse in the novel," in *The Dialogic Imagination*, 411–12.
10 ibid., 288.
11 cf. the literalization of the metaphor of "worlds" in Cortázar's early fiction, discussed in Chapter 5, "A world next door."
12 Halliday, *Language as Social Semiotic*, 111 and *passim*.
13 On Eliot, see Alan Wilde, *Horizons of Assent: Modernism, Postmodernism and the Ironic Imagination* (Baltimore and London, Johns Hopkins University Press, 1981), 20–5. On Dos Passos, see Wladimir Krysinski, *Carrefours de signes: Essais sur le roman moderne* (Le Haye, Paris, New York, Mouton, 1981), 298–303.
14 Donald Barthelme, *Snow White* (New York, Bantam, 1968), 45–6.
15 ibid., 46.
16 Donald Barthelme, "The Police Band," in *Unspeakable Practices, Unnatural Acts*, 76. Actually the clash of registers here is transparently motivated by the pun in the title: "Police band," in the sense of a radio frequency reserved for use by the police, vs "police band," in the sense of a group of musicians.
17 Interestingly, "Icicles" is in this respect nearly a perfect mirror-image of the other stories from the collection in which it appears, Gass's *In the Heart of the Heart of the Country* (1968). In the other stories, such as "The Pederson Kid," "Mrs Mean," and "Order of Insects," the intrusion of a character upon somebody else's domestic space precipitates an outburst of extravagant and highly unnaturalistic language; see Chapter 5, "A world next door." In "Icicles," conversely, the intrusion of an alien discourse into the closed discourse-world of real-estate "shop talk" leads to the protagonist feeling "haunted" or "possessed" within the privacy of his own domestic space.
18 See M. A. K. Halliday, "Antilanguages," in *Language as Social Semiotic*, 164–82; cf. also Kress and Hodge, *Language as Ideology*, 70–7.
19 Roger Fowler, "Anti-Language in Fiction," *Literature as Social Discourse*, 157.
20 William Burroughs, *Naked Lunch* (New York, Grove Press, 1966), 2, 7, 15.
21 Fowler, "Anti-Language in Fiction," 155.
22 William Burroughs, *The Ticket That Exploded* (New York, Grove Press, 1968), 27.
23 Barthelme, "A Picture History of the War," in *Unspeakable Practices, Unnatural Acts*, 143.
24 See Baxtin, "Discourse in the novel," 279–85.
25 James Joyce, *Finnegans Wake* III.4 (Harmondsworth, Penguin, 1976), 564.

26 See Margot Norris's analysis of a comparable passage of superimposed discourses from *Finnegans Wake* II.2 in her *The Decentered Universe of Finnegans Wake: A Structuralist Analysis* (Baltimore and London, Johns Hopkins University Press, 1976), 114–18.

27 Donald Barthelme, "Kierkegaard Unfair to Schlegel," in *City Life* (New York, Pocket Books, 1978), 92.

28 See M. M. Baxtin, *Problems of Dostoevsky's Poetics*, ed. and trans. Caryl Emerson (Minneapolis, University of Minnesota Press, 1984), 101–6; *Rabelais and His World*, trans. Hélène Iswolsky (Cambridge, Mass., and London, MIT Press, 1968), *passim*. For a more skeptical view of the relation between carnival and the novel, with interesting analyses of "carnivalized" texts by Mann, Gombrowicz, and Carpentier, see Wladimir Krysinski, "Variations sur Bakhtine et les limites du carnaval," in *Carrefours de signes*, 311–44.

29 Baxtin, *Problems of Dostoevsky's Poetics*, 107–8; "Discourse in the novel," 366–415. cf. also Northrop Frye's account of what he prefers to call "anatomy," *Anatomy of Criticism: Four Essays* (Princeton, NJ, Princeton University Press, 1966), 308–12.

30 Baxtin, *Problems of Dostoevsky's Poetics*, 110–11.

31 Precursors of the postmodernist traveling-circus motif include such fantastic texts as Charles G. Finney's *The Circus of Dr Lao* (1935), Ray Bradbury's *Something Wicked This Way Comes* (1962), and Peter S. Beagle's *The Last Unicorn* (1968). See Brian Attebery, *The Fantasy Tradition in American Literature: From Irving to LeGuin* (Bloomington, Indiana University Press, 1980): "Circuses and carnivals seem in this country [i.e. the United States] to be like reservations or wildlife preserves where the unknown and the marvelous can be locked up for safekeeping, and peered at from time to time from behind bars. Finney, Beagle, and Bradbury generate considerable effect by opening the cages" (139).

32 Monique Wittig, *Les Guérillères*, trans. David LeVay (London, The Women's Press, 1979), 93.

33 ibid., 73.

12: Worlds on paper

1 Ronald Sukenick, "The new tradition" (1972), in *In Form: Digressions on the Act of Fiction* (Carbondale and Edwardsville, Southern Illinois University Press, 1985), 206.

2 See e.g. Father Ong's *Orality and Literacy: The Technologizing of the Word* (London, Methuen, 1982), 123–9.

3 Sukenick, "The new tradition," 206: cf. W. J. T. Mitchell, "Spatial form in literature: toward a general theory," *Critical Inquiry* 6: 3 (Spring 1980), 550–1: "The spatiality of English texts as physical objects is normally backgrounded, but this does not negate the significance of this aspect of their existence."

4 Jacques Derrida, *Glas* (Paris, Galilée, 1974), 88.

5 See e.g. David Lodge, *The Modes of Modern Writing: Metaphor, Metonymy and the Typology of Modern Literature* (London, Edward Arnold, 1977), 231–5.

6 Among the postmodernist texts which employ this spaced-out format are Samuel Beckett's *How It Is* (1961), Jerzy Kosinski's *Steps* (1968), Donald Barthelme's "Alice" (from *Unspeakable Practices, Unnatural Acts*, 1968), "Views of My Father Weeping" (from *City Life*, 1970), and "The Genius," "The Rise of Capitalism," and "The Temptation of St Anthony" (from *SADNESS*, 1972), Monique Wittig's *Les Guérillères* (1969), Ishmael Reed's *Yellow Back Radio Broke-Down* (1969), Robert Coover's "The Magic Poker," "The Gingerbread House," "Quenby and Ola, Swede and Carl," and "The Babysitter" (all from *Pricksongs and Descants*, 1969), Kurt Vonnegut's *Breakfast of Champions* (1973), Clarence Major's *Reflex and Bone Structure* (1975), Ronald Sukenick's *98.6* (1975), Roland Barthes's *Fragments d'un discours amoureux* (1977), Guy Davenport's "Au Tombeau de Charles Fourier" (from *Da Vinci's Bicycle*, 1979), and Raymond Federman's *The Twofold Vibration* (1982).

7 Monique Wittig, *Les Guérillères*, trans. David LeVay (London, The Women's Press, 1979), 143.

8 Other postmodernist examples of the spacing-with-headlines format include

Barthelme's "Robert Kennedy Saved from Drowning" (from *Unspeakable Practices*), "Paraguay" (from *City Life*) and "Daumier" (from *SADNESS*), J. G. Ballard's *The Atrocity Exhibition* (1969), Leonard Michaels' "Eating Out," "Downers," and "I Would Have Saved Them If I Could" (all from *I Would Have Saved Them If I Could*, 1975), and Walter Abish's "Minds Meet" and "How the Comb Gives Fresh Meaning to the Hair" (from *Minds Meet*, 1975). We might read the title of this last text by Abish as a metaphor for spacing: the comb of spacing (and what is a comb if not a spaced-out object?), passed through the conventional solidly-printed page of prose fiction, gives it "fresh meaning."

9 Italo Calvino, in *If on a winter's night a traveller*, has described the effect on the reader of a misbound book in which blank pages mistakenly alternate with printed pages of a densely detailed naturalistic fiction: "And so you see this novel so tightly interwoven with sensations suddenly riven by bottomless chasms, as if the claim to portray fullness revealed the void beneath"; trans. William Weaver (New York and London, Harcourt Brace Jovanovich, 1981), 43. Much the same sort of vertigo is experienced when the reader encounters the blank pages in Cabrera Infante, Sukenick, and Gray.

10 Jerome Klinkowitz, "Raymond Federman's visual fiction," in Richard Kostelanetz (ed.), *Visual Literature Criticism: A New Collection* (Carbondale and Edwardsville, Southern Illinois University Press, 1979), 123–4.

11 Dick Higgins, *Horizons: The Poetics and Theory of the Intermedia* (Carbondale and Edwardsville, Southern Illinois University Press, 1984), 32. For other recent essays on concrete poetry and related phenomena, see the special issue "Poetics of the avant-garde," *Poetics Today* 3:3 (Summer 1982).

12 Raymond Federman, *Double or Nothing* (Chicago, Swallow Press, 1971), 56, 144, and *passim*. See Carl D. Malmgren, "Paginal space and *Double or Nothing*," in *Fictional Space in the Modernist and Postmodernist American Novel* (Lewisburg, Bucknell University Press, 1985), 180–2.

13 *Thru* (London, Hamish Hamilton, 1975), 4, 56, 156. In fact, both of these icons do double, triple, multiple duty throughout the text. The rectangular word-grid appears in the early pages of the text as an iconic representation of a rear-view mirror, then later metamorphoses into an academic timetable, then into the classroom, and so on, forming a chain of icons of shifting meaning, spanning the text. The word-pattern of broken arches occurs only twice, here on p. 156 and earlier, in a slightly different version, on p. 37, but its signification is multiple each time. It seems to refer not only to a lecture-hall, but also to the patterns of light cast by streetlights on a wide boulevard – "great curved beams of pale light equispaced but staggered each to the other laterally, the quarter arches never meeting even on an imagined curve except quite distantly along the canyon of tall blocks" (17; an ironic intertextual allusion to Virginia Woolf's "series of giglamps symmetrically arranged"?) – as well as to a more abstract "object" of representation, discussed below. I wish to thank Christine Brooke-Rose herself for reminding me of the proliferation and slippages of meaning among the concrete prose passages of *Thru*.

14 Ronald Sukenick, *Long Talking Bad Conditions Blues* (New York, Fiction Collective, 1979), 22.

15 Brooke-Rose, *Thru*, 36.

16 Raymond Federman, *Take It or Leave It* (New York, Fiction Collective, 1976), Ch. XVI (no pagination).

17 Federman, *Double or Nothing*, 138.

18 Postmodernist texts illustrated with photographs or with drawings from other sources include Richard Brautigan's *Trout Fishing in America* (1967), Julio Cortázar's *La Vuelta al día en ochenta mundos* (1967), Gass's *Willie Masters' Lonesome Wife*, Donald Barthelme's "At the Tolstoy Museum" and "Brain Damage" (from *City Life*) and "The Flight of Pigeons from the Palace" (from *SADNESS*), Italo Calvino's *The Castle of Crossed Destinies* (1969/73), Ishmael Reed's *Mumbo Jumbo* (1972), and several recent texts by Robbe-Grillet which have been "illustrated" by works of David Hamilton, René Magritte, and Paul DelVaux. Texts illustrated or decorated by the authors themselves include Kurt Vonnegut's *Slaughterhouse-Five* (1969) and *Breakfast of Champions*, Guy Davenport's *Tatlin!* (1974) and *Da Vinci's Bicycle*, Clarence Major's *Emergency Exit* (1979) and Alasdair Gray's *Lanark* (1981), *Unlikely Stories, Mostly* (1983), and *1982, Janine* (1984).

19 Joseph Frank, "Spatial form in modern literature," in *The Widening Gyre: Crisis and Mastery in Modern Literature* (New Brunswick, NJ, Rutgers University Press, 1963), 3–62. In its Winter 1977 and Spring and Winter 1978 issues, *Critical Inquiry* conducted a kind of informal symposium, in which its contributors undertook to review and reconsider the "spatial form" idea. These issues include articles by Eric S. Rabkin, William Holtz, and Frank Kermode, as well as two contributions by Joseph Frank himself. See also W. J. T. Mitchell's "Spatial form in literature," *Critical Inquiry* 6:3 (Spring 1980).

20 Frank, *The Widening Gyre*, 13–14.

21 For the alternate-page format, see Steve Katz's *The Exagggerations of Peter Prince* (New York, Holt, Rinehart, and Winston, 1968), 116–50, and Rayner Heppenstall's *Two Moons*; for different texts on alternate lines, see Cortázar's *Hopscotch* (*Rayuela*, 1963), Ch. 34. A related format involves the chapter-titles in J. G. Ballard's *The Atrocity Exhibition* (1969) and Italo Calvino's *If on a winter's night a traveller*, which, when placed end-to-end and read consecutively form a separate text running parallel to the main text.

22 Postmodernist texts in which marginal glosses run parallel to the main text include Kenneth Patchen's *The Journal of Albion Moonlight* (1941), Barthelme's "To London and Rome" (from *Come Back, Dr Caligari*, 1964), Sukenick's "Momentum" (from *Death of the Novel and Other Stories*, 1969), Brigid Brophy's *In Transit* (1969), Steve Katz's *The Exagggerations of Peter Prince*, Alasdair Gray's *Lanark*, and *Finnegans Wake* (1939) II.2. In the latter two texts, marginal gloss is combined with footnotes. Other texts which exploit the footnote format (printing the notes sometimes at the foot of the page, sometimes in a separate section at the end of the book) include Flann O'Brien's *The Third Policeman* (1940/67), Cortázar's *Hopscotch* (Ch. 95), Gass's *Willie Masters' Lonesome Wife*, R. M. Koster's *The Dissertation* (1975), and Manuel Puig's *Kiss of the Spider Woman* (1976).

23 Parallel-column postmodernist texts include more or less long sections of Patchen's *Albion Moonlight*, Brophy's *In Transit*, Katz's *Peter Prince*, Federman's *Double or Nothing*, Major's *Emergency Exit*, Sukenick's *98.6*, and Alasdair Gray's *1982, Janine* and "Logopandocy" (from *Unlikely Stories, Mostly*).

24 Derrida, *Glas*, 7.

25 Alasdair Gray, *Lanark* (Edinburgh, Canongate, 1981), 483.

26 In neither case, however, does the alternative ordering interfere very profoundly with the structure or stability of the fictional world. "Hopscotching" through Cortázar's text does not in fact alter the order of events in the "normal" sequence, or even the order of chapters, but merely interpolates additional chapters. As for *The Unfortunates*, this text is framed as a classically modernist interior monologue, in which present experience is interwoven with memories of the past, triggered by elements in the present scene. Given this frame, *any* ordering of the text's sections would be plausibly verisimilar: the fluidity of memory and its interactions with present experience guarantee this. In other words, both *Hopscotch* and *The Unfortunates* are late-modernist rather than postmodernist texts.

27 Nevertheless, it was not *Hopscotch* but his subsequent novel *62* (1968) that Cortázar subtitled *A Model Kit* (*Modelo para armar*). And with considerable justification: for although *Hopscotch* is the text that offers us alternative orders of reading, *62* is the one that foregrounds fiction's ontological structure, and thus lays bare the process of world-building.

28 "*Lector in Fabula*: Pragmatic Strategies in a Metanarrative Text," in *The Role of the Reader: Explorations in the Semiotics of Texts* (Bloomington and London, Indiana University Press, 1979), 246.

29 Guy Davenport, *Da Vinci's Bicycle* (Baltimore and London, Johns Hopkins University Press, 1979), 106.

30 Raymond Federman, *The Twofold Vibration* (Bloomington, Indiana University Press, 1982), 116.

31 ibid., 117.

32 ibid., 118.

33 Italo Calvino, *The Castle of Crossed Destinies*, trans. William Weaver (London, Pan Books, 1978), 116.

34 ibid., 119.

13: Authors: dead and posthumous

1 John Fowles, *The French Lieutenant's Woman* (London, Pan Books, 1969), 85.
2 Gabriel Josipovici writes of frame-breaking novelists like Fowles: "First they lull us into taking the 'picture' for 'reality,' strengthening our habitual tendencies, and then suddenly our attention is focused on the spectacles through which we are looking, and we are made to see that what we had taken for 'reality' was only the imposition of the frame." *The World and the Book: A Study of Modern Fiction* (London, Macmillan, 1971), 297. Other postmodernist gestures comparable to the breaking of the frame in Chapter 13 of Fowles's *French Lieutenant's Woman* are easily found: for instance, at the mid-point of Sukenick's *Out* (1973), or on the last page of Robert Pinget's *Mahu, or, The Material* (1952) and B. S. Johnson's *House Mother Normal* (1971).
3 Ronald Sukenick, "Thirteen digressions (1973)," in *In Form: Digressions on the Act of Fiction* (Carbondale and Edwardsville, Southern Illinois University Press, 1985), 25.
4 Roland Barthes, "The death of the author," in *Image-Music-Text*, trans. Stephen Heath (New York, Hill and Wang, 1977), 145.
5 ibid., 146.
6 Jorge Luis Borges, "Borges and I," repr. in *A Personal Anthology*, trans. Anthony Kerrigan (London, Jonathan Cape, 1968), 200–1.
7 ibid.
8 Barthes, "The death of the author," in *Image-Music-Text*, 142.
9 Michel Foucault, "What is an author?" in Josue Harari (ed.), *Textual Strategies: Perspectives in Post-Structuralist Criticism* (Ithaca, Cornell University Press, 1979), 144.
10 ibid., 158.
11 Sukenick, "Thirteen Digressions," in *In Form*, 24.
12 Sukenick, "The Death of the Novel," in *The Death of the Novel and Other Stories* (New York, The Dial Press, 1969), 85.
13 Ronald Sukenick, *Up* (New York, Dell, 1970), 325.
14 Steve Katz, *The Exagggerations of Peter Prince* (New York, Holt, Rinehart & Winston, 1968), 158.
15 Raymond Federman, *Take It or Leave It* (New York, Fiction Collective, 1976), Ch. XIX; Federman's ellipses.
16 Steve Katz in Tom LeClair and Larry McCaffery (eds), *Anything Can Happen: Interviews with American Novelists* (Urbana, Chicago, London, University of Illinois Press, 1983), 226.
17 Kurt Vonnegut, *Slaughterhouse-Five* (New York, Dell, 1971), 125.
18 Barthes, "From work to text," in *Image-Music-Text*, 161.
19 Ronald Sukenick, *Out* (Chicago, Swallow Press, 1973), 164. For strong, if somewhat problematical, discussions of *Out* in the context of postmodernist characterization in general, see Thomas Docherty, *Reading (Absent) Character: Towards a Theory of Characterization in Fiction* (Oxford, Oxford University Press, 1982).
20 Gilbert Sorrentino, *Imaginative Qualities of Actual Things* (New York, New Directions, 1971), 111.
21 ibid., 144.
22 ibid., 149–50.
23 ibid., 225.
24 ibid., 80.
25 The most interesting disclaimer appears in *The Tokyo–Montana Express* (1980), where a prefatory note seems to warn us against identifying the "I" of this text too directly with its author: "The 'I' in this book is the voice of the stations along the tracks of the Tokyo–Montana Express." This formulation, presenting the subject as a series of positions successively occupied and then vacated, accords well with notions of the author's plurality that we find in Foucault or Thomas Docherty.
26 Vladimir Nabokov, *Pale Fire* (Harmondsworth, Penguin, 1973), 236.
27 Vladimir Nabokov, *Look at the Harlequins* (Harmondsworth, Penguin, 1980), 76. Cf. John Barth's "Life-Story": "Was the novel of his life for example a *roman à clef*? Of that genre he was . . . contemptuous . . . ; but while . . . it seemed obvious to him that he didn't 'stand for' anyone else, any more than he was an actor playing the role of himself . . . he had to admit that the question was unanswerable, since the 'real' man to whom he'd

correspond in a *roman à clef* would not be also in the *roman à clef* and the characters in such works were not themselves aware of their irritating correspondences." *Lost in the Funhouse* (New York, Bantam, 1969), 122.

28 Nabokov, *Look at the Harlequins*, 30.
29 James Joyce, *Finnegans Wake* (Harmondsworth, Penguin, 1976), 186–7.
30 ibid., 185–6.
31 William Gass, "Philosophy and the form of fiction," in *Fiction and the Figures of Life* (New York, Random House, 1972), 20.
32 Kurt Vonnegut, *Breakfast of Champions* (New York, Dell, 1974), 200.
33 ibid., 206.
34 Withdrawing behind a coy editorial *we*, Nabokov's narrator nevertheless reserves to himself the right to manipulate his characters' strings – but gently: "Direct interference in a person's life does not enter our scope of activity. . . . The most we can do when steering a favorite in the best direction, in circumstances not involving injury to others, is to act as a breath of wind and to apply the lightest, the most indirect pressure such as *trying* to induce a dream that we *hope* our favorite will recall as prophetic if a likely event does actually happen"; *Transparent Things* (Harmondsworth, Penguin, 1975), 95. At the opposite extreme lies Coover's shamelessly manipulative narrator, who improvises props, decor, characters, and events before our eyes: "I wander the island, inventing it. I make a sun for it, and trees – pines and birch and dogwood and firs – and cause the water to lap the pebbles of its abandoned shores. This, and more: I deposit shadows and dampness, spin webs, and scatter ruins"; *Pricksongs and Descants* (New York, New American Library, 1970), 20.
35 Stanley Elkin, "Plot," in "Current trends in American fiction," *Sub-Stance* 27 (1980), 70.
36 ibid., 71.
37 ibid., 73.
38 Flann O'Brien, *At Swim-Two-Birds* (Harmondsworth, Penguin, 1967), 9.
39 Julio Cortázar, *62: A Model Kit*, trans. Gregory Rabassa (London, Marion Boyars, 1976), 20.
40 See Roman Jakobson's "Shifters, verbal categories, and the Russian verb," in *Selected Writings* (The Hague, Mouton, 1971), II, 130–47. For Roland Barthes, it is precisely the "shiftiness" of the first-person pronoun that guarantees the author's death: "Linguistically, the author is never more than the instance writing, just as *I* is nothing other than the instance saying *I*: language knows a 'subject,' not a 'person,' and this subject, empty outside of the very enunciation which defines it, suffices to make language 'hold together,' suffices, that is to say, to exhaust it"; "The death of the author," 145.
41 Cortázar, *62: A Model Kit*, 25.
42 Federman, *Take It or Leave It*, Ch. III.
43 Sukenick, *Up*, 328.
44 Vonnegut, *Breakfast of Champions*, 240–1.
45 ibid., 294.
46 John Fowles, *Mantissa* (Boston, Little, Brown, 1982), 94.
47 ibid., 183.

14: Love and death in the postmodernist novel

1 John Gardner, *On Moral Fiction* (New York, Basic Books, 1978); Gerald Graff, *Literature Against Itself: Literary Ideas in Modern Society* (Chicago and London, Chicago University Press, 1979); Charles Newman, "The post-modern aura: the act of fiction in an age of inflation", in *Salmagundi* 63–4 (Spring-Summer 1984), 3–199.
2 Graff, *Literature Against Itself*, 179–80.
3 ibid., 208.
4 Newman, *The Post-Modern Aura*, 183.
5 Graff, *Literature Against Itself*, 12.
6 On Borges, see Graff, *Literature Against Itself*, 55–6; on Gide and Musil, see 211–12. For Graff's justification of postmodernist satire, including Barthelme, see 224–39; for his negative views on science fiction, see 74–5 and 99–100.

7 See Gardner, *On Moral Fiction*, 110, 140–2, 194–5.
8 Gardner, *On Moral Fiction*, 91, 112–13; see also pp. 203–4.
9 Graff, *Literature Against Itself*, 164–5.
10 See René Girard, *Deceit, Desire, and the Novel: Self and Other in Literary Structure*, trans. Yvonne Freccero (Baltimore, Johns Hopkins University Press, 1965).
11 *The Characters of Love: A Study in the Literature of Personality* (London, Chatto and Windus, 1968 [1960]), 7–8 and *passim*.
12 Ross Chambers, *Story and Situation: Narrative Seduction and the Power of Fiction* (Minneapolis, University of Minnesota Press, 1984), 218, 217.
13 For the "turned back" motif of modernism, see Allon White's discussion of Henry James, where he makes the gesture of characters turning their backs on one another into an emblem of early-modernist obscurity: "The obscurity of modern writing is inseparable from a widespread tendency for the novelist to turn away from the reader, leaving him the odd, uncomfortable, or even insulting view of his turned back. . . . it is above all in the 'turned back' that both the desire for security and the pathos of exclusion find their perfect image"; *The Uses of Obscurity: The Fiction of Early Modernism* (London, Routledge & Kegan Paul, 1981), 161, 159.
14 Italo Calvino, *If on a winter's night a traveller*, trans. William Weaver (New York and London, Harcourt Brace Jovanovich, 1981), 141. Of course, Italian grammar forces Calvino to specify the number and gender of his Reader in the original text – the Reader is, at the outset, masculine, singular – which somewhat cuts down on the potential for equivocation in the second person. In this respect, English is a good deal more ambiguous.
15 W. S. Merwin, *The Miner's Pale Children* (New York, Atheneum, 1970), 116.
16 ibid, 117.
17 Thomas Pynchon, *Gravity's Rainbow* (New York, Viking, 1973), 271–2, 131, 472, 267 respectively. For analyses of these and other instances of the second-person pronoun in *Gravity's Rainbow*, see my essay, "'You used to know what these words mean': misreading *Gravity's Rainbow*," *Language and Style* 18:1 (Winter 1985).
18 John Barth, "Life-Story," in *Lost in the Funhouse* (New York, Bantam, 1969), 123; William H. Gass, *Willie Masters' Lonesome Wife* (Evanston, Northwestern University Press, 1968), unnumbered; *Gravity's Rainbow*, 695–6; Gilbert Sorrentino, *Imaginative Qualities of Actual Things* (New York, Pantheon, 1971), 66. Barth explains in one of the "Seven Additional Author's Notes" to the 1969 edition of *Lost in the Funhouse* (p. xi), that "the deuteragonist of 'Life-Story,' antecedent of the second-person pronoun, is you." This certainly clarifies things.
19 Ronald Sukenick, *The Death of the Novel and Other Stories* (New York, The Dial Press, 1969), 71.
20 Peter Handke, *Offending the Audience*, trans. Michael Roloff (London and New York, Methuen, 1971), 35.
21 William Gass, *On Being Blue: A Philosophical Inquiry* (Boston, Godine, 1975), 43.
22 Sorrentino, *Imaginative Qualities of Actual Things*, 146–7.
23 Tzvetan Todorov, "Les hommes-récits," in *Poétique de la prose* (Paris, Seuil, 1971), 78–91.
24 Ronald Sukenick, "The Death of the Novel," in *The Death of the Novel and Other Stories*, 55.
25 cf. the curious and chilling argument in Francis Barker's *The Tremulous Private Body: Essays on Subjection* (London and New York, Methuen, 1984), 103–12. According to Barker, the bourgeois discursive order seeks an ultimately adequate narrative closure, and will only be able to find it in what he calls a "nuclear dénouement."
26 cf. Alan Wilde's accurate, if rather unsympathetic, reading of Federman's fiction in *Horizons of Assent* (Baltimore and London, Johns Hopkins University Press, 1981), 138–9.
27 Raymond Federman, *The Twofold Vibration* (Bloomington, Indiana University Press and Brighton, The Harvester Press, 1982), 51.
28 Walter J. Ong. "*Maranatha*: death and life in the text of the book," in *Interfaces of the Word: Studies in the Evolution of Consciousness and Culture* (Ithaca, Cornell University Press, 1977), 232–3. Cf. Michel Foucault, "What is an author?", in Harari (ed.), *Textual Strategies: Perspective in Post-Structuralist Criticism* (Ithaca, Cornell University Press, 1979): "this relationship between writing and death is also manifested in the effacement

of the writing subject's individual characteristics. Using all the contrivances that he sets up between himself and what he writes, the writing subject cancels out the signs of his particular individuality. As a result, the mark of the writer is reduced to nothing more than the singularity of his absence; he must assume the role of the dead man in the game of writing" (142–3).

29 Maggie Gee, *Dying, in other words* (Brighton, The Harvester Press, 1981), 161.
30 Borges, *A Personal Anthology*, trans. Anthony Kerrigan (London, Jonathan Cape, 1968), 200–1.
31 Ong, "*Maranatha*," 231.
32 Gabriel Josipovici, *The World and the Book: A Study of Modern Fiction* (London, Macmillan, 1971), 296–8.
33 Douglas R. Hofstadter, *Gödel, Escher, Bach: An Eternal Golden Braid* (Harmondsworth, Penguin, 1980), 698.
34 Robert Alter, *Partial Magic: The Novel as Self-Conscious Genre* (Berkeley and Los Angeles, University of California Press, 1975): "The impulse of fabulation, which men had typically used to create an imaginary time beautifully insulated from the impinging presence of their own individual deaths, was turned back on itself, held up to a mirror of criticism as it reflected reality in its inevitably distortive glass. As a result it became possible, if not for the first time then surely for the first time on this scale of narrative amplitude and richness, to delight in the lifelike excitements of invented personages and adventures, and simultaneously to be reminded of that other world of ours, ruled by chance and given over to death" (244–5).
35 Gardner, *On Moral Fiction*, 115–16.

Coda

1 James Joyce, *Finnegans Wake* (New York, Viking Press, 1959), 540, 3.

INDEX